"*Restoring the Soul of the University* makes it clear that the Christian failure to sustain universities in service to God was the result of the failure of Christians to think through their most basic convictions. But this is not a negative book. It is an insightful and historically illuminating account of how the university became fragmented, institutionally and in the souls of those who teach and study in the university setting. An imaginative theological proposal is developed that is a practical and hopeful alternative for restoring the soul of the university."

Stanley Hauerwas, Gilbert T. Rowe Emeritus Professor of Divinity and Law, Duke University

"This work calls all of us to recover a commitment to the 'higher' work in higher education. Reviewing the rich tapestry of university life over the centuries, the authors remind us of the ways that colleges and universities have contributed to human flourishing in big and small ways while also suggesting a hopeful way forward. This is a joy to read!"

D. Michael Lindsay, president, Gordon College

"All universities search for a soul, for some unifying vision of identity and mission. So say the authors of this remarkable book, and they comb through the history of universities in the West to show what kinds of souls they have—whether a heart for God's way and will in the world, for unifying and building a national culture, or for creating more personal wealth and prowess. And they show what a fragmented sprawl of competing visions and ambitions contemporary American universities have become. Can their souls be saved? Only if, the authors insist, they recover a pervasively theological vision, drawing on the only reality that can comprehend all that there is: God. Then they suggest ways in which theology might reintegrate university life. What a grand, sweeping book. I have been trying for forty years to learn how to be a Christian higher educator and to make higher education Christian, and this book humbles me with its breadth of knowledge and depth of wisdom. It should be required reading for this field, especially for those called to lead in it."

Joel Carpenter, Calvin College

"The travails of the contemporary university have been dissected and diagnosed by scholars and pundits alike. The authors of this provocative volume locate our current crisis in a sense of fragmentation that is endemic to modern universities, a flaw that secular universities are not equipped to remedy. Glanzer, Alleman, and Ream argue that a unified, coherent vision for higher education is possible only when that vision is based in the triune God and God's story of redemption. Their book provides a prophetic critique of secular education and an attractive—albeit challenging—vision to Christian educators of what a learning community can be when truly centered in the triune God."

Rick Ostrander, vice president for academic affairs and professional programs, Council for Christian Colleges & Universities

RESTORING THE SOUL OF THE UNIVERSITY

UNIFYING CHRISTIAN HIGHER EDUCATION IN A FRAGMENTED AGE

Perry L. Glanzer, Nathan F. Alleman, and Todd C. Ream

IVP Academic

An imprint of InterVarsity Press
Downers Grove, Illinois

InterVarsity Press
P.O. Box 1400, Downers Grove, IL 60515-1426
ivpress.com
email@ivpress.com

*InterVarsity Press® is the book-publishing division of InterVarsity Christian Fellowship/USA®, a movement of
students and faculty active on campus at hundreds of universities, colleges, and schools of nursing in the United
States of America, and a member movement of the International Fellowship of Evangelical Students. For
information about local and regional activities, visit intervarsity.org.*

*All Scripture quotations, unless otherwise indicated, are taken from THE HOLY BIBLE, NEW INTERNATIONAL
VERSION®, NIV® Copyright © 1973, 1978, 1984, 2011 by Biblica, Inc.™ Used by permission. All rights reserved
worldwide.*

*Short original portions of this book were previously published in academic journals. A similar summary of
European secularization developments in chapter three first appeared in Perry L. Glanzer, "The Role of the State in
the Secularization of Christian Higher Education: A Case Study of Eastern Europe," Journal of Church and
State 53, no. 2 (2011): 161-82. Some paragraphs from chapter twelve first appeared in Todd C. Ream, "Reviving
Sophia: The Search for Transcendent Wisdom—A Review Essay," Christian Scholar's Review 43, no. 3 (2014):
279-88. A table in chapter thirteen first appeared in Nathan F. Alleman, Perry L. Glanzer, and David Guthrie,
"The Integration of Christian Theological Traditions into the Classroom: A Survey of CCCU Faculty," Christian
Scholar's Review 45, no. 2 (2016): 103-25 (copyright ©2016 by Christian Scholar's Review; reprinted by permission).
Finally, small parts of chapters eight and fifteen are derived in part from the article Perry L. Glanzer,
"Building the Good Life: Using Identities to Frame Moral Education in Higher Education," Journal of College and
Character 14, no. 2 (May 2013): 177-84, available online: www.tandfonline.com/doi/abs/10.1515/jcc-2013-0023.
We are thankful to the publishers for permission to use those portions.*

Cover design: Cindy Kiple
Interior design: Jeanna Wiggins
Images: blue sky: ©MO:SES/iStockphoto
*   classic building: ©MilosJokic/iStockphoto*

ISBN 978-0-8308-5161-4 (print)
ISBN 978-0-8308-9163-4 (digital)

Printed in the United States of America ∞

Library of Congress Cataloging-in-Publication Data

A catalog record for this book is available from the Library of Congress.

| **P** | 25 | 24 | 23 | 22 | 21 | 20 | 19 | 18 | 17 | 16 | 15 | 14 | 13 | 12 | 11 | 10 | 9 | 8 | 7 | 6 | 5 | 4 | 3 | 2 | 1 |
| **Y** | 34 | 33 | 32 | 31 | 30 | 29 | 28 | 27 | 26 | 25 | 24 | 23 | 22 | 21 | 20 | 19 | 18 | 17 |

To All of My Teachers
Perry L. Glanzer

∎ ∎ ∎

To David D. Alleman and Julia H. Alleman
Nathan F. Alleman

∎ ∎ ∎

To Tyler W. Ream and Trevor S. Ream
Todd C. Ream

Not only am I handicapped by ignorance, but also frequently—indeed too frequently—I make false statements, or maintain the truth with arrogance and pride, until reproved and corrected by God. Hence it is that I earnestly beseech my reader and listener to remember me in his prayers to the Most High, and to petition God to grant me pardon for my past offenses, security against future falls, knowledge of the truth, love of what is good, and devotion to Himself, as well as that we may accomplish, in thought, word, and action, what is pleasing to His divine will.

JOHN OF SALISBURY, *THE METALOGICON: A TWELFTH-CENTURY DEFENSE OF THE VERBAL AND LOGICAL ARTS OF THE TRIVIUM*

CONTENTS

ACKNOWLEDGMENTS

The process of writing a book from the cultivation of the initial idea to the completion of the final manuscript is a long and, at times, challenging process. In order to complete such a process in relation to this topic, we needed the encouragement of friends and colleagues who knew us best. Offering our appreciation to these individuals is thus the least we can do. While we are in their debt, we also encourage you as the reader to in no way hold them accountable for any inevitable deficiencies, for which we alone are responsible.

At Baylor University, Cara Cliburn Allen and Britney Graber offered their valued assistance in editing the manuscript. In particular, we are grateful to Cara for offering numerous broad insights and editorial suggestions that influenced the shape of the final manuscript. Barry Hankins was also gracious enough to read and comment on chapter four. Jim Halverson of Judson University kindly read and offered feedback on chapter one.

At Taylor University, Steve Bedi, Scott Gaier, Tim Herrmann, Heather Sandlin, Kelly Yordy, Emilie Hoffman, Jessica Martin, Drew Moser, and Skip Trudeau all provide a context that goes beyond the boundaries of a traditional department, rising to the level of friendship that makes the contemplation of these questions a true joy. The same can be said for lunch conversations shared with Tom Jones and Bill Ringenberg. Their value as students of the university is matched by their value as friends. Finally, Taylor University's new president, Lowell Haines, served as a great source of encouragement before and after he accepted the enormous responsibility of leading the university.

CrossRoads Christian Fellowship in Bigfork, Montana, Jerome Christian Church in Greentown, Indiana, First Baptist Church of Woodway, Texas, and Hope Fellowship, Waco, proved to be homes that made reflection on the themes present in this book possible.

This book emerged out of our contemporary experience in these communities as well as our past attempts (in Todd and Perry's previous coauthored works) to address the impact of the Christian faith on scholarship, the moral problems facing higher education, and the unique challenges to the growing Christian university (*The Idea of a Christian College: A Reexamination for Today's University*). We wanted to write a book that touched on a core problem that we think has continually haunted the university.

From Perry—I dedicate this book to my educators who graced me with their wisdom and support. My parents and brother, Bryan, have been the most important and vital early educators in my life, but I also am grateful for others in the church who educated me such as Patricia Trollinger, Harry Schanker, Dave Rattan, Leroy Kemp, Rick Hove, Craig McConnell, and countless other Bible study leaders and Sunday school teachers. I am also grateful for the professors who took a special interest in developing my intellectual life, such as Thomas Haskell, Michael Beaty, John Orr, Don Miller, Dallas Willard, and many others. Finally, I'm thankful for the support of my wife, Rhonda, and the gift of our children, Bennett and Cody, who continue to teach me that being able to think and write about Christianity and Christian education is much easier than living out those ideals in everyday life. I'm thankful for their education, patience, and grace.

From Nathan—I am deeply grateful for the generosity of heart and mind extended to me by those who have taught me the disciplines of thinking and writing but also of right loving and living. Foremost I think of my family and particularly my parents, David and Julia, whose own educational journeys and thoughtful life choices influence me always. My contributions to this book and the academic preparation that led to it would not have been possible without the loving patience of my wife, Karen, and the loving impatience of our daughter Annabelle. Thank you to the faculty at Eastern Mennonite High School (most notably Elwood Yoder, Gloria Diener, and Vivian Beachy) for their essential role in my formation on many levels. My love and regard go also to the "boys" at Geneva College (in particular, David Guthrie) and to Dot Finnegan for her academic tough love and abiding friendship. Thank you to my brothers and sisters who are the community of Hope Fellowship in Waco, from which streams of living water flow. Finally, my thanks to Walter Brueggemann for his prophetic vision and to the unnamed provosts and presidents who thoughtfully responded to that vision for the "Reimagining Academic Leadership" chapter. I value your insights and respect the difficult path God has called you to walk.

From Todd—As always, my greatest debt of gratitude is owed to my wife, Sara, and my daughters, Addison and Ashley. Sara and I met during English class at a research university. She then walked alongside me while I did graduate work at two more research universities. I was then fortunate enough to walk alongside her during her own journey through a fourth. She has thus lived these questions with me and, to her credit, never tired of hearing them. Perhaps my only way of repaying her is that what is in these pages may in some small way make the opportunities afforded to Addison and Ashley deepen what is best about the research university.

I also owe a debt of gratitude to my own brothers, Tyler W. Ream and Trevor S. Ream, for many of the lessons that weave themselves into any significant effort one encounters later in life. To the two of you, I thus dedicate this book. The days we resided with Mom and Dad at 507 Las Riendas Drive are unfortunately now well behind us. However, experiences as seemingly frivolous as learning how far a lemon will fly when hit with a tennis racket or making impromptu calculations concerning how much force a window can withstand when struck by just about any ball continue to yield immense value. I am thus forever in debt to the two of you for the lessons we learned together. May such comparable blessings find their way to your own children and the relations they share with their siblings.

Perry L. Glanzer
Hewitt, Texas

Nathan F. Alleman
Waco, Texas

Todd C. Ream
Greentown, Indiana

Seventeenth Week of Pentecost, 2016

INTRODUCTION

Can the Soul of the University Be Saved?

...

What good will it be for someone to gain the whole world,
yet forfeit their soul? Or what can anyone give
in exchange for their soul?

MATTHEW 16:26

B Y MOST MEASURES, AMERICAN UNIVERSITIES appear to have gained virtually the whole academic world. According to certain rankings, America hosts seventeen of the top twenty-five universities in the world,[1] boasts anywhere from 84 to 90 percent of the world's wealthiest universities,[2] and is home to sixty-two of the one hundred universities that produce the most millionaires.[3] Moreover, scholars experience an amount of academic freedom unparalleled to the rest of the world.[4] In terms of money, prestige, power, and freedom, American universities outrank every other country. Professors and students from all over the world hope to become part of these institutions, and according to these measures, American universities appear to be a definite success story.

Despite all of this success, over the past few decades, various critics of American higher education have used prophetic, even apocalyptic language to describe the loss of something they believe should be or was there among these universities but no longer exists. They describe American universities as being "in crisis," "ruins," "decline," and "collapsing," often referring to some sort of moral or spiritual core the university has lost.[5] One writer aptly

1

called this body of higher education critique the "funeral dirge" genre.[6] The metaphor is quite appropriate since most of these authors claim something, perhaps the most important part, has died inside the body of the American university. One writer even goes so far as to claim that that the top American universities are producing "excellence without a soul."[7] In other words, certain critics wonder whether American universities gained the whole world but lost their soul in the process.

One important first question to ask, though, is what exactly it means for a university to have a soul. The author of *Excellence Without a Soul*, Harvard University's Harry Lewis, provides a helpful example of the common way the term is used. For Lewis, when a university loses its soul, it neglects its core mission or missions.[8] More specifically, Lewis laments that while universities "succeed, better than ever, at being creators and repositories of knowledge," one part of their mission, they "have forgotten that the fundamental job of undergraduate education is to turn eighteen- and nineteen-year-olds into twenty-one and twenty-two-year olds, to help them grow up, to learn who they are, to search for a larger purpose for their lives, and to leave college as better human beings"—what Lewis appears to believe is the soul of their mission.[9] What is interesting about Lewis's formulation is that he suggests universities should not only expose students to different views of the good life but also actually form or change students into better human beings. This task requires that the university possess some understanding of core human identity and a moral ideal about what makes a better human being.

Lewis's talk about soul, a substantive view of the good life, and the competing goals of the contemporary research university are not new. Indeed, although universities have been around for centuries, we appear increasingly confused about the soul of the university. As a result, we find ourselves always asking the question: what are universities for?[10] Not surprisingly, then, over a half century ago, the one-time head of the University of California system Clark Kerr discussed the soul of a university in a similar way. The difference is that Kerr wondered whether the contemporary research university could really have a singular soul. He claimed:

> The university started as a single community—a community of masters and students. It may even be said to have had a soul in the sense of a central animating principle. Today the large American university is, rather, a whole

series of communities and activities held together by a common name, a common governing board, and related purposes.[11]

Kerr called this new type of university with multiple purposes something unique, a *multiversity*. Kerr was not as hopeful as Lewis is that the many purposes of the multiversity could be reconciled, due to the competing purposes. He thought it important to recognize that the contemporary research university—the multiversity—"is an inconsistent institution."[12] Kerr recognized the freedom, growth, and prosperity the research university enjoyed brought with it the possibility, and even the reality, that a university would lose its singular soul. The reason was that it consisted of several communities with diverse purposes. He therefore identified "the community of the undergraduate and the community of the graduate; the community of the humanist, the community of the social scientist, and the community of the scientist; the communities of the professional schools; the community of all the nonacademic personnel; the community of the administrators."[13] Today we would likely add the athletic department. In addition, external constituencies, such as alumni, government agencies, foundations, and more have unique concerns with all of these different parts. The outcome, Kerr recognized, resulted in fragmentation and conflict. The multiversity, he then went on to contend, "is so many things to so many different people that it must, of necessity, be partially at war with itself."[14] Ultimately this war tears the purpose, or the soul, of the university into pieces. He thus claimed:

A community, like the medieval communities of masters and students, should have common interests; in the multiversity, they are quite varied, even conflicting. A community should have a soul, a single animating principle; the multiversity has several—some of them quite good, although there is much debate on which souls really deserve salvation.[15]

For Kerr, the singular soul of the university could not be saved. In contrast, it must end up multiplied. He believed we must recognize that the university and the university's soul are now fragmented by this multiplicity, and we can only talk about which aspects are worth saving.

Although Kerr wrote about the university having multiple souls, he perhaps reinforced the image of the soulless university by suggesting that we should not consider the multiversity a living organism where head, arms, and legs are inextricably bound together, in which any attempt to remove one part would cause bloodshed and perhaps kill the organism.[16] In contrast, the multiversity, he argued, is more like a machine or mechanism held together by a common budget, administrative procedures, and a name. As a machine, different parts can be added or subtracted without necessarily harming the entity. Similarly, a multiversity might add or discard different parts.

Perhaps not surprisingly, academic leaders do not appreciate these impersonal metaphors, nor a bodily metaphor that talks about fragmenting or dividing souls. They view multiplying souls as almost akin to dividing one's soul as something evil, the activity of malevolent, fictional characters such as Voldemort in the Harry Potter series. They want to save all that gives the university prestige, those things that make it a multiversity, and yet they also want to keep their singular soul as well. For instance, the president of Emory University James Wagner wrote about trying to preserve a singular soul within the institution. He noted in a discussion about his university's strategic plan that the term *multiversity* described

> the opposite of what we believe Emory truly is, and what it should remain—a UNIversity—with the emphasis on oneness of community, oneness of vision, oneness of purpose and aspiration, oneness of enterprise. We do not want to be multi in the sense of being divided, having schools and programs that work at cross purposes, or assuming a zero-sum game in which the advantage of one part necessarily disadvantages all the others.[17]

Yet Wagner also admitted his university was now a multiversity as Kerr understood the term. Emory now sought to be a "knowledge factory," which means it is now seeking to be "a major research institution to which policy wonks turn for expertise, industrialists turn for research, government agencies turn for funding proposals, and donors turn for leveraging their philanthropy into the greatest impact on America and the world."[18]

Such advances in scholarship require increased specialization, and lead both to a "diminished concentration on educating undergraduates as the core mission of the university" and to the "fragmentation of learning."[19] Wagner still hoped that something transcendent could supply the soul to their emerging university. For Wagner what appeared to replace it seemed to be some sort of broad value for "community."

Indeed, Wagner saw the major problem with the multiversity as its "anti-communitarian" vices. How he suggested his institution attempt to address this danger, however, seemed oddly shallow. It largely consisted of vague desires. He wanted their faculty to place some of their energy and focus in the university and not merely the national academy. He mentioned "regretting that a cadre of student-life professionals has had to replace the faculty in mentoring and caring for students" and hoped to maintain their informal community despite the "increased administrative scale and complexity." Want, lament, and hope were his suggested means of battling back the fragmenting forces of the multiversity. Wagner concluded by setting out the hope that they were attempting to create an institutional organism, "a unique institution that has the muscle and energy and creative intelligence of Kerr's multiversity, while retaining the spirit, the soul, of the university."[20] Unlike Wagner, however, we remain doubtful that regrets, longings, and hopes alone can save the soul of today's university. We need something more.

Can the Soul of the University Be Saved?

The aim of this book is to explore what it means for the soul of the university to be saved. Saving the soul of the university requires, we believe, understanding that the soul of the research university is not merely a purpose. It also includes its central *identity* and the *story* that connects that identity to the transcendent story of the universe and its Author. This identity and its story provide the source for the university's ultimate *moral ideals* and various *purposes*, such as the moral ideal about what it means to be human that Lewis hoped the university would pass on to students.

We believe this understanding proves particularly at home in the ecclesial university. The church, similar to the Christian university, seeks to be a body and not a soulless knowledge or doctrine factory. Moreover, the church can and should remain unafraid of the university's growing into a multiversity with many parts, since the church itself, as Christ's body, has this characteristic. As 1 Corinthians 12:12-14 states:

> Just as a body, though one, has many parts, but all its many parts form one body, so it is with Christ. For we were all baptized by one Spirit so as to form one body—whether Jews or Gentiles, slave or free—and we were all given the one Spirit to drink. Even so the body is not made up of one part but of many.

As this passage indicates, individuals are also divided. One way individuals are divided is in their various identities and their associated moral practices. Individuals are often trying to be excellent in various identities that may sometimes be in conflict. We, in particular, are trying to be good Christians, spouses, parents, friends, professors/students, neighbors, citizens, and more.

The question, then, is not whether these identities will sometimes compete against each other. They will. The real question is how one orders these identities and the associated loves. To order one's identities and loves, one needs an overarching identity and story with a substantive vision of the good, the true, and the beautiful that allows one to prioritize multiple, competing purposes. Individuals have this need and, we believe, so do universities. Robert Maynard Hutchins captured this need for prioritization when he wrote, "Real unity can be achieved only by a hierarchy of truths which shows us which are fundamental and which subsidiary, which significant and which not."[21] We would merely specify that the truths have to do with one's fundamental identity or story.

Almost every university tries to find such an identity or story, whether they admit it or not. Like Wagner, most university leaders do not want the university to simply be a knowledge machine or factory with interchangeable parts and no soul. They want the university to be experienced as an organic whole like a body. Yet if one continues to have this vision of the university as an organic whole, it is important to have a soul that holds everything together and that provides a source of spiritual, moral, and intellectual virtues. To lose one's soul speaks to a loss of a core identity, story, and source of moral insight and inspiration. When an entity loses its core identity, fragmentation abounds and the negative implications of a split personality then become a possibility. The university at times may end up at war, trying to hold together its fragmented selves.

Part of our argument in this book is that the advent of the contemporary research university, or what Kerr calls the multiversity, did not suddenly introduce this problem. We think Christians and certain other scholars may too easily blame the development of the secular research university or the multiversity for the problems with the university's soul. We think the problems with the soul of the university started much earlier.

We address this issue in part one. According to the common telling of the history of the university, the early universities in Europe and then in America supposedly always had a singular soul—an identity and story that held them together and gave a coherent unity. In fact, scholars discussing what it would mean for a university to have singular soul usually refer to the older medieval universities as an example.[22] In this view, God supplied the soul, or more particularly, the study of God—theology—supplied it. In contrast, we argue that the mistake of many Christians is the belief that since universities in Europe and colleges in America began in a dominant Christian era that the early structures of how the soul of theology informed the university were somehow closer to the ideal of what a university should be. We wonder if the recent growth of classical education seems to reflect this assumption.[23] We thus contend that Christians need to think critically about past educational structures and institutions they helped to build and perhaps where they went wrong.

We, in turn, contend that the particular habits of thinking and building the curricular body of the early university actually contributed to the problem. In other words, the inability to sustain the soul of the university started much earlier than the multiversity. This problem had its origins in the structure of the first universities and later the early American colleges. University leaders picked up the habit of reducing the vital discipline that nourished the soul and body of the university, which we identify as a certain way of understanding theology, into a particular professional discipline long before the multiversity. We need to recognize that Christians in both Europe and North America played a role in the sequestering and marginalization of Christian theology within most of Christian higher education. In early European universities, there was a fear of bringing theology to the masses. In America, educators feared theology was too distinct and too sectarian to nourish the soul of universities that needed to serve the needs of a new nation with significant religious pluralism, particularly its need for some sort of moral foundation. Of course, there have been those who have tried to keep theology circulating throughout the whole university—this volume highlights some of those innovators, who, to date, have lost.

Part one also seeks to help us understand the additional historical trends that led to the multiversity and the possibility for even greater fragmentation of the university's soul. The emerging secular multiversity, of course, did not look to theology to nourish its soul. As Hutchins wrote in 1936, "To look to theology to unify the modern university is futile and vain."[24] The leaders of the new multiversity abandoned the university's traditional Christian identity and narrative to gain the freedom to independently pursue different identities and stories. Since university leaders still wanted the university to have a soul, however, they still sought to find unity in other sources, such as national identity or the story of nature as understood through science.[25] These developments also helped cultivate the origins of the multiversity.

The advent of the research university and the development of the multiversity merely magnified the already existing problems with the university's soul. The parts and identities of research universities multiplied, and the areas in which it sought to be excellent expanded. Part two then examines the sources of and reasons for this fragmentation in the range of university communities: professors, the curriculum, students, administrators, athletics, and ultimately the bodily location of the university itself. Ultimately this fragmentation brought the various communities of the university a sort of freedom and also allowed the university to embrace pluralism and diversity. American higher education not only hosts what might be called a tournament of narratives[26] but has also fragmented into multiple competing factions. This fragmentation divided the university's soul.

Consequently, despite the celebration and support of pluralism and freedom in the university, the leaders of the multiversity still have good reasons to fear the tournament of identities and narratives. One reason is that the demise of a singular soul results in a loss of coherence and unity. Educational leaders still appear to hold the view articulated by Christian Smith: "The commitment to coherent knowledge about what is true and real is a good to prize. Fragmentation and schizophrenia are not."[27] Consequently its leaders have continued to look for other sources of transcendent unity for the different components of the university. Most of them seek to identify what Burton Clark terms an "organizational saga"[28] and not a coherent vision of goodness, truth, and beauty. The saga is a quasi-religious story that provides an identity and purpose for the university, but it is not simply a story. It also has a cadre of believers who view the story not simply as history but as a source of pride, moral ideals, and identity. The saga remains fairly narrow though. It does not encompass the entirety of the universe, but it only refers to a particular narrow human or organizational identity (i.e., professional, national, or institutional). When educational leaders create this type of saga it produces "an emotional loading, which places their conception between the coolness of rational purpose and the warmth of sentiment found in religion."[29] This quasi-religious saga often helps participants and outsiders avoid envisioning the university as a soulless machine.

Usually, as Wagner's appeal to the saga of university community indicates, educational leaders want the saga to point students, faculty, and alumni to something beyond themselves. For instance, they expect universities to help students with life beyond self-focused purposes, such as personal competence and success in a particular career. They fear the university becoming merely a business that provides services to meet the needs of individual students instead of an institution with some kind of larger beyond-the-self moral ideal.[30] They expect higher education to be a certain kind of broad, missional community, although they disagree about what the mission should be. They may believe the purpose of higher education should be the interpretation, advancement, and transmission of a national culture[31] or that it should provide "the knowledge to be a reasonably informed citizen in a democracy."[32] Others claim that higher education's "original and enduring purpose" is "to challenge the minds and imaginations of this nation's young people, to expand their understanding of the world, and thus of themselves."[33] Despite these disagreements about the exact purpose, the critics are united in that they want a university to still have a quasi-religious soul—a broad identity, story, and purpose that transcends the individual.

In addition, most of these critics agree that this broad mission should also provide some sort of overall coherence to the curriculum and help both students and faculty move beyond self-centered reductionism and fragmentation. To judge from critics, though, the success of this quest has questionable results. Many still lament the reduction of higher education to higher training, the focus on self-oriented goals, and the university's continual fragmentation.[34] As one scholar recently complained:

The growing number of college and university faculty members focused on their research and publishing careers has led to a conflict between the preoccupations of professors and the needs of students. As the interests of these faculty members become more specialized and the subjects of their publications more esoteric, the curriculum becomes increasingly fragmented and the educational process loses its coherence as well as its relevance for the broader society.[35]

Although critics believe a relevant, beyond-the-self purpose goes together with a coherent curriculum and that they need some sort of unifying story, they do not believe they have yet found something that can save the university's soul.

In part three, we set forth an argument for how the Christian university can perhaps save the university's soul while also freeing it to embrace the different communities and complexity found in an expanding university. The temptation of Christian universities is to follow the pattern of secular multiversities. If they want to do something different, though, they need to understand the fragmenting dangers of certain aspects of the multiversity described in part two and develop different models. Unfortunately Christians sometimes have their own nostalgia problem. While looking for help from the early medieval universities or the early American institutions is perhaps helpful in some ways, as part one reveals, it is problematic in many others. We should also note that we can learn quite a bit from current colleges and universities that exhibit "quality with soul," as the title of Robert Benne's book so helpfully puts it.[36] Yet we also believe that even these colleges and universities need help regarding how to think in a visionary manner in our post-Christian times.

Redeeming the Christian university's soul starts by recognizing that if we are made in God's image and the world is made by God, we must first know God if we are to truly know who we are and what the world is. This is the first and foremost liberating art. Christian theology, which we define as the worship, love, and study of God, becomes central to the university's attempt to gain knowledge and wisdom. It is the lifeblood of the university body. Since it is the lifeblood, it must flow into every area of the university in some way. In this respect, we need to rethink how theology can serve and nourish the university. In particular, we must recognize that what makes theology unique is that it is the only field of study that can properly worship the subject that it studies—God. Every other discipline and every other part of the university must learn how to seek excellence without idolatry, and it can only do this with the help of theology.

A focus on the worship, love, and study of God results in an emphasis on wholeness and coherence, whether vested in an understanding of whole persons or an appreciation for the whole body of knowledge about God's world. As the lifeblood of the university, this type of Christian theology can sustain and hold together the university's disparate parts by nourishing the whole body (curricular and cocurricular) that is the dwelling place of the university's soul—our shared identity, story, and purpose. Worshiping, thinking, and loving in the light of God and God's story can foster the integration of professors' practicing teaching, scholarship, and service as well as their identity and life purpose. As image bearers of God, they can faithfully pursue a coinherence reflected in the Trinity. In the curriculum, this means Christians must recognize that there is nothing magical about a liberal arts education. Indeed, a liberal arts education can be quite corrupting. Although we must not abandon the liberal arts for a narrowly specialized education, we must realize that teaching the liberal arts must be preceded by the liberating arts of worship and the imitative practice of God's creativity and virtue in order to be truly liberating.

By talking about recovering and integrating the practice of the liberating arts throughout the university, such as theology and creativity guided by the practice of God's virtue, we do not mean that past universities actually ever fully practiced them in the manner we will describe. We are thus not calling for a return to some golden age of the medieval or Reformation university, as if during those times a grand Christian idea of the university was ever fully incarnated. Nonetheless, we do argue the *idea* that the Christians university should be governed by ideals and practices of a story-formed community engaged in the liberating arts of worship, confession, theological reflection, mutual love, and humble service partially existed at times in the past and continually needs to be resurrected and practiced today. In this regard, even past and present arguments from Christians who rightly practiced theology that deserves a place in the university curriculum often prove to be too small. In contrast, we argue that God himself, along with the liberating arts that give us a deeper understanding of God, must nourish the soul of the Christian university if it hopes to demonstrate virtues such as coherence, unity, and a concern with overall human flourishing. It needs God and the liberating arts to sustain its soul.

Audiences

This book is written with at least two audiences in mind. First, it is written for Christians in the multiversity. Only by understanding its fragmentation and the distorted ways the multiversity tries to overcome this challenge through quasi-religious forms of coherence can one free oneself to create a different kind of coherent learning experience. One can then encourage secular multiversities to stop being quasi-religious and embrace the fact that they are arenas for the tournament of narratives in America. Their job is to attempt to maintain some semblance of justice in this tournament. It is not to take over the tournament by enforcing some substitute religious narrative.

Second, it is also written for those seeking to nurture and build coherent Christian universities. The problem today is that secular multiversities are the model to follow. Our message to faith-based universities is to be aware of the fragmenting influences of secular multiversities and chart their own path forward. Despite the rich Christian past, Christian educators do not have a singular model to follow that can illumine a different path than the one offered by the multiversity. Today there is talk of Benedictine or Augustinian options,[37] but the challenge today is that Benedictine and Augustinian universities, while embodying many positive qualities, may still practice some of the dangerous habits that led to the loss of the university's Christian soul in the first place.[38] If Christian universities are truly to survive and prosper in non-Christian societies, we need to think in radical new ways about the practices of the contemporary university.

A Final Note About University Metaphors

Before we continue with the core of our argument, we want to say a final word about the metaphors we use to talk about the university. We believe these metaphors are vital to our deepest longings and our imaginative vision of what the university can and should become. In their book about metaphors for education, David Smith and Susan Felch observe, "The visions we adopt will help shape the kinds of teachers and learners that we become. . . . The renewing of our minds is about visions as well as beliefs."[39] In their book, they discuss three important metaphors used in Scripture and often applied to education: journeys, gardens, and buildings. This last one in particular was applied to the early university, and we will draw on it in this book at times, especially in part one. Indeed, the concern about a lack of unity in the university has often been expressed using a building metaphor. For example, one constantly hears concerns about the dangers of disciplinary *silos* in the university. Underneath this talk lies a concern that a complex entity is actually breaking apart into something that is no longer held together by something in common. It reveals a longing for a unified university structure with a common foundation and pinnacle—an image continually used in the first five hundred years of the university, which we discuss in part one.

As the title and argument of this book reveal, we will prioritize the use of the metaphor of the university as a living organism with a soul. This metaphor also draws on Scripture and has historical precedent.[40] We should note that we must be careful not overextend the metaphor and thus cheapen the idea of a "soul." We realize that institutions do not literally have souls. Metaphors are helpful, but we need to keep their limits in mind. Thus we want to remind readers once again that we use the term *soul* as merely shorthand for a university's core identity, story, and mission. Moreover, we contend that for the soul to be healthy, it cannot and should not simply be an organizational saga. This central *identity, story, and purpose* must connect to the transcendent story of the universe and its Author—the triune God.

PART ONE

BUILDING THE UNIVERSITY

...

In PART ONE, WE ADDRESS how educational leaders of the past built universities with soul. The mixing of metaphors in this phrase is purposeful. The metaphor of the university as a body with a soul was less dominant during the medieval period. Instead, one of the dominant metaphors scholars drew on during the first half millennium was the idea of learning as a structure—such as a castle, tower, palace, or house for the queen of wisdom.[1] This metaphor was especially appropriate when the university was yet in the initial "construction" phase. During this period, early thinkers were particularly interested in ways that curricular structures and institutions could help organize and further a person's learning. This building was to occur inside the student and provide a place for God (often described as Wisdom) to dwell.

We think both metaphors, the university as a structure and the university as an organic body with a soul, are legitimate and helpful ways to think about the university (although we will focus on the latter in the second part of this book). As we will demonstrate in part one, however, picturing the university as some kind of structure means that it is vitally important to establish the proper foundation (akin to the importance of the soul for the body).

Unfortunately, the early blueprint of the academic building resulted in a particular weakness with regard to how it approached theology and what today we might describe as the role of faith in animating learning. Theology only implicitly and not explicitly served as the foundation of the university. The discipline of theology itself served more as the palace or peak of the structure. This approach had important consequences for the university, particularly when the unified theology of the Roman Catholic Church broke further apart during the Reformation. As a result, the foundation of the university, which had never been firmly established in its dependence on God and the study of God, was replaced by other foundations. This first part tells this important story, a story that is somewhat different from the common secularization story.

1

CREATING THE
ORIGINAL BLUEPRINT
OF A UNIVERSITY

...

Let no man excuse himself. Let no man say, "I am not able to build
a house for the Lord; my poverty does suffice for such an expensive
project; I have no place in which to build it." . . . You shall build
a house for the Lord out of your own self. He himself
will be the builder; your heart will be the place;
your thoughts will supply the material.

HUGH OF ST. VICTOR

The more we are conformed to the divine nature,
the more do we possess Wisdom. . . .
We find many who study but few who are wise.

HUGH OF ST. VICTOR

FEW HUMAN CREATIONS LAST for any significant period of time. Universities, however, have proved to be an exception. The oldest universities in Europe, North and South America, and Asia have lasted longer than the governments of the nations in which they reside and virtually every other institution minus the church.[1] Interestingly, among the many purposes suggested for a university education today is that it is essential for defending liberal democracy.[2] While understandable, the fact that many older universities preceded the rise of liberal democracies raises the question of what universities were for in the thirteenth century when they began.

The thinkers who provided the intellectual scaffolding on which the earliest universities were built did not compose mission statements. Nevertheless, these scholars still offered rationales for the unique project in which they were engaged. Within these justifications one finds a unique way of thinking that departed from earlier Greek and Roman justifications for what today we call a liberal arts education. This distinctive vision, we contend, is crucial for understanding the larger identity, story, and purposes that nurtured the creation of the university and the development of its soul.

Hugh of St. Victor

We begin our story with Hugh of St. Victor, who died in 1141. Unfortunately, we actually know very little about Hugh's life, including his birth date. He described himself as an earthly resident alien ("From boyhood . . . I have dwelt on foreign soil"[3]). He later came to Paris, France, where he studied and began to teach and write. Eventually he became a master and head of the school at St. Victor from 1120 to 1141. Hugh's position at this school proved important for a number of reasons. As European cities grew during this time, centers of education began moving from monasteries to cathedral schools in the cities. A tension soon developed, however, between the monastics and those teachers now educating in the cities. The strain arose because monastics believed that educators in the new city-based schools placed too much emphasis on the nuggets of intellectual gold acquired through the pagan writings independent of faith in God and downplayed the importance of both orthodox belief and virtuous living for gaining wisdom.[4]

The School of St. Victor, overseen by Hugh, became one of the schools that addressed this tension. It existed just outside the city walls, less than a mile from the royal residence. In the words of Jim Halverson, the school did not represent "the flight to the desert by a weary ecclesiastic."[5] Its founders played a central role in the political and ecclesiastical life of the city. They opened the school to the wider public in the hopes of attracting some of the top minds coming to the city. The priests who ran the school were not monks but a group known as canons regular. They combined the disciplines of a monk with the active ministerial life of priests in urban churches. They saw their educational work of preparing students for various worldly callings as part of their ministerial work.[6] This unusual combination of monastic spiritual disciplines and leading academic work built on previous educational approaches, but it also proved ground-breaking in important ways.

Both the continuities and the distinctives can be found in Hugh's *Didascalicon*, which contains his ideas about how to justify and organize education. Although earlier Christian thinkers such as Augustine, Boethius, Varro, Cassiodorus, and Isidore had also created classification schemes for knowledge, these types of organizational schemes started to blossom during Hugh's time.[7] In the century preceding the rise of the university, the fields of academic knowledge began to expand rapidly. As a result, systematizers such as Hugh arose within the various types of monastic and cathedral schools and tried to organize both old and new forms of knowledge. These scholars began writing manuscripts known as *didascalicons*, which sought to introduce students to the various writings they should read to be educated.[8] These documents were basically instruction manuals for building the substantive content of what they called the academic house or palace for wisdom.

Although Hugh's *Didascalicon* was clearly influenced by early Christian scholars in how he thought about education, particularly Augustine of Hippo, his blueprint for learning departed from previous approaches in one important way.[9] Previous Christian classifications had often been written as a critical response to pagan systems of knowledge. For instance, in *On Christian Doctrine*, Augustine created a classification of knowledge in order to help Christians discern which pagan liberal arts were suitable for Christians and which arts were not (e.g., medicine—yes, magic—no). In contrast, Hugh created a positive vision and classification of learning that, while taking pagan knowledge into account, focused more on the creative endeavor of placing the whole educational enterprise within the expansive Christian narrative.[10] In other words, he set forth a comprehensive blueprint of how to build the academic structure that answered questions about who we are, why we should learn, what we should learn, and how we should learn it.

The Foundation: A Grand Reason to Discover Wisdom

As with any building, the foundation remains vitally important. During Hugh's time, two foundational concepts were used. Some organizers simply classified their system under the word *scientia* (knowledge), but others used the term *philosophia* (which in Greek means the love of wisdom).[11] The latter term drew on both Greek thought as well as Hebrew Wisdom literature such as Proverbs. *Philosophia*, or philosophy, would be the term that won the day at the time when universities began. For example, for Hugh philosophy served as the overarching category on which to build the academic house since he considered it "the art of arts and the discipline of disciplines."[12] In contrast to contemporary conceptions of philosophy, this wide-ranging view of philosophy included what today we would consider theological questions. "Philosophy" was an all-encompassing term. For example, Hugh believed that "philosophy is the discipline which investigates demonstratively the causes of all things, human and divine."[13] This comprehensive use of philosophy still persists as part of contemporary universities. The highest level of graduate students in the fields of arts and sciences receive a doctorate of philosophy, or PhD. Most students, and even many professors, do not understand why someone receiving the most advanced degree in chemistry should receive a doctorate in philosophy. This language points to the earlier means of conceiving and constructing knowledge that developed during the time leading up to the establishment of the universities.

Yet we have completely lost two important understandings of philosophy that proved central to Hugh's blueprint for education. First, according to Hugh (as well as other early Christian thinkers), philosophy involved the pursuit of wisdom and not merely the pursuit of certain technical skills such as the use of logic. Echoing Proverbs he opened his first chapter with the claim, "Of all things to be sought, the first is that Wisdom in which the Form of the Perfect Good stands fixed."[14] A second important point is that wisdom for Hugh was found in the ultimate perfect Good—the persons of the Trinity. Consequently Hugh spoke in relational terms about philosophy (i.e., wisdom), since it involved pursuing and getting to know a Being and not simply abstract truths.

> Philosophy, then, is the love and pursuit of Wisdom, and in a certain way, a friendship with it; not, however, of that "wisdom" which is concerned with

20

certain tools and with knowledge and skill in some craft, but of that Wisdom which, wanting in nothing, is a living Mind and the sole primordial Idea or Pattern of things. This love of Wisdom, moreover, is an illumination of the apprehending mind by that pure Wisdom and, in a certain way, a drawing and a calling back to itself of man's mind, so that the pursuit of Wisdom appears like friendship with that Divinity.[15]

In other words, just as friendship involves getting to know the thoughts of another person and drawing closer to each other in the process, Hugh believed the study of philosophy required developing an intellectual friendship with God. Only by getting to know God could one then begin to understand the causes and "Pattern of things." Indeed, this belief that through friendship with God one could understand the cause and pattern of all things in a systematic way, God's ordering of the world, became instrumental in the building of the first universities.[16]

For Hugh, humans also needed to seek God's wisdom for another important reason related to our fundamental identity and the story we tell about our identity. Hugh understood human identity according to the basic outlines of the Christian narrative. We are all made in God's image, but the fall marred this image. Thus, he claimed, "This is our entire task—the restoration of our nature and the removal of our deficiency."[17] Since Christ is "the image of the divine Wisdom, the second person of the Trinitarian Godhead, through whom . . . the Father has established the universe and through whose mysteries, from the fall to the end of time, he accomplishes the work of redemption," we need Christ (i.e., Wisdom) to be reconciled with God.[18] While contemporary Protestants often emphasize Christ's role in atoning for our sin to accomplish "the removal of our deficiency," Hugh also focused on what would involve "the restoration of our nature," or to use language more familiar to Christians today, to become like Christ, the human incarnation of divine wisdom.

Whereas writing about being an imitator of God (Eph 5:1) or becoming like Christ today usually focuses on the ethical ways we are to imitate Christ's virtue, such as sacrificial love, humility, forgiveness, and service,[19] for Hugh the way students can participate in God's restoration of our divine image is through both "the contemplation of truth and the practice of virtue."[20] Contemplating truth involves becoming reconciled to God and then learning God's wisdom through an intimate, loving friendship. In the process, the student joins with the triune God, the ultimate builder, to build in one's heart and mind a place for the divine wisdom.[21] While contemporary thinkers may talk about constructing knowledge or making meaning without reference to some final ideal, Hugh wrote about the need for all humans to discover and construct a place for wisdom in their hearts and minds that adhered to a blueprint provided by God.

> Let no man excuse himself. Let no man say, "I am not able to build a house for the Lord; my poverty does suffice for such an expensive project; I have no place in which to build it." . . . You shall build a house for the Lord out of your own self. He himself will be the builder; your heart will be the place; your thoughts will supply the material.[22]

Hugh believed this motivation for education could apply to all Christians. For Hugh, an educational institution should assist with this majestic endeavor by being God's instrument for helping rebuild the image of Christ in humanity.

In light of the importance of discovering and knowing the wisdom (i.e., Christ) necessary for restoring the divine image, learning proves essential not only for the elite but for all humanity. Everyone's flourishing is aided by growing in wisdom and virtue. In this regard, Hugh had a wider audience in mind than many earlier Christian writers. Previous Christian thinkers often wrote guides about how to organize and think about various forms of knowledge for clergy, clerks, and monastics. A few sought to set forth "an impersonal digest of universal knowledge, an encyclopedic source book."[23] Hugh believed restoring the image of God entailed establishing a friendship with God that supplies us with wisdom—"a living Mind and the sole primordial Idea or Pattern of things."[24] Moreover, this pursuit is meant to be undertaken by the whole of humanity and not merely a chosen few.

Hugh's answers to the *who are we?* and *why learn?* questions provided a rich theological foundation for all of learning. As Ian Wei notes, "It was above all Hugh of St. Victor who fully articulated the monastic view of the proper relationship between life and learning, but also established a place for scholarship practiced on its own terms."[25] Humans, as image bearers of God, Hugh believed, should seek to understand and discover God's ideas through natural and special revelation, especially through Christ, the incarnation of wisdom. Hugh recognized that since humans are made in God's image, they can only more fully bear that image by acquiring the wisdom and character qualities of God we are made to reflect. If Christ is the ultimate incarnation of wisdom, it changes one's whole understanding of philosophy.

Designing the Academic Castle: Creating and Organizing the Curriculum

How does one get to know the triune God, the source of wisdom and the one who can restore our full humanity? For Hugh the liberal arts supply the tools to illuminate both special and natural revelation, which gives us insight into the triune God's living Mind. This wisdom then helps us develop and rebuild our marred image of God. As Hugh contends, "This, then, is what the arts are concerned with, this what they intend, namely, to restore within us the divine likeness, a likeness which to us is a form but to God is his nature."[26] In Hugh's view, the particular arts that constituted philosophy were not a lower form of secular knowledge. With Christ as the foundation, the liberal arts become vitally important because they serve as tools supplied by God's common grace for understanding wisdom, acquiring virtue, and repairing fallen humanity.

Hugh's expansive view of the arts also pertained to how he classified them. As opposed to the traditional seven liberal arts mentioned by various Greek and Roman thinkers and established formally in the fifth century, the *quadrivium* (arithmetic, geometry, music, and astronomy) and the *trivium* (grammar, logic, and rhetoric), Hugh set forth a much grander curriculum containing twenty-one arts (see table 1).[27]

Table 1. The arts within philosophy

Theoretical	Practical (Ethical)	Mechanical	Logical
mathematics	ethics	weaving	grammar
arithmetic	economics	defense	theory of argument
music	politics	navigation	demonstration
astronomy		agriculture	probable
geometry		hunting	argument
physics		medicine	sophistic
theology		theater	

What is important to recognize is that Hugh believed all these arts should be taught within the same institution. In other words, students should not learn about theology in a separate seminary that is somehow disconnected from the other arts. Instead, all of these liberal arts should fit within one educational structure, since we need all of them to discover God's multifaceted wisdom.

It is important to grasp how Hugh's understanding of theology within this vision differed from our contemporary understanding, but we must realize also how he contributed to the way we treat theology today. What today we would describe as the Christian narrative and Christian theological premises actually guided Hugh's whole outlook. Scholars such as Hugh thought about the purposes of education and the curriculum as a whole within the context of the broader Christian theological narrative. As one historian notes of philosophy and theology during this time, "The two were not easily separable in the thinking of that age, and the philosophers . . . were pretty certain to have their fling at purely theological questions."[28] Part of the reason is that church fathers such as Augustine did not envision that subject matter about God should somehow be placed within its own separate category as an academic discipline within the older liberal arts. As G. R. Evans writes, "For Augustine *theologia* is far from being a mere subdivision of *philosophia*. It is the measure against which philosophy's highest achievements are to be tested."[29] Hugh also thought philosophy or wisdom could not be understood apart from friendship with God.

Yet early medieval thinkers, including Hugh, made an important and fateful decision regarding the subject they described as theology that would have a tremendous influence on the original idea of the university. During this time, the curricular systematizers did something unique. They created a special place in the curriculum for something they called the discipline and faculty of theology.[30] The practice of making theology a particular subject within this broad conception of philosophy perhaps originated with Boethius (475–524). In his *Theological Tractates*, he labeled theology as a subdivision of philosophy concerned with God.[31] Hugh copied this practice, which had also been used by earlier Christian systematizers. Although he initially described theology in a broad manner as "discourse concerning the divine, for *theos* means God, and *logos* discourse or knowledge,"[32] he later described the separate art of theology in

24

a more narrow fashion as addressing discussions about "some aspect either of the inexpressible nature of God or of spiritual creatures."[33]

It is important to realize that if one thinks of the curriculum as a structure, as Hugh did, placing theology in a separate academic discipline changed its relationship to other fields of knowledge. Theology becomes no longer understood as Augustine originally conceived it—the foundation that supports all the other disciplines—or to use another common classical analogy, the light by which one more clearly sees all other knowledge. As Hugh's way of organizing knowledge demonstrates, if one sees the disciplines as various rooms, theology appears to be merely a room in the palace.

The idea that theology is merely a room in the palace, however, fails to capture either its exalted status during this time or Hugh's view of it. It is better understood as the pinnacle or upper palace room. Artists at this time depicted theologians as sitting atop the academic tower.[34] Evans observes of this time, "A philosopher may try to acquire any kind of knowledge and be rated a lover of wisdom, although the highest *sapientia* [wisdom] is a knowledge of God. But a theologian must by definition want to know about God."[35] In the language of these systematizers, theology actually served as the royal throne room or pinnacle of all learning. In another source, Hugh called theology the "peak of philosophy and the perfection of truth."[36]

The foundation to the structure of learning was actually supplied by a different set of disciplines. Hugh believed that a student should start with the seven liberal arts found in quadrivium and trivium and even claimed, "It is in the seven liberal arts, however, that the foundation of all learning is to be found."[37] Again, though, it should be noted that for Hugh a theological vision of wisdom informed the whole understanding of why someone should learn the arts. In Hugh's mind, both the reason for learning the liberal arts and the content of the liberal arts were inseparable from theology. Hugh sought to elevate the importance of the liberal arts and not devalue theology. Yet the structures we create sometimes have unintended consequences.

How Do Students Learn?

When it comes to how students should be educated in the arts, Hugh described what today might be called a student-centered approach to learning. In recent times, this language is often used to support the claim that we should fixate on students' needs as the students perceive them. In contrast, Hugh had a clearly defined understanding of what students needed in order to achieve excellence in life in general and in the various arts in particular. First, students required some natural aptitude. Second, they needed certain basic skills (e.g., reading analysis and how to memorize) and a proper environment. Perhaps due to his own experience Hugh recommended studying in a foreign country since "all the world is a foreign soil to those who philosophize."[38]

Third and most importantly, he believed they required virtues that do not come naturally but must be formed through practice. The virtues of discipline and eagerness to inquire, what we might call inquisitiveness, helped. Parsimony or frugality also motivated students since "a fat belly . . . does not produce a fine perception."[39] Although some virtues Hugh listed could be considered common to various traditions of moral thought, particular virtues emphasized within the Christian moral tradition shaped how he understood the best scholarly practices. For instance, Hugh stressed the importance of the Christian virtue of humility for the practice of learning wisdom: "Although the lessons of humility are many, the three which follow are of special importance for the student: first, that he hold no knowledge and writing in contempt; second, that he blush to learn from no man; and third, that when he has attained learning himself, he not look down upon everyone else."[40] Failure to practice humility would undermine all of one's learning, since one sought to acquire the virtues of Christ. Student-centered learning for Hugh meant expecting virtues, especially certain Christian virtues, of students.

This expectation also applied to the habits students must acquire in order to learn. Hugh drew on the monastic tradition to set forth a set of practices one could not employ without attention to the realities described by the Christian narrative. He described five steps the student must undergo: instruction, meditation, prayer, performance, and contemplation. Moving through each of these steps required explicit forms of Christian direction and focus. For example, Hugh drew on the constructive monastic practice of meditation versus what today might be described as the deconstructing task of critical thinking. He claimed:

> Meditation takes its start from reading but is bound by none of reading's rules or precepts. For it delights to range along open ground, where it fixes its free gaze upon the contemplation of truth, drawing together now these, not those causes of things, or now penetrating into profundities, leaving nothing doubtful, nothing obscure. The start of learning, thus, lies in reading, but its consummation lies in meditation. . . . And when through the things which God has made, a man has learned to seek out and to understand him who has made them all, then does he equally instruct his mind with knowledge and fill it with joy. From this it follows that in meditation is to be found the greatest delight.[41]

Instead of deconstructing truth, Hugh saw meditation as building up divine truth, a truth that would lead one to joy instead of emptiness or cynicism. As one proceeds from meditation to performance, one needs prayer.

> Since the counsel of man is weak and ineffective without divine aid, arouse yourself to prayer and ask the help of him without whom you can accomplish no good thing, so that by his grace, which, going before you has enlightened you, he may guide your feet, as you follow, onto the road of peace; and so that he may bring that which as yet is in your will alone, to concrete effect in good performance.[42]

Of course, even in performance, Hugh insisted that a person must realize that he or she is coworking with God. The one who works and walks with God along life's road can eventually come to the ultimate wisdom, the contemplation of God.

It should be noted that, for Hugh, one does not simply proceed up this five-step stairway of learning, but one must continually go up and down the various steps. In other words, one needs to be a lifelong learner who becomes a continually discerning thinker, meditator, pray-er, performer, and contemplator. Hugh maintained that learning required not merely a well-ordered curriculum but also a particular kind of community that acquired certain kinds of virtues and engaged in certain kinds of practices. In this regard, Hugh supplied an amazingly comprehensive vision. He wanted to combine the best of the monastery with the best of contemporary learning to transform the world. The school at St. Victor closed soon after Hugh died, however, perhaps because maintaining such a grand vision that subjects a wide range of students to such a high vision of intellectual, moral, and spiritual excellence proved too difficult.

Building the University

The degree to which scholars credit Hugh and the educational program at St. Victor with influencing the origins of one of the first universities, the University of Paris, varies by whether scholars believe the university represented a break with the past or actually demonstrated continuity with earlier educational visions.[43] Stephen Ferruolo argues that Hugh's school represented an important blueprint: "The Victorine educational program endured as an ideal, as a set of intellectual methods and values against which the other developments in the other schools of Paris were measured, and as a standard that ultimately played a vital role in the formation of the university by the masters and scholars of the city."[44] Certainly, there are ways the University of Paris developed that showed continuities with Hugh's vision regarding the who, why, what, and how of learning, although there were some important discontinuities as well.

The most important continuity pertained to the overall vision of knowledge and its relationship to God. Students studied to understand and discover God's comprehensive and unified wisdom. One recent scholar describes the epistemological assumptions that dominated the early University of Paris:

> It was assumed that the materials given for study—the texts of the tradition, but also the inner and outer world about which they spoke—were amenable to articulation: they had a God-given harmony or beauty about them, even if it was hidden to the untutored eye. It was assumed that to discover that harmonious ordering was not simply an intellectual game, but one of the means (or part of the means) for discovering the good ordering of human life before God, including the good ordering of social life.[45]

The curriculum set forth in the early University of Paris was not nearly as extensive as Hugh of St. Victor's curriculum, but it did include teaching the seven traditional liberal arts in a school of liberal arts and the advanced arts of medicine, law, and theology. Since the seven arts were considered the foundation of learning, the early statutes stipulated that the teachers had to be at least twenty-one years old and have studied these arts for at least six years.[46]

Similar to Hugh's curricular vision, theology was considered the most exalted among the other faculties of medicine, law, and the liberal arts. Later in the twelfth century, scholars had expanded Hugh's narrow conception of theology to include the study of the Bible, Christian doctrine, and Christian practice. Due to these scholars' efforts to create a more systematic account of these sources, they created the academic discipline of theology, which was part of the larger disciplinary palace being built as universities emerged.[47] As Evans observes, "It is not coincidence that the forming of theology as an academic discipline went hand in hand with the slow development of the twelfth-century schools into the first universities."[48] Scholars used the language of politics to describe theology as the "queen of the sciences,"[49] which meant they considered it the most prestigious and rigorous. As a consequence, theology was studied only after one had mastered the liberal arts. A doctorate in theology at the University of Paris, for example, required one to be thirty-five years old and to undergo sixteen years of study.[50]

The methods of learning also showed continuity with Hugh's vision. Although Enlightenment devotees such as Hastings Rashdall have claimed the University of Paris prospered by cultivating forms of critical thinking separate from the past Christian tradition,[51] scholars today believe that approaches to thinking in early universities actually shared much with Hugh's Christian vision. In an early university such as the University of Paris, "reason emerges not *over and against* Christian devotion, but *as a form of* Christian devotion."[52] In other words, the development of practices that strengthened one's reasoning abilities were not a means of escaping the Christian tradition but were actually "a new form of medieval devotional practice or . . . spiritual discipline" that had its origins in the monastic tradition.[53] Early thinkers in the university, similar to Hugh, used certain kinds of meditation not as a means to escape God but as a means to better understand God and God's plan for their lives and the world.

The two particular methods emphasized in the University of Paris were the careful reading of and meditation on authoritative texts, which one then sought to systematize (known as *lectio*) and debate (known as *disputatio*). Regarding the former, Michal Higton claims *lectio* was "*the* central practice of the emerging university."[54] Similar to what Hugh set forth, this process required particular kinds of intellectual virtues and practices (e.g., humility, piety, patience) previously nurtured in the monastic orders but now practiced in the world. As Higton states, "Reason seriously practiced is a means by which the reasoned is called out of himself; it waits humbly upon an articulation that it cannot simply invent, attending to an ordering in things that is understood as God's good gift."[55] This kind of meditative reading seeks to discover the order that God has already provided in the world.

While *lectio* provided this opportunity for the individual learner, *disputatio* supplied the social means by which to sharpen one's view of God's world. Here perhaps is where the ideas about learning added to Hugh's original vision, which he derived from monastic ideas. At the early University of Paris, the implementation of *disputatio* meant that through dialogue with others, one's ideas were sharpened. Again, however, this practice required the peaceful hospitality and listening that one found in the monastic setting in order that intellectual debate did not descend into fractious or perhaps violent fights.

Of course, numerous cultural, economic, and political factors beyond philosophical blueprints such as that found in Hugh's *Didascalicon* played a role in bringing about the creation of the University of Paris. One of these external factors proved to be the church. The church placed a high priority on the emerging masters (i.e., teachers) and scholars and labeled them the "mirror of the church," since the church's leadership increasingly came from the academic world.[56] Paolo Nardi observes that so many church leaders came from academic circles "that the world of study appeared to be identical with the church itself."[57] In return for the support provided by the academic masters in advancing rationally intelligible doctrine against heresies, strengthening the institutional church, and providing educated staff, the church granted students and masters certain "universal" rights and privileges that transcended local authorities (such as towns, dioceses, principalities, and states) and applied them throughout geographical Christendom.[58] Masters and students were placed under the protection of papal authority and given legal protection by the church against local and regional political and ecclesiastical authorities; and the degrees conferred allowed graduates to teach not only in local areas but across Christendom.[59]

The church also provided one other important function in that it nurtured academic freedom. As William Hoye writes, "Both the idea of the university and the idea of academic freedom can be called gifts of medieval Christianity to the modern world."[60] Since this claim flies in the face of some popular views of the medieval church, it helps to explain Hoye's argument. Hoye points out that the first mention of the scholastic freedom (*libertas scholastic*) of universities, or what today we would define as academic freedom, was made by Pope Honorius III in 1220 in the midst of a conflict between the University of Bologna, usually considered one of the original universities, and local civic government. The city government insisted that the students pledge an oath of allegiance to the city, while the pope encouraged the university to defend its scholastic freedom and resist such attempts. Throughout this time and later, the church would defend students and professors against abuses by local governments or even local ecclesiastical authorities, encourage broad freedom of travel, and provide professors the right to teach anywhere in Christendom.[61] The church's role was aided by its transnational character and the fact that universities were also initially transnational entities. As Hugh's understanding of the purpose of higher education and the curriculum make clear, national political interests did not take a primary shaping role.

The Fallen Realities

Despite the existence of these early high ideals that were put into partial practice, this time was not an unspoiled age to which the university can and should return. It is helpful to remember that some early thinkers even saw the first universities themselves as an impediment to learning. The theologian and poet Philippus de Grevia, who served as chancellor at the University of Paris from 1218 to 1236, made this complaint about the new institution:

> At one time, when each *magister* taught independently and when the name of the university was unknown, there were more lectures and disputations and more interest in scholarly things. Now, however, when you have joined yourselves together in a university, lectures and disputations have become less frequent; everything is done hastily, little is learnt, and the time needed for

study is wasted in meetings and discussions. While the elders debate in their meetings and enact statutes, the young ones organize villainous plots and plan their nocturnal attacks.[62]

University administrators today could relate to this eight-hundred-year-old problem. The original universities, while nourished by particular Christian ideas, were flawed institutions that never fully incarnated the original ideals set forth by scholars such as Hugh.

One of the cracks in the original foundation concerned, as mentioned before, the creation of theology as a separate faculty and its placement in the curriculum. For the curriculum that Hugh of St. Victor envisioned to succeed an important combination had to be maintained. One could not simply separate theology and philosophy and consider Scripture the source for theology and creation the source of philosophy. They must be integrated. Indeed, Hugh claimed that one had to maintain an important distinction, not between theology and philosophy, but between worldly theology and true theology.

> But worldly theology adopted the works of creation and the elements of this world that it might make its demonstration in these. . . . And for this reason, namely, because it used a demonstration which revealed little, it lacked ability to bring forth the incomprehensible truth without the stain of error. . . . In this were the wise men of the world fools, namely, that proceeding by natural evidences alone and following the elements and appearances of the world, they lacked the lessons of grace.[63]

In contrast, the study of God's wisdom (philosophy) found in *both* creation and God's special revelation, Hugh contended, leads us to bear the image of God in fuller ways. Hugh understood divine revelation through Scripture as the preeminent source for this restoration, but "natural considerations" and "natural arts" should also play a role.[64] In other words, Hugh believed the liberal arts were needed to interpret Scripture, and both the liberal arts and Scripture were needed as sources for theology.

Furthermore, for Hugh the stairs in this academic palace should go both ways. Theology and Scripture were also needed to properly interpret and apply the liberal arts and to fit together a comprehensive understanding of philosophy or wisdom as a whole. The content of Christian faith must be integrated with the ways we learn the liberal arts. Figures such as Hugh tended to emphasize the creative and redemptive role that the liberal arts can play for the one who already subscribed to the Christian theological outlook.

Later medieval scholars such as Thomas Aquinas, a theologian at the University of Paris, would carry forth an important part of this vision. They believed the ends of the university must be linked to an understanding of humans as made *imago Dei*, in the image of God. As Alasdair MacIntyre writes, "The ends of education, that is to say, can, on Aquinas's view, be correctly developed only with reference to the final end of human beings and the ordering of the curriculum has to be an ordering to that final end."[65] Unfortunately, as MacIntyre notes, this thought "was remarkably uninfluential in determining how universities developed."[66] Part of the problem, we contend, was that scholars such as Aquinas actually created an academic structure that, by the very way it was constructed, conceived of philosophy as increasingly separate from theology. The stairs also became less traveled. MacIntyre observes about the difference between Aquinas's view of the relationship between theology and philosophy and Augustine's: "Although Aquinas as both theologian and philosopher moves easily between them, he is always alert to the distinction. Although he is unflinchingly Augustinian in his theology, he treats philosophy as an independent form of enquiry in a way and to a degree that Augustine never did."[67] It is also a distinction Hugh of St. Victor did not draw, since he saw theology as the "peak of philosophy and the perfection of truth."

Aquinas also drew a sharper distinction between natural theology/philosophy and biblical theology.[68] The former could rely on human reason untutored by biblical revelation. This distinction would later make it easier to secularize conceptualizations of knowledge and limit one's understanding of God's relationship to knowledge, particularly when the university abandoned monastic forms of discipline and practices. While this distinction placed biblical theology in an elevated position, it also isolated it from the liberal arts. This change meant students received less guidance regarding how broad Christian theological content and narratives animate the rest of the liberal arts curriculum.

The result is perhaps best related in a picture from Gregorius Reisch's *Margarita Philosophica* (1503), an illustrated encyclopedia of academic knowledge composed just before the Reformation.[69] The drawing depicts theology at the top of a tower of knowledge but separate from the other liberal arts on which it was built (see figure 1). Moreover, the other liberal arts in this drawing were simply learned from pagan authors such as Aristotle, Cicero, Pythagoras, Euclid, Ptolemy, and Seneca without theological input. The connection between theology and the liberal arts supplied by a common theological story that Hugh envisioned had diminished and perhaps even disappeared.

Figure 1. Tower of Philosophy, woodcut from Gregor Reisch, *Margarita Philosophica*, c. 1503

The methods for learning these different forms of knowledge also transformed over time. Hugh emphasized the importance of friendship with God, the need for virtues such as humility, and the necessity of Christian practices such as meditation and prayer when learning the liberal arts. One finds this vision depicted visually closer to Hugh's time. In the Tower of Learning developed by John of Metz (1310), depicted in figure 2, one finds a vision of Christian wisdom where the virtues prove instrumental for obtaining wisdom.

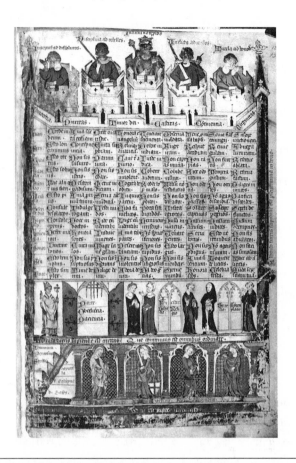

Figure 2. Miniature of the Tower of Wisdom, from the De Lisle Psalter. Courtesy of the British Library Catalogue of Illuminated Manuscripts.

The Christian virtue of humility serves as the tower's foundation. Although the four key supporting pillars are the cardinal virtues emphasized by pagan and Christian writers alike (prudence, justice, fortitude, and temperance), to reach the top of the tower one must climb the stairs using the Christian virtue of "charity," the key to all the virtues listed within the tower. Furthermore, one must enter through the door of "obedience" and "patience." The stones on the left that constitutes the castle list key virtues such as honesty, mercy, and compassion. The stones to the right specify nine actions that help one develop those virtues, such as "flee vainglory" or "be upstanding."

35

What became lost as the medieval vision of the university developed was the need for the Christian story and Christian theology to undergird and inform the development of these virtues and practices for learning. After all, this foundation must support the whole structure of wisdom. The absence of this foundation occurred due to the growing confidence in human reason. Philosophy became that which could be known through human reason, and theology pertained to that understood by faith and grace. Any attempt to teach the liberal arts without the benefit of theology would have surprised an earlier church father such as Augustine. For someone such as Augustine, the dangers of learning the liberal arts outside of a loving friendship with God were quite apparent. In his *Confessions*, Augustine claimed,

> From my nineteenth year to my twenty-eighth, I went astray and led others astray. I was deceived and deceived others, in varied lustful projects—sometimes publicly, by the teaching of what men style "the liberal arts"; sometimes secretly, under the false guise of religion. In the one, I was proud of myself; in the other, superstitious; in all, vain![70]

Later he confessed in language that recalls Plato's allegory about the cave:

> And what did it profit me that I could read and understand for myself all the books I could get in the so-called "liberal arts," when I was actually a worthless slave of wicked lust? I took delight in them, not knowing the real source of what it was in them that was true and certain. For I had my back toward the light, and my face toward the things on which the light falls, so that my face, which looked toward the illuminated things, was not itself illuminated.[71]

In particular, Augustine lamented his lack of gratitude to God for the ability to be able to understand the various arts.

> Whatever was written in any of the fields of rhetoric or logic, geometry, music, or arithmetic, I could understand without any great difficulty and without the instruction of another man. All this thou knowest, O Lord my God, because both quickness in understanding and acuteness in insight are thy gifts. Yet for such gifts I made no thank offering to thee. Therefore, my abilities served not my profit but rather my loss.[72]

For Augustine, the so-called liberal arts, when taught outside the Christian theological narrative and community, and the practice of particular Christian virtues such as humility and gratitude to God, did not furnish one

36

with liberation; they merely amplified one's enslavement. When university scholars exalted the liberal arts as the road to knowledge without the need for divine revelation, they departed from what Augustine and Hugh thought of as the way to build wisdom.

These fateful developments about how to build, organize, and teach knowledge, we will argue, created a structure for knowledge that did not make theology and the resulting Christian virtues the foundation. Instead, theology became the queen of the sciences placed in a room at the top of the academic structure. In other words, Hugh's organization of the curriculum created an easier road to compartmentalization. Although Hugh integrated theology throughout his vision, he also created a separate academic room for it. Making theology the pinnacle of education resulted in the loss of theology as the foundational curriculum.

We simply do not want theology to be the top of the tower or the throne room of the palace. Indeed, this is one reason we think it may have been helpful to switch metaphors regarding the university and its associated curriculum to a more organic one. If we are made in God's image and the purpose of the university is to help us rebuild that image by acquiring God's wisdom, the whole university must be engaged in building friendship with God. This remains the soul of the university, and the whole body of the university must be connected to it and involved with it. In this regard, theology can and must be understood as essential to the soul of the university. It enlivens and connects to every discipline or every part of the academic body. It cannot be isolated to a particular part of the body.

The church's active role in the medieval university prevented the problem of theology's separation and isolation from other disciplines from becoming apparent in the early university's life. Today, however, the problem is quite apparent. Philosophy pertains to something quite different from the divine wisdom Hugh of St. Victor envisioned. Indeed, the idea that philosophy encompasses learning theology and God's wisdom is lost. It is no wonder that two scholars who recently interviewed Catholic leaders of higher education concluded,

> While many admired the traditional framework of the Catholic intellectual tradition, the role of philosophy in communicating that tradition to current students is hazy in the minds of many senior administrators we interviewed,

who simply did not point to philosophy as a major vehicle for presenting aspects of the Catholic tradition today.[73]

The reason for this development will be explained in the next chapter. The growing distinction between theology and philosophy would also create a crack in the foundation of the university that would split even more when the church broke into separate pieces.

2

A CRACKED PINNACLE AND SHIFTING FOUNDATION

Attempting to Repair the University (1517–1800)

...

Refinement and elegance of speech, the acuteness of reason,
adroitness in mathematics and geometry, knowledge of the heavens
and the whole world will be brought together in order to form
the soul, to give it a pattern, to set it firmly,
to render it elegant and perfect.

PETER RAMUS

The very notion of the nature and order of things,
of a single universe, different aspects of which are objects of enquiry
for the various disciplines, but in such a way that each aspect needs
to be related to every other, this notion no longer informs the
enterprise of the contemporary American university.
It has become an irrelevant concept.

ALASDAIR MACINTYRE

ONE OF THE CENTRAL IDEAS medieval university professors taught was the belief that universal wisdom existed and could be known. The core premise behind this idea was that all knowledge emanated from the triune

God. The wisdom of God embedded in God's creation could be discovered through God's revelation both in nature and in special revelation. Part of obtaining wisdom involved understanding the different relationships between particular disciplines, general knowledge as a whole, and human flourishing. As the last chapter chronicled, the Catholic Church sought and gave support to this unified vision of wisdom while it supported the formation and growth of universities.[1]

Although the church had already fractured in the eleventh century (1054 officially) when the Roman Catholic and Eastern Orthodox branches separated, this split did not have a significant influence on early universities and their respective curricula. The invention of the European university occurred solely in Catholic lands. In contrast, the Eastern Orthodox Church did not participate in the governance of any new European universities.[2] The seventy universities existing in 1500 still officially represented only one outlook—that of the Catholic Church. Theology also retained its preeminent position as the pinnacle or upper palace room in the academic castle, both shaping and giving unity to the university curriculum even up until the Reformation.[3]

The Reformation changed everything. The reforms initiated by Martin Luther in 1517 and continued by John Calvin and others resulted in different confessions taking over existing universities. The Reformers also helped create something new in the history of the university. When Lutheran, Reformed, and Anglican universities sprang into being, the denominational university was born. By its very nature, the denominational university posed a particular problem for the idea of universal truth and wisdom. How could a divided church with disparate theology faculties still support a unified vision of truth in the post-Reformation world? Moreover, how could theology still reign as the queen of the sciences in the upper palace room if different types of theology departments now existed throughout European universities? The queen of the sciences proved unable to retain her crown over a divided kingdom. The theological pinnacle or upper palace room was breaking apart. Could anything be done to repair the damage? Moreover, what would be the results of this fragmentation for the foundation of the university, the liberal arts? This chapter chronicles two noble figures who tried to provide solutions to these problems. They proposed an approach that sought to make Christian theology the foundation on which everything should be built. Unfortunately, their efforts could not stem changes that shifted the university's central focus from God to nature. As in the past, humans began to believe that nature and not God could serve as the foundation for the castle of wisdom they hoped to build.

The Attempt to Repair the Foundations of the Medieval University

On August 26, 1572, blood stained the streets of Paris as mobs ran wild. Inspired by political rulers, the Catholic mobs murdered at least two thousand French Protestant Huguenots in what become known as the Massacre of St. Bartholomew's Day. Not even small children and women were spared. Geoffrey Treasure summarizes the fate of one woman who broke her legs trying to escape over a roof after her husband was killed: "She was caught, dragged by the hair through the streets, her hands cut off at the wrists to secure her bracelets; she was impaled on a spit before being dumped in the Seine."[4]

Among those murdered during this ghastly spectacle was a Protestant professor named Pierre de la Ramée, commonly known in English as Peter Ramus. The motivation for the murder remains subject to scholarly debate.[5] One scholar claims it stemmed from academic revenge. Another professor, Jacques Charpentier, still smarting from Ramus's attacks on his competence six years earlier, is said to have hired assassins to murder Ramus. Others simply maintain he was killed for his allegiance to the French Protestant Reformation. Whatever the motive, we do know that Ramus met his end in one of the University of Paris's colleges. His body was thrown out a window, decapitated and whipped by students, dragged around the streets, and then thrown in the Seine.

Ramus certainly had plenty of enemies. In fact he made enemies most of his life. One colleague even described him as "either rabid and demented or else perverse and criminal," and the king of France called him "ignorant, impudent, arrogant, and a liar."[6] Modern scholars have also found him irritating, with one placing a less than flattering quote from one of Ramus's contemporaries as an epigram to his title page: "You will never be a great man if you think that Ramus was a great man."[7]

41

What did Ramus do to outrage and irritate everyone? He sought to reform the university. For example, he thought that everyone should have the chance to attend a university, to afford a university education, and to learn the liberal arts in their own language. "It is a most unworthy thing," he complained, "that the road leading to knowledge of philosophy be closed and forbidden to the poor, even when they are wise and learned."[8] He also believed that faculty appointments should be based on merit and not social and political connections, that the students should not support idle faculty, and that universities should be publicly funded in addition to student fees—certainly crazy ideas!

Ramus's own experience informed his critique. He was orphaned at a young age and had few of the aristocratic benefits and connections of his fellow students (for example, his grandfather was a charcoal burner). As a student of modest means, he had not been able to rely on wealth and prestige to advance.[9] He recalled of his early educational experience, "I confess that my whole life has been one bitter struggle. . . . As a young boy under every possible handicap I came to Paris to study the liberal arts. Twice I was forced to return from Paris, but the more studies were denied me, the more I wanted to study."[10] His struggles would lead him to advocate throughout his life for ways to make complex ideas more accessible to a wider audience.

Perhaps the most outrageous part of Ramus's efforts to reform the university concerned the curriculum. Ramus thought the very curricular foundations of the medieval university needed to be repaired. It was also, as every professor who has dealt with revisions to the general education curriculum knows, the most dangerous and important place to start. The university was now typically divided into four faculties: theology, law, medicine, and the liberal arts/philosophy. The idea that the liberal arts faculty address a separate realm known as philosophy was a development Hugh of St. Victor would not have understood, since he saw all the arts as philosophy, the study of wisdom. The liberal arts/philosophy faculty was the largest of all the faculties in a university, since it was also where most every university student started.[11] As Wilhelm Schmidt-Biggemann observes, "It was the faculty of the beginning and the beginner. . . . Though it occupied the lowest rung on the ladder of knowledge, it was the faculty that determined what ordered rational knowledge was."[12]

The problem with the liberal arts, according to Ramus, stemmed from the university's attempt to build its foundations on the pagan Greek philosopher Aristotle. Medieval scholars such as Thomas Aquinas had attempted to synthesize Aristotle's philosophy with Christianity, suggesting that natural human reason could lead pagan thinkers to common truths also found in Scripture. Yet, as mentioned in chapter one, Aquinas also reinforced a sharper distinction between theology and philosophy in ways previous Christian thinkers had not.[13]

As a result, professors in the lower-level arts faculty of the university often taught Aristotle's ethics and metaphysics with little additional theological critique. Indeed, as we noted at the end of the last chapter, theology became a separate academic palace (or pinnacle) at the top of the learning castle. Moreover, the stairs between the theology and arts faculty were not exactly well trod and, in fact, were quite decayed. As one scholar notes of Ramus's time, "Generally speaking, professors of philosophy and theology tended to go their separate ways."[14] Of course, the liberal arts faculty at this time still touched on key theological issues such as the existence and nature of God and the immortality of the soul, but their treatment of logic, rhetoric, ethics, and metaphysics relied heavily on Aristotle's works with limited modification.

Ramus wanted to challenge Aristotle's dominance in the liberal arts. It remains unclear whether Ramus actually began his critique with the less than subtle master's thesis "Everything that was said by Aristotle is inconsistent."[15] Nonetheless, Ramus mounted a full-scale attack on the extensive use of Aristotle and the arid scholasticism associated with philosophy at that time, instead arguing that the arts always had to be practical and that they should be taught in practical ways. As Ramus complained of Aristotle's logic, "Ordinary people don't talk like that," and people would laugh if anyone did.[16] In contrast, Ramus argued that since every person came into the world possessed of a natural, God-given ability to reason, people tend to use the arts, such as logic, in actual daily practice. The examples for arts, such as logic and rhetoric, should then be derived from daily practice.[17]

Critics were not impressed. One English scholar lamented that Ramus sought to overthrow "the grounds, principles, and rules of that most illustrious and thrice renowned *Aristotle*." His disciples, he feared, "shall with their owne furious and witles conceits, set the whole world in combustion."[18] Ramus's attacks on Aristotle resulted in King Francis I labeling Ramus "ignorant, a liar, arrogant, and impudent" and led him to ban Ramus's books.[19]

The attacks and ban did not work. The popularity of Ramus's works rose throughout Europe. What proved particularly attractive was Ramus's fundamental belief and general insistence that the liberal arts should be made accessible to a wider audience and that knowledge and its teaching should be focused on the practical results it would have on one's life. Ramus's non-hierarchical perspective would be one reason his views proved popular among the Puritans, particularly the Puritans at Harvard during its first hundred years.[20]

What also made Ramus's perspective attractive to these new Puritans was the fact that he became one of them. Ramus converted to the Protestant faith at age fifty-four in 1569. Many Catholics were not sad to see him leave, since many considered his attacks on Aristotle as attacks on the Catholic faith.[21] He had also criticized the theology faculty in 1562 for placing too much emphasis on the scholastics and not enough on teaching the Old and New Testaments in their original languages. Indeed, Ramus's late interest in theology would prove to be particularly influential among Puritans.

Ramus's full views might not have been known, except for one unusual historical event (which his followers considered providential). The night Ramus was murdered, his attackers also ransacked and destroyed his library. Yet one particularly important unpublished manuscript survived, Ramus's commentary on the Christian religion. It contained the materials others would use in their attempt to build a new foundation for the liberal arts and the university, and not merely a new upper theological palace room.

In this work, Ramus set forth a vision that would once again make Christian theology and ethics foundational to the liberal arts. He defined theology in a broad fashion as the "doctrine of living well" for God.[22] It involved faith and actions. This foundational theology, Ramus believed, should serve as a replacement for Aristotle's metaphysics and ethics. For Ramus, the contrast was quite simple: "Theology is comprised in faith in God and the actions of faith, but human philosophy [Aristotle] embraces happiness by the contemplation of wisdom and the action of courage, temperance, and justice."[23] He also believed Aristotle came to the wrong conclusions about God, faith, providence, sin, worship, and eternal life. In contrast, he insisted, "Let us speak the words of Holy Scripture; let us use the language of the Holy Spirit. For the Spirit is the most true teacher of wisdom and the most eminent rhetorical teacher of eloquence."[24] Ramus's insistence on teaching a biblically rooted view of knowledge represented a radical break from the typical approach to the liberal arts at the time.

How successful was Ramus in convincing others to put his radical ideas into action? One biographer concluded, "He was not successful at all,"[25] at least in France. In England, however, as noted above, Ramus's radical ideas found a following among the Puritans studying and teaching at Christ's College, University of Cambridge. The Puritans agreed with Ramus that what Protestant reformers needed was a way of approaching knowledge and the arts that could be "free of Aristotelianism and popish scholasticism," as well as "pagan atheism or popish doctrines."[26] In order to redeem the university from these influences, the Puritans realized they needed to reorganize the structure of knowledge. Ramus became their inspiration and guide. One Puritan in particular, William Ames, became "the foremost seventeenth-century Puritan Ramist."[27]

William Ames (1576–1633)

Ames, like Ramus, became an orphan at a young age. As a result, he was brought up by a Puritan uncle who also provided him with an education. He eventually attended the University of Cambridge, where he experienced a profound religious conversion while also drinking deeply from Puritan thinking. It was at Cambridge that Ames encountered Ramus's thought[28] and where Ames came to consider Ramus "the greatest master of the arts."[29]

One of Ramus's most important influences on Ames, as well as other Puritans, concerned his interest in something called *technometria*, "the science of defining and delineating the arts according to their nature and use."[30] What made this science possible centered on a particular Christian conviction about knowledge. Ramus and the Puritans believed that knowledge is one and that "God, the Alpha and Omega, creates all things and governs all things by eternal, immutable laws."[31] God also creates and distributes knowledge. "God put knowledge into things, where man through his senses can find it and through his reason understand it. . . . Knowledge originates from God and through his benevolence is carried to men, at least in some essentials."[32]

Although a unified church no longer provided curricular unity, Protestants still wanted a common Christian narrative to guide contemporary views about the curriculum. Christians, Ames believed, could use *techno-metria* to discover broad, God-ordained laws found in the world of knowledge and organize the arts into an "*encyclopaedia*, the circle or totality of the arts."[33] Knowledge of all the arts would be *pansophia*, or universal wisdom. In Ames's work, one finds echoes of Hugh of St. Victor's vision for finding, through the curriculum, a universal wisdom rooted in God.

Inspired by Ramus, Ames proposed something remarkably original for his time as he set forth the view that theology should play a role in his new construction of the liberal arts. As Norman Fiering points out, "Such an arrangement was unheard of in medieval universities."[34] Ames no longer believed that theology should serve as the premier discipline that would only be studied by a chosen few. He believed everyone in the university needed to study theology. In other words, theology needed to be taught in the liberal arts and not merely to those who today we would consider the most advanced graduate students. One historian called this position a declaration that theology is meant to be an art "for every man, not reserved for the expert or the *perfectiones*."[35] It held the potential to transform the soul of the university at the time.

In one respect, though, Ames still categorized knowledge in a similar fashion. Ames listed theology as one of six major arts, with the others being logic, grammar, rhetoric, mathematics, and physics.[36] For Ames, this view did not mean theology was somehow unrelated to the other arts: "To God the truth of knowledge is obviously single and undivided, but as it is reflected in creation like the refraction of a ray of light, it appears to man as multiple kinds of truth discernible as the arts."[37] In Ames's refracted vision, theology should be divided further into two parts, faith and observance, which take the place of classical medieval metaphysics and ethics taught using Aristotle (see table 2). Like Ramus, Ames thought the teaching of Aristotelian ethics and metaphysics corrupted students. He approvingly quoted from Ramus that he would prefer philosophy be taught to students out of the gospel by a learned theologian of proven character than out of Aristotle by a philosopher. A child will learn many impieties from Aristotle which, it is to be feared, he will unlearn too late. He will learn for example, that the beginning of blessedness arises out of man; that the end of blessedness lies in man; that all virtues are within man's power and obtainable by man's nature, art and industry; that God is never present in such works, either as helper or author, however great and divine they are; that divine providence is removed from the theatre of human life; that not a word can be spoken about divine justice; that man's blessedness is based on this frail life.[38]

Table 2. Ames's organization of the arts

General Arts	Special Arts
logic	mathematics
grammar	physics
rhetoric	theology
	observance
	faith

He also pointed to history to demonstrate that few lovers of Aristotelian metaphysics came to Christianity, while many Platonists did. The reason why, he believed, is that Aristotle's metaphysics "presumed to teach about God without the Father, God without the Redeemer, God without the Sanctifier—in short, God without God."[39] It would be better if faith and observance replaced Aristotle's metaphysics and ethics since "the theologian who lives best is the best theologian. The person who is only an observer and teacher of theology is no theologian."[40] To provide an imperfect comparison, such a change today might be like replacing two required general education courses in philosophical ethics and metaphysics with Christian theology and Christian ethics courses.

Moreover, for Ames, the other five arts were largely skills or tools without moral content. To use a building metaphor that Hugh of St. Victor preferred, Ames set theology, which for him included both actions and cognitive beliefs, as the foundation for learning and considered the other arts merely to be helpful tools used for building the academic structure. The rooms built on the theological foundation should be the results of the uses of these various arts (e.g., politics, household economics, jurisprudence). Nonetheless, they all should relate to the foundation of theology, since for Ames "there is no precept of universal truth relevant to living well in domestic economy, morality, political life, or lawmaking which does not rightly pertain to theology."[41] Ames always placed his primary focus on theology. "Technometria and logic help to systematize and analyze, but theology alone speaks the message of truth."[42] The American Puritan John Cotton claimed of Ames that his "very sinews and marrow were theological."[43] One biographer of Ames notes, "Hardly a page survives from Ames that is not theological."[44] The reason why is that, as Ames claimed, "the highest kind of life for a human being is that which approaches most closely the living and life-giving God," and that "theology is the doctrine of living to God."[45] Theology was for Ames "as wide as human experience and as long as life."[46] It could and therefore should serve as the foundation, or what we would prefer to call the soul, for understanding all the other arts since it was "the ultimate and noblest of all teaching arts."[47] "Other arts teach how to reason, to speak, to communicate, to count, and to understand nature, but theology alone teaches how 'to live.'"[48]

Ames's book *The Marrow of Sacred Divinity*, which set forth his approach, gained a wide following among Puritans and became particularly influential among those who immigrated to the New World. According to Increase Mather, Ames accepted an invitation to teach at the new college being started in the American colonies, Harvard. Mather later wrote that if not for that "particular *diversion* given by the hand of heaven," Ames would have come. That diversion happened to be Ames's death at age fifty-seven in the Netherlands. His wife and children eventually moved to Cambridge, Massachusetts, and some of Ames's grandchildren attended Harvard. Furthermore, his *Marrow of Sacred Divinity* later became a well-used text at both Harvard and Yale.[49]

Ames's vision, like Ramus's, however, only succeeded for a short period of time, and even the way in which his writings were used demonstrated its actual failure. For example, the colonial colleges used *The Marrow of Theology* for a number of years. A detailed listing of the Harvard curriculum in 1723 lists Ames's *Marrow of Theology* as a required text in, of all places, natural philosophy—the reason being that Harvard still required traditional ethics and metaphysics instead of theology courses. Theology remained a course of study only for those entering the ministry who had already earned a bachelor's degree. The idea that all undergraduate students should study theology failed to take hold even in a Puritan Protestant American college.[50] The failure to build a new foundation for the university meant that the old, broken theological palace room remained over a building that appeared to have many foundational problems. Indeed, theology, or divinity, would increasingly be removed as the apex of American curricular life. What took its place in the growing number of American universities is an important story.

The Fragmented Church and the Decline of Theology

One might expect that since the religious divisions produced by the Reformation created religious conflict that spilled into the academy, streets, and battlefields, universities would have been devastated by the conflicts. Yet, while particular universities did suffer, in general the religious divisions produced by the Reformation created intellectual competition that actually led to a growth in the number of universities. The Lutheran, Reformed, and Anglican Churches took over eleven existing universities, but they also created new ones. By 1700, Calvinists claimed or created nine new universities, Lutherans fourteen, and Anglicans three. Altogether Protestants had created or started twenty-six universities. The Catholics were also not idle and actually outpaced the Protestants, starting sixty-four new universities. The Jesuits alone started or influenced the founding of thirty-one of these institutions. From the start of the Reformation in 1517 to 1789, the number of universities in Europe would more than double to 143.[51]

A similar competition on a lesser scale also took place in the New World. In the British colonies, from the founding of Harvard by Congregationalists in 1636 and William and Mary by Anglicans in 1693, six more colleges were begun by a wide variety of Protestant traditions (see table 3). The Catholics would not be quite so successful in the American colonies, although they did found Georgetown in 1789. More importantly, they founded over thirty universities in Latin America and Canada between 1551 and 1791.[52] Even into the nineteenth century, new colleges and universities would be created throughout the Americas.

Table 3. Origins of American colleges, 1700–1776

College	Denomination	Date of Founding
Yale	Congregationalist	1701
Princeton (College of New Jersey)	Presbyterian	1746
Columbia	Anglican	1754
Brown	Baptist	1764
Rutgers	Dutch Reformed	1766
Dartmouth	Congregationalist	1769

Although religious competition may have been good for the spread of colleges and universities, it was not good for the academic study of theology. Before the Reformation, theology was the leading faculty. Because of the Reformation, however, it lost this position.[53] As Wilhelm Schmidt-Biggemann notes:

> The result of the doctrinal conflict between the three main confessions, which had been made possible by theology as the leading science common to all three, was the paralysis of theology's claim to truth. If the confessional theological experts in the universities and colleges were unable to reach consensus on central questions, it could be argued that there was nothing there on which to agree. The polemical debate which dragged on for generations no longer discredited only the respective opponents but also the entire area of confessional theology.[54]

Yet if the church and church-sponsored theology departments could no longer find and incarnate some semblance of a unified truth, what other entities and academic fields would come forward to provide unity and a foundation for the university? The substitute entities that did emerge, ironically, would actually end up radically transforming parts of the academic structure even further.

The Solution to Theological Sectarianism

The pressing question for leaders and academics in the emerging nation-states, particularly those with a significant amount of Christian pluralism, pertained to finding moral agreement. How does one arrive at moral agreement on which to make laws, particularly in lands where deep theological and ecclesiastical differences exist? The answer could not be found in theology since "confessional theology was in the long run clearly incapable of fulfilling its role of political legitimation any more than it proved itself a unifying theological force as polemical theology. Theology was no longer credible."[55] Scholars also did not turn to another option that could have been possible, focusing on what C. S. Lewis famously called "mere Christianity" or what others have called the common Christian worldview—the theological foundations and beliefs that all Christian confessions have in common.

Instead, the new approach of intellectuals was to turn to a source of knowledge beyond the Bible that all humans had in common—a move that Ames had foreseen and tried to guard against. As Norman Fiering notes, "Ames' prescient fear was that the divines in his time would deteriorate into the moral philosophers of old, abandoning revelation and relying only on the inbred law and the Sinai of nature."[56] Ames was right. Scholars began turning to an understanding that God had created a moral order that could be discerned through nature. As one scholar of the university curriculum observes, "The discredit in which the theologies had fallen was partly compensated for by the rise of the law of nature."[57]

The "law of nature" would not be the only term used. Other writers called it natural law, natural theology, natural philosophy, and so on. The key underlying belief behind this approach was that while humans may disagree on theological truths determined through special revelation, they could agree on moral knowledge determined through nature. Appeals to nature became the source for justifying everything political—social contract theory, human rights, violating a nation's laws, and more. It seemed to be the one source of unity that could provide a common point of reference and hold back the growing power of various political leaders.

In this situation, the fields of law and philosophy came to be seen as the most important disciplines for helping students think about the legal and moral implications of nature. Yet philosophy ended with a distinct advantage. Schmidt-Biggemann summarizes the development as follows:

> The paralysis of confessional theology had rendered new theological foundations and a new but still political legitimation of sovereignty necessary. Both these tasks had been accomplished by the revision of the concept of nature, by the concept of natural theology and that of natural law. But because

theology remained confessional and jurisprudence became political, philosophy was able to become the leading science, a position to which it laid claim during the Enlightenment and in the end attained.[58]

In America, a certain kind of moral philosophy would prove to be a key new discipline in the young colleges.

Nature Claims a Christian University

The increasing emphasis on nature as a primary source of moral authority can be illustrated by looking at "the most national of America's colonial colleges," the College of New Jersey, or what today is known as Princeton.[59] In 1768, John Witherspoon emigrated from Scotland to colonial America to become the new president of the college. Educated at the University of Edinburgh during the Scottish Enlightenment, he brought with him evangelical piety, a strong orthodox faith, and a hearty confidence in what nature could reveal and teach students regarding moral knowledge. This last element would help him introduce a new moral philosophy.[60]

Although rooted in an orthodox faith, Witherspoon would also be an effective evangelist for the new way of thinking. In fact, Garry Wills claims, "Witherspoon was probably the most influential teacher in the entire history of American education."[61] Witherspoon's key course was called Moral Philosophy. Although not the first to teach it at Princeton, he was "the first college head in America to set forth in his classroom lectures a definitive *system* of ethics."[62] In this system, Witherspoon claimed that by the light of nature, "we can or do discover by our own powers without revelation or tradition."[63] This proved particularly helpful when thinking about politics, since Witherspoon believed that "the political law of the Jews contains many noble principles and equity and excellent examples to future law givers, yet it was so local and peculiar that certainly it was never intended to be immutable and universal."[64]

How does one then distinguish the light of nature from fallen nature? Witherspoon recognized that there will be those who "will be apt to plead for everything or for many things as dictates of nature which are in reality propensities of nature in its present state, but at the same time the fruit and evidence of its departure from its original purity."[65] The trick is to use one's "remaining power of natural conscience" by which "to detect and oppose these errors."[66] Much of his lectures involved unpacking what the natural conscience is and what it teaches individuals. Some of these lessons even included exploring how the light of nature leads one to believe in a creative and virtuous God.[67]

This type of course would soon become the model capstone course for American colleges and universities, and Witherspoon's lectures influenced dozens of future American politicians who took his class, including James Madison. Witherspoon's most recent biographer claims, "Through them Witherspoon almost single-handedly gave a philosophy to the embryonic nation and helped transform a generation of young idealists into hard-headed politicians of the first rank."[68] The quote is instructive as the university's primary focus and audience had changed. Witherspoon was not forming a church but a new nation. Mark Noll claimed that Witherspoon's most lasting influence was to replace "the Christian ministry with patriotic public service as Princeton's primary contribution to morality, liberty, and social cohesion."[69] Indeed, Princeton became known as the "seminary of sedition" with Witherspoon leading the way. One British soldier complained of Witherspoon, "he poisons the minds of his young students and through them the continent."[70]

Witherspoon would go on to become the only pastor and university president to sign the Declaration of Independence—which used an appeal to nature to justify the existence of a set of natural rights that could be used to critique England's political ruler. As the first words of the Declaration of Independence read, "We hold these truths to be self-evident." The Declaration would go on to list twenty-seven natural rights that King George had violated. Later, Witherspoon would become a member of the Continental and Confederation Congresses (1776–1782) and a participant in the New Jersey convention ratifying the US Constitution (1787).[71]

Witherspoon's teaching and politics would be a sign of the changes to come. While rooted solidly in the Christian tradition, Witherspoon's course of teaching and political interests proved to be radically new. He found in nature, unhinged from the biblical revelation, a guide for both moral philosophy and political guidance. He also found in nature what he wanted. In a sermon on the day of national thanksgiving on April 19, 1783, he proclaimed:

Nothing appears to be more manifest than that the separation of this country from Britain, has been of God; for every step the British took to prevent, served to accelerate it, which has generally been the case when men have undertaken to go in opposition to the course of Providence, and to make war with the nature of things.[72]

Ames would not have been surprised by the exaltation of nature and the marginalization of biblical theology in Witherspoon's thought and the Princeton curriculum, but he would have been saddened. He would also not be surprised that Princeton became less of a Christian college and more of a national institution. Educators' quests to find a common moral and political outlook for a diverse population within the colonies fostered the turn to nature. Consequently, they became more concerned with national interests than universal knowledge as others soon followed Princeton's lead.

The development of courses in moral philosophy would prove to be one of the most significant changes in eighteenth-century American colleges.[73] Harvard, Yale, William and Mary, and other new colleges adopted the practice of making a moral philosophy course the capstone of the required curriculum. In this way the new moral philosophy soon took over the place held by theology. Frederick Rudolph claims, "Between 1700 and 1850 [the moral philosophy course] took its place in the curriculum as 'the semi-secular way station between the great era of theological dominance' of the Middle Ages and the twentieth century, when objective science presses so hard on all other modes of experience."[74]

In a university/college and culture that took Christian theology seriously, students encountered a universe filled with subjects, angels, demons, the devil, and, most importantly, God. The final authority and source of knowledge was the Being who created the world. In moral philosophy, the metaphysical world diminished in favor of this world. Appeals to God's authority, while undertaken, became secondary.

As with Witherspoon's moral philosophy, the attempt to downplay certain contentious elements of the Christian tradition in this course did not necessarily involve its abandonment. "The basis of moral authority," Norman Fiering notes, "shifted slowly to 'reason' and 'nature' from Scripture and revelation, but it was a Christianized reason and a Christianized nature that came to the foreground, albeit well camouflaged."[75] When reason appeared to show particular limitations, these thinkers often referred to Scripture or God's moral law. Donald Meyer concludes his study of these American moral philosophers by observing, "Although they dealt dutifully with the logic of ethics, and realized that God's naked will is not a proper basis for a rational theory of duty, they all relied ultimately on their faith that God's will and the moral law coincide."[76] In the end, the moral philosophy presented in most American colleges still drew from the Christian tradition and was considered compatible with it.[77]

Yet later thinkers would unpack the limits of appeals to "the light of nature." Nature's revelation was not always clear, particularly when it came to political and moral matters. Schmidt-Biggemann summarizes the situation as follows:

> At the end of the eighteenth century, enlightened despotism, individual human rights, or an economy aiming at personal happiness could all alike claim to be "natural." In the eighteenth century, conformity with nature could be regarded as a basis for theology, politics, law or claims to property. The concept of "nature" had come an astonishingly long way since the seventeenth century. . . . But what sort of concept of "nature" was this? Was there any concept more polyvalent than this? Nature was almost everything at the same time: external nature, nature of the reality into which insight is possible, stabilizer of political or economic conditions, legal guarantee yet at the same time object of experience and reason.[78]

These various appeals to nature all shared one common element: they were "always connected with some claim or other of a truth confronted by human arbitrariness and caprice. It was a guarantee of objectivity."[79] Controlling human caprice through appeals to some sort of objectivity would become a common concern in coming centuries.

Appeals to the objectivity nature provided proved particularly important to protecting freedom. For some, such as the American founders, it promised freedom from political abuse. One could appeal to natural rights that existed before the state and over and against the state's power. For others, such as the leaders of the French Revolution, it promised freedom from religious authorities. For others still, such as Jean-Jacques Rousseau, it promised freedom from any and all humanly made institutions. Nature—and not nature's God—provided freedom.

The problem would be, however, that nature was inconsistent. Moreover, its supposed moral knowledge was not always clear and convincing. The solution to this problem would ultimately rest on two approaches. The first merely relied on the use of political power to override the claims to nature. The second solution would be to find a new story and method by which to understand and interpret nature. In other words, university leaders increasingly began to search for a new soul for the university that did not need to be nourished by theology. The next two chapters describe the attempts to find this new soul for the university.

3

THE STATE TAKES OVER
THE ACADEMIC PALACE IN
EUROPE (1770–1870)

...

*University reform was part of the agenda of enlightened absolutism
(the term generally preferred today to "enlightened despotism"). . . .
[The rulers] had wider political and cultural aims: to strengthen
the territorial state and increase its military and fiscal efficiency,
to create a loyal class of bureaucratic servants, to weaken the
independent power of the aristocracy and the obstacles to strong
government posed by particularism and corporate privilege,
and to subordinate the church to the interests of the state.*

R. D. ANDERSON

I N 1773, WITH ONE STROKE OF THE PEN, Pope Clement XIV undercut the
most successful and extensive system of Christian higher education in the
world. He disbanded the Jesuits. At that time, the Jesuits were in charge of
over seven hundred educational institutions around the globe, including
over two dozen European universities.[1] Education for the Jesuits had been
the primary ministry of the order. Moreover, the education they undertook
in their schools was meant for those engaging in secular or worldly vocations outside the ministry.

Understanding the reason for the pope's action, however, must begin with the story of a Jesuit mission outreach to the Guaraní people of Paraguay that began in 1611. The mission proved to be incredibly successful. A later scholar would call it "the loveliest days of a new-born Christianity," while another has identified it as "a vigorous civilization comparable to the Incas."[2] An ex-Jesuit described it as reaching a degree of civilization "perhaps as high as the new nations could reach and certainly anything existing in the new world."[3] What impressed scholars was how the Jesuits nurtured, protected, and helped the Guaraní population, leading them to build a highly centralized communal civilization that appeared to reflect the New Testament vision in which all worked for the common good. It became known as the Jesuit Republic of Paraguay.

In political terms, the Jesuit Republic was located in a territory under Spanish rule. A 1750 Spanish treaty with Portugal, however, gave the land with the Guaraní settlements to Portugal. More importantly, the treaty required the Guaraní to move a number of miles across the Uruguay River. The Jesuits from the theological faculty at Córdoba University (founded in 1613), led by Jesuit Padre Rábago, made a spirited attack on this controversial part of the treaty. Rábago argued that natural law required the king provide compensation to the Guaraní for the enormous cost of the move. If the crown did not, he concluded that the Jesuits could not consider it safe "to obey a civil and human law that is so plainly in contradiction to the laws of nature, God, the Church, and the State."[4] The crown refused, and in the end, the Guaraní engaged in a failed rebellion that would later become the basis for a Hollywood movie.[5]

The rebellion sparked the fire that led to the destruction of a major segment of European Catholic higher education. Various Portuguese politicians, led by the prominent politician the Marquis of Pombal, blamed the Jesuits for the rebellion. The Marquis saw the Jesuit-sponsored settlements of Guaraní, as well as the other Jesuit educational communities, as rival political entities. Throughout the world, the Jesuits had created numerous educational institutions and communities that were not directly overseen by a national government, what today we would call civil society.[6] This kind of transnational institution-building worried government leaders such as Pombal. Thus, when an assassination attempt of King Joseph I took place in

1758, Pombal took advantage of the situation to accuse the Jesuits of fomenting the attack. In the aftermath, the Jesuits were confined to their homes, suppressed, and deported. A number of Jesuit leaders were left to rot in prison, and one was executed.[7]

Soon afterward, similar movements against the Jesuits eventually spread into France and Spain. By 1773, Pope Clement XIV disbanded the order altogether, under pressure from European political leaders, in what John Henry Newman called "one of the most mysterious matters in the history of the Church."[8] This left the more than two dozen European universities founded or overseen by the Jesuits without clear leadership. Political leaders and their followers willingly stepped into the educational void and transformed Jesuit educational institutions in their territories into national educational institutions that marginalized both theology and the church.[9] This nationalization of European universities, which would extend to other Christian universities, would help to transform the purpose of many European universities.

What do we mean by nationalization of the university? Originally universities were sanctioned and emerged from partnerships between ecclesiastical and extranational political authorities (e.g., emperors). As we noted in chapter one, the church and the theological faculty had almost always played a vital role particularly in sustaining the idea that universities should be universal institutions. Wisdom and truth from God were universal. Such an idea did not negate the importance of particular political identities, but it did focus the university's quest on common human ends. The fragmentation of the Church during the Reformation, however, weakened one of the most powerful forces standing against elevating the use of the universities for particular national agendas.

Protestant universities, in particular, began to be overseen by national leaders who not only protected the nation's Protestant churches but also saw the nation's well-being as their first priority. Nationalization describes this change in the balance of university control from the church and extranational political authorities to national rulers. The nationalization of the university would also entail changes in the purposes, structure, and curriculum of universities across Europe so that the universities prioritized serving national ends over the broader interests of an international community. In other words, educational leaders placed universities in what we would call a national saga. Ultimately, national identity, a national story, and national purposes took over the soul of the university. It would never be the same again. The new soul of the university became a focus on "freedom," although the freedom meant to further the university proved to be one-dimensional.

The late 1700s in particular brought about nationalization since a number of national political revolutions occurred during that time. Secular thinkers and political revolutionaries who rejected religious thought argued that the nation-state should control universities to further their Enlightenment-inspired end: the promotion of liberty. Freedom from any form of external authority, not universal wisdom or knowledge, became their concern, and they saw politics and political entities as the source and way to bring about their new freedom. Church-related universities, they contended, restricted free thought, caused divisions, and did not always produce the types of graduates that met the needs of the nation.[10]

Ironically, the thinkers and revolutionaries behind the Enlightenment that claimed to advance reason and academic freedom actually helped nurture the political revolutions which unleashed the chaos that would lead to the destruction of two-fifths of Europe's universities. The Enlightenment-inspired French Revolution and the Napoleonic conquests that soon followed devastated Europe's university system, particularly the Catholic institutions. Between 1789 and 1815, 60 of Europe's 143 universities ceased to exist, leaving only 83 traditional universities.[11] Most of the 60 lost universities were Catholic. The majority disappeared in Western Europe. Germany lost 18, Spain lost 15, and France lost all 24 universities.[12] Europe would not reach the same number of universities again until the late nineteenth century. The growing influence of the state and its authority over European universities did not always lead to the flourishing of actual universities. It did, however, lead to their transformation.

As a consequence, similar to the funeral-dirge genre of literature described in the introduction, the eighteenth century in Europe had its fill of intellectual leaders complaining about the crisis in the universities. Notker Hammerstein observes of this time, "The number of publications demanding reform grew fivefold."[13] Critics lamented that student numbers were stagnant or falling, smaller universities were becoming financially unviable, curricular innovation had ceased, and professors read lectures from the texts students could otherwise read on their own. From this frustration there emerged a desire to re-create or redeem the university. The political leaders and entities that had exacerbated these problems faced the daunting task of figuring out how to fix them. Soon a variety of new ideas about the university emerged with a different view of its mission, curriculum, and structure. The intellectual founders behind these changes sought to deconstruct what they perceived to be the deformed soul of the university currently in place. The question is whether they deformed the soul of the university even more by either nationalizing the university's soul or in some cases destroying it altogether.

The French Take the Lead

France undertook the most radical nationalization of universities of any European country. One could argue that the nation that perhaps did the most to nurture the Enlightenment would also do its utmost to destroy the soul of the university and to build something new. At the time when French political authorities dissolved the Jesuit order in 1762, the Jesuits ran one-third of the colleges, many of which provided the basic liberal arts education for the universities. After the order's dissolution, political authorities abolished a quarter of these colleges. Others were consolidated or taken over by other religious or political entities.[14]

The most far-reaching changes, though, would come after the French Revolution, whose leaders championed reason over revelation and a militant form of secular nationalism.[15] The confiscation of church property and endowments in 1789 weakened the universities, as did the imposition of an oath of loyalty to the constitution, which resulted in large-scale resignations and emigration of the clergy. In September 1793, the French Revolutionaries abolished the twenty-four French universities, including all the Catholic universities. In their place they created a set of new institutions meant to serve the state.[16]

The complaints against the old Catholic universities shared similarities to those made by Protestant Reformers of the last chapter, but the Revolutionaries' answer was not to repair the university's original foundation. Instead, they wanted to destroy the whole foundation and start anew. The focus would not be on the liberal arts as found in the old curricular structure. A liberal arts education was now deemed elitist and contrary to the espoused principles of the Revolution. After all, such a curriculum "was more likely to produce obscurantist theologians and contentious lawyers . . . than creative scientists, good craftsmen, and enlightened citizens."[17] The new Revolutionaries wanted good professionals and citizens with specialized training. The elite polytechnique educational institutions established by the Revolutionaries were meant to prepare young men for military careers with the state or to learn specific scientific fields valuable to the state such as physics, chemistry, mining, and civil engineering.

When Napoleon took power in 1799, he basically continued along the same path and, in fact, strengthened the state's educational monopoly. Although he restored some educational rights to the Catholic Church, he did not restore its role in university education. Instead he made sure the French state continued to play the key leadership role in order to "give direction to the 'public mind' and 'have a means of directing political and moral opinions.'"[18] As part of his reforms, Napoleon set up narrowly focused secularized academies governed by state officials that met particular national needs for training in engineering, law, and medicine. These institutions were not universities as traditionally understood, which meant that during that time France actually had no universities. Napoleon also created new secondary-educational institutions (*lycées*) that adhered to a rigid secular curriculum and through reforms passed in 1806 and 1808 created new institutions to train secular teachers for the centralized French educational system. Fritz Ringer aptly summarizes the situation: "Since 1808 intense centralization and state control have been salient characteristics of the French educational system."[19]

Overall, the Enlightenment-inspired French Revolution and the Napoleonic conquests that spread the new French approach toward traditional universities helped devastate a large portion of Europe's university system. "Where French armies went," Fritz Ringer observed, "French reforms such as the confiscation of church lands and dissolution of corporations and religious orders followed. The immediate effects on universities were as disastrous as in France."[20] One other region, however, would take a very different path, and in doing so would also contribute to the transformation of the university's soul.

Prussia/Germany

Not surprisingly, the increasing political control created problems for the faculty. Part of the problem was that political authorities in Protestant countries took the place of ecclesiastical leaders in seeking to protect certain forms of theological orthodoxy. As a result, the faculty sought to free themselves from the influence of both the state and the church. In most cases they only succeeded in the latter and, instead, became dependent on other narratives that merely reinforced the power of the state. In order to gain freedom, they transferred the university's soul to the state.

Kant and the beginning of German nationalization. The story of one important conflict that contributed to the university's nationalization began a year after the philosopher Immanuel Kant published his famous work *Religion Within the Boundaries of Mere Reason* in 1793. A government official wrote a letter to Kant on behalf of the Prussian ruler Frederick the Great to express the emperor's disapproval of the work's treatment of the Bible and Christianity. Although Kant defended his views to some degree, he was unwilling to endure punishment for his opinions and initially acquiesced by promising to "refrain altogether from public discourses on religion, in both lectures and writings, whether natural or revealed."[21] After Frederick died in 1797, however, Kant considered himself free from his promise and went about establishing the intellectual groundwork for greater intellectual freedom from political control. To obtain this freedom, he set forth an argument about how to distinguish between the four major university faculties, which he titled *The Conflict of the Faculties*.

Kant's reasoning appeared quite simple. He wanted to recover the academic freedom the university had lost to political authorities so that philosophy could be free from the state and able to build its own academic structure. His argument proved to be a masterful deconstruction of the old blueprint of the university on a number of different levels. In contrast to Hugh of St. Victor, who sought to organize a unified vision of knowledge in reference to God, humanity, and nature, Kant framed his discussion of the organization of knowledge primarily in reference to the political authorities. Furthermore, instead of defending the unity of knowledge and the faculty, Kant created divisions within the university, so he could purposefully abandon the other three faculties to the state's control. He wrote,

"The faculties are traditionally divided into two ranks: *three higher* faculties and *one lower* faculty. It is clear that this division is made and this nomenclature adopted with reference to the government rather than the learned professions."[22] In Kant's narrative, neither the church nor God is part of his organization of the university's curriculum. In other words, Kant claimed that the three "higher" vocational faculties (theology, law, and medicine) are really only higher due to the government's interest in them: "A faculty is considered higher only if its teachings—both as to their content and the way they are expounded to the public—interest the government itself."[23] The government wanted to approve or sanction these fields since it seeks the "means for securing the strongest and most lasting influence on the people, and the subjects which the higher faculties teach are just such means."[24] It should be noted that Kant did not believe the state had the competence to determine the truth of these teachings.

Kant contended that the lower liberal arts faculty, broadly described as philosophy, should be "independent of the government's command with regard to its teaching."[25] This faculty would then be free to evaluate everything, since it concerned itself only with truth and not with imperatives such as "Believe!" but only "I believe." Kant called the philosophy faculty "lower," he claimed, because "a man who can give commands, even though he is someone else's servant, is considered more distinguished than a free man who has no one under his command."[26]

Kant also sought to further divide the faculties by distinguishing among their methods. Unlike the early University of Paris, where scholars understood the cultivation of critical reasoning as a form of Christian devotion, Kant drew a sharp contrast between the reliance on various written authorities used in the higher disciplines (theology—the Bible; law—the law of the land; medicine—medical regulations) and those used in philosophy (reason). Kant understood reason as the power to judge freely according to the principles of thought in general. Academic freedom, as defined by Kant, was "to answer, on behalf of the state, the questions that the state sets, but to do so without regard to the answers that the state prefers."[27]

Overall, Kant's deconstruction of the synthesis envisioned by medieval thinkers such as Hugh of St. Victor was powerfully influential. Kant helped demote theology from the pinnacle of all learning to being merely one more room in the academic palace. More importantly, he reaffirmed the liberal arts (broadly defined as philosophy based only on reason) as the foundation on which the university should be built. He wanted philosophy and not theology to become its soul.

A research university for the state: The University of Berlin. Although Kant gained freedom for the philosophy faculty, his narrative ceded academic authority to the state. Not surprisingly, within a decade (in 1806) churches in Prussia lost virtually all their ecclesiastical authority when their affairs were handed over to the Department of Ecclesiastical Affairs and Public Education.[28] Around this time, the philosophical movement of German idealism emerged, which "in effect, magnified the state as a cultural and ethical force . . . and subordinated the church to the state's own quasi-sacral purposes."[29] This movement would influence the founding of an important new university in Prussia.

The purpose of discovering truth that would in turn serve the state would eventually become the new mission envisioned by German scholars for the university. Consequently, the political purpose of the university began to be seen as preeminent. The concern with the nation partly stemmed from the defeat of the German principality of Prussia by France in 1806. A defeated people, the Prussian Germans sought to rise again by renewing both the idea of the university and the idea of a unified Germany.

When the source of the unity of knowledge is no longer God's wisdom and the soul of the university is no longer understood as a relationship with God, scholars must find other sources for unity and another soul for the university. Heinrich Steffens, who originally coined the phrase "the idea of the university" as a title for a series of his lectures, proposed an answer in those lectures in 1808–1809.[30] He argued that the problem of his time was that the citizen has become "something separate from the state."[31] Steffens would go on to argue that a state could be developed where everyone works for the good of the whole. The university can be the "means by which the wisdom of this organically unified state is to be developed and maintained."[32] Thus, in contrast to Hugh of St. Victor, who saw the liberal arts as a means to learning God's wisdom, the university for the new nineteenth-century German intellectuals became the means to provide a new unified German state with wisdom.

Johann Gottlieb Fichte, one of Kant's scholarly colleagues, exemplified this new nationalistic vision. Although Fichte had once contemplated going to seminary, later in life he became a deist who identified God as a personified expression of the abstract moral order. In place of an earlier religious devotion, Fichte reserved his devotion and loyalties to the state. The radical nature of his nationalism can be understood by his belief that children should be taken from their families and educated communally by the state.[33]

Fichte gave a famous set of addresses to the German nation in Berlin in 1807 and 1808, a few years after Napoleon's victory over the most powerful German principality, Prussia. In those addresses, he expounded on the German people's unique educational gifts and their calling to be "pioneers and models for the rest of mankind."[34] Sounding like an Old Testament prophet, he declared that Germans should be a people set apart: "It is only by means of the common characteristic of being German that we can avert the downfall of our nation which is threatened by its fusion with foreign peoples."[35] For Fichte, salvation could come to the German people through education. Overall for the German thinkers,

> The state became for them a reinvented church: a church without the divisions of particular denomination from particular denomination; a church in which each citizen would be able to speak on his own behalf to every other citizen, rather than allowing the conversations of the state to be locked within denominational silos.[36]

The university would now focus on serving the state's needs instead of the needs of the church. To further this education, German principalities needed a new system of education. Fichte himself would help build a new type of university to make this happen.[37]

In 1810, the Germans helped make Kant and Fichte's vision a reality by founding what many consider the first research university, the University of Berlin. As Thomas Albert Howard describes it, they put forward "secular or only vestigially religious ideals to guide the university—ideals in many respects antithetical to the lingering confessionalism that had justified theology's institutional centrality in the post-Reformation period."[38] Since the mission was to serve the future united German nation-state, its need for the creation of secular approaches to knowledge and reason meant that the practice of philosophy must be separated from the practice of theology and from ecclesiastical communities. Howard summarizes the momentous change to structure that this new purpose entailed.

> The University of Berlin was the first German university, at least in the formulation of its founders if not entirely in actual practice, to sever the centuries-old tie between confessionally defined Christianity and university education. It was the first European university founded under purely national, secular auspices, bearing the imprimatur of neither emperor nor pope.[39]

Although the university would contain the remnants of the earlier university model, such as the traditional faculties of philosophy, medicine, law, and theology, it embodied Kant's new ideal. And though a theology faculty still existed, the philosophy faculty replaced the theology faculty as the queen of the sciences and the lifeblood of the university. This concept began to reshape the very soul of the university, and indeed the idea of what constitutes knowledge throughout the West. Knowledge had to be rational and secular.

The overall result was that education became the new source of salvation in German principalities and, in many respects, replaced the church as the institution that could transform society. In fact, undergirding this hope behind the new German idea of the university were older conceptions grounded in the university's Christian past. German scholars still exalted the unity of knowledge. As one scholar summarizes this vision, "All aspects of truth were part of a single higher and developing reality, whose inner meaning could be grasped by the trained mind through a form of intuition rather than through positivist analysis."[40] A couple German scholars even began the inaccurate historical claim that universities derived their name from the concept of the universality of truth.[41]

Since they marginalized theology, the universities needed a new orienting purpose. They found it in science as expressed in *Bildung*—"an ideal of personal self-development through the pursuit of truth."[42] In this process, the role of the university no longer primarily involved passing along inherited knowledge. It encompassed, in the words of one of the founding visionaries, stimulating "the idea of science in the minds of students, to encourage them to take account of the fundamental laws of science in all their thinking."[43] To do so, they should be taught how to discover new knowledge. Since the university was the place to experience *Bildung*, this made it, in one German scholar's words, "the most important and most sacred institution which mankind possesses."[44]

Like the church, the new German research university proclaimed freedom to its members, but this concept of freedom contained a whole new element. It was not freedom from sin. Instead, as Kant insisted, it was freedom from external constraints that might inhibit the pursuit of truth. Inspired by Kant and his successors, the leaders of the German research university believed that it must be guided by two types of freedom. To students, university leaders granted the freedom of learning (*Lernfreiheit*). This freedom referred to the absence of administrative regulations in relation to the education of students. As an attempt to free their minds for scholarly pursuits, students were deemed free to live wherever and study whatever, given they passed the exam awaiting them at the end of their course of study. This also meant they had no compulsory classes, and their attendance was not monitored.

To teachers, the German research university granted the freedom of teaching (*Lehrfreiheit*). This freedom granted professors the ability to inquire, subject to the rules of academic detachment, about any problem and report their findings in published works. This freedom proved particularly attractive to the scientists within the liberal arts faculty, who were increasing in importance. For them, if discovering the laws of nature proved the best source of knowledge, the field of study that supplied the methods to discovering those laws would be the highest. By the end of the nineteenth century, science would claim to be queen among what had traditionally been understood to be the liberal arts or philosophy (a term that would become increasingly narrow in usage).

The freedom experienced by German scientists housed within that faculty as well as the medical faculty proved quite unusual at the time, and it led to significant scientific advances. Walter Rüegg observes,

> By the mid-century, Germany had surpassed France in the natural sciences. . . . By the mid-century, practically all researchers in the natural sciences and medicine in Germany were active either as heads or collaborators of institutes or university laboratories, while in Great Britain and France research in these fields remained the preserve of the private initiative of amateurs or individual scholars or of institutions outside the university.[45]

Consequently German research universities gained supremacy and became the archetype for educators looking for models of the university.

England

The thinking behind the University of Berlin would eventually spread to other European countries, with England remaining one of the last holdouts.[46] At the turn of the eighteenth century, England still represented the old ideal of one church and one kingdom, and the two historical universities of Cambridge and Oxford helped enforce it. Over six hundred years old, Oxford and Cambridge Universities remained Anglican, and the colleges within the universities continued to be Anglican corporations. The fellows who taught had to be Anglican Church members, and the students had to declare their allegiance to the Anglican Church either upon matriculation (Oxford) or before graduation (Cambridge).[47]

By the early nineteenth century, however, English political leaders increasingly complained that student and faculty admission to Oxford and Cambridge should not be limited to members of the Church of England. As one critic noted at the time, "Oxford ought to be a national institution but is bound hand and feet by the clergy of one sect."[48] Eventually both religious and secular minorities that could not gain admission to Oxford or Cambridge sought to found a new institution. The English poet Thomas Campbell conceived the idea for the institution during a visit to Germany.[49] Impressed by the new University of Berlin, as well as other new German universities, he admonished a member of Parliament, Henry Brougham, to start a similar university. As a result, a unique partnership between secular utilitarians, Jews, Catholics, and Nonconformists (e.g., Baptists) who were excluded from Oxford and Cambridge came together to form the third major university in England, the University of London, in 1828. Supporters argued that Cambridge and Oxford excluded "so great a body of intelligent youth" that the University of London must be "designed for the most important occupations in society, from the highest means of liberal education."[50] Furthermore, the University of London provided for "persons of all religious persuasions" the opportunity to obtain a degree "without the imposition of any test or disqualification whatsoever."[51]

To achieve this end, the founders required no Anglican entrance or exit requirements or theology courses. Such a fact earned it such titles as "the godless institution of Gower Street" and "the Synagogue of Satan."[52] To temper such criticisms, the founders still required a course in the "moral sciences," but it too clearly departed from the older model of the university that considered the theology faculty the queen of the sciences. A few decades later, in 1860, T. H. Huxley, known as Charles Darwin's bulldog, pushed to have science recognized as a faculty and placed "on the same footing with regards to Arts, as Medicine and Law."[53] The usurping of theology proved complete. In light of the growing pluralism in English society, one could understand the appeal of science (which appeared to overcome differences and provide a common language) over and against theology (which appeared extremely divisive in a pluralistic society).

The final authority, however, lay not with the scientific academy but with the political powers. The government's control over the university was all-encompassing, down to whether a porter could receive an additional shilling a week.[54] As the most recent historian of the university testifies, "The University of London—the metropolitan university, the national university, the imperial university—was the government university."[55] The University of London would eventually join with Oxford and Cambridge to dominate English university life, with the three universities usually matriculating two-thirds of all college students in England during the nineteenth century.[56]

Nationalization Across Europe

Overall, the placement of universities' identity and purpose within a national saga would influence every element of university life. Some of the general trends of influence identified by educational historians are listed below:

1. Legal standing or academic legitimacy: The state granted legal legitimacy, and emerging academic professions were granted academic legitimacy. In addition, the state increasingly took away special legal privileges previously accorded to university students by church authorities.[57]

2. Governance/leadership and funding: The state took over both the funding and governance of universities, often with the help of a centralized Ministry of Education.[58]

3. Identity and purpose/mission: The state "more and more intensively regulated, visited, and controlled" the universities because it saw them "as 'factories' for civil service and clerical recruits whose education was subject to the utilitarian norms of the *respublica*."[59]

4. Structure: Whereas discussions about science had previously been international, newly founded national scientific academies, such as the Royal Society of London and the Académie Francaise, created more nationally focused discussions.[60]

5. Membership in the community for faculty, staff, and students: The state increasingly introduced and supported lay teachers.[61] In addition, student admissions based on national identity became more important than religious identity. International student movement declined, and universities began to be more regional in nature. More forcefully, countries even prohibited their students from studying at foreign universities and began requiring study in one's own country.

6. Transmission of scholarship and teaching: The state also played an important role in changing the language of study from Latin to the national language since such changes reinforced political cohesion. The result was that universities tended to become less international and started to attract largely national students interested in the learned professions and state service.[62] Latin, which provided an international language for scholarly discussion, began to be replaced in universities by national vernacular languages.[63] Consequently, scholarship in journals and books became confined within national boundaries, with only a few exceptions.[64]

7. Curriculum: Clerical training and teaching about theology began to lose importance to those subjects and disciplines which would serve the nation-state, such as secular forms of jurisprudence. As Hammerstein writes, "Universities and similar institutions were expected to teach not metaphysics or theology but disciplines like economics, technology, medicine, natural sciences. . . . Theology lost its leading place in the universities and ceased to be the fundamental science."[65] The theology faculty lost its position of leadership, and in countries such as France, Spain, and Italy, it was abolished.[66] Where theology faculties continued to exist, the state and not the church appointed the professors.[67] Institutional differentiation became

more pronounced through the establishment of separate seminaries or schools of theology outside the university.[68] Law or jurisprudence became the leading university faculty since it best served the interests of the state. In some cases, the state would prescribe the university curriculum or create the examination requirements for graduates.[69]

8. Religious practices and ethos: Since an increasing number of students studied secular disciplines such as law instead of theology, the social ethos of universities became more aristocratic. "Instead of the clerical manner and behaviour of the students of philosophy or theology, those of the lay *honnête home*, or the elegant *studiosus*, dominated the academic scene."[70] Even dress changed, with students wearing clerical-academic dress in the sixteenth century and nobleman's clothing in the seventeenth.

As these developments make clear, beginning in the eighteenth century, political reformers thoroughly transformed universities into instruments for creating a strong national state.[71]

Although the nationalization of the university removed theology as queen of the academic castle, this change did not mean Christianity was wholly driven from the academic structure. As R. D. Anderson observes of Europe, "Although by the early nineteenth century universities were essentially secular institutions in the sense that the state rather than the church was the directing authority, religion had by no means lost its importance."[72] Unlike America, many European countries still supported state churches and therefore sponsored theology departments in state universities (e.g., Catholicism, Calvinism, or Lutheranism). In addition, confessional hiring requirements often continued to exist, and professors with controversial religious views continued to face various types of repercussions.[73] Chapel requirements and a religious ethos still existed at many schools.[74] In fact, nationalism and Christianity fused quite easily throughout Europe.[75] Thus, while nationalization was promoted throughout the system, secularization initially remained far from complete. The nationalization of the universities, however, would open the door for the latter step of secularization and the continued reliance on science as the foundation of the university. Anderson writes of Europeans, "By the 1870s, most scholars thought that religion was a matter of private belief, and that objective truth was attainable by the application of agreed scientific methods."[76]

A Final Argument and Prophetic Warning

John Henry Newman's magisterial work *The Idea of a University* could be said to be the last-gasp attempt of a European educational leader to thwart the marginalization or elimination of theology from structure of the European university. First published in a more limited book form in 1853 and then published in its more expanded form as *The Idea of the University Defined and Illustrated* in 1873, Newman's argument regarding theology is particularly striking for a number of reasons.

Newman's starting point for his argument shows how the view of theology in the university had changed. He had to start with the basics by arguing that "the systematic omission of any one science from the catalogue prejudices the accuracy and completeness of our knowledge."[77] He then maintained that "religious doctrine is knowledge, in a full a sense as Newton's doctrine is knowledge."[78] In other words, it is not simply private belief. Consequently, he maintained, "University Teaching without Theology is simply unphilosophical. Theology has at least as good a right to claim a place there as Astronomy."[79] By theology, Newman meant "the Science of God, or the truths we know about God put into system just as we have a science of the stars, and call it astronomy, or of the crust of the earth, and call it geology."[80] What is important to note is that Catholics had gone from exalting theology as queen of the sciences to now having to formulate an argument for allowing theology a room in the modern European academic structure.

Yet, like some of the thinkers reviewed earlier, Newman still tried to set forth an understanding of theology that did not view it simply as a separate room in the academic structure that could be discarded from the university without consequence. He believed that God, the subject of theology, will shape our understanding of and connect to all the other academic disciplines. For example, humans receive gifts from God through God's creation that relate to every field.

> To Him must be ascribed the rich endowments of the intellect, the irradiation of the genius, the imagination of the poet, the sagacity of the politician, the wisdom (as Scripture calls it), which now rears and decorates the Temple, now manifests

itself in proverb or in parable. . . . All that is good, all that is true, all that is beautiful, all that is beneficent, be it great or small, be it perfect or fragmentary, natural as well as supernatural, moral as well as material, comes from Him.[81]

Newman extended this argument even further and maintained that theology, when properly understood, is an essential discipline to the quest for truth, knowledge, and various academic disciplines and not simply a discipline helpful in discovering one part of truth: "Religious Truth is not only a portion, but a condition of general knowledge. To blot it out is nothing short, if I may so speak, of unravelling the web of University Teaching."[82] Newman's argument harkens back in one way to Hugh of St. Victor. He did not want to make theology just a room in the academic house but something closer to a foundation.

Yet Newman's justification for making theology a foundational discipline was different from Hugh's. Hugh grounded the need to discover God's wisdom as necessary to restoring the image of God within us. Moreover, for Hugh, finding wisdom knows of no boundary between God, God's revelation, and every dimension of the created order. God created the object of study of every discipline, including humans, and therefore we know God by all of God's creation. Due to this theological vision, Hugh saw learning in relational terms. Learning wisdom that restores God's image involved friendship with God.

In contrast, despite Newman's defense of theology, he articulated and defended the ends of learning in less personal, less theological, and more rationalistic ways. Newman focused on learning as the discovery of objective truth.

> Truth means facts and their relations, which stand towards each other pretty much as subjects and predicates in logic. All that exists, as contemplated by the human mind, forms one large system or complex fact, and this of course resolves itself into an indefinite number of particular facts, which, as being portions of a whole, have countless relations of every kind, one toward another. Knowledge is the apprehension of these facts.[83]

For Newman, truth is a unified set of facts about the world. Thus Newman goes on to build his argument for theology using this understanding of the end of learning:

> In order to have possession of truth at all, we must have the whole truth; that revealed truth enters to a very great extent into the province of science, philosophy, and literature, and that to put it on one side, in compliment to secular science, is simply under colour of a compliment, to do science a great damage.[84]

Yet he goes on to admit that theology and the knowledge it offers, if omitted from the university, may not touch on or influence certain disciplines.

> I do not say that every science will be equally affected by the omission; pure mathematics will not suffer at all; chemistry will suffer less than politics, politics than history, ethics, or metaphysics; still, that the various branches of science are intimately connected with each other, and form one whole, which whole is impaired, and to an extent which is difficult to limit, by any considerable omission of knowledge, of whatever kind, and that revealed knowledge is very far indeed from an inconsiderable department of knowledge, this I consider undeniable.[85]

The weakness with this argument was that for an increasing number of educators throughout Europe, it was deniable. Educators preoccupied with building universities to serve emerging nation-states instead of discovering universal truth began to see theology as less important and perhaps even a hindrance to their fundamental task.

Newman did understand the consequences of this change. He followed his argument in favor of including theology in the university with a description of what would happen if theology was removed from the university. Although Newman did not appeal to any metaphors, we will use the building metaphor common during the first half millennium of the university to summarize his argument. Basically he argues that if the room in the academic castle is vacated, particularly one as exalted and important as theology, it does not merely remain empty. Other disciplines attempt to move into the room (particularly if it is the upper palace room).

The problem with this new development, as Newman observed, is that any science, no matter how comprehensive, "will fall largely into error, if it be constituted the sole exponent of all things in heaven and earth, and that for the simple reason that it is encroaching on territory not its own, and that undertaking problems which it has no instruments to solve."[86] In other words, the loss of theology leads to the expansion of the power of certain other sciences or groups into domains over which they have little expertise or insight. It thus leads to their perversion. As an example, he notes that the anatomist will proclaim, "There is no soul beyond the brain."[87] Ultimately science will become distorted when theology does not exist to defend its own boundaries. In sum, then, "supposing Theology be not taught, its province will not simply be neglected, but will be actually usurped by other sciences, which will teach without warrant, conclusions of their own in a subject-matter which needs its own proper principles for its due formation and disposition."[88]

As this chapter demonstrates, Newman's understanding of what would happen certainly applied to developments in the university in Europe. By the last quarter of the nineteenth century in Europe, Christianity, or more accurately theology, had lost its role in providing either a foundation or upper palace room for the academic castle. The state, and the related discipline of law, had moved to fill the gap left by the church and theology.[89]

As a consequence, the soul of the university changed. Instead of its purpose being concerned with shaping flourishing human beings, the new state universities sought to educate citizens. Instead of drawing on a story concerned with the kingdom of God and how a vision of this kingdom might shape the university's contribution to the common good, university leaders sought to focus on the story of the nation-state and how the university could contribute to its strength. If the early university had an unfortunate habit of partitioning theology into a separate disciplinary upper palace room, the new universities, such as the University of Berlin, simply tore down the upper palace room or placed theology in the basement.

Since theology as a discipline was then marginalized or abolished, a new focus on practical disciplines that furthered the interests of the nation-state emerged. Yet by focusing the soul of the university on the nation-state, the university lacked a story that held all the disciplines together. As Alasdair MacIntyre observes of this change, "The university thus soon became a place where it is nobody's responsibility to relate what is learned and taught in any one discipline to what is learned and taught in any other."[90] In America, however, a new approach would initially be taken, one that at first did not rely extensively on national identity, story, and purposes, and one that looked to the new field of science to nourish the university's soul.

4

THE AMERICAN IDEA OF THE UNIVERSITY

Freedom Within the Bounds of Science (1825–1900)

...

Supposing Theology be not taught, its province will not simply be neglected, but will be actually usurped by other sciences.

JOHN HENRY NEWMAN

Science is rapidly lifting the mist which has rested upon the conditions in which the human race is placed.

DANIEL C. GILMAN

IN THE EARLY 1800s, American higher education appeared to be an exception to the increasing nationalization of universities found in Europe, for two reasons. First, the churches funded and helped administer most American colleges. Francis Wayland, president of Brown University (1827–1855), speaking in 1835 observed:

> The legislatures of this country have never done for even professional [higher] education one tithe of what has been done by the various denominations of Christians among us. In many cases, the State has done nothing; at best it has generally done but little, and I fear it is too true that even that little has been done badly.[1]

This reality only changed slowly over the next one hundred years. Indeed, the majority of American college students attended private, mostly religiously affiliated, higher education institutions until 1951.[2] Since American higher education remained largely private, a tremendous amount of *institutional* freedom and diversity emerged. In fact, throughout the 1800s, America contained the most diverse set of higher education institutions in the world. Nowhere else on the globe could one find Anglican, Baptist, Catholic, Congregational, Lutheran, Methodist, Presbyterian, and Quaker colleges existing in one country.

The second reason for American exceptionalism had to do with the fact that the Christian denominations initially created colleges instead of universities. These colleges focused on teaching the liberal arts and did not create advanced faculties in theology, law, or medicine like those that existed in European universities. Of course, the fairly uniform classical curriculum in each college still exhibited a broad Christian theological and moral outlook.[3] The shared Christian worldview within the denominational colleges proved to be important in sustaining both moral and theological inquiry within America's diverse pluralistic context, as well as a particular form of character education.[4] By meditating on the classics, acquiring mental discipline through learning Latin and mathematics, and gaining the ability to discern God's design in nature and science classes, students underwent a general form of theological and moral formation. Likewise, college chapel services, daily prayers, and an in loco parentis model served this end.

When Americans created their first research universities, it initially appeared that America would continue to be an exception to the nationalization trends in Europe. The Johns Hopkins University and other early research universities, such as the University of Chicago, Stanford University, and Harvard, began as and continue to be private institutions. Yet, since America's educational leaders admired the unified national focus exhibited by the European institutions of higher education, they sought a similar unity. They wanted the new European soul.

For these leaders, religious sectarianism appeared to be an important enemy to creating a university with a singular soul. As a result, the antisectarian sentiments that shaped the founding of the University of Berlin and the University of London also appeared in the United States. These sentiments found fertile soil in America because higher education leaders increasingly grew quite fearful of the institutional pluralism produced by the freedom within the American system of higher education and the possibility of controversy and disunity that resulted. They believed strongly that an objective truth existed, but pursuing that truth within a pluralistic context often meant avoiding conflict rather than seeking to build institutions that initiated students into conflict from a particular point of view.

Institutionally the avoidance of metaphysical conflict emerged earliest with the foundation of the University of Virginia. Indeed, as we will outline in this chapter, the University of Virginia would go even further than the University of Berlin in its marginalization of theology. Interestingly, it would also face difficulty with moral formation. Later the antisectarianism, the fear of theological conflict, and the difficulties with moral formation that characterized the University of Virginia would become pervasive during the mid-1800s. Consequently other American private research universities, such as Johns Hopkins, Stanford, and Harvard, would eventually be guided by an antisectarian and, at times, even an antitheological approach. Moral concerns would also shift from a preoccupation with the whole student to a focus on the professional and civic identity of the student.[5] Not surprisingly, denominations played a minimal role in constructing and shaping the new research universities, and theology was gradually removed or sidelined from playing any role in nourishing the soul of the university.

Thus, while the American system of higher education and its growing group of research universities would retain certain distinctive features, particularly in the importance of private higher education, American leaders' ideal for the university would change. And although the nationalization that occurred in Europe would eventually make its way to America, another factor would play an even more important role—the fight against religious diversity. Of course, this fight was actually articulated as a fight for something more positive. American universities, both public and private, still sought first and foremost the unity of truth. They still wanted a soul—a common identity, story, and purpose. Yet after marginalizing theology they could not find an overarching narrative and structure that could embrace theological diversity or even a common vision of moral formation and inquiry. Consequently, the myth that excluding theology from the curriculum would bring a unity of objective knowledge to the university emerged. The fight against sectarian diversity would, as this chapter explains, be promulgated as an effort to emphasize Christian unity, but in the end it contributed to the secularization of the academy and the marginalization of moral education.[6]

Yet educational leaders still wanted a university with soul. The unity on which the new soul of the research university would be built in the United States was partly supplied by the national narrative of freedom and liberal democracy, but the robust private sector of American education meant that something more would need to provide a unifying story and identity. The growing discipline of science, which had ascended to the throne of knowledge, played a key role and emerged as the most important force for unity in the modern research university. It also provided an alternative saga for the university. Modern science and the associated belief in scientific naturalism became the reigning paradigm for how scholars navigated the natural world, a world from which God became increasingly marginalized and even absent.[7]

Avoiding the Theological Gladiators

Before the founding of the University of Berlin, the fathers of the American Revolution supported building a national university in America. In 1788, Benjamin Rush proposed that the federal government fund a university that students could attend after finishing college. The purpose of the university, he envisioned, would "prepare our youth for civil and public life."[8] For Rush this meant that the whole curriculum should be designed around political purposes. For example, he thought the university should only teach those subjects that promote the well-being of the nation-state, such as political history, agriculture, manufacturing, and commerce. He wanted the liberal arts reduced so that the faculty would teach "those parts of mathematics which are necessary to the division of property, to finance, and to the principles and practice of war."[9] The university would only offer parts of natural philosophy "which admit to an application to agriculture, manufactures, commerce and war."[10] Reminiscent of ancient Sparta, it would also provide "all those athletic and manly exercises."[11]

Notably, Rush's imagined curriculum omitted theology, and moral philosophy was nowhere to be found. Although Rush's envisioned university was quite narrow in its purpose and scope, he understood it to be superior to impractical European education.

> While the business of education in Europe consists in lectures upon the ruins of Palmyra and antiquities of Herculaneum, or in disputes about Hebrew points, Greek particles, or the accent and quantity of the Roman language, the youth of America will be employed in acquiring those branches of knowledge which increase the conveniences of life, lessen human misery, improve our country, promote population, exalt the human understanding, and establish domestic, social and political happiness.[12]

Rush remained far from alone in his desire for such an institution. The first six presidents supported a national university.[13] George Washington's reasoning was as follows: "The more homogenous our citizens can be made in these particulars the greater will be our prospect of permanent union; and a primary object of such a National Institution should be, the education of our Youth in the science of *Government*."[14] While today we celebrate diversity, the founders were actually quite fearful of it, particularly theological diversity.

In addition, a certain utopian-like hopefulness drove their expectations of what a national university could accomplish. For instance, James Madison used religious language in claiming that a national university, or what he called a "seminary," would be "universal in its benefits" in that

> by enlightening the opinions, by expanding the patriotism, and by assimilating the principles, the sentiments, and the manners of those who might resort to this temple of science, to be redistributed in due time, through every part of the community, sources of jealousy would be diminished, the features of national character would be multiplied, and greater extent given to social harmony.[15]

Today it is difficult to see how expanding patriotism is a "universal" benefit, but at this time the nation had become almost a universal expression of human unity.

When writing about establishing an institution of higher education in Virginia, Thomas Jefferson and James Madison expressed a similar fear of ideological diversity and comparable utopian hopes in nonreligious forms of unity. For them, the worst approach to take would be to support "sectarianism"—a divisive expression of truth based on particular religious doctrines. Jefferson thought theology, being filled with arguments about sectarian differences, should be excluded from the new idea of the university he had in mind, the University of Virginia. Madison, who supported Jefferson's vision, related the mindset advancing this thinking.

> A University with sectarian professorships, becomes, of course, a Sectarian Monopoly: with professorships of rival sects, it would be an Arena of Theological Gladiators. Without any such professorships, it may incur for a time at least, the imputation of irreligious tendencies, if not designs. The last difficulty was thought more manageable than either of the others.[16]

Interestingly, this vision did not mirror the principles for dealing with religious pluralism that Jefferson and Madison had implemented in politics. Their political solution, both in Virginia and in the US Bill of Rights, was to allow something closer to the second option (the "Arena of Theological Gladiators"). Yet, while the option of allowing rival religious confessions to exist would be tested in German theology departments,[17] Jefferson and Madison feared trying it in the more pluralistic context of American higher education. The conceit, of course, was that the new university they envisioned would be neutral. The reality was otherwise.

At the University of Virginia, Jefferson hoped to establish unity by avoiding discussions about theological systems and focusing on what he thought all Americans could agree on—a general belief in God as the creator, ruler, and originator of the universe and its moral order. In a report of the Rockfish Gap Commission on the Proposed University of Virginia chaired by Thomas Jefferson, the committee indicated,

> In conformity with the principles of our constitution, which places all sects of religion on an equal footing . . . we have proposed no professor of Divinity; and tho rather, as the proofs of the being of a god, the creator, preserver, & supreme ruler of the universe, the author of all relations of morality, & of the laws & obligations those infer, will be within the province of the professor of ethics.[18]

Although supposedly accommodating all religions, the reality is that Jefferson and his colleagues sought state funding to teach an approach that undermined robust intellectual discussion about theology and the possible moral differences that emerged from different theological traditions. This vision, not surprisingly, was consistent with Jefferson's own religious views, particularly his deep faith in reason and his optimism about human nature and the capacity of humans to find moral agreement through reason.

Not surprisingly, Jefferson integrated his faith in human reason into the whole university. He placed the library (and not a chapel) in the middle of the university. But Jefferson's faith influenced more than structural decisions. He also created what he considered a student-centered curriculum at his new University of Virginia. Like Rush's national university model, Jefferson's curriculum abolished Latin and theology courses. He departed from Rush, however, in that he based the curriculum on an elective system in which students would choose classes based on their own interests. In the spirit of democracy, there would not be a president of the university, and student discipline would focus on appealing to students' "pride of character, laudable ambition, and moral dispositions."[19]

The students, however, took advantage of this freedom in ways Jefferson did not anticipate. One recent history summarizes the students' escapades during the early years of the university.

> The students brandished guns freely, sometimes shooting in the air, sometimes at each other. They secreted dirks and daggers and, with little to no thought and even less hesitation, stabbed each other. They pummeled, kicked, bit, and gouged each other. They brawled with town merchants, they scuffled with the local wagoners. They cheated at cards for money. They robbed graves. They gambled on cockfights. They beat slaves. They cursed each other, townsfolk, and professors. They vandalized property (even taking a hatchet to the front doors of the Rotunda, the university's signature building) and mutilated cows. They drank and drank and drank. And rioted.[20]

They also attacked and beat professors. One student attempted to target a professor with a bomb—twice. The behavior started in the first year of the school's existence. The professors eventually threatened to leave unless a campus police force was established. At this point, the eighty-two-year-old Jefferson faced his rebellious students only seven months into the university's existence, despondent over their behavior, and he broke down crying.[21] Jefferson's belief that gentleman did not need to be forced to do the right thing was proved false by his students' antics.

Indeed, the student court established to encourage self-government and address such issues failed since students proved unwilling to punish their peers. Ultimately the leaders had to enforce a stricter set of rules to overcome the initial student-caused unrest facing the university. Yet even these standards did not stop the parade of mischief described above from continuing. The university constantly had to fight to save its reputation and state funding.

Interestingly, Jefferson was not alone in discovering the dangers of student freedom. German state authorities would eventually find untethered reason to prove unwieldy and dangerous. They would later come to believe human reason still needed a helpful tutor. For instance, Wilhelm von Humboldt, who helped found the University of Berlin, shifted within fifteen years "from being a champion of the freedom of the individual to being a champion of state regulation in culture."[22] After disbanding the old religious restraints in favor of student freedom, political power now had to be asserted to control the unwieldy students. University communities, even nonsectarian ones, still required rules and officials who enforced those rules. Eventually the University of Virginia did provide a model of a certain kind of state university that eventually became the dominant model in America, although its influence at this time was negligible. Part of this limited influence was due to the fact that the denominational college continued to be the norm in American higher education until after the Civil War.

Moreover, the religious fervor unleashed after the Second Great Awakening spurred a whole new round of institution building. While only 29 permanent Protestant colleges existed before 1830, 133 would begin between the years 1830 and 1861.[23] This growth included a variety of denominations that did not have universities in Europe. By the start of the Civil War, Presbyterians could boast 49 colleges, the Methodists 34, the Baptists 25, Congregationalists 21, and the Catholics 13. Altogether, 162 of the 182 colleges in America were under the control of Christian denominations.[24]

Ironically, the Second Great Awakening also helped solve the University of Virginia's student-conduct problem. Peter Onuf notes that students converting to evangelical Christianity during the Second Great Awakening created "a new culture on the campus—a more evangelical, religious culture."[25] In the end, what changed the students at Jefferson's university "wasn't the Enlightenment, because they didn't get enlightened. But they did get Jesus. . . . And that's the irony, because this was supposed to be a secular place. Jefferson needed serious Christians at his school for it to fulfill his original vision."[26]

One strand of Jefferson's thinking regarding higher education, however, would be much more successful. The antisectarian reasoning exemplified by Jefferson and Madison would start to spread through American higher education. An increasing number of commentators questioned the legitimacy of denominationally affiliated colleges.[27] They longed for a university devoid of sectarianism. For example, one of those critics complained in 1829:

> Why colleges should be sectarian, any more than penitentiaries or than bank, road or canal corporations, is not very obvious. Colleges are designed for the instruction of youth in the learned languages—in polite literature—in the liberal arts and sciences—and not in the dogmatical theology of any sect or party. . . . Are they to inculcate sectarian Greek, sectarian mathematics, sectarian logic, history, rhetoric, philosophy?[28]

Critics believed that unity should be pursued by focusing upon the moral and theological beliefs that Americans held in common rather than encouraging institutional diversity that allowed each college to pursue its own unified vision of the true and good.

In reality, though, denominational colleges already focused a great deal on inculcating a common set of moral beliefs through the teaching of a capstone moral philosophy course. The course, usually taught by the college president, focused less on controversial theological or moral questions and more on practical matters concerning one's obligation to God and fellow humans.[29] The basis of moral authority in this course "was a Christianized reason and a Christianized nature that came to the foreground, albeit well camouflaged."[30] As Douglas Sloan notes, "The entire college experience was meant, above all, to be an experience in character development and the moral life as epitomized, secured, and brought to a focus in the moral philosophy course."[31] In this respect, moral philosophy became the new lifeblood for the university. This effort to avoid sectarian differences and focus on a form of common morality later influenced the emergence of the American research university.

German Research University Envy

The National Teachers Association asserted in 1869, "We have as yet no near approach to a real university in America."[32] What they meant was that a research university did not exist in America. The perception that American colleges lagged behind had existed since the start of the colonies. In 1814, Yale president Timothy Dwight would compare his own institution and Harvard to advanced high schools in Europe.[33] Before the Civil War, America did not have any institutions of higher education with graduate study at the time. Only in 1861 did Yale offer the first American PhD.[34] As one early historian of America's first research university wrote, "We could fling railroads across the continent but our accomplishments in pure science were negligible."[35] As mentioned in the last chapter, however, the Germans had proved to be much more capable in the latter. One of the first Americans to study in Germany was George Tickner, who later became a Harvard professor of French and Spanish languages. He wrote home to Thomas Jefferson in 1815,

> No man can come into their country and see their men of letters & professors, without feeling there is an enthusiasm among them which has brought them forward in forty years as far as other nations have been three centuries in advancing & which will yet carry them much further—without seeing that there is an unwearied & universal diligence among their scholars—a general habit of laboring from fourteen to sixteen hours a day—which will finally give their country an extent and amount of learning of which the world has before had no example.[36]

Through the influence of such reports, during the one hundred years after the University of Berlin was founded (1810), over ten thousand Americans traveled to Prussia and other German territories to study.[37] More than half studied at philosophical faculties (versus theology, medicine, or law), and half of these enrolled at the University of Berlin.[38]

The reasons why so many Americans came to seek knowledge from German philosophical faculty, particularly the revolutionary new state-sponsored University of Berlin, had more to do with their scientific advancement than their agreement with democratic principles or their opening up education to the masses. In fact the German investment in research universities coincided with a decline in university enrollment. After a high of 15,838 students in 1830, enrollment at German universities dropped to 11,899 by 1835 and would not reach 14,000 again until 1870.[39]

Other practical reasons also compelled Americans to travel to Germany. The English universities, Oxford and Cambridge, were closed to non-Anglicans. The French institutions of higher education had fallen behind due to radical restructuring, and the French Revolution had soured many Americans toward French ideas. As a result of postrevolutionary developments, the French approach to higher education appeared extremely narrow and rigid to Americans. It consisted of specialized colleges that were

> subjected to severe, often military discipline, strictly organized and controlled by an enlightened despotism that governed to the last detail the curriculum, the awarding of degrees, the conformity of views held concerning official doctrines, and even personal habits such as the ban on the wearing of beards in 1852.[40]

This approach contrasted sharply with the freedom provided to German professors and students and the freedom Americans admired. In light of the limits of the other options and the success of the German model, learning from the German universities proved much more attractive.

One of the visitors to these universities would ultimately lead America's first research university. On February 22, 1876, Daniel Coit Gilman was inaugurated as the first president of Johns Hopkins University.[41] Gilman had traveled to Germany as a youth, and he was well aware that Johns Hopkins was inspired by the German research university model, although he cautioned, "In following, as we are prone to do in educational matters, the example of Germany, we must beware lest we accept what is their cast off; lest we introduce faults as well as virtues, defects with excellence."[42] The virtue he wanted to introduce was the faculty freedom to focus upon research.[43] In Gilman's estimation, the faculty at Johns Hopkins should be defined by "its power to pursue independent and original investigation, and to inspire the young with enthusiasm for study and research."[44] This vision would propel Johns Hopkins to stand as the most influential institution in higher education in the United States for at least the first twenty years of its history.[45]

With freedom, however, came the fear of disunity and fragmentation. Gilman's opening remarks also demonstrated a concern with avoiding two types of conflicts that could tear at the unity of a nation or an institution. He claimed that the university would strive for "freedom from tendencies toward ecclesiastical or sectional controversies."[46] To avoid ecclesiastical or sectional controversies, Gilman specified that when hiring he wanted professors with attitudes toward religion and politics that "precludes the uncalled-for expression of these differences which are likely to impair the usefulness of the University."[47]

The two concerns would appear a bit uneven. Just eleven years after the Civil War, it remains unsurprising that the university would be eager to avoid "sectional" political controversies. Although Johns Hopkins University was not a state institution, it still found unity in its national identity. D. G. Hart points out that the justification for the modern research university "arose from a desire to serve and shape the recently reunified nation. This nation-serving character of the university movement meant that all higher education worthy of distinction was public, not in the sense that funding came from the state, but in the sense that it served public or national ends."[48]

The fact that *sectarian* was just as problematic of a word as *sectional* would appear to be odd. In that same 1876 inaugural event, however, Harvard's Charles Eliot provides a rationale for this fear. He claimed, "A university can not be built upon a sect, unless, indeed it be a sect which includes the whole of the educated portion of the nation."[49] For Eliot, similar to the new German research universities, the concern about unity stems from a concern with finding a unity that is satisfactory not to the church but to a nation. Trying to engage with the diversity of Christian traditions, negatively defined as sectarianism, proved too threatening for these educational leaders. Instead of hoping to build a pluralistic group of universities with particular identities, the founders sought a more uniform set of institutions that would avoid theological controversy.

Without a particular theological narrative to guide the university, Johns Hopkins drew from a broader, more general educational vision that contained remnants of religious language. This approach reflected the reduction to a "what we hold in common" approach. Gilman used this kind of language when describing the law that governs the work of the faculty: "with unselfish devotion to the discovery and advancement of truth and righteousness, they renounce all other preferment, so that, like the greatest of all teachers, they may promote the good of mankind."[50] Yet only certain kinds of truth were really pursued. Gilman's research university was concerned with unified answers to truth and not with disciplines such as theology that teach controversies about truth but fail to come to a unified solution.

This vision had important ramifications for the curriculum. If unity could not be found in an academic field such as theology, the field would be avoided, and those fields and methods where unity could be found, such as science, became the exalted field of study. Gilman committed the bulk of his resources to the natural sciences, since the natural sciences were not a discipline that courted conflict but rather provided common answers.

Although Johns Hopkins remained hostile to Christian sectarianism and open to the sciences, Gilman did not believe it was hostile to Christianity. The sciences, in Gilman's view, were friendly to Christianity, although he would not use so specific a word at the risk of sounding sectarian. The favored word would be *religion*. As Gilman proclaimed in his inaugural address, "Religion has nothing to fear from science, and science need not be afraid of religion. Religion claims to interpret the word of God, and science to reveal the laws of God. The interpreters may blunder, but truths are immutable, eternal and never in conflict."[51] Moreover, undertaking research in the scientific method, he believed, actually shaped the character of the student, which he saw as the key objective when it came to students.

Again, hoping to focus on what scholars agree on, he proclaimed ten points of commonality in his inaugural address. One of these points included the following claim:

The object of the university is to develop character—to make men. It misses its aim if it produced learned pedants, or simple artisans, or cunning sophists, or pretentious practitioners. Its purport is not so much to impart knowledge to the pupils, as whet the appetite, exhibit methods, develop powers, strengthen judgment, and invigorate the intellectual and moral forces. It

89

should prepare for the service of society a class of students who will be wise, thoughtful, progressive guides in whatever department of work or thought they may be engaged.[52]

For undergraduates, this objective would be aided by requiring a course in moral philosophy, which would spend less time lecturing and attempting to address moral conflicts than it would on inculcating agreed-on moral beliefs shared by those in the nation.[53]

Science also fulfilled this moral objective by requiring students to develop rigorous intellectual habits. In other words, "the modes of observation, of comparison, of eliminating error and of ascertaining the truth" built character.[54] It also reinforced certain Christian sentiments such as the mystery of creation, an awe and reverence for the universe, the need for diligence, and zeal in the pursuit of truth. Indeed, in Gilman's view, the research university would aid the building of a "better state of society" and quench the thirst for intellectual and moral knowledge.[55] As Hart claims, it was a "blend of faith and intellect that guided the architects of the research university."[56]

Despite all this rhetoric about belief in the unity of science and religion, Johns Hopkins University did not include a course that had always existed in the liberal arts curriculum of the older colleges. The course, natural theology, or as it was called at Yale at the time, "Natural Theology and Evidences of Christianity," placed science within a larger theological narrative. It began to disappear from most college curricula in the mid-nineteenth century. In fact, Yale would be one of the last colleges to teach the course, which it did up until the 1880s. The reason for its disappearance from Johns Hopkins University and other institutions could be linked to an important development—the saga of science that Johns Hopkins professors adopted.[57]

The Unified Story of Nature

Building knowledge and the associated concept of truth on a unified story about nature brought important changes. As the last chapter noted, the shift began by depersonalizing God and ended by depersonalizing the natural order. This change meant that final epistemological authority slowly became vested not in a Being but in an object. To be objective was to take the standpoint of (increasingly) impersonal nature, and it would slowly come to be perceived as the best stance to take as a scholar. The best way to discover impersonal nature's story would then become the discipline that specialized in learning about nature—science.

This search for nature's story was aided and complicated by the publication in 1859 of Charles Darwin's *Origin of Species*. John Dewey, who received his PhD from Johns Hopkins in 1884, summarized one of Darwin's key tenets: "The conceptions that had reigned in the philosophy of nature and knowledge for two thousand years . . . rested on the assumption of the superiority of the fixed and final."[58] The *Origin of Species* upset that assumption because it provided evidence that nature is always changing. If nature never stayed the same, what could be said about knowledge and the truth? Natural laws no longer seemed quite as lawlike. As Julie Reuben summarizes the problem, "Science could not be considered the discovery of regularity in nature because nature was not necessarily regular."[59] This change in perspective would also lead to an alteration in one key idea guiding the university. For Dewey and the progressives who followed him, human development would become the aim of education.[60]

Science became indispensable in providing the tools to help learn about that form of development. Charles Sanders Pierce, an early philosophy professor at Johns Hopkins, provides an example of the understanding during this time. Science, he wrote,

> is a living and growing body of truth. We might even say that knowledge is not necessary to science. . . . That which constitutes science is not so much correct conclusions as it is correct method. . . . That which is essential, however, is the scientific spirit, which is determined not to rest satisfied with existing opinions, but to press on to the real truth of nature.[61]

The key parts of this method included openness to inquiry and the verification of hypothesis. How would the verification of hypothesis lead to better knowledge? Reuben notes,

> Philosophers and scientists did not fully justify how their method of hypothesis testing would lead to better knowledge. Instead, they assumed that intellectual progress could be identified by agreement. They believed that scientists studying the same problem could eventually come to the same solution.[62]

Whereas when theology was queen of the sciences, disputation or debate proved to be a key academic method. Science, like the nation-state, was more invested in finding agreement. As Reuben observes, "The emphasis on consensus as the *sign* of scientific progress contradicted intellectuals' simultaneous commitment to conflict as a *source* of scientific progress."[63]

The emphasis on consensus also contributed to what George Marsden labels as methodological secularization. He summarizes it in this way: "One of the major dynamics of complex modern societies arises from the principle that many tasks are done most efficiently by isolating and objectifying them.... In effect, one creates a mechanism for addressing the issue and applies it to a practical problem."[64] Marsden cites efforts to improve the efficiency of a steam engine as an example. Although religious motives may have inspired or guided the worker, religion was largely left out of the process. This approach proved particularly important in scientific laboratories: "Diversities of religious beliefs also made it particularly important for scholarly cooperation that their substance be kept out of the laboratories."[65] Since this approach produced results that brought benefits to humanity, religious believers in general found nothing wrong with this form of methodological secularization.

Yet this new conception of science challenged the older conceptions of natural theology taught in American colleges and universities. Earlier scholars supported the idea of the existence of natural laws by connecting the concept to natural theology. If science was no longer understood as the discovery of natural laws, but instead was constantly in flux, it was difficult to bring scientific knowledge and specific unchanging theological doctrines into agreement. Theology began to be seen as the source of the problem within natural and moral philosophy courses. G. Stanley Hall, who would teach at Johns Hopkins University from 1882 to 1888, wrote in 1876 that one problem with moral philosophy courses was that they used "a score of moral treatises on 'moral science' which deduce all ground of obligation from theological considerations."[66]

Intellectual leaders created a solution by reframing the problem. The conflict, as Reuben describes it, "was not between scientific truth and religious truth, but between the openness of scientific inquiry and the dogmatism of theology. They suggested that if religion would rid itself of dogmatic theology, science and religion would be harmonious."[67] Reuben cites the example of the Johns Hopkins' professor of chemistry Ira Remsen, who wrote "that science can do true religion no harm, but can only strengthen it. It may modify, and has modified, dogmatic theology, but dogmatic theology is one thing and religion is another, and true religion must find a broader and broader foundation in knowledge."[68]

Overall, by drawing on religion and not theology, educational leaders, such as those at Johns Hopkins, hoped they could create a new kind of research university that took both religion and science seriously. In reality, it took science much more seriously and simply avoided theological controversy. Since metaphysical unity proved difficult, professors at universities such as Johns Hopkins would look to find unity in the story of the physical world. Oddly, in an institution supposedly devoted to exploring intellectual controversies, the research university sought instead the peace of intellectual agreement that science brought. Science's promise of helping find a unified view of physical and moral knowledge, however, would fail to provide unity within the new research university. Ultimately the false harmony between science and religion that cleared the way for the preeminence of science could not save the research university's soul.

Discovering Science's Moral Limits

One of science's chief limits pertained to the moral vision necessary to sustain a university's soul. Initially scholars had great hope for the moral insights one could derive from science. Some claimed scientific advances in agriculture could lead to world peace, and developments in biology could help us understand history and foreign policy.[69] Eugenics research, university leaders contended, was one of the ways the university could contribute to the progress of a nation and humanity. In this view, the scientific method would lead to increased knowledge of both the true and the good.[70] Moreover, they believed that this knowledge would be free from the conflicts that plagued both theology and philosophy.

Practitioners of the new social sciences that arose from the old moral philosophy course proved especially interested in using their scientific findings for moral ends. Early economists, political scientists, psychologists, and sociologists debated not about the objectivity of their results but also the moral ways science should be used.[71] One of the most popular expressions was authored by John Dewey and James Tufts, who set forth a scientific conception of ethics rooted in evolutionary theory instead of supernatural belief in God.[72] Instead of being based on dogmatic theological premises, they thought science could provide a new moral foundation based on objective truth.

The idea that science could provide the basis for a new source of curricular unity ultimately failed. Scientists could not escape conflict any more than theologians could.[73] Consequently a new group of scientists reverted to the "what we have in common" principle. They claimed that scientists exceeded their authority when they used science to answer moral questions that went beyond its methods. Science, they argued, could not provide a unified view of the world any more than philosophy or theology.

As the views of this new group of scientists began to dominate the academic culture, scientists began to place increasing emphasis on the need for researchers to be objective or value-free.[74] This approach, it was argued, was needed to arrive at an accurate knowledge of the facts. The scientific method, however, could not discover what "ought" to be. Because moral claims were merely issues of value and not fact, ethics began to be seen as subjective. Consequently, by the 1920s two things occurred. First, natural and social scientists believed that practicing the scientific method required objectivity and ethical detachment. Second, this attitude effectively undermined attempts to find a unified source of knowledge based on science.[75] Focusing and teaching about the subject matter on which we could find agreement ultimately meant avoiding not only theology but also ethics.[76]

Restricting the university so that it avoided theology and marginalized moral concerns produced a uniform, if not boring, shell of an institution—a contrast to the ideologically substantive work carried forward previously. Abraham Flexner, when describing the American university in 1930, used these uninspiring words to describe the university at the time: "an institution consciously devoted to the pursuit of knowledge, the solution of problems, the critical appreciation of achievement, and the training of men at a really high level."[77] He made no reference to philosophical pursuits such as wisdom, truth, or goodness. Instead he used vacuous and morally bereft terms related to problem-solving or "training" at a "really high level," without any reference to a larger narrative in which those problems or standards of excellence might make sense. The university graduate simply used knowledge to solve problems. The idea of the university had been reduced to that of being a successful producer of practical knowledge. Not surprisingly, critics began to find fault with this result.

5

FRACTURING THE SOUL

The Creation of the American Multiversity (1869–1969)

...

The multiversity is a confusing place for the student.
He has problems of establishing his identity and sense of security
within it. But it offers him a vast range of choices, enough literally
to stagger the mind. In this range of choices he encounters the
opportunities and the dilemmas of freedom. The walking wounded
are many. Lernfreiheit—the freedom of the student to pick
and choose, to stay or to move on—is triumphant.

CLARK KERR

THE REJECTION OF THE CHRISTIAN TRADITION AND THEOLOGY as
sources of unity for the university, we have argued, led education leaders to
find other quasi-religious sources to provide the university a substitute narrative or saga to nourish and unify its soul. Many sought a unity grounded
in national political ideology (in Europe, as discussed in chapter three) or
science and the scientific method (in America, as discussed in chapter four).
The most successful American effort would combine both elements. As we
recount in this chapter, Charles Eliot, the president of Harvard for forty
years (1869–1909), assembled a vision grounded both on the liberal democratic notion of freedom and the use of science to provide empirical truths
by which to live that helped set in motion the changes in higher education

that helped create today's multiversity—a university that exalts the freedom to experience a fragmented education and life. This vision, however, would also lead to the fracturing of the university's soul and leave it with multiple competing identities, stories, and purposes. A few educational leaders, particularly Robert Maynard Hutchins, would attempt to preserve the university's soul through an appeal to a liberal arts education nourished by common great texts that provide metaphysical insight into our common human condition. Eventually, though, some educators, such as Clark Kerr, argued that we really cannot hope to save the singular soul of such a complicated beast as the multiversity. We merely have to learn to live with the multiversity's fractured soul.

Charles Eliot: Father of the Multiversity

Measured by the sheer volume of his influence, Charles Eliot (1834–1926) stands as a central figure in the emergence of the American research university and what others would eventually call the multiversity. His forty years at Harvard resulted in revolutionary changes to Harvard's identity, narrative, purpose, and structure. Fueled by his Unitarian faith and the trust it led him to place in human freedom, Eliot transformed his university. His efforts successfully marginalized theology from the university and paved the way for the fragmentation definitive of today's multiversity.

Eliot's academic career, however, began in apparent failure. Although he graduated from Harvard College in 1853 as a promising student who had studied mathematics and the emerging field of chemistry, after five years as an assistant professor of chemistry and mathematics back at Harvard, he failed to be promoted. After spending two years studying chemistry in Germany, Eliot would assume a position as professor of chemistry at the Massachusetts Institute of Technology. The professor once denied promotion would then return to his alma mater to assume its presidency after publishing a series of high-profile articles on the future of education in *Atlantic Monthly*.[1]

Inspired and motivated by Daniel Coit Gilman's innovations at the new Johns Hopkins University, Eliot wasted little time laying the groundwork for how he envisioned Harvard's transformation into a research university.[2] In his inaugural address, given on October 19, 1869, Eliot contended, "The [educational] practice of England and America is literally centuries behind the precept of the best thinkers of education."[3] Recitations and the memorization of information from texts had been the norm at Harvard. In contrast, Eliot wanted to unleash ways of knowing that depended on "objects and instruments in hand,—not from books merely, not through the memory chiefly, but by the seeing eye and informing fingers."[4] He further declared, "The notion that education consists in the authoritative inculcation of what the teacher deems true may be logical and appropriate in a convent, or a seminary for priests, but it is intolerable in universities."[5] Eliot sought to recast authority, epistemology, and pedagogy in higher education. Instead of passing down to students a system of fixed knowledge and known truths from faculty and texts, he envisioned the university as a place where new knowledge was created through scientific means. He saw the scientifically guided university as serving the chief end of the nation. Since a fundamental ideal of liberal democracy involved the freedom to choose one's worldview and vision of the good life, he believed what the nation needed was a new university guided by its fundamental value of freedom.

According to Eliot's most recent biographer, Eliot's exaltation of freedom arose from his religious and social philosophy.[6] A concise example of this connection came in a speech he gave at Harvard Divinity School titled "The Religion of the Future." In front of a group of students who had gathered that summer, Eliot argued, "religion is not a fixed, but a fluent thing. It is therefore wholly natural and to be expected that the conceptions of religion prevalent among educated people should change from century to century."[7] Eliot's religious views reflected his devotion to the Unitarian tradition that had usurped or evolved from (depending on one's perspective) New England's Congregational roots. What this outlook retained from its Reformed roots was the belief that both political and religious authorities could be corrupted. For Eliot, "The religion of the future will not be based on authority, either spiritual or temporal. The decline of the reliance upon absolute authority is one of the most significant phenomena of the modern world."[8] Authority for Eliot would not simply disappear though. It would simply not be vested in every individual and not in those with political or religious positions. As a result, for Eliot the pursuit of divine truth could proceed by any number of paths taken by individuals, who were free to choose the best path for them.

Charles Taylor describes this ontological approach, only beginning to emerge in Eliot's time, as indicative of a phase of secularization he calls "the Age of Authenticity."[9] Self-orientation and expressive individualism then became the de facto modality of modern existence. Presaging this culture-wide development, Eliot's ideas of individual freedom also informed his views of how the scholars, the students, the curriculum, and the emerging cocurricular dimension were to be understood at Harvard as it made its transition from a college to a research university.

One of the ways that Eliot "freed," but also fragmented, the university pertained to the role of the professor. For Eliot, "The virtue of an institution of learning lies in the qualities and attainments of its faculty."[10] In that inaugural address, Eliot noted that "the professors, lecturers, and tutors of the University are the living sources of learning and enthusiasm."[11] In order for such enthusiasm to find its proper expression, not only did universities need well-trained faculty members with initiative, but those faculty members must also find themselves in environments where they were, in Eliot's terms, fully free. For scholars, freedom—in particular, academic freedom—was an essential quality of their very identity. Eliot believed universities were incapable of running well if faculty were hindered from offering responsible and free advice.[12] Faculty members also needed to be free in relation to how they taught their courses.

Perhaps most critical, however, was that faculty needed to be free to pursue truth through their research in whatever direction that process led them. Due to Eliot's Unitarian views, the Harvard president firmly believed that all earnest pursuits of truth would lead well-meaning individuals to comparable ends. As a result, limiting those pursuits through some externally imposed authority would only lead faculty members to something less than the truth they were called to pursue. Eliot assumed that freedom would not lead to the fragmentation of the university's soul but would instead allow for a more organic and freely chosen form of unity.

In many ways, those same views were also extended to students. Prior to Eliot's arrival at Harvard, higher education in America was dominated by a prescribed curriculum. Students had little to no input into what they studied. First-year students all took a particular set of courses, which were then followed by a comparable set of prescribed courses during the three subsequent years. Critics charged that this traditional lock-step approach to study was a useless remnant of tradition, exemplified by the requirement that students take "dead languages" such as Greek and Latin.[13]

Although the pressure to revise the curriculum was certainly mounting prior to the beginning of Eliot's tenure as president, his views on freedom and how those views applied to the curricular offerings for students were also ahead of their time. Eliot believed that students, in order to pursue truth, needed to be free to follow wherever their intellectual interests might lead. The German term for a student's right to unfettered inquiry was previously noted as *Lernfreiheit*. In particular, during his inaugural address, Eliot made his intentions clear concerning the role students should play in deciding their course of study. In contrast to the prescribed curriculum that was predominant at that time, Eliot argued:

> All the studies which are open to him [the student] are liberal and disciplinary, not narrow or special. Under this system, the College does not demand, it is true, one invariable set of studies of every candidate for the first degree in Arts; but its requisitions for this degree are nevertheless high and inflexible, being nothing less than four years devoted to liberal culture.[14]

For Eliot, granting undergraduates the freedom to determine a course of study was not an expression of declining expectations but a move deemed necessary to achieve the highest of possible standards.

In his estimation, "the young man of nineteen or twenty ought to know what he likes best and is most fit for."[15] The university should recognize that imperative and revise its expectations accordingly. The reason why is that

> the elective system fosters scholarship, because it gives free play to natural preferences and inborn attitudes, makes possible enthusiasm for chosen work, relieves the professor and the ardent disciple of the presence of a body of students who are compelled to an unwelcome task, and enlarges instruction by substituting many and various lessons given to small, lively classes, for a few lessons many times repeated to different sections of a numerous class.[16]

Eliot's view rejected the Puritan emphasis on human sinfulness that had previously shaped the institution and turned to a more optimistic understanding of human nature. As Eliot explained, according to this perspective, a young man is much affected by the expectations which his elders entertain of him. If they expect him to behave like a child, his lingering childishness will oftener rule his actions; if they expect him to behave like a man, his incipient manhood will oftener assert itself. The pretended parental or sham monastic régime of the common American college seems to me to bring out the childishness rather than the manliness of the average student; as is evidenced by the pranks he plays, the secret societies in which he rejoices, and the barbarous or silly customs which he accepts and transmits.[17]

For someone such as Eliot who wanted to dispense with the negative idea of human nature held by the Puritans, one need merely adapt college policy to the preferred set of student ideals, "and in time the evil fruits of a mistaken policy will disappear."[18]

Not surprisingly, one criticism of what came to be known as the elective system was that it weakened the common curriculum that united members of a class. Eliot acknowledged this criticism in his speech and ironically based his rebuttal on the fact that the emerging structure of the university already made such a bond unlikely, if not impossible. According to Eliot, "The increased size of the college classes works a great change in this respect. . . . This increase is progressive."[19] In order to pursue truth on all of the various paths it may offer, a university of increasing size was necessary. Compounding that growth was the ever-expanding array of interests guiding both faculty and students.

When giving an address almost halfway into his forty-year presidency, Eliot also noted that the elective system not only allowed faculty and students to follow their interests but also provided them with the "opportunity to win academic distinction in single subjects or special lines of study."[20] He believed that "the uniform curriculum led to a uniform degree, the first scholar and the last receiving the same diploma."[21] By its very nature "a university could not be developed on that plan."[22] The university he envisioned, and the research university that would emerge in the wake of his efforts, must "encourage students to push far on single lines; whence arises a demand for advanced instruction in all departments in which honors can be won."[23] As a result, the university needed to provide opportunities for its students to excel. According to Eliot, those opportunities should come in a wide array of opportunities or disciplines. Given the emerging emphasis on faculty and student freedom, it should perhaps be little surprise that Eliot created structures to allow faculty greater freedom from supervising students.

As a result, Eliot asked LeBaron Russell Briggs to serve as the first dean of men at Harvard in 1890. The creation of this new role, as Julie Reuben notes, shifted concern for student morality from the faculty to the college staff.[24] Over the course of the next eleven years, Briggs established "a reputation as that to the end of his life he was a student's friend."[25] According to Samuel Eliot Morison, "the key to his [Briggs's] character was a unique balance of kindness and shrewdness. He believed in human nature without being soft."[26] He became a source of encouragement to students while also providing guidance, direction, and of course correction. Ultimately he served as a substitute for what the faculty had once offered.

The creation of this new position and what would ultimately become known as the cocurricular realm indicated that despite the promise of giving students freedom, certain problems accompanied this arrangement. For example, a cocurricular advising presence was "more needed in an era when personal liberty and free election bewildered many students, left them drifting without rudders, the sport of every breeze."[27] As the tendrils of the influential elective movement spread across the country, other university leaders also realized they needed to appoint judicious colleagues to comparable roles. As time passed and more comparable appointments were made, a new professional class initially referred to as student-personnel administrators became a fixed component of university administrations.

What nurtured the soul of this new university was the democratic story and its ideal of freedom from any external authority. In Eliot's understanding of the "free" university, theology and religion played only a marginal role. In a speech made at Harvard Divinity School near the end of his presidency, Eliot proclaimed, "The religion of the future will not be based upon authority, either spiritual or temporal."[28] In essence, he believed that the "tendency toward liberty is progressive, and among educated men irresistible."[29] He was quick to note that individuals of his day were no less willing to be led than members of previous generations. The difference was that authority needed empirical verification, and it needed to demonstrate usefulness. In his eyes, "the authority both of the most authoritative churches and of the

Bible as a verbally inspired guide is already greatly impaired."[30] In contrast, he believed people yearn for truth that is not only verifiable but also useful.

Although for Eliot theology or religion could provide little help with offering useful knowledge or empirically derived authority, it did provide one thing—it motivated people to long for the good beyond oneself. He noted, "In the religious life of the future the primary object will not be personal welfare or safety of the individual in this world or any other."[31] In contrast, "The religious person will not think of his own welfare or security, but of service to others, and of contributions to the common good."[32] In the dedicated pursuit of the common good here and now, the power of religion would be readily evident. Religion would motivate people not to focus on their own well-being or even on the well-being of other individuals. Instead it could motivate them to focus on the common good.

By providing this motivation, religion could actually lead to one form of knowledge. Eliot asserted, "The race has come to the knowledge of God through knowledge of itself; and the best knowledge of God comes through knowledge of the best of the race."[33] Humans needed to look no further for God than within themselves. Theology, as previously practiced, was no longer needed to hold the university together. Eliot also did not see the need to find unity in the sciences or some other discipline. Instead freedom would be the primary unifying source. In other words, American higher education, he believed, should serve politically related ends such as "freedom" and "democracy."

The Failure of an Alternative Humanistic Vision

Although Eliot's emphasis on freedom dominated the conversation about the ends of higher education for the next century, his vision would also be challenged by other thinkers. One of these critics was Robert Maynard Hutchins. Hutchins, who served as president of the University of Chicago from 1929 to 1951, inherited an institution defined in many ways by the ethos Eliot sought to inspire at Harvard. As a newly installed president, Hutchins believed that the Harvard curriculum Eliot initiated was fragmented and thus incoherent to the students who encountered it and the professors who delivered it. In his most influential work, *The Higher Learning in America*, Hutchins began by arguing, "The most striking fact about higher learning in America is the confusion that besets it."[34] The organic whole or soul that Eliot had assumed would emerge had failed to develop. The specialized nature of the academic disciplines had made it difficult for faculty members to address big questions across disciplinary lines. Although they could apprehend with great clarity their ever-increasingly small part of the whole, no one seemed capable of seeing the whole, much less taking any ownership of it.

Hutchins claimed that the underlying problem was that educators were no longer aware of the common end to which they were preparing their students. According to Hutchins, the compounding challenge was that

> we do not know what a good education is. We do not know how to communicate it to those who cannot read. We must find the answers to both of these questions. It is possible that if we can discover what a general education is the problem of communication may partially solve itself; for it might be the first fruits of an intelligible curriculum would be an interest in understanding it, even on pain of doing so through books.[35]

For Hutchins, students should not to be left to follow their own passions and thus design a curriculum they think is best for them. The elective approach, in its purest form, ran counter to the aims of the university and the democracy it was called to serve.

Hutchins even went so far as to argue, "The free elective system as Mr. Eliot introduced it at Harvard and as Progressive Education adapted it to lower age levels amounted to a denial that there was content to education."[36] For Hutchins, academic freedom was thus "simply a way of saying that we get the best results in education and research if we leave their management to people who know something about them."[37]

Hutchins's search for a solution to this problem led him to Mortimer J. Adler, a newly minted PhD in philosophy from Columbia. Hutchins first met Adler while Hutchins was leading the Yale Law School. A devout New Yorker who did not savor the thought of moving to a quaint village such as New Haven, Adler was eventually persuaded by Hutchins to join him in Chicago. Searching for some form of soul that would hold the university together, Hutchins found it in the "great conversation" Adler sought to initiate through the required study of a canon of literary classics.[38] Adler initially led discussion-based seminars in which even Hutchins participated despite his busy schedule. Absent the theological soul that previous generations had depended on, Hutchins staked his legacy as an educator on the ability of this canon to hold as the unifying force within the university.

Hutchins argued that the unifying quality of the great conversation centered on what it revealed about humanity: "One purpose of education is to draw out the elements of our common human nature. These elements are the same in any time or place." As a result, in order to identify these texts, one must first look to "books which have through the centuries attained to the dimensions of classics."[39] Foremost to Hutchins were those texts that had endured regardless of passing trends and the fickle whims of society.

In addition, for Hutchins, books that populate the core of a general education do so "because it is impossible to understand any subject or to comprehend the contemporary world without them."[40] For example, one cannot understand the current nature of law unless one reads works such as Plato's *Republic*, Augustine's *City of God*, and Jean-Jacque Rousseau's *The Social Contract*, to name only a few. For Hutchins, ideas do not exist in vacuums nor does the manner in which they might evolve in the future. One must see the whole of the ideas that define our common existence, roots and all, in order to adequately participate in a vibrant democracy.

Two years removed from the presidency of the University of Chicago, Hutchins developed his ideas concerning the university as the head of the Ford Foundation with the publication of *The University of Utopia*.[41] Freed from the daily pressures of his former office, Hutchins sought to envision a university with soul to which we could aspire. He started by enumerating the plagues besetting the university. In particular, he described the worst elements of industrialization, specialization, philosophical diversity (or "the problem of forming a community in the absence of communication"[42]), and social and political conformity that hold the university back from reaching its full potential.

To Hutchins, the critical question in the end was "whether it is possible to have the University of Utopia without having Utopians." The answer he offered "would seem to be in the negative."[43] However, for Hutchins it was not essential for Utopians to achieve the full aspirations of their ideals to establish such a university. "Apparently they have to only be this far along the road to Utopia: they have to want to get there."[44] What this meant for Hutchins is that we only need optimistic liberal democrats. The reason is that for Hutchins, education and democracy share an interdependent relationship. He wrote, "The educational system is a means to the country's ideals."[45] The founders of state universities in the nineteenth century would have been pleased.

Although Hutchins and Eliot held opposing opinions about curricular structure, they held similar beliefs about what justified their preferred approach. In a secularizing society, Eliot flung wide the doors to the curriculum while Hutchins tried to justify requiring students to read the canon of vital texts. Both did so on the grounds that it furthered the well-being of liberal democracy. Hutchins opined that if students were unable to look beyond their own individual desires to the common political good, democracy and the education that served it would disintegrate. Hutchins was not the first (see discussions of Jeremiah Day and the Yale Report of 1828 in chapters seven and eleven) nor the last (see Neil Postman's *The End of Education*[46] and many others) to make this argument. However, try as he did, the seed of the university with soul Hutchins labored to cultivate in the wake of Eliot's experiment would not take root.[47] Similarly, Eliot's desire for a free and open curriculum was often embraced more in spirit than in practice, as many institutions continue to cling to the notion of a curricular "core." What did rise to prominence was the notion that the end of the university was to produce autonomous critical thinkers, and that the university should provide a forum for school choice. In this regard, drawing on liberal democracy to form the university's soul did not provide sufficient unifying power to ground the purposes of higher education in something beyond the self. Like the larger democratic society, the freedom the university bestowed would often become merely a means of advancing the dizzying array of self-interests. The emergence of the multiversity would have confirmed Hutchins's worst fears.

The Multiversity and the Spirit of Eliot

Among Hutchins's critics, as previously mentioned, was the one-time head of the University of California Clark Kerr (1958–1967). In a piece titled "Disagreeing with Hutchins," Kerr offered, "Long live the classical model—as one of many."[48] At the heart of Kerr's sentiments was a belief, similar to Eliot, in the plurality of options, whether those options are curricular or even institutional. To Kerr, America needed institutions such as St. John's College in Annapolis, Maryland, that offered students a great texts curriculum. In addition, he believed America needed research universities that offered students an almost dizzying array of options. Kerr opened his book *The Uses of the University* by arguing, "Universities in America are at a hinge of history: while connected with their past, they are swinging in another direction."[49] He then quickly noted that "analysis should not be confused with approval or description with defense."[50]

The themes he highlighted he addressed in more detail in the following years. For example, in the first volume of his memoir, Kerr noted, "Federal research dollars in the hundreds of millions were available to our universities" and led to "often unrelated activities; the resulting new attention to graduate studies and research; and the neglect of undergraduates and the humanities."[51] The result, he then contended, included "restless undergraduates, dissension within the faculties, the rise of more and more restricted specialties, and the loss of a sense of integrated intellectual community."[52] These contextual details would lay the groundwork for what Kerr would describe as the *multiversity*.

The multiversity, according to Kerr, "is so many things to so many different people that it must, of necessity, be partially at war with itself."[53] Kerr asserted that *The Idea of a University* as described by John Henry Newman had not only a clear ideological center but also a clear set of boundaries. In contrast, the multiversity attempt to be everything to everyone leaves it lacking such qualities. At one of his more sarcastic points later in his presidency, Kerr would contend that the defining priorities of a university administrator included parking for faculty, sex for students, and intercollegiate sports for alumni.[54]

The multiversity was not without its virtues. Kerr did drily note that "no bard sings its praises; no prophet to proclaim its vision; no guardian to protect its sanctity. It has its critics, its detractors, its transgressors. It also has its barkers selling its wares to all who will listen—and many do." However, he argued that "it also has a reality rooted in the logic of history. It has an imperative rather than a seasoned choice among elegant alternatives."[55] This imperative would allow the multiversity to acquire unprecedented resources and thus produce unprecedented research. The permeable nature of the multiversity's boundaries and thus the wide variety of constituents the multiversity could attract could allow for an array of efforts previously unimagined. As a result, Kerr noted that throughout history nothing compares with the intellectual vitality of such a community.

These opportunities, however, also came with a correlative array of challenges. For example, "There is less sense of community than in the village but also less sense of confinement. There is less sense of purpose within the town but there are more ways to excel. There are more refuges of anonymity—both for the creative person or the drifter."[56] Individuals with vision and the requisite resources thrive in such an environment. An absence of vision and resources, however, makes success unlikely at best. For graduate students in particular, who arrive on campus with the developmental lessons of their undergraduate experiences behind them along with considerable vocational clarity, the multiversity often proves to be an invigorating place. They are not looking to form a relationship with the university as a whole but simply one or perhaps two particular subcultures.

Most undergraduate students, however, lack those advantages. Having recently departed their homes, they need the solidarity of some subgroup, and Kerr notes that some find it in anything ranging from Greek organizations to athletic teams. At this point, Kerr makes his most striking assessment of what is at stake in the student experience, which we first quoted in the epigraph to this chapter.

> The multiversity is a confusing place for the student. He has problems of establishing his identity and sense of security within it. But it offers him a vast range of choices, enough literally to stagger the mind. In this range of choices he encounters the opportunities and the dilemmas of freedom. The walking wounded are many. *Lernfreiheit*—the freedom of the student to pick and choose, to stay or to move on—is triumphant.[57]

Students are thus left to wrestle with how to embrace their freedom, to pick and hopefully choose wisely. If so, what may come just might prove to be considerable. If not, a high casualty rate awaits. Absent a foundation that held the university together, students were left to their own way among an "intellectual world [that] has been fractionalized."[58] Ironically, Kerr would experience the results of this frustration in the Free Speech Movement in

California universities. As Mario Savio, widely recognized as the student leader of the Free Speech Movement, once argued in relation to Kerr and the University of California:

> There is a time when the operation of the machine becomes so odious, makes you so sick at heart, that you can't take part. You can't even passively take part! And you've got to put your bodies upon the gears and upon the wheels, upon the levers, upon all the apparatus, and you've got to make it stop! And you've got to indicate to the people who run it, to the people who own it—that unless you're free, the machine will be prevented from working at all![59]

This rage against the impersonal machine of the university resounded with feelings of alienation. The university that Savio experienced was far from a vibrant home for hospitality, learning, and human flourishing. Feeling used and exploited by the university machine is not anyone's idea of the ideal university.

Freeing the university from the unifying confines of a particular soul, as Eliot did, resulted in the creation of the multiversity. For some thinkers, such as Kerr, the creation of the multiversity opened up numerous new options. It also raised the question of whether it offered students a false freedom and the divided university appeared a slave to multiple personalities. Try as they might, educators such as Robert Maynard Hutchins could not fill the void left by theology. As a result of theology's absence, and the resulting multiversity described by Clark Kerr, the soul of the university began to fragment. In part two we will turn our attention to the ramifications of this fragmentation on scholars, the curriculum, students, administrators, the expanding athletic department, and the larger institution. When the soul of the university fragments and it must turn to various secular sagas to hold together different parts of the university, the consequence is that each part develops its own saga, whether it be an interest in democratic ideals such as freedom, a desire to pursue scientific knowledge, a longing to serve the interests of students (whatever they may be), the pursuit of transcendent athletic glory, or the hope for financial ascendance and growing institutional prestige. Each part of the fragmented multiversity now competes against the other to achieve its particular purposes.

PART TWO

THE FRAGMENTATION OF THE MULTIVERSITY

...

PART ONE CHARTED THE history of the displacement of theology within the university, ending with the emergence of the American multiversity and its associated fragmentation. In part two we explore some of the specific manifestations and consequences of this fragmentation, focusing on faculty, curriculum, cocurriculum, administrators, athletics, and online/for-profit activities and institutions. The fragmentation Clark Kerr[1] identified as indicative of the multiversity is also indicative of our postmodern/hypermodern age. This "incredulity toward metanarratives," as Jean François Lyotard phrased it, decries the violence claimed to be inherent in all universal stories.[2] The specialization and partitioning of the disciplines, of curriculum and cocurriculum, and of faculty themselves are congruent with the desire of our age to show deference to the tribal and the marginalized. Fragmentation, then, can be seen as a desirable outcome for postmodernists. While we think Christians should acknowledge, affirm, and even promote what we consider the most appropriate response to postmodernism in policy—what scholars have called principled pluralism[3]— we argue that the multiversity and its stakeholders pay a high price for this fragmentation.

In part two, a key aspect is what Robert Maynard Hutchins titled "external conditions"[4]: assumptions of the purposes of higher education that are embedded in society and create pressure for access (seen in online/for-profit and administrative expansion responses), curricular options (seen in extreme specialization), and policy influence (seen in athletics, curriculum, and online/for-profit). One of these external conditions is the context and subtext of America's emerging post-Christian culture. When we say American culture is *post-Christian* what we mean is that tacit societal norms can no longer be expected to reflect the theological commitments and associated behavioral expectations of followers of Jesus. Perhaps more to the point, the twenty-first-century American college student may be shocked that they ever did.[5] The soul of the American university thus splintered. We describe some concomitant implications in this section that we believe show its unsatisfactory outcomes, and ultimately the need for theological reenvisioning by Christians, particularly those leading Christian universities.

6

THE FRAGMENTED SOUL
OF THE PROFESSOR

...

Classes will dull your mind,
destroy the potential for authentic creativity.

JOHN NASH (PLAYED BY RUSSELL CROWE), *A BEAUTIFUL MIND*

Ron Howard's *A BEAUTIFUL MIND*, based on the book by Sylvia Nasar, won four Academy Awards in 2001, including best picture. Drawing on the life of John Nash, the mathematician who won the 1994 Nobel Prize in economics, the film opens in 1947. In a wood-paneled room, mathematics doctoral candidates clad in coat and tie are being welcomed to Princeton University by the department chair. The young John Nash (played by Russell Crowe) then hears that "mathematicians won the war. Mathematicians broke the Japanese codes and built the A-Bomb. Mathematicians, like you."[1] Noting the rising threat of the Soviet Union, the chair goes on to admonish his students that "to triumph, we need results—publishable, applicable results."[2] Along with this call to research, nothing is mentioned to these entering students about the call to teach or the call to serve, often construed as the other two legs of the three-legged stool defining the academic vocation. The end of the calling they are being formed to inherit is simply research.

After absorbing those lessons, creating his truly original idea—governing dynamics—and graduating at the top of his class, Nash selects a position at MIT's Wheeler Defense Laboratories. Like MIT's Lincoln Laboratory, the fictitious Wheeler is a joint venture between the Department of the Defense and the university. In a scene that opens at Wheeler shortly after Nash returns from a trip to the Pentagon, where he breaks an otherwise indecipherable Russian code, the emerging star in his field is greeted with the news that he made the cover of *Fortune* "again," and he has ten minutes until his class begins. Nash responds by asking how he can get out of class, going so far as to ask, "Can I not get a note from a doctor or something?"[3] He then arrives, albeit late, and promptly informs a student that "your comfort comes second to my ability to hear my own voice."[4] He goes on to say, "Personally, I think this class will be a waste of your, and what is infinitely worse, my time."[5]

The laughter this scene engendered in theaters was undoubtedly driven by the ability of moviegoers to recall comparable details from their own college years (though perhaps not always involving Nobel Prize–winning mathematicians). One of us had a professor who rarely showed up for class, came late when he did, read from a textbook, and then challenged the views we expressed in his teaching evaluations—indicating he had intercepted them prior to their arrival at the dean's office. Compounding matters, that professor was also the department chair, supposedly tasked with serving the department and the students within that department. These kinds of practices highlight what can often be the broken condition of the three-legged stool that currently defines the academic vocation of professors: research, teaching, and service. In short, professors often unsuccessfully navigate the competing purposes that tear at the soul of the multiversity.

Defining the Good Professor

Since universities have been around for over eight hundred years, one would think that we would have a fairly stable understanding of the academic vocation and what constitutes a "good" professor. Yet, like most vocations, the standards of excellence for the academic vocation have always been subject to debate and discussion. From the start, though, being a master, doctor, or professor was associated with achieving "excellence in a given domain" whose "formulations approximate ever more closely to the truth."[6] This true knowledge would be transmitted by lectures and disputations.

Furthermore, the ideal professor should demonstrate certain Christian virtues especially applicable to their position. Since professors were dealing with knowledge, they needed to demonstrate humility. As Jacques Verger describes it, the ideal medieval professor

> was meant to be humble before God, the source of all knowledge, and before the providential order of the creation, which the hierarchical arrangement of disciplines merely reproduced. He was therefore warned not to stray from his own domain, a warning which was especially aimed at philosophers in the arts faculties who were tempted to free themselves from the control of theology, or indeed, to invade its domain.[7]

In other words, disciplinary specialization was understood as something that Christian humility required—a product of the blueprint of the university first established by thinkers such as Hugh of St. Victor. Additionally emphasized virtues included "impartiality, goodwill towards his colleagues and his pupils, keenness in work."[8] Beyond the primary endeavor of teaching, faculty members and administrators were also called on to engage in scholarship and serve the university and the public.[9] They were to be individuals who could make new discoveries and draw on the intellectual reserves of their given disciplines as a means of addressing questions plaguing a particular community, such as the church or the common good, through scholarship and service. As the chancellor of the University of Paris, John Gerson, declared in a 1405 speech, "One does not learn solely in order to know but also in order to demonstrate and act."[10] Overall it was hoped that this ideal would lead professors to be "lights of the church, shining as brightly as stars in the firmament."[11]

Of course, since universities and professors are fallen, critiques have always emerged when the practices of professors failed to adhere to this ideal. In fact, Verger's words quoted above point us to a problem with the early theology faculty we will return to in chapter twelve. Theologians sometimes jealously sought to guard their exalted status instead of seeking to serve all the other disciplines and involve them in common endeavors. Instead of nourishing and partnering with other disciplines, they either cut themselves off from them or sought to control them.

Of course, professors in every discipline had problems. Within the first centuries of the university, complaints emerged about teachers simply dictating to their classes, teaching only part of the course material, failing to show up, awarding degrees to undeserving candidates, or asking lower-qualified individuals to teach their courses for them.[12] With regard to their service to the public, one former master of arts in Paris complained in the fourteenth century regarding university professors, "These men wreck all piety, make fun of ordinary folk, and deceive the people."[13] The sixteenth-century scholar Erasmus in *The Praise of Folly*[14] made fun of scholars who "blacken paper with sheer triviality."[15] Such scholars, he noted, are "pitiable" as they torment themselves to labor in the construction of a work that will only reach a small handful of individuals.[16] Part of the reason for the limited appeal of the scholars' work was the fact that the chosen writing style was nearly incomprehensible. He noted, "The scholar considers himself compensated for such ills when he wins the approbation of one or two other weak-eyed scholars."[17] Some things, including the vices of professors, never change. The ideal professor would, hopefully, avoid these vices and exalt the virtues associated with the tasks of each of the three legs of the scholarly stool: teaching, scholarship, and service.

What did change though was the emphasis the various tasks received at different types of universities. The general view before the eighteenth century was that teaching was the foremost activity of the professor. A few scholars even argued that professors had no obligation to advance scholarship, although the dominant view was that scholarship should be valued.[18] The priority given to teaching would begin to change, however, due to the secularization and nationalization of the university and the emergence of the professional professor. From the sixteenth to the nineteenth century in Europe and North America, laypersons replaced clergy as professors and as leaders of universities.[19] Governments also started to take over universities and the supervision of faculty.[20] Peter Vandermeersch summarizes the way European governments limited the freedom of professors during this time.

> State commissioners were sent to the university to verify the professional orthodoxy and diligence; chancellors appointed by the crown . . . involved themselves in the day-to-day control of the academic and religious life of both senior and junior members of the universities; the subjects to be taught were imposed by the government; the publications of the professors were submitted to a governmental *approbatio*; the professor became a civil servant

whose *licentia docendi* [license to teach] was controlled and whose *libertates, immunitates et honores* [liberties, immunities, and honors] were both guaranteed and limited by the civil authorities.[21]

In America, where the state did not control colleges, professors faced less government control. A different kind of change, however, would shape professorial expectations in both America and Europe.

The Professional Professor

The famous sociologist Talcott Parsons once asserted, "The development and increasing strategic importance of the professions probably constitute the most important change that has occurred in the occupational systems of modern societies."[22] As Thomas Haskell tells the story, professionals arose in the context of a period of doubt about causal attribution, plausibility, and truth, particularly triggered by Darwin and historical criticism of the Bible.[23] In Europe they also emerged as a counterculture to state control.[24] Professionals constructed "safe institutional havens for sound opinion."[25] These havens appeared when experts in a particular field of study joined together and engaged in intense interaction with a community of peers. To accomplish this end, they began creating professional societies, publishing journals, and holding annual meetings in which they discussed their research findings. A closed group, one could only enter these new professions through convincing one's peers of one's expertise in the discipline; as Haskell puts it, "All had to submit to the potential tyranny of the majority of the competent."[26] One usually gained the expertise for joining these groups through study under a mentor. In thirteenth-century Paris, this academic apprenticeship, known as *inception*, certified the legitimacy of novitiates and provided entrée into the collegium, or community of scholars.[27] During colonial times this mentorship occurred in the context of professional practice (apprenticing with a lawyer or an architect, for example), since the rise of the professions in the nineteenth century, it began to extend to fields within the university.

Professors in the sciences first developed this system. The first use of the word *scientist* appeared in 1840, and the first professional scientific society began the same year, marking the beginning of professional self-consciousness.[28] Most of the early leaders were involved in the American

Association for the Advancement of Science (AAAS), founded in 1847. The social sciences followed eighteen years later, with the formation of the American Social Science Association (ASSA) in 1865.[29] Although the American Philosophical Society began in 1743, for the most part the humanities would be the last to form professional societies, with the foundation of groups such as the Society of Biblical Literature (1880) and the Modern Language Association (1883).[30]

These professional societies, however, did not come without their own problems regarding authority and knowledge. Haskell highlights the obvious risk of these professional societies as well as the argument for them: "The danger that such self-justifying communities will drift into a truly circular scholasticism, utterly divorced from reality, is not to be dismissed lightly, but what better general criterion of intellectual authority can be found in the competitive mental world of an interdependent universe?"[31]

In the past, the danger Haskell identified (the insularity of the new professional disciplines) was checked by the interdependence of the disciplines nurtured in the university. In particular, university leaders expected (in the ideal situation) that each discipline would have to engage in a dialogue with theology, the metadiscipline in the university. The problem was that this dialogue often was a one-way conversation, with theologians doing most of the talking.

The professionalization of the disciplines, however, now allowed professors in the growing and expanding group of disciplines to build independent groups of authorities and peers apart from the university and apart from theology through professional societies and journals. Moreover, with the increasing doubt about the basic Christian narrative and the social isolation of theology to a separate discipline and eventually separate seminaries, those in the emerging professional societies did not engage in substantial dialogue with theology and saw no need for it.

The creation of the professions also unleashed a new dynamic in the university. Even as most professions valued the production of knowledge meant to promote the internal goods of their discipline, competition for resources and survival in the university meant that academic disciplines also needed to gain prestige and power. Although university presidents believed teaching and research "could and should be united,"[32] professors became less committed to providing a coherent understanding of truth for their students and more interested in advancing the particular knowledge base associated with their profession. When discussions about general education would later take place, the professional professor became more concerned with defending his or her profession's portion of knowledge than in providing students with a holistic view of the world or contributing to holistic student development.

As a consequence, influence within one's professional association soon eclipsed the importance in professional value of a professor's influence on campus. Robert L. Geiger observes that universities, in order to compete for the best professors, started to provide what came to be known as research professorships or professorships that came with reduced teaching loads so that faculty could spend more time conducting their research. Despite the intentions of presidents to see teaching and research as united, Geiger concludes that the practices of teaching and research were "being pulled in opposite directions."[33] Teaching may have garnered a faculty member some distinction on campus; however, research soon became the only practice that would garner distinction beyond the campus. As a result, the two practices were eventually seen as distinct efforts with one earning much more distinction and value than the other.[34] As we will discuss more extensively in chapter nine, professionalization also eventually meant that tasks faculty formerly provided as service to the university soon became separate positions staffed by professionals.

This development fostered two other important changes in the conception of the academic vocation. First, in order to further their career, professors needed to engage in specialized research. Second, this need for specialization also meant they should no longer be expected to serve as moral guides who could help students live the good life. Max Weber provides the starkest example of this critique. With regard to scholarship, Weber insisted, "Only strict specialization can make the scholar feel confident, for once and perhaps for the only time in his life, that he has achieved something that will really last."[35]

In relation to teaching, Weber rejected the idea that a professor should seek to provide broad forms of moral inspiration for life to students or that they should serve society by being some kind of moral leader. "The error of that part of our youth," Weber argued, "is that they seek in the professor something other than what stands before them—a *leader*, not a *teacher*. But our place at the lecture is solely that of a *teacher*."[36] The reason for this understanding, Weber claimed, involved a professor's lack of qualifications to be a moral leader.

> Fellow students! With these demands on our qualities of leadership you come to our lectures and you fail to say to yourselves beforehand that out of the hundred professors at least ninety-nine not only do not and should not claim to be football coaches in the field of life; they cannot even claim to be "leaders" in matters of conduct.[37]

For Weber, scientific academics were to focus less on broad forms of service or teaching that impart moral instruction and more on their specific scholarly quest and the specific form of teaching associated with it. In Weber's words the science and social-science professor's job "today is a 'vocation' conducted through specialist disciplines to serve the cause of reflection on the self and knowledge of relationships between facts, not a gift of grace from seers and prophets dispensing sacred values and revelations."[38]

The Fractured Professor

Today's professors at research institutions could be said to have expanded Weber's outlook even further. Teaching in research institutions is understood as secondary to specialized scientific research. To illustrate this point, Mark Schwehn points simply to the common complaint one hears from professors at research universities: "Because this is a terribly busy semester for me, I do not have any time to do my own work," which reveals that they view their vocation primarily as "writing, composing, and experimenting."[39] We would note, though, that teaching still has some moral pull (or at least the threat of consequences from failure to complete it) since the professors set aside their research to engage in it. Schwehn attributes the socialization process that occurs in graduate school as the primary reason for this attitude.

> There students learn, regardless of their field of study, that research and publication constitute their tasks and that all other activities—teaching, lecturing, university service—somehow just go with the territory. . . . The results of five

to ten years of graduate training are unmistakable. Publication, graduate students discover, is *the* vocational aspiration.[40]

As for service, Richard A. Posner argues in *Public Intellectuals: A Study in Decline* that the university is to blame for the decline of one major form of service—that of being a public intellectual.[41] Research universities socially sequester their faculty members in highly specialized professional guilds. By contrast, teaching institutions sequester their faculty members in arenas of direct service to their own campuses. Either way, the wider public service is, at best, an afterthought in comparison to research or teaching. Research universities may grant public service some credence in relation to offices held by faculty members in disciplinary associations or positions on editorial boards for specific publications. Teaching universities may grant it some credence in relation to the number of campus committees faculty members fill. Yet neither one of these approaches serves the broader public. Not surprisingly, Posner blames the modern university.

> Its rise has encouraged a professionalization and specialization of knowledge that, together with the comfortable career that the university offers to people of outstanding intellectual ability, have shrunk the ranks of the "independent" intellectual. . . . At the same time, by fragmenting the educated public into slivers of specialists (people who know a lot, but only about a few subjects) and destroying a common intellectual culture, the university-induced specialization of knowledge has made the audience for public-intellectual work undiscriminating.[42]

We ourselves wonder if Posner overstates this point, because his understanding of service focuses on the arts and sciences. When one looks at the service professional disciplines carry out in fields such as education, social work, nursing, and so on, this claim may need to be qualified. Still, this "specialized scholarship is my work" conception of the academic vocation is now culturally dominant and shapes the flow of influence in academe. Trends in higher education often begin with the leading research institutions and work their way down this culturally established hierarchy.

Although many of the leading research universities in America are still private, they are now subject to substantial research-funding incentives from the federal government. Geiger points out that the post–World War II era witnessed a substantial increase in funding for research offered by various federal agencies as well as a number of other private clients universities attracted. The Cold War "altered the flow of research funds to universities"[43] in some ways, but often not as some historians argue. According to Geiger, "Most of this applied and developmental activity was both peripheral to the main lines of academic research and also a net addition."[44] As the Cold War, especially the highly symbolic launch of Sputnik, may have provided an emotional stimulus for the federal government to become more involved in funding research, more sustainable forms of investment came through agencies such as the National Institute of Health, the National Science Foundation, and even the National Endowment for the Humanities. In conjunction with increased financial support for students to attend college (such as the Servicemen's Readjustment Act of 1944, known as the GI Bill), the impact of such efforts was an expansion of the university not previously witnessed in history.

This expansion has had important implications for teaching. Unlike the German university, where attendance at lectures was generally optional, with exams required, the American university generally required students to attend lectures and take exams. The challenge, however, for the American research university came with the increase in the size of its courses. The rationale behind herding students into such large lectures was not only rooted in the inherited tradition of the lecture but also in economics. Enrolling students in a British tutorial-type class in numbers of six, eight, or perhaps even fifteen simply proved to be far more expensive than enrolling students in quantities of 425, 675, or 925 in a lecture class. In order to compensate the professor for his or her research expertise, the economics of lecture courses proved to be a financially favorable pedagogical model.

One additional advantage to the lecture-type course is that it creates a safe space for the professor to share his or her expertise. In environments where the professor is, at times, referred to as the "sage on the stage," the class session is almost guaranteed to follow a preset pattern.[45] For example, a professor can outline in advance exactly what he or she plans to cover in a given session. Students attend the lecture and take notes based on the material presented. If students are given the opportunity to interact with the professor in some manner, the professor can no longer know ahead of time exactly what he or she will cover. However, the lecture is a safer and more predictable pedagogical format than other class formats since it reduces the variables down to ones that the professor alone controls.[46] The lecture hall thus becomes a space where intellectual transactions are made. Professors share information and students receive it. This form of education has been described as the "instruction paradigm."[47] It stands in contrast to the "learning paradigm" where students are expected to take responsibility for their learning and are trusted to be sources of knowledge creation rather than receivers only. In the instruction paradigm, other dimensions of human identity that can reduce the safe and predictable nature of the lecture are, by implicit design, denied a presence.

Although professors who give lectures are the face of this challenge in American higher education, we would note once again that they are not entirely to blame. On one level, they are heirs of a Germanic system that prized the lecture and the expertise of the person who gave it. On another level, they were formed by virtue of their professional preparation as doctoral students to perform at their best in such environments. For example, in his chapter in *Envisioning the Future of Doctoral Education*, Kenneth Prewitt argues, "Although prepared to do original research, they [faculty members] seldom are adequately prepared for their teaching duties or their more general professional obligations [perhaps such as service]."[48] In a subsequent volume on doctoral education, a group of scholars press this argument even further. After reviewing the data they gathered related to the formative process afforded to doctoral students, they conclude:

> Where teaching is available, it may not be required. And where it is required, there is no guarantee (or structure to ensure) that experience actually leads to greater understanding of the complicated dynamics of teaching and learning. In teaching, as in other complex practices, more experience does not automatically lead to more expertise.[49]

In particular, the authors go on to note that at the highest level, approximately 65 percent of doctoral students in history that were at the dissertation phase reported that they had the "opportunity to develop increasing responsibility as a teacher."[50] At the lowest level, approximately 15 percent of doctoral students in chemistry reported that they had the same opportunity.[51]

Under the best circumstances, these scholars acknowledge that "faculty enter academe because of a desire to advance knowledge and teach young minds; they are passionate about their fields and committed to their students."[52] Over the course of their respective careers, however, "many slide into less noble, more pragmatic, and, yes, selfish motives tied up with questions of prestige, funding, and their own advancement."[53] Unfortunately the university's means by which to prevent such a slide are limited. In an attempt to manage their burgeoning size, universities have become more bureaucratic, as have the means by which they measure their professors.

Identifying and Evaluating the Good Professor

Identifying and evaluating what it means to be a good professor now proves extremely difficult. For example, in 2015 the American Association of University Professors sought to answer a variety of questions about teaching and how faculty are evaluated. Survey responses gathered by the committee from some nine thousand professors revealed "diminishing student response rates for course evaluations, too much focus on such evaluations alone in personnel decisions—especially for non-tenure-track faculty—and a creep of the kinds of personal comments seen on teacher rating websites into formal evaluations."[54] It also found that students are often the sole evaluators of teaching and the means by which students make their determinations run the risk of being infrequent and capricious. Peer evaluations are only occasionally practiced.

Indeed, one reason why teaching has been eclipsed by research is the fact that research is easy to quantify and teaching is not. Research productivity offers administrators clearer paths for assessment. Although research may prove to be more quantifiable and thus a more comfortable domain by which administrators can make evaluations of faculty members, the list of arguments against using research as the primary metric to assess whether a professor is "good" is a lengthy one. Here we note four of the most compelling.

To begin, the most often noted criticism being offered today is the emergence of a "publish or perish" culture. In a chapter simply titled "Publish or Perish" in his book *Higher Education in America*, Derek Bok notes: "Reinforcing the pressure to publish, faculty salaries have been increasingly linked to publications at all types of four-year colleges. The more books and articles professors produce, the higher their salaries. The more hours per week they spend in the classroom, the smaller their paycheck."[55] We find it worth noting that Bok claims the pressure to publish, whether explicit or implicit, is present across all four-year institutions. If true, most faculty members cannot escape this pressure, nor do we think they should be able to escape it. The problem comes when, as Bok notes, pressure to research is distinct from the pressure to teach well. As one higher education scholar has noted, "The greatest paradox of academic work in modern America is that most professors teach most of the time, and large proportions of them teach all the time, but teaching is not the activity most rewarded by the academic profession nor most valued by the system at large."[56] Ideally the commitment to teaching and research, along with the commitment to service, is integrated into a larger understanding of the academic vocation.

Second, the pressure to conduct research also raises the question concerning the end or purpose for which such work is done. In many ways, the pressure to produce scholarly work has spawned an industry. Faculty members are pressured to produce such material, journals and publishing houses make it available to the public, and libraries house it. When we pause to consider in what ways scholars use this work, some quite unfavorable data emerges. Later in his chapter, Bok notes, "A staggering 98 percent of all published articles in the arts and humanities are never cited, and the corresponding figure in the social sciences is 75 percent, a figure only slightly less dismaying. Writings in the sciences fare better: only 25 percent are reportedly never cited."[57] Such staggeringly low citation rates thus make many faculty pause and wonder what the impetus is behind the need for them to publish.

Third, critics are quick to note that part of the reason why academic work is rarely of use is because so much of that work is defined by jargon only accessible to a few people who speak the same language (and that is assuming, given the statistics Bok cited, that those few people care). In many ways, people who spend time in a particular community or subcommunity (as is more often the case now) understandably develop a unique iteration of language that allows them to detail the specifics of their common concerns. However, anyone outside of that community or subcommunity may have a difficult time appreciating what those individuals have to offer. Fortunately, some professors have begun to acknowledge this challenge. For example, Kristin Sainani says, "I think scientists really need to know how to write well. . . . Why shouldn't [the general public] be able to understand why research and work is being done?"[58] She also observes that "this creates a situation where things are hard to read even for scientists."[59] As a result, she began teaching a MOOC (Massive Open Online Course) known as "Writing in the Sciences."[60]

Finally, Mark C. Taylor, in *Crisis on Campus: A Bold Plan for Reforming Our Colleges and Universities*, contends that the current state of research only exacerbates the nature of fragmentation in academe. In particular, he notes that this reality is an unintended outgrowth of the globalization of higher education. According to Taylor, the globalization of higher education did not begin with the advent of the World Wide Web in the 1990s but with cheaper airfare in the 1950s and 1960s. Prior to that point in time, "most academic meetings were local or at-best regional affairs; faculty members attending drove or took buses or trains."[61] But "with this development, new professional organizations and societies were established and new global networks emerged."[62] Instead of reaching across previously existing disciplinary lines, the result was further subdivision and fragmentation—"so-called cutting edge research became more and more about less and less."[63]

This fragmentation also now extends to teaching institutions, albeit perhaps in a different manner. Although the majority of public concern (and rightfully so) is focused on universities where research is the only functional leg of the stool, institutions that refer to themselves as "teaching institutions" harbor a quality that proves equally problematic. In such a context, faculty may succumb to a two-legged understanding of the academic vocation that omits research. Consequently they soon fall behind and become incapable of preparing their students to engage in a particular field at even a modest level. Compounding this challenge is the fact that such faculty members may also be incapable of modeling a level of studiousness that reflects a proper love for a given subject. If teaching faculty disengage from their fields, they facilitate the demise of their institutions and the vocational aspirations of the students they are called to serve.

Although the criticisms of the lack of proper balance among research, teaching, and service (particularly the prioritization of research over teaching and service) are numerous, the solutions are few. For instance, Donald Kennedy, a former Stanford president, addresses the various tasks of the professor in his book *Academic Duty*. In addition to the usual three mentioned above ("to teach, to serve the university, and to discover knowledge"), he adds "to mentor," "to tell the truth," "to reach beyond the walls," and to "change."[64] What ties all these activities together? As the title of the book indicates, they are one's academic duty. An inspiring narrative about why one should do one's duty is never really offered, although at times he makes vague references to an organizational saga connected to the common good and national interests.

The Best Hope for Multiversities Without a Soul

Perhaps the most noteworthy and hopeful of recent solutions came from Ernest L. Boyer in the form of *Scholarship Reconsidered: Priorities of the Professoriate*, published in 1990. A recent review of the rate at which Boyer's report is cited concludes, "To be sure, 'staggering' best depicts the number of citations received for *Scholarship Reconsidered: Priorities of the Professoriate*."[65] In his book Boyer recognizes the pressure the fragmenting multiversity has on professors and "that the faculty reward system does not match the full range of academic functions and that professors are often caught between competing obligations."[66] After reviewing the empirically collected details concerning perceptions that professors hold regarding the practice of research and the relationship it shares with the other components of the academic vocation, Boyer launches into his proposal for a four-part understanding of scholarship. Each part, as he defines it, draws on different yet significant efforts. As a result, they do not exist in any form of hierarchy, so that different colleges and universities can utilize them in ways that best fit with their respective missions. In essence, Boyer's efforts are aimed at "enlarging the conversation."[67]

First, Boyer begins by defining what most people think of as research— efforts that lead to the results recorded in academic journals and books—as the *scholarship of discovery*. At this point, he acknowledges that this form of scholarship, "at its best, contributes not only to the stock of human knowledge, but also to the intellectual climate of a college or university. Not just the outcomes, but the processes and the passion give meaning to the effort."[68] Universities do need to encourage their faculty to participate in the practice of scholarship. In one sense, this scholarship can expand human understanding. However, Boyer is also quick to point out that the value of such a practice does not reside merely in the outcome but also the struggle. "The advancement of knowledge can generate an almost palpable excitement in the life of an educational institution."[69]

As previously noted, Boyer's goal is to enlarge the conversation concerning research. As a result, he defines a second category he refers to as the *scholarship of integration*. In contrast to many critics of academe, Boyer is not completely convinced that disciplinary subdivision is harmful. However, he states that he longs for universities to recognize efforts made by scholars who make "connections across the disciplines, placing the specialties in a larger context, illuminating data in a revealing way, often educating nonspecialists too."[70]

Given the way the disciplines were structured at Boyer's time (and still are today), Boyer knew the difficulties faced by faculty who practiced the scholarship of integration—in particular, neither academic journals nor publishing houses were set up to receive and disseminate such work. We would also add that departments and universities are not set up to reward it. Although Boyer viewed such work as critical, he also knew that its mere recognition was fraught with challenges.

Third, Boyer identifies a category that has come to be known as the *scholarship of application*. He acknowledges that "colleges and universities have recently rejected service as serious scholarship, partly because its meaning was so vague and often disconnected from serious intellectual work."[71] However, he also argues that the scholarship of application is crucial to universities seeking to be relevant contributors to the wider world. As a result, in order to qualify as such a form of scholarship "service activities must be tied directly to one's special field of knowledge and related to, and flow out of, this professional activity. Such service is serious, demanding work, requiring the rigor—and the accountability—traditionally associated with research activities."[72]

Finally, Boyer defines what has come to be known as the *scholarship of teaching*. Like the scholarship of application, too many faculty members feel tempted to simply see the performance of teaching as the scholarship of teaching. In contrast, Boyer seeks to inspire faculty members to become more formally reflective about their efforts in the classroom. In particular, he asks, what would it mean to study the successes and failures that occur in the classroom and present those findings in ways accessible to other faculty members?

As a result of the success of the scholarship of teaching, publishers began producing books on collegiate teaching. New journals emerged in almost every major discipline to share the results related to particular pedagogical practices. Overall, although the scholarship of teaching may have inspired such new outlets for faculty work, the success of Boyer's four-part understanding as a whole remains much debated. Discussions about Boyer's *Scholarship Reconsidered* between faculty members and administrators often boil down to something like "Often cited, rarely implemented."

Despite these trends, we think the John Nashes of the world are not as numerous as some believe. Yet we also think we need to recognize their actions for what they are. Such faculty members have simply adapted to the value structures and subsequent practices that define the multiversity. Good professors in a university without a soul will likely focus on one or two legs of the stool defining the academic vocation, because they are rewarded for doing so. Attempting excellence in research universities with a split soul necessitates figuring out which part of the soul to please. Unless a university has a unified soul where integration and other various forms of scholarship that Boyer described are prized, we should not be surprised by emergence of more professors like John Nash.

7

FALLING TO PIECES

Declaring Independence from Curricular Coherence

...

A little French Literature of the 19th Century here, a little Animal
Behavior there. Throw in a statistics class and an introduction
to gender studies and you have . . . well, what do you have?
No one quite knows, because most college curricula today
are completely incoherent.

NAOMI SCHAEFER RILEY

F OR SOME ODD REASON, we still think the college curriculum should have some coherence. It should be guided by a soul, a consistent identity, narrative, and purpose, as well as by academic authorities who have a big picture of the whole. One finds a recent example of this expectation in a magazine article in *The Atlantic* titled "The Future of College?" There the author quotes Ben Nelson, the founder and CEO of a new online university called Minerva. Nelson makes the complaint that

> general education is nonexistent. It's effectively a buffet, and when you
> have a noncurated academic experience, you effectively don't get edu-
> cated. You get a random collection of information. Liberal-arts education
> is about developing the intellectual capacity of the individual, and
> learning to be a productive member of society. And you cannot do that
> without a curriculum.[1]

Nelson uses two contrasting metaphors to make his point about the incoherence of current curricular approaches. First, he calls it a buffet. A buffet still offers the possibility of a healthy curricular meal (which appears to be Nelson's assumed ideal). What bothers Nelson is the lack of a wise guide or a curator to assist students in navigating the meal options (which switches the analogy). The new choice of words is important. Using the word *curator* is a more palatable way to say to intelligent people that you need an authoritative guide to organize and present information to you. A museum curator still provides a buffet of art or historical artifacts, but the buffet is chosen and organized in light of some overarching purpose or ideal.

It should be no surprise that the curator example remains one of the last analogies that antiauthoritarian intellectuals may find acceptable. Yet even this image may no longer be palatable. In a *Wall Street Journal* story titled "Everyone's a Curator," the writer tells how museums "are increasingly outsourcing the curation of their exhibits to the public—sometimes even asking the crowd to contribute art, too."[2] The bottom line is that such an approach helps "produce quick and often inexpensive shows that boost ticket sales."[3] The idea that the curator can provide some source of coherence to a story line that the audience needs to know has given way to a different idea about authority: "It's no longer only the highly trained professionals who decide what belongs on the gallery wall, but the audience, too."[4] The same is true for the curriculum. Today students exercise a significant amount of freedom over their curricular choices. The pendulum has swung dramatically from the prescribed curriculum of the early nineteenth century to today's curricular openness.

We think it is helpful to switch back to the food-buffet analogy. Nelson assumes we long for some coherent version of the curriculum in the same way we long to eat healthy meals at a buffet. For some reason, he thinks the education a university provides should have some coherence. Administrators should make sure students do not eat five desserts, such as taking a variety of courses on video games, rock music, and sex. Like Nelson, other scholars writing laments about higher education also hope that the curriculum provides some coherence. Mark C. Taylor notes that "the education bubble is about to burst."[5] In defense of his assertion, Taylor claims that as the interests of "faculty members become more specialized and the subjects of their publications more esoteric, the curriculum becomes increasingly fragmented and the educational process loses its coherence as well as its relevance for the broader society."[6] Taylor does not explain why he thinks coherence and relevance are the standards of evaluation. Naturally, perhaps, humans do not want to live a divided and fragmented life, and the university, scholars expect, should somehow provide that coherence. What exactly underlies the longing for coherence and what provides that coherence prove important questions.

Another important question is what constitutes the curricular fruits and vegetables to which Nelson refers. The article does not tell us, but we do get some idea of his ideal meal. Nelson mentions the phrase "liberal arts education." Why and what exactly is the substance of a liberal arts meal is not clear from the quotation, although we are given two ideas of the ends of this education: developing the intellectual capacity of the individual and helping one to be "a productive member of society."

From the beginning of universities, as chapter one revealed, scholars took seriously the coherence and systematic division and organization of knowledge. Theology, as discussed earlier, provided some basis for coherence by providing the overarching pinnacle, but its role was not central.[7] In contrast, the arts faculty through which every student would transition provided the foundation. It also served as the source from which the early idea of coherence emerged. Hugh of St. Victor argued that the seven liberal arts (grammar, rhetoric, logic, arithmetic, geometry, astronomy, and music)

> so hang together and so depend upon one another in their ideas that if only one of the arts be lacking, all the rest cannot make a man into a philosopher. Therefore, those persons seem to be to be in error who, not appreciating the coherence among the arts, select certain of them for study, and leaving the rest untouched, think they can become perfect in these alone.[8]

In this respect, Nelson's appeal to the liberal arts as a source of coherence merely copies an eight-hundred-year-old view.

Although Nelson's and Taylor's appeals to a common liberal arts curriculum are similar to this old appeal, there are numerous ways the appeals made by Nelson, Taylor, and Hugh of St. Victor are also worlds apart, particularly regarding the justification for the liberal arts, their content, and the university structure in which they are delivered. This chapter tells a short story of how those understandings and views changed as well as the consequences of those changes.

A Curriculum with Soul

In chapter one, we noted Hugh of St. Victor believed that the coherence of the liberal arts was not found within the arts themselves but outside of them in God. The arts, he believed, were meant "to restore within us the divine likeness."[9] Moreover, he contended, "The more we are conformed to the divine nature, the more do we possess wisdom, for then there begins to shine forth again in us what has forever existed in the divine Idea or Pattern, coming and going in us but standing changeless in God."[10] Hugh recognized that since humans are made in God's image, they can only fulfill that image by acquiring those character qualities of God we are made to reflect. The liberal arts help us do that with the particular virtue of wisdom. God ultimately remains the source of coherence for both wisdom and the liberal arts. According to this conception, we should determine the content of the arts by asking what provides us with God's wisdom.

How humans organized this wisdom and the curriculum associated with the liberal arts would constantly change throughout the history of the university. For example, by the middle of the thirteenth century, the seven-part classification of the liberal arts had been supplemented with a general classification of the three philosophies that constituted the arts: natural, moral, and metaphysical.[11] In addition, more subjects would be placed within the arts faculty, such as the historical, geographic, and linguistic arts. For instance, faculty chairs in history began to be added to the university in the sixteenth and seventeenth centuries.[12] These new arts were often considered to be necessary precursors to learning in the three philosophical subject areas.[13] In fact, they would eventually be removed from the university curriculum and considered pre-university requirements.

The American college curriculum would follow this approach. The three-part classification of philosophy would influence the organization of knowledge in the American college curriculum. In addition, the linguistic arts (Latin and Greek) and eventually mathematics, history, geography, and

English were added to the curriculum. By the mid-1800s, however, these subjects would become precollegiate requirements.[14] Protestant colleges in America added one prominent exception. Since their tradition emphasized knowledge of the original biblical languages in order to properly understand God, they added the teaching of Hebrew.[15] American colleges required this type of curriculum of all their students.

Although the content of the curriculum changed, the philosophy under-girding the curricular unity and coherence had roots in a common set of ideas held by those from Hugh of St. Victor to William Ames. For these thinkers, the curriculum gave insight, through both substantive instruction and teaching in various methods of knowledge, into the wisdom of God, whether found in the natural order designed by God or God's special reve-lation. Following the proper methods, one could discover God's divine order and the coherence it contained. The curriculum, it was believed, should reflect this order and coherence and thus God's wisdom.

The difficulty with connecting the curriculum to the divine nature, however, is that human methods for helping us obtain divine wisdom may need to change as human knowledge expands and transforms. After all, God's world and human knowledge of it are not static. The world and our knowledge of it constantly expand and grow. Consequently, a curriculum that fails to develop no longer addresses the specific and diverse types of wisdom students require in a growing and changing world. In other words, as Taylor noted above, it loses "relevance."

One important change that influenced the curriculum was the estab-lishment of the United States. This new political reality transformed the existing colonial system of higher education in ways that undermined the coherence of the past foundation. The change ultimately emerged from the new church-state relationship in America. In countries with an estab-lished church, it was expected that the university curriculum would mirror the coherent Christian view of the world. However, with the creation of the United States, a liberal democracy without an established church, leaders in higher education began to view colleges in America as serving the country first and foremost. Since a major ideal of liberal democracy involved ex-panding human freedom, college leaders began to believe that the structure of the university and the curriculum should also enhance that same freedom.

As Charles W. Eliot's story illustrated in chapter five, instead of finding the end of education in discovering God and God's wisdom, the end of learning began to focus more on the capacities and knowledge necessary for democratic citizenship and practical living.[16] This emphasis resulted in important structural and curricular changes.

The first alterations in this area were subtle. At the beginning of the nineteenth century, a development occurred in the United States that mirrored the development that had stymied the growth and development of universities in Eastern Europe. It emerged after a challenge to the Christian foundations of Harvard. In 1805, Henry Ware, a Unitarian, was selected to be Hollis Professor of Divinity at Harvard. Orthodox Congregationalists responded by creating a separate postgraduate seminary in 1808, Andover Theological Seminary, and other denominations would follow. One early twentieth-century scholar called the creation of separate seminaries "disastrous" because "it separated the education of ministers from that of men going into other callings."[17] Unlike in traditional Western and Central European universities, those undertaking theological graduate study in the United States would now be undertaking their study apart from those pursuing a liberal arts degree at the same university. The training of ministers, one of the foundational purposes of early American colleges, would become assigned to seminaries separate from liberal arts colleges. This removal of theology from the house of liberal learning certainly contradicted the vision set forth by thinkers such as Hugh and Ames.

Consequently theology became even less central and integrated in the colleges. As George Marsden notes:

> Theology remained a point of intellectual reference at most colleges, but often in a residual capacity. So the potential was already there for the distinctly Christian aspects of the intellectual enterprise to be jettisoned, or broadened into vestigial platitudes, without threatening any of the fundamental functions of the educational enterprise.[18]

An example of the jettisoning of theological rationales for the curriculum can be found in the Yale Report of 1828. The authors, Yale President Jeremiah Day and associated faculty, never mentioned God, and theology received only a passing reference as a form of advanced graduate study. When

defending the classical curriculum, the authors used more pragmatic arguments such as the following:

> He who is not only eminent in professional life, but has also a mind richly
> stored with general knowledge, has an elevation and dignity of character,
> which gives him a commanding influence in society, and a widely extended
> sphere of usefulness. His situation enables him to diffuse the light of science
> among all classes of the community. Is a man to have no other object, than to
> obtain a *living* by professional pursuits? Has he not duties to perform to his
> family, to his fellow citizens, to his country; duties which require various and
> extensive intellectual furniture?[19]

Interestingly, the faculty even neglected to list the church as a sphere where
the educated person can use one's knowledge.

The reference to furniture fits with the various structural metaphors used
in part one (castle, palace, etc.). The faculty understood that one of the important functions of a collegiate education is to provide the rooms of the
mind with furniture (knowledge) from the various disciplines. Yet they
noted that something else proved more important: "The two great points to
be gained in intellectual culture, are the *discipline* and the *furniture* of the
mind; expanding its powers, and storing it with knowledge. The former of
these is, perhaps, the more important of the two."[20] The phrase "mental discipline" appealed more to an athletic image. For the authors, it was vital that
"*all* the important mental faculties be brought into exercise."[21] This emphasis
focused less on subjects and more on particular intellectual *capacities*.

> The art of fixing the attention, directing the train of thought, analyzing a
> subject proposed for investigation; following, with accurate discrimination,
> the course of argument; balancing nicely the evidence presented to the
> judgment; awakening, elevating, and controlling the imagination; arranging,
> with skill, the treasures which memory gathers; rousing and guiding the
> powers of genius.[22]

This focus on developing individual capacities instead of knowledge of
subjects continues today. What gives coherence to the particular capacities
proposed often proves quite varied. In the Yale Report, it was "balance of
character."[23] Later it would involve appeals to the capacities necessary for
being a good citizen, such as critical thinking. What is clear though is that

the capacities are not chosen or justified using an appeal to God's character, wisdom, or other theological criteria. They are chosen in reference to some other social identity.

The marginalization of theology and an increasing focus on human capacities would lead to a second step, the breaking up of the common liberal arts curriculum of the undergraduate college in favor of the elective system. In other words, the secular reasoning used to preserve the classical curriculum in the Yale Report ultimately did not work. As a result, to use the opening analogy, the introduction of the elective system that started at Harvard in late 1800s introduced the curricular buffet. As historians Richard Hofstadter and Wilson Smith claim:

> The abandonment of the old required classical curriculum and its replacement by a more complex curriculum in which the undergraduate was required to exercise a large amount of choice in the selection of studies was the most important single consequence for the undergraduate college in the development of the modern university.[24]

Overall, the elective system supported a move from a curriculum focused on the unity that God provides to an educational system that would simply find unity in the desires and preferences of the students. That students might still need wise guides to help them with curricular choices was not an idea incorporated into the policy, at least initially.

Looking for Checks, Balances, and Coherence

What is surprising about Eliot's approach to the curriculum is that he failed to follow the democratic blueprint offered during America's founding. He never set up significant checks and balances to prevent the abuse of curricular freedom that the system allowed. In essence, students could eat a meal of desserts from the curricular buffet. Of course, critics picked this up. One critic, the president of Princeton William B. McCosh, claimed in 1885, "I am for freedom, but it must be within carefully defined limits."[25] Every student, he believed, needed a balanced curricular diet, which must include language and literature, science, and philosophy. "Without this," McCosh claimed, "man's varied faculties are not trained, his nature is not fully developed and may become malformed."[26] The failure to choose a well-balanced curricular meal, he claimed, would result in the deformation of one's understanding and senses: "There should be physical science, but there should also be mental and moral science required of all. In knowing other things our young men should be taught to know themselves. When our students are instructed only in matter they are apt to conclude that there is nothing but matter."[27] In contrast, McCosh proposed a system that combined required classes and some electives. The required classes would help provide coherence. To support this point, he used a scientific example.

> Nature is a system like the solar, with a sun in the centre and planets and satellites all around, held together by a gravitating power which keeps each in its proper place, and all shining on each other. You cannot study one part comprehensively without so far knowing the others. In like manner, all the parts of a good college curriculum should be connected in an organic whole. Make a man a mere specialist and the chance is he will not reach the highest eminence as a specialist. The youth most likely to make discoveries is one who has studied collateral subjects.[28]

McCosh's defense of curricular coherence demonstrates the rise of scientific authority at the time. Unlike a Hugh of St. Victor, McCosh defends curricular coherence using nature instead of nature's God, as well as pragmatic reasoning.

This does not mean that McCosh was totally oblivious to theological rationales and thinking. Indeed, he closed his defense of college authority by relating what he could conceive of an imaginary father saying accusingly to a college such as Harvard:

> I sent my son to you believing that man is made in the image of God, you taught him that he is an upper brute, and he has certainly become so; I sent him to you pure, and last night he was carried to my door drunk. Curse ye this college; "curse ye bitterly," for you took no pains to allure him to good, to admonish, to pray for him.[29]

Ironically, though this hypothetical father claims the university has lost an appeal to humans as creatures made in God's image, any appeal to theological rationale was also absent from McCosh's defense of curricular unity.

By the early 1900s it became clear that the elective system needed some checks, especially because faculty believed students no longer perceived any coherence in the curriculum. For example, the president of the University of Michigan Marion LeRoy Burton complained, "Students have imagined that the universe, in some mysterious way, is actually departmentalized, just as a university is. They have not sensed the unity of all knowledge."[30] He unpacked his argument with a provocative image: "The *disjecta membra* of the body of knowledge have rarely been fashioned by them or for them into a living, unified organism."[31] Later he would use the same image: "At present the dazed undergraduate is suddenly ushered into the gross anatomy laboratory of knowledge and vigorous groups of specialists hurl at him heart, lungs, and other vital organs of the body of knowledge."[32] The students' job is supposedly to "fashion these *disjecta membra* into a harmonious living organism."[33] Not surprisingly, he was not optimistic.

The metaphors of a structure, a body, a solar system, or a meal—entities that have complex parts with a supposed unity—were popular descriptors for the structure of the curriculum. The president of Harvard Lawrence A. Lowell even used the museum metaphor mentioned earlier, albeit in a negative way: "The ordinary student is too apt to treat courses as Cook's tourists do the starred pictures in foreign galleries, as experiences to be checked off and forgotten. To have taken a course is by no means always equivalent to possessing any real command of a subject."[34]

Overall, the criticism of the elective system rested on three points. First, critics claimed it led to haphazard course selection. College students who chose courses based on their interests and whims gathered no big-picture view of the world. Second, it led to overspecialization, with the students knowing a great deal about a narrow field without gaining a broad view of knowledge. The growing number of courses and academic departments did not help. Julie Reuben observes that within twenty years the University of California course catalog went from less than thirty pages to over two hundred.[35] At first, the course catalogs would list the academic departments according to their "logical" relations (e.g., foreign languages came after classical languages), but this approach was eventually discarded for an alphabetical listing. Of course, in the arena of curricular competition that the elective system created, academic departments sought to increase their market share.

Finally, critics considered the elective system too individualistic. For instance, Woodrow Wilson used two different metaphors while president of Princeton to discuss the purpose of higher education. First, he argued that the purpose of college was to give each generation "a view of the stage as a whole before it was drawn off to occupy only a little corner of the stage and forget the rest, to forget the plot as a whole in the arrangement of its position of it."[36] Next, he would go on to use the image of a traveler and the need for the university to provide a conceptual map by which to orient the traveler. He noted:

> I have often thought it was an extremely inaccurate expression when a man has lost his way in a desert or a jungle to say that he had lost himself. That is the only thing he has not lost. What as a matter of fact he has lost is the rest of the world. If he knew where any other thing of definite position was in the rest of the world, he would have something to steer by and he could get out. Orientation I understand to be illustrated by that. A man has found where he is in relation to the intellectual and moral content of the world and having ascertained his relations to other things and to other persons and to other forces, he knows more accurately where he himself is located.[37]

The reality, though, was that elite American universities had abandoned providing a metaphysical map that could guide students. At most, Wilson hoped it would give students a map that provided a certain more limited understanding of themselves—first and foremost that they were citizens of a nation that needed them to use their talents for the national good. In addition, the common mental-capacities approach to justifying the curriculum meant that universities focused more on equipping students for their journey, even though they did not provide an overarching map and destination. Instead, students were supposed to create their own maps and destinations. The university would focus on giving them general capacities that could support a variety of journeys.

Critics pointed out that equipping students for a variety of journeys did not necessarily mean that universities equipped students to choose among journeys. In 1938, William Brown asked:

> What if what you ask of the university is not that it furnish you with any one of the particular kinds of knowledge that it has to offer but that it teach you how to choose between them? Then you would be asking for a wisdom which

it may be that some or one of the professors who make up our faculties has won for himself but which the university as such would be the first to confess it cannot give you.[38]

To change the analogy, what the university offered was a larger and larger buffet of courses and professions, but the courses of study did not help students make choices regarding the buffet. Part of this problem had to do with the fact that professors developed the unusual expectation that they were only responsible for providing students with expertise related to their academic profession, but they were no longer expected to provide wisdom for life as a whole. They no longer believed it was their job to help students determine what a healthy meal/life would be. They merely cooked and offered their special dish.

The combination of a world of fragmented and competing professionals and disciplines contributed to the multiversity described above in chapter five and later made an important contribution to the rise of the professional administrator described below in chapter nine. Christian universities proved to demonstrate little capacity or awareness of the possible dangers. As one scholar notes of this time period, "In the end, the churches fell back on and accepted uncritically, often enthusiastically, the dominant university conceptions of knowledge."[39]

Understandably, many who experienced this multiversity found it far from satisfactory, especially if they hoped to bring together all the various capacities one developed and the knowledge one encountered into some coherent whole. David Sloan Wilson describes the overall situation in this manner:

> The Ivory Tower would be more aptly named the Ivory Archipelago. It consists of hundreds of isolated subjects, each divided into smaller subjects in an almost infinite progression. People are examined less with a microscope than with a kaleidoscope—psychology, anthropology, economics, political science, sociology, history, art, literature, philosophy, gender studies, ethnic studies. Each perspective has its own history and special assumptions. One person's heresy is another's commonplace.[40]

Not surprisingly, students found this experience frustratingly incoherent. Parker Palmer and Arthur Zajonc write of their own experience within this system,

But early on in our academic careers, we found that the disciplinary silos in which we had been educated—and the fragmentary and fragmenting assumptions about knowledge and humanity that often lay behind them—obscured as much as they revealed about the nature of reality and how to inhabit it as whole human beings.[41]

Attempting to provide some semblance of unity, the defenders of liberal education have struggled to find new justificatory narratives. The soul holding the curriculum together had fragmented, and they had only limited ways of trying to put it back together.

The Usual Justifications

The context created by these developments means that the contemporary justificatory narratives and sagas for defending the liberal arts in American universities today have become quite predictable. Scholars almost always make reference to the development of certain human capacities, such as critical thinking and the American national story and interest. Michael Roth's *Beyond the University: Why Liberal Education Matters* is only the latest such example. In the introduction he lists the usual national justifications: "Access to a broad, self-critical and pragmatic education has been and remains essential for a culture that prizes innovation and an economy that depends on it. It also remains essential for a society that aspires to be democratic."[42] Later, Roth also claims, using Thomas Jefferson and Ralph Waldo Emerson, that our universities are paradoxically supposed to do two contradictory things: (1) produce research and knowledge and spread it to others, and (2) teach students critical thinking that undermines the received wisdom from the research and knowledge produced.

Roth perceives these two impulses as paradoxical because he does not offer a justificatory narrative that can account for them. For Christians, this tension is explained by the biblical narrative. Humans are made in God's image to discover and create knowledge. Yet due to our human limitations and fallenness, our discoveries and creations will always be limited and corrupt. Therefore we need those coming after us to continually transform (or in some cases discard) the previous creative structures and knowledge frameworks. For Roth, however, these two tasks stand in tension.

Near the end of his book, Roth does set forth some big-picture justifications. He notes that since we are unable to find a set of texts or skills on which we all can agree, the closest common end for liberal education becomes critical thinking. Yet, as a college president, he knows that students become very good at showing how things or people "don't make sense," but they do not acquire the "capacity to find or create meaning and direction in the books they read and the world in which they live."[43] The critical thinking they acquire, especially in postmodern forms, becomes like a sledgehammer used to destroy rather than a bag of tools that helps one create. Consequently, "they wind up contributing to a cultural climate that has little tolerance for finding or making meaning, whose intellectuals and cultural commentators delight in being able to show that somebody else *is not be to be believed*."[44] Understandably, Roth wants students to do something more with the liberal arts tools a college gives them.

To change this outcome, Roth makes two proposals. First, he suggests emphasizing an additional set of human capacities that he hopes will help students make choices: the capability for intellectual and moral empathy, understanding others from their point of view, and understanding cultures from their internal rationale. Second, he believes a liberal arts education should help students be "explorers of the normative."[45] "Explorers" is the key word since Roth has an allergy to professors engaging in moral judgmentalism.

> As guides, not judges, we can show our students how to engage in the practice of exploring objects, norms, and values that inform diverse cultures. Through this engagement, students will develop the ability to converse with others about shaping the objects, norms, and values that will inform their own lives.[46]

Overall, according to Roth's vision, colleges should equip students with the general capacities of critical thinking, empathy, and exploring objects, norms, and values for an undefined journey. In that way students learn how we create legitimate meanings, norms, and values (whatever those are) and how to add "value to the organizations in which they participate"[47] (whatever "value" may be). Along the way, students "will often reject roads that others have taken and they will sometimes chart new paths."[48]

143

What provides the basis for rejecting particular roads or charting specific new paths beyond the usual pragmatic "whatever helps our liberal democracy" standard remains unclear. Ultimately this form of liberal education provides students the "ability to find together ways of living that have meaning and direction."[49] Meaning and direction, though, are things that the individual creates on his or her own. Universities, professors, and their disciplines may provide various maps of the world or the good life for observation, but they do not help students chart the path to a particular destination in a way that gives specificity and direction to the human capacities that one should develop. Lack of particularity and direction define Roth's outlook. The obvious advantage is that this vision offends virtually no one and includes nearly anyone. In the end, what provides the only form of coherence for the contemporary curriculum is that it provides the intellectual tools for students to build whatever they want.

Still, the idea and longing for curricular coherence persistently shapes the university. Alasdair MacIntyre claims one can still find its remnants in our institutions and curriculum:

> Even now the organized institutions of the academic curriculum and the ways in which both enquiry and teaching are conducted in and through those institutions are structured to a significant degree as if we still did believe . . . [and] behave as if there is some overall coherence to and some underlying agreement about the academic project.[50]

After all, the fact that the university still attempts to teach a range of majors and subjects together in one institution assumes the importance and need for some sort of coherence. It still operates as if it has a soul. Not surprisingly, some are starting to question these assumptions. In an article titled "What Universities Have in Common with Record Labels," Martin Smith argues that universities of the future will increasingly have to unbundle their content just as record labels had to start offering individual songs for sale: "The individual course, rather than the degree, is becoming the unit of content. And universities, the record labels of education, are facing increased pressure to unbundle their services."[51]

Although there are good reasons to doubt the reality of this development, not the least being that parents and students buy universities as a whole based on their reputation and not individual professors or courses,[52] it still illustrates an important development in thought. Today, an education with coherence supplied by a university with some sort of soul is no longer necessarily an ideal or perceived need. Some results of this view will be detailed in chapter eleven. Whether there is a vision that can once again provide coherence and bring together the various disciplines is a subject for chapter fourteen.

8

FRAGMENTING STUDENTS

The Curricular/Cocurricular Division

...

If there is one thing that should raise the question of the secular university's irrelevance it might especially be in the failure to justify or even make sense of the concept of the human.

C. John Sommerville

PROFESSORS ARE SUPPOSED TO be trained to teach—to help students learn the knowledge, wisdom, and practices associated with the course subject matter. Yet some American colleges and universities still have the odd idea, not always shared by other university systems around the world, that they should educate the whole person.[1] Thus they task cocurricular educators with this tremendous responsibility. Indeed, the cocurricular sphere of the university is larger than the curricular sphere because students spend more time outside of class than in it. For example, at most, undergraduates will spend 18 hours per week in formal classroom-type settings. With 168 hours in a week, 150 hours are then left for students to spend elsewhere. We hope they spend about 56 hours (seven days × eight hours) a week sleeping but suspect that is highly unlikely. We hope that students enrolled, for example, in 18 credit hours spend about 54 hours (eighteen credits × three hours) per week studying, but unfortunately we know that is not even close to being true.[2] Even if our hopes are fulfilled, students still have forty hours to spend engaged in other activities that leave an imprint on their identity. Not only do cocurricular educators set the tone for where students sleep and quite often where they study, but they also set the tone for much of what fills those remaining hours.

In this chapter, we outline why educating whole persons today is difficult in the contemporary multiversity with a fragmented soul where a curricular and cocurricular division of labor exists. This situation is not surprising in a fragmented multiversity where different parts function as silos with their own unique identities, narratives, and purposes. In fact, contemporary American higher education often creates a situation where curricular educators and cocurricular educators rarely meet. Students simply shuffle back and forth between them and are thus left to piece together some conception of human flourishing and the good life. Although this gives the student freedom to engage in what scholars today like to call "meaning-making" and "self-authorship,"[3] it also leaves students without relationships that cross into their various areas of life or common frameworks by which to make sense of the whole of life. Indeed, multiversities with fragmented souls, by their very nature, avoid taking responsibility for helping students discover wisdom—a holistic view of knowledge and the good life. As a result, students lack mentors who may help them think about the various dimensions of their life as a whole and what it means to be a good human being.[4]

In contrast to this experience, consider a vignette shared by Rod Dreher after the death of his sister, Ruthie Leming, that resulted from living in a community where such sharp lines of division did not exist. Ruthie's doctor and his wife, Tim and Laura, came to the Leming's home after Ruthie's death and talked with the family, including Ruthie's daughter Hannah. Dreher shares his reflections of the experience.

> I watched Tim and Laura sitting in rocking chairs in Ruthie's front porch, flanking Hannah [Ruthie's oldest daughter], talking to her about grief and what it means both emotionally and theologically to face death. . . . It struck me that although my sister was dead, and Tim's service to her as a physician was over, he didn't see it that way. There was still healing to be done to Ruthie's family, the kind of healing that medicine, strictly speaking, could not effect. Because Tim approached his vocation as a work of love, he found the strength, the direction, and the inner resources to treat the Lemings in ways beyond

147

the reach of standard medical practice. Here was a family doctor treating his patients like family.[5]

In the context of higher education, this kind of instance when a professional faculty or staff member might move beyond a limited professional role to a more holistic form of care is increasingly rare, especially when the curricular and cocurricular are fragmented and operate in silos with their internal sagas.

This fragmentation is also exacerbated by another difficulty facing the contemporary multiversity. These institutions have largely discarded the Christian metaphysics and narrative for determining what a flourishing human being is and the way to achieve that end. Moreover, they have adopted a particular American conception of freedom that encourages individuals to make their own choices about what it means to be a flourishing human being. Although we understand this approach among public universities, we often underestimate its implications for student life. Student life personnel in these situations are faced with the difficult task of both honoring student freedom while also somehow encouraging students to develop toward some commonly agreed-on understanding of what a flourishing human being should be. Such a task proves extremely difficult in a multiversity with a fragmented and uncertain soul. This chapter recounts the growth of the curricular and cocurricular divide and how higher education addressed the problems that came without thick forms of agreement about the end of human development and human flourishing.

The Development of the Cocurricular Realm

As faculty members in American higher education began to focus their attention more on research and on teaching in a lecture format in the early twentieth century, they had less time for shaping other aspects of the university experience, such as the moral formation of students or attending to other needs. As a result, universities started to hire staff to take care of additional tasks that faculty would or could not perform.[6] In the beginning what exactly student personnel administrators were responsible for remained somewhat ambiguous. At first they focused on tasks related to career placement. For example, in 1919 C. S. Yoakum believed the primary responsibilities of a student personnel program were "to obtain accurate data on each student, to codify the requirements of different professions, to supervise the use of tests and to provide means whereby each student may become acquainted with his abilities and the requirements of the occupations in which he is interested."[7]

As the next decade progressed, student personnel administrators began to expand and clarify their functions. One example is Francis F. Bradshaw's 1936 essay "The Scope and Aim of a Personal Program." Rooted in the historical perception that "as colleges grew in size and the faculty became increasingly unwilling to spend time not directly germane to their teaching and research,"[8] Bradshaw included services ranging from admissions to physical and emotional health services as valued offices in a student personnel program. In addition, other universities began to include the moral health of students. For example, Yale created a dean of students position in 1919 to "deal with all the collective problems of public morals and public order which confront the University as a whole."[9] Advocates claimed that these new specialized experts, more often referred to as student development administrators or student affairs administrators, could take responsibility for the emotional, physical, moral, and spiritual identity of their students outside of class in what we previously referred to as the "cocurricular" realm.[10]

However, this new class of administrators often lacked a comprehensive philosophy to guide their work. In 1919, W. H. Cowley, arguably the most important figure in the development of an understanding of student personnel work, began to encourage his colleagues to embrace an understanding of their work as efforts designed to meet the educational needs of whole students. In "The Nature of a Student Personnel Work," Cowley argued that student personnel

> administrators are interested in his [student's] emotional and social development, in his health, in his selection of courses as they relate to his personal objectives, in his place of residence, in his extra-curricular activities, in his financial needs, and in any number of other considerations which bear upon his education when broadly considered.[11]

In essence, students needed administrators in their life who could aid in their full development apart from responsibilities taken on by faculty in instructional spaces such as the classroom, laboratory, or recital hall.

The language of "whole person" would formally come to the front of a document produced at an American Council of Education meeting in Washington, DC. With the *Student Personnel Point of View*, student personnel administrators now had a document that philosophically elaborated why their work on campus was critical. Drafted by Cowley and eighteen other colleagues at that meeting, the *Student Personnel Point of View* brought attention to the reasons why colleges and universities should emphasize "the development of the student as a person, rather than upon his intellectual training alone."[12] As a result, the *Student Personnel Point of View* thrusts on

> educational institutions the obligation to consider the student as a whole—his intellectual capacity and achievement[,] his emotional make-up, his physical condition, his social relationships, his vocational aptitudes and skills, his moral and religious values, his economic resources, his aesthetic appreciations.[13]

In the void left by faculty members who increasingly limited their vocational practices to research, teaching, and narrow forms of service, Cowley and his associates argued that student personnel administrators would be present to work with students as whole persons.

What exactly would characterize a developed "whole person" upon leaving college, however, was usually not specified or was referred to in broad generalities. Two decades after this vision was articulated, Herbert Stroup decried the lack of progress made toward specific theory-building, fearing that the catchphrase "students as a whole" masked a great deal of nuance.

> To an impressive extent, the task of theory is answered quickly by many student personnel workers with the phrase "the student personnel point of view." This rejoinder means that the field is not seriously in need of theoretical advancement because its theoretical needs have been met with a philosophy or a point of view. . . . If it is a philosophy or theory of student personnel work, it is decidedly vapid and sentimental rather than precisely theoretical in its intention and analysis.[14]

This breadth and inclusivity would present other challenges as well. For instance, the report insisted that universities had the moral obligation "to assist the student in developing to the limits of his potentialities and in making his contribution to the betterment of society."[15]

These potentialities included social relationships, physical condition, and moral and religious values. The report then assumed that colleges and universities could agree on the improvement of things such as "personal appearance" and "manners" as well as "progression in religious, emotional, social development, and other non-academic personal and group relationships."[16] It also claimed that "an effective educational program" would include student personnel engaged in "supervising, evaluating and developing the religious life and interests of students" and "maintaining student group morale by evaluating, understanding, and developing student mores."[17] The new profession quite quickly and officially tasked itself with undertaking forms of student development, such as moral and religious development, increasingly cast off by the faculty.

Agreement about what the developed student would look like proved to be much more difficult to find when, shortly after the close of World War II, the student populations at research universities increased in size at record rates. To address this issue, leaders among student personnel administrators, now most commonly referred to as student life administrators, student development administrators, or student affairs administrators, drew on two sources. The first source was the common political identity held by students and the associated liberal democratic ideals for which America had fought in World War II. For instance, when the American Council on Education eventually revised its 1937 statement in 1949, the statement articulated the profession's goals as "education for a fuller realization of democracy in every phase of living."[18] Democracy in the statement no longer served as a political philosophy, but became an encompassing approach to education and life. The student life movement justified its approach with a religious appeal to democracy by claiming, "Our way of life depends upon a renewed faith in, and extensive use of, democratic methods, upon the development of more citizens to assume responsibilities in matters of social concern, and upon the active participation of millions of men and women in the enterprise of social improvement."[19] Colleges and universities therefore needed to inculcate in students "a firm and enlightened belief in democracy."[20]

Democracy, however, could not provide a sufficient theory base. Consequently, student life personnel turned to a second source. They saw themselves as functioning as the mediators and interpreters of advances in the science of student psychology by "assist[ing] the student in developing an understanding of proper concepts of behavior, ethical standards, and spiritual values consistent with his broadened horizons resulting from newly acquired scientific and technical knowledge."[21] Science, instead of religious revelation, would now illuminate the way forward, and student life professionals would be their guides. Science showed great possibilities in this area because it could be used to appeal to the whole array of diverse students now attending the university.

The Fragmentation of the Cocurricular

The 1968 report *The Student in Higher Education* continued to lament the narrow focus on intellectual development since "it becomes virtually impossible to separate intellectual from moral and emotional growth."[22] This report argued for developmental education since "even technicians cannot be trained unless it is recognized that they are something more than functionaries—that they are also human beings."[23] Oddly, although student affairs administrators were supposed to focus on the holistic development of students, at that time, rather than seeking to study students as whole persons, most theories they adopted focused on important yet singular strands of human identity.

In brief, the spirit of fragmentation, one that plagued the faculty and the disciplines they served, also plagued cocurricular educators. Instead of first focusing their efforts on what defined a student as a whole person, student development theorists primarily trained in psychosocial stage theory, subdivided human identity into smaller and smaller blocks of understanding. The assumption in their thinking was that the cumulative weight of the parts yielded a coherent whole. That assumption would only continue to be extended in the years to come as significant theories of human identity related to gender, race, and sexual orientation, to name only three, were added to the list of components defining a whole person. Again, the challenge is not that such forms of identity were added to what defines a whole person. The challenge is whether the sum of the parts, as with the academic disciplines, makes for a coherent whole. In most cases, cocurricular educators define the whole student only in reference to the intersection of parts with no overall sense of what a flourishing human being is. Without a soul—a coherent identity, narrative, and purpose—cocurricular educators are left with not only subdivided disciplines but also now with subdivided students.

One obvious place where this approach has occurred pertains to the moral dimension of college life. On a residential college campus, as with any group living together, there always have to be moral ideals in place that allow the communal living arrangement to work. The problem with most college campuses is that these elements are often fashioned without a larger guiding vision of human flourishing at both an individual and corporate level. For example, in September 2011 Harvard administrators made an attempt to require freshmen to sign a "Freshman Pledge." The core of the pledge stated:

> In the classroom, in extracurricular endeavors, and in the Yard and Houses, students are expected to act with integrity, respect and industry, and to sustain a community characterized by inclusiveness and civility. As we begin at Harvard, we commit to upholding the values of the College and to making the entryway and Yard a place where all can thrive and where the exercise of kindness holds a place on par with intellectual attainment.[24]

Why should students uphold the virtues of integrity, respect, industry, civility, inclusiveness, and kindness? The pledge does not really say. What about the definitions and different understandings? Will one person's honesty be another person's incivility? The pledge offers students little guidance with this critical issue. The Harvard Pledge only provides virtues without any of the other elements necessary for thinking about what it means to be a good community member at Harvard. Students do not receive an explanation of the moral origins of these virtues, definitions, or readings that might explain the rich reasons for them. This is the reason why Lawrence Kohlberg in 1971 criticized this type of moral education as the "bag of virtues" approach.[25] The problem, Kohlberg observed, is that "everyone has his own bag."[26] Moreover,

> a vague consensus on the goodness of these virtues conceals a great deal of actual disagreement over their definitions. What is one person's "integrity" is another person's "stubbornness," what is one person's honesty is "expressing your true feelings" is another person's insensitivity to the feelings of others.[27]

What Kohlberg did not appear to recognize is that virtues only appear to be randomly selected and arbitrarily defined if one scrapes away a wider moral tradition from one's vision for the ideal human. Why a person should choose to acquire a particular virtue only makes sense in light of a larger story that explains human flourishing.

To offer an alternative, Kohlberg identified how people progressed from lower to higher forms of moral reasoning through six distinct stages.[28] The theory proved immensely popular, and a number of student development scholars claim that "Kohlberg's ideas were a dominant force guiding moral development research for over forty years."[29] What the theory did not do, however, was provide substantive answers to the actions and affections that the good life might entail.

Indeed, the situation at Harvard is merely the product of the failures of student life administrators to find theories that can supply a substantive vision of the good life. Instead, they have relied on theories that provide an understanding of the form of moral development without attention to its substance. For instance, a popular student development textbook dedicates an entire chapter to exploring William Perry's 1968 theory and its impact on the work of individuals who would follow.[30] In essence, Perry's schema begins by noting a young person starts by engaging rather dualistic or "black-and-white" forms of thinking. Ideas are either good or bad. Forms of behavior are either right or wrong. As a person matures, Perry notes that he or she potentially progresses through four basic categories, from simple dualism, to complex dualism, to relativism, to commitment in relativism. Perry understood his theory as encouraging complex thinking as well as moral commitment. In other words, the task of the educator is to guide students from relativism, which in its failure "to provide orientation for the individual makes its structure highly unstable,"[31] and toward commitment. In fact, he believed this responsibility should rouse the scholar from any neutral, objective stance. He argued, "It is no longer tenable for an educator to take the position that what a person does with his intellectual skills is a moral rather than intellectual problem and therefore none of the scholar's business."[32] Scholars should be committed to taking students toward commitment.

Encouraging thoughtful and critical student commitment, however, does not necessarily answer the question of what a flourishing human life might be. For instance, Perry does not address the role of the university in actually suggesting that there might be better commitments than others or in differentiating among commitments. Following his theory merely leaves any person promoting student development with promoting commitment in general.

Overall, these types of developmental theories lack a soul—a larger narrative understanding of human flourishing and the human purpose that can guide the direction of development. As a result, what we know best are particular components of a student's identity, and subsequent research is focused on slicing those forms of identity into smaller and smaller domains. The vast array of theories that followed in the wake of the historically significant ones, such as the two we just noted, unfortunately follow that same trajectory. The means by which cocurricular educators understand their students become not that different from how faculty members appreciate the disciplines. Compounding this problem is the administrative gulf separating cocurricular and curricular educators. Again, the question is whether the sum of all these parts forms a coherent whole.

Ultimately this is the problem with Harvard's approach, not the advocacy of virtue. In contrast, we must agree on the purpose of a particular role or the end of life as a whole in order to agree on the virtues necessary for the flourishing of that particular role or of life as a whole. Harvard's attempt to instill virtue is similar to a Catholic university asking incoming students to sign their commitment to the seven cardinal virtues without explaining the origins of these virtues, what they mean, what they might look like in actual practice, or the larger purpose and metanarrative that gives them meaning and significance.

This last omission is the most serious. Rules or definitions of virtue can only be effectively established when communities conceptualize a specific human and communal end derived from a particular identity and narrative. Based on this conception of human flourishing, communities then seek to establish certain rules and embody, prioritize, and exemplify particular virtues.[33] Yet many higher education programs appear to seek an intellectual community devoid of a guiding tradition or narrative about human flourishing because such trappings prove restrictive. The mission of Harvard College (which is the undergraduate program at Harvard University) even boasts that "Harvard seeks to identify and to remove restraints on students' full participation, so that individuals may explore their capabilities and interests and may develop their full intellectual and human potential. Education at Harvard should liberate students to explore, to create, to challenge, and to lead."[34] In other words, instead of the Catholic university example, it might be more appropriate to say that asking someone to sign the Harvard Pledge is like asking someone to learn to dribble and throw a ball without providing him or her any context of the game for which such a virtue might be helpful. Harvard College has no story and no saints. Granted, Harvard College probably does not hope to form moral saints. One might argue that it merely wants kind and civil students. A pledge written by a committee supplies a basic community ritual, so perhaps it remains a small beginning to forming a slightly more vigorous moral community. Yet assortments of virtues designed to focus on community citizenship will likely be less compelling than advancing a robust vision of human flourishing. If college administrators and staff wish to reenvision what they hope to accomplish with students outside of the classroom, they will need the former and not simply a grab bag of virtues and programming ideas.

Holistic Student Development and Learning

Just as Ernest Boyer's *Scholarship Reconsidered* was an effort to rectify the divided nature of the academic vocation in multiversities without a soul, so others have sought to craft ways to bridge the chasm separating curricular and cocurricular educators. The problem, though, is that cocurricular professional associations are unable to provide a comprehensive understanding of what a developed, whole student should look like.[35] In light of this failure it is not surprising that an important shift in language has now occurred within these associations. Today major statements by professional student life organizations speak less about the more comprehensive notion of "development" and more about "learning."[36] Such a shift is understandable since "learning" does not carry with it certain metaphysical assumptions about the human person. It is also much easier to measure, which is the focus of many new initiatives. Especially at state-funded institutions that are more accountable to the public, it proves much simpler and less controversial to talk about learning than development. In fact, it may even be appropriate since some of the assumptions about what a developed human being looks like that guide student life programs at state universities may actually ignore the deep metaphysical disagreements among the public students attending.

As a result, the contemporary multiversity currently undertakes a number of ad hoc strategies that seek to at least broker partnerships between curricular and cocurricular educators. Although they have been met with mixed results, we will conclude this chapter by at least noting three such efforts. First, the "Student Learning Imperative" made a considerable impact on the way cocurricular educators view their work. Drafted in 1996 by representatives of the American College Personnel Association (ACPA), the "Student Learning Imperative" opened by noting that the "key to enhancing learning and personal development is not simply for faculty to teach more and better, but also to create conditions that motivate and inspire students to devote time and energy to educationally-purposeful activities, both in and outside the classroom."[37] The context for this document was first and foremost a larger environment of accountability that was beginning to demand demonstrable proof from colleges and universities that various efforts did favorably influence student learning. In addition, at least among cocurricular educators, a perception had developed that the gap between the efforts they were making outside the classroom and the efforts that faculty were making inside the classroom were too distinct from one another. Somehow campuses needed to find ways to integrate the programming that took place in those two realms.

As a result, the authors of this statement attempt to reposition the student affairs division as one that "complements the institution's mission, with the enhancement of student learning and personal development being the primary goal of student affairs programs and services."[38] Like Boyer's *Scholarship Reconsidered*, perhaps the best way to identify the effect of the "Student Learning Imperative" is that it is widely cited but seldom understood. In its wake, more scholars produced research that focused on how educators could program for and assess student learning.[39] What is important to note, though, is that the shift from "development" to "learning" in many ways signals that these associations want to focus less on any grand theory of what it means to be a flourishing human being and more on a measurable outcome that is primarily cognitive in nature. For instance, "student learning" does not necessarily include students' affections or behaviors (although it can). This propensity demonstrates the reductionistic tendencies that can be associated with increasing pluralism and a form of postmodernism that discourages any sort of metanarrative in favor of positive self-selected change or outcomes on which all can agree (so learning instead of developing fits right in).

One also finds this trend in the sheer volume of campuses that have redesigned at least portions of their residence life programs to focus on creation of learning communities. Following the general demise of the in loco parentis model in the late 1960s and early 1970s, residence life programs arguably became utilitarian in terms of their interaction with students—don't leave your hot plate unattended, don't burn the building down, don't harm your roommate—and the rest was up for negotiation. Conversations on a number of campuses, as facilitated by statements such as the "Student Learning Imperative," soon determined that such approaches were insufficient. Resident directors (RDs) and resident assistants (RAs) were asked to identify and assess their learning goals for programming. As a result, today floors and even entire residence halls are given over to large, interdisciplinary themes that drive the programming within those areas for an entire year. Faculty members are often asked to serve as partners in such efforts. Students are then given the option to sign up for housing with the selection of such themes as part of their decision-making process.

When designing "living-learning" spaces from scratch, cocurricular educators and architects often now begin with a new focus to their work. As noted by one group of scholars, "Residential learning communities can enhance interaction, particularly at large schools. Some institutions are now adding classrooms, other teaching facilities, and faculty housing directly in the dormitory buildings."[40] Although such spaces often are more expensive on a cost-per-square-foot construction basis, empirical assessments of student-learning outcomes are beginning to point to favorable results.

Finally, one of the most formal ways of achieving the benefits of a living-learning community is through a residential college. Rooted again in the British system of higher education, where students, as previously mentioned, live on campus and in close proximity with individuals responsible for their learning, residential colleges are often referred to as the Oxbridge system. While living on campus was often a part of the American educational experience from the beginning, the residential college system was introduced at Harvard University and Yale University in the 1930s.[41] At Harvard, all first-year students live together in "The Yard" and then are assigned to one of the houses as they are called. At Yale, first-year students are assigned to a residential college after admission and then move in when they arrive on campus to begin their educational careers.

According to Yale's admissions website, the "residential colleges have been called 'little paradises,' each with its own distinctive architecture, courtyard, dining hall, and library as well as activity spaces such as a movie theater, recording studio, printing press, dance studio, and gym."[42] Harvard's houses are designed along comparable lines. However, more important than the design is the way these universities staff their houses or colleges. In particular, most are led by a master who is a senior member of the faculty and provides leadership and vision. A dean works in partnership with the master as the senior cocurricular educator and is responsible for day-to-day operations.

In the United States, the Oxbridge system is not only in place at Yale and Harvard. Other institutions such as Rice University and the University of California at Santa Cruz also have comprehensive college systems. When taken as a whole, the Claremont Colleges operate in many ways as a residential college system. The University of Notre Dame has a system of halls that are single-sex and where almost all students live for four years. Such facilities are led by a rector but are also served by a priest or religious sister who also lives in residence.

Although far from universal in consideration and implementation, concepts such as the "Student Learning Imperative," living-learning communities, and residential colleges do aid in integrating the efforts being made by curricular and cocurricular educators, and they do advance learning. Yet there is a big difference between amassing learning and acquiring wisdom, virtue, and a love of truth. A robust understanding of the human person in a university with a soul requires that we expand our view of what human development might entail. Consider what one recent comprehensive account of human personhood suggests are the five highest-order capacities of human development: (1) interpersonal communion and love, (2) aesthetic judgment and enjoyment, (3) forming virtues, (4) moral awareness and judgment, and (5) truth seeking.[43] Similar to Hugh of St. Victor, who thought the way students can participate in God's restoration of our divine image is through "the contemplation of truth and the practice of virtue," these five elements point to broad capacities rooted in a particular—we would argue, Christian—conception of human personhood.

Unfortunately, the emphasis on the diffuse concept of student learning also means that it is unlikely the student affairs professional associations will attempt to craft a comprehensive understanding of student identity and development that also integrates the important subdivided qualities that are currently proliferating. Indeed, we doubt that in multiversities with fragmented souls such an endeavor would be rewarded unless it contributed to simple pragmatic ends such as student retention or graduation rates. For now, students are generally left to themselves to make sense of the subdividing culture they are asked to navigate, proving that when the university loses a unified soul it becomes something less than its name indicates.

9

CHIEF FRAGMENTATION OFFICER

The Advent of the Professional Administrator

...

The normal American goal in any occupation is administration.

E. P. CHASE

The general rule is that administration everywhere becomes,
by force of circumstances if not by choice,
a more prominent feature of the university.

CLARK KERR

O N CLEAR MORNINGS, the glow of the forthcoming day long precedes the actual appearance of the sun. On an overcast morning, identifying the "moment" of sunrise becomes a futile exercise without scientific calculations. In a similar way, the "rise" or growth and proliferation of the professional administrator (that is, an employee of a university whose task is not directly or explicitly instructional) has been gradual, and yet clearly this profession has "risen." How American higher education developed from a time when a college president was an institution's sole administrator in the colonial era to the vast bureaucracy of the modern university is a fascinating and complex story.

This narrative of expansion and specialization matters here because of the difficult questions it raises about the identity, story, purposes, and necessary functions of a university. The importance of the rise of the professional higher education administrator is nested in a long-standing dispute not simply about the presence of this labor segment but, most significantly, its legitimacy and its impact on the enterprise as a whole. Beneath this ongoing squabble over university control are ideals—those held by academics and those often derisively attributed to administrators—that are grounded in assumptions about what and whose the university should be. Administrators are often the ones who struggle most with the question about how to prevent the growth of their professional class from turning the multiversity into an impersonal machine instead of a community with soul. The increasing number of administrators, after all, is often associated with soulless bureaucracies that lose sight of any larger identity and purpose.

Clark Kerr lamented that one of the problems of the university is to "relate administration more directly to individual faculty and students in the massive institution."[1] He realized that an increased administrative class makes it more difficult "for an institution to see itself in totality rather than just piecemeal and the sweep of history rather than just at a moment of time."[2] In other words, a large bureaucratic institution tends to lose a singular soul. In this chapter we explore the nature of administrative professionalism, proceed by examining the roots of administrative expansion in higher education, and end by investigating the legitimacy of this labor segment and what the rancor often targeted at it indicates about the perceived nature of the soul of the university.

The Beginning

Administratively speaking, appreciating just how modest an enterprise most colleges and universities were even well into the nineteenth century provides perspective on the roots of the administrative profession and its recent dramatic proliferation. In 1920, Samuel P. Capen, then director of the American Council on Education, spoke of the changes that were already vast.

> The future historian of American higher education will be impressed by the development of administrative organization and administrative technique. In a short generation, American universities and larger colleges have grown from one-man concerns, which presidents handled without assistance and

often without advice, to larger and complicated enterprises. In the same period, one administrative function after another has been delegated to special officers—deans, comptrollers, directors, and registrars. An administrative hierarchy has grown up which has no counterpart in the university organization of any other country.[3]

Reflective of this sea change, Earl James McGrath, in his 1936 dissertation, outlined the expansion of administrative roles and functions that occurred over the prior fifty years.[4] McGrath identified two basic trends: some offices were recent inventions of necessity, reflecting the increasing number of institutional functions. These included the librarian (which, owing to the lack of books or restricted access to books by students in a prior era was a recent innovation), the alumni secretary (now commonly associated with titles such as director of alumni relations), and chief business officer. The second and more common trend was the gradual emergence of administrative roles that were at first shaped largely by the necessities of bookkeeping and oversight. Over time, they expanded in function and complexity as the curriculum and student bodies grew. Offices such as academic dean, registrar, dean of men/dean of women, and so on multiplied in number and technical expectancy at the turn of the twentieth century.

As McGrath suggests, the office of the registrar may be the prototype for this increase in scale and required expertise. Prior to 1915, at twenty-one of the thirty-two institutions in McGrath's nationwide study, the office of the registrar was combined with other duties. McGrath argues that these combined roles imply a relatively light administrative load. Quoting Samuel Capen, McGrath chronicled the modest origins of the office and its subsequent acceleration toward specialization.

> In the beginning, the registrar's office was concerned with the simplest kind of recording. The office was generally treated—and in many institutions it is still treated—as an adjunct of the president's office, or of a dean's. Sometimes the duties of the registrar were performed by an experienced clerk. Sometimes they constituted a kind of supererogatory task for some professor whose schedule was not heavy and whose salary might by this device be increased. The next stage in the evolution of the office shows it as a large clerical undertaking demanding the full time of a trained man and several assistants.[5]

With startling rapidity, the basic *functions* of the registrar (maintaining lists of students and their academic progress) coalesced into the *position* registrar. McGrath notes that in the early to mid-1800s most registrars also had instructional responsibilities (or perhaps more accurately, some faculty also had registrar responsibilities); by 1933, "only" 21 percent of registrars still had teaching duties. Presently, that dual role is functionally nonexistent. It now resides solely in the hands of professional administrators known as registrars.

Factors in the Rise of the Professional Administrator

In the following subsections, we discuss the factors behind the rise of the professional administrator. It is vitally important to understand the implications of this expansive and expanding profession before we discuss its implications for the soul of the university. Primarily so, since the forces that gave rise to its present form are often indicted for their role in the fragmentation of the university's soul.

Although the factors behind the rise of the professional university administrator are manifold, we suggest four important drivers: the advent of rationalism and scientific principles applied to management and then to higher education, the massive expansion of higher education access in the Progressive Era, a resulting increase and increasing perception that students needed to be understood and sorted, and the rise of governmental intervention requiring mechanisms for collecting and reporting institutional data. In each case social, economic, cultural, and demographic forces beyond the control of higher education pressed colleges and universities to keep pace with changing environmental demands, often resulting in conflicting ideals related to the scope, purpose, and oversight of higher education.

Applying scientific principles to management. The age of scientific empiricism bore many progeny, all carrying a strong family resemblance. Empiricism is a philosophy of science that emphasizes the importance of systematic evidence gathering and analysis, particularly through observation and testing. Within academia, the various branches of natural and physical sciences were among the firstborn of this perspective. Soon after, scholars applied principles of rationalism and scientific inquiry to human social systems, resulting in the fields (or modifications to the fields) of sociology, psychology, and more importantly to this discussion, organizational management.[6] By the mid-1930s, industrialists clamored for organizational processes that mimicked the production processes that had made manufacturing so successful. Dexter S. Kimball, dean of engineering at Cornell University and a leader in industrial management, noted that "the extension of the principles of standardization to the human element in production is a most important and growing field of activity."[7]

Fredrick W. Taylor was among the first to apply scientific principles to business management. By the early 1900s his work on time and motion efficiency in business and industry had become widely influential.[8] One of Taylor's protégés, Morris L. Cooke, collaborated with the newly established Carnegie Foundation on a study of eight higher education institutions. His findings, published in 1910 under the title *Academic and Industrial Efficiency*, were both of and ahead of their times.[9] Educational researcher William H. Cowley noted in 1937, "Management engineering did not strongly influence most administrators, however, until the 1930s; and at many institutions, it has still to pass beyond the elementary stage."[10] Cooke's volume nevertheless initiated academic awareness of the concept of functional organization. Cooke identified three areas for focus and improvement: *functional organization* (identifying and separating roles and associated tasks), *efficiency* (maximizing resources and processes), and *operational research* (gathering internal performance and process data). College and university leaders heeded this call and responded with new positions and institutional functions. At Cornell University's opening, President Andrew Dickson White appointed a vice president and several associate positions. As previously mentioned, Charles Eliot appointed the nation's first undergraduate deanship.[11] All three of these areas (functional organization, efficiency, and operational research) have since developed into clear and central concerns of university operation today.

In each case, the increased mandate for data generation, analysis, and adjustment was paralleled by an increasing expectation of training specific to the office and function. The result of this and other regularization efforts was the diffusion and specialization of university administration.[12] *Diffusion* describes the distribution of responsibilities among an increasing number of administrators. *Specialization* refers to the necessity of specific knowledge linked to related subsystems, such as the aforementioned office of the registrar. The combined effect was an expansion of university administration and administrative requirements that ushered in an era of professional expectation and ushered out an era of collegiate presidential provincialism. As C. H. Judd explained in a 1924 address:

> Our higher institutions of learning have moved steadily in their recent evolution in the direction of decentralization of administration. This is a natural consequence of the specialization which is characteristic of modern times and of the rapid increase in the size of universities and colleges. There is little or nothing left today of the old-fashioned type of personal administration about which one reads in the records of the college of two generations ago where the president was a kind of patriarchal overlord with full knowledge of the student body and of the personal traits and academic doing of each of the members of the faculty.[13]

And yet institutional leaders in the early twentieth century understood that theirs was an industry that also resisted the full application of regularization. Unlike the factories and mills down the hill where mechanization and efficiency techniques turned raw materials into measurable products, "the university could not aspire to tight functional integration."[14] Management, in the sense that other industries used it, was not fully available since education is a doggedly inefficient enterprise and highly resistant to solutions of increased scale and directive oversight popular at the time. Bureaucratic administration was the necessary compromise. Thus rationalism and scientific empiricism provided at least the basic foundation for a new kind of university, but the turn of the twentieth-century enrollment boom provided additional urgency to the university's development.

Enrollment expansion. American institutions of higher education, no matter how grand in current form, typically emerged from humble beginnings on the wobbly legs of inadequate funding, modest physical plants, and minimal instructional faculty. Even Harvard University began as a wilderness outpost housed in a single structure at its founding in 1636.[15] Nationally, higher education proliferated considerably in enrollment and number of institutions through the 1800s, yet the total number of college-going students remained proportionally small: by the 1870 school year, institutions averaged 211 students.[16] Only 63,000 students were attending higher education institutions, amounting to about 1 percent of the population.[17] Even by the 1880s many institutions now recognized as flagship universities were modest enterprises: Maine College of Agriculture and Mechanic Arts (now University of Maine) had nearly 100 students; the Ohio State University (375), University of North Carolina, Chapel Hill (405), and the University of Illinois (833 students) were all below one thousand full-time matriculates.[18]

Driven in part by immigration and rising population rates, the increased opportunity for professional training afforded by the Morrill Acts, and the increasing cultural interest in postsecondary collegiate life, college-going numbers rose dramatically after the turn of the twentieth century. In the first decade of the new century, enrollment rose by 50 percent, by another 68 percent in the decade that followed, and through the 1920s jumped again by a dramatic 84 percent.[19] In the 1926–1927 school year the total student population first exceeded one million enrollees. With this rapid growth in enrollment numbers came a parallel rise in the number of professional (noninstructional) staff. Snyder notes that "the ratio of students to staff has remained remarkably stable for more than 100 years. In 1869–70 there were 11 students for every professional, and in 1989–1990, there were 9 students for every professional."[20]

New ideas about how to manage organizations were thus fueled by the opportunity and necessity of rapid enrollment growth. However, the students that made up this enrollment spike were not the same sort of students that had filled the rolls and halls the centuries before. Rather than legacies, new matriculates were more likely to be first-generation students with little or no anticipatory socialization to the norms of collegiate life.[21] That difference, and attempts to understand and manage that difference, also fed the perceived necessity for an increasing number and variety of professional staff. Historian John Thelin notes that even at institutions that decided to limit enrollment severely, college presidents were still left with the growing problem of an "unruly, autonomous student culture."[22] Both student culture and general lack of oversight would be remedied through heavy doses of administrative oversight.

The result at most colleges after 1900 was an expansion of the administrative bureaucracy to include a growing number of deans and assistant deans whose main responsibility was policing student conduct. At the larger universities, mutual avoidance had increased the gulf between students and faculty. Into that void entered the new student-affairs officials who acted as both mediators and enforcers.[23]

However, for this new university employment segment to fully blossom from mere conduct enforcers to respected administrative professionals a shift was required in thinking about students and how to approach their peculiar behavior.

The rise of college student psychology. Prior to World War I, psychologists had begun performing basic experiments on college students, focusing on a wide and eclectic range of aptitudes and abilities such as suggestibility, memory span, color naming, and endurance grip.[24] Although primitive and at times marginally scientific, these early attempts to sort and categorize students provided evidence that students and their universities could benefit from systematic testing. At the University of Texas–Austin psychologists correlated students' grades to their performance on such tests, with an attempt to "throw light on the differences in the intellectual capacity among" them.[25]

Although the advent of World War I temporarily depressed college enrollments, this event was a boon for the emerging testing movement. The military was at first reluctant to embrace the tools of psychology as a mechanism for sorting and training soldiers. However, pioneers of psychological testing and training such as Walter Dill Scott, later president of Northwestern University and the American Psychological Association, were able to demonstrate the utility of their methods. Intelligence tests, such as the Stanford-Binet Scale, also grew in popularity and sophistication thanks to the ready subjects the war effort provided.[26]

In the 1920s the postwar enrollment boom pressed colleges and universities to seek out new means for selecting the most able students and aiding those selected by identifying areas of deficiency. The Stanford-Binet Scale and early SAT tests were adapted for collegiate admissions purposes.[27] From this data collection, administrators soon concluded that proactive and coordinated efforts were necessary to ameliorate collegiate transition, socialization, and academic preparedness issues. At the University of Rochester, a newly instituted "Week of Instruction" included "a preliminary series of lectures, banquets, and examinations . . . [including] the Columbia psychological tests . . . and an examination covering the work of the week."[28] In 1923, newly installed University of Maine president Clarence Cook Little informed parents that his innovative new Freshman Week program aimed to "provid[e] an opportunity, before the rush of the returning upperclassmen starts, to study carefully the individual problems of freshmen and to assist in estimating their ability to meet the responsibilities and difficulties of college life."[29] The importance of innovations like Freshman Week lay not only in growing assumptions of institutional responsibility for student success but also in the union of psychological sciences and organizational management that flowered into an entire new subgenre of administrative professionals: the student personnel movement.

By the early 1930s, insights from the SAT and other scholastic entrance exams coalesced with emerging concerns about student retention and persistence to motivate institutional leaders to consider new forms of intervention and, with them, new administrative types. Two particular innovations drew disparate roles into a shared professional identity: the establishment of student personnel offices (forerunner of today's office of student affairs) and the articulation of an ethos for this nascent profession in the form of the previously described *Student Personnel Point of View*. Then president of Northwestern University Walter Dill Scott hired former associate L. B. Hopkins to head the first student personnel office in the early 1920s.[30] The primary function of the personnel office was to establish a detailed psychological record of each student using data gathered through annual interviews and to catalog all students based on their psychological profile. The aim, as he conveyed to the students in a speech in 1923, was for students to maximize their talents: "I don't expect that all of you will make grand opera singers; I don't assume that all of you can run one hundred yards in ten seconds. I do expect that there are some things that each of you can do better than you can do other things. We want to help you find out what things you can do best."[31]

Although student personnel work would gradually gain momentum, it was not until the American Council on Education adopted its cause and convened a series of conferences and standing committees to explore further the application of testing and sorting that national interest was engaged.[32] It was through the work of one of these subcommittees, the Committee on Student Personnel Work, that the *Student Personnel Point of View* (or *SPPV*), the defining document of the profession, was published in 1937. The *SPPV*, updated and expanded in 1949 and again in 1987, describes the profession as concerned about students as "whole persons" and "defines the role of student affairs as the delivery of services enhancing educational experiences of college students."[33]

Today this "delivery of services" and the concurrent trend toward colleges using appurtenances such as lavish exercise facilities, branded dining services, and apartment-style housing to lure talented and full-paying students have contributed to the escalating share of student-services costs, even in a down economy. For example, between 2004 and 2014, student-services spending increased 16.4 percent at public research universities and an incredible 29.8 percent at private research universities, the highest increase of any category and far higher than instructional spending (which increased by 4.4 percent and 18.7 percent, respectively).[34] Student affairs administration represents only one type of institutional reaction to the expansion of student enrollment and institutional purpose. Offices of admissions, financial aid, institutional research, and academic support services, in addition to libraries, medical centers, and many other functions, have stretched the boundaries of higher education to include an incredible variety of services and functions almost unimaginable even a century ago.

Nevertheless, the importance of this branch of university administration and its emergent professional self-consciousness in the context of this book is what it represented in terms of the shifting ideals and purpose of higher education. In an era when moral authority was removed from (or in some cases rejected by) the faculty, students' moral and religious development was relegated to the cocurriculum.[35] The *SPPV* noted that the collegiate years were often a time when students became detached from the religious moorings of their youth. Naturally, then, the student personnel worker (as they were then known), equipped with the latest empirical psychological tools, would be a ready guide. However, psychometrics (testing, but also theories of development) disguised preferences for types of student being and purpose in objective and apparent value-free language. As we discussed in chapter eight, underlying values of scientific objectivity and democratic liberalism influenced perceived ideal student outcomes. The nature of the guidance they were to provide as neutral, scientifically equipped counselors was not at all clear.

Government intervention. The story of the rise and proliferation of student affairs professionals highlights the reactionary nature of postsecondary education. Applications of psychological testing, organizational management, and precollege preparation interventions were all primarily motivated by environmental changes and innovations that were adapted internally but originated externally to the university. Yet of these environmental influences, one of the most pronounced over the past century has been the increasing impact of government legislation, funding, regulation, and intervention at state and federal levels. Some of the federal government's most notable and influential higher education policies were not developed with the advancement of colleges and universities as the primary goal. The Morrill Acts (1862, 1890) were designed as means for the federal government to divest itself of thousands of acres of Western land, protecting them from speculators and others who would exploit an open market sale.[36] The solution—to distribute "land grants" to the states and earmark either the land use or the proceeds from land sales for public universities—functionally created a new category of institution: the land-grant university. Mechanical arts, agriculture, cadet training, and the liberal arts were all specified curricular targets of the Morrill Acts.

American higher education also benefited from the surge of returning World War II servicemen. Once again the benefit was a latent one, not directly intended to produce the expansion of services and infrastructure that resulted. Faced with the daunting transition from a wartime to a peacetime economy and the challenge of employing millions of veterans returning to the workforce, Congress authorized the Servicemen's Readjustment Act.[37] Known more commonly as the GI Bill, this legislation provided generous financial aid and college choice opportunities in coordination with colleges and universities nationwide. Universities, in nature and organization, would be re-formed as a result. As Thelin notes, "The GI Bill demonstrated how a quantitative change—in student financial aid and in the number of newly

171

enrolled students—elicited a qualitative change in the character of 'going to college' and the American campus."[38] Historians primarily focus on how this landmark bill affected students, perceptions of access, and American society generally.[39] However, on the university side, the GI Bill required enrollment and financial tracking and reporting mechanisms on a scale not previously seen, which created an additional impetus for upscaled student services. National historical data on the higher education workforce bears this out: between 1934 and 1941, the number of professional, noninstructional staff grew by an average of nearly 11,000 employees each year (from 108,873 to 151,980). In the five years following the authorization of the GI Bill, that average jumped to 40,939—a nearly fourfold increase (from 165,324 to 246,772).[40]

A similar proliferation of reporting, data gathering, compliance assurance, and other roles followed subsequent legislation. By contrast, much of it was aimed directly at supporting or redirecting the focus of or access to higher education. These injunctions included the National Defense Education Act of 1958 (which provided research funding to bolster math, science, and technical education), the Higher Education Act of 1965 (which established federal financial assistance for students through the Pell Grant program), and Title IX of the Education Amendments of 1972 (which established equal access to programs and activities, including athletics, regardless of sex).[41] These legislative acts, and the financial resources tied to them, opened the way for unprecedented growth in enrollment and expansion in the variety of university services. These combined forces and influences significantly shaped the direction of university development and attention. As Kerr argues (or perhaps concedes),

> Universities are not directionless; they have been moving in clear directions and with considerable speed; there has been no "stalemate." But these directions have not been set as much by the university's visions of its destiny as by the external environment, including federal government, the foundations, the surrounding and sometimes engulfing industry. The university has been embraced and led down the garden path by its environmental suitors; it has been so attractive and so accommodating; who could resist and why would it, in turn, want to resist?[42]

172

As research universities were increasingly transfixed by the siren's song of additional institutional resources and prestige, one of the byproducts of access to federal research and student aid funding was the accompanying role, expansion, and proliferation of administrative specialists. The cost of administrative expansion, however, might not have been the only price paid.

The Purpose of the Professional Administrator

Thus far we have identified the origins, roles, and purposes of postsecondary administrators and largely resisted the implications of this expansive and expanding profession for the soul of the university. We have argued, implicitly and explicitly, that the proliferation of professional administrators in higher education is the product of a range of historical, contextual, environmental, and conceptual shifts through which universities became huge unwieldy enterprises—what Clark Kerr called "multiversities"—less a coherent set of functions aimed at a common purpose than a loose assemblage of enterprises united under a common mascot.[43] In this sense, analogies for higher education might cast it not as a ship without a rudder but as a patch of flotsam related only in proximity and condition but lacking any essential purpose beyond accumulating size and environmental impact.

As in our prior argument, the study of theology, while treated as a specialization and set aside as a pursuit only a few undertook, previously served the university by providing a unifying identity, purpose, and narrative.[44] More specifically to the topic at hand, one effect of this absence of a unifying purpose is that support systems for higher learning threaten to become, functionally, their own self-serving purpose. Higher education historian Laurence Veysey argues this very point, noting how the mechanisms that developed to keep the university running over time also became the glue that held it together in the absence of larger telos.

> Bureaucratic administration was the structural device which made possible the new epoch of institutional empire-building without recourse to specific shared values. . . . Techniques of control shifted from the sermon and the direct threat of punishment toward the more appropriate devices of conference, memorandum, and filing system. . . . Bureaucratic codes of conduct served as a low but tolerable common denominator, linking individuals and

factions who did not think in the same terms but who, unlike students of the 1860s, were usually too polite to require threats.[45]

The great irony of the rhetoric that administrators are meddling obstructionist managers of other people's creative works is that administration has often simply accommodated the demands of faculty and valued constituents, developing new policies, functions, and areas of expertise to support the pursuit of research dollars and picky prospective students.

Nowhere is this development clearer than in the murky world of technology transfer (which is university speak for turning the intellectual creations of faculty into marketable products). In her book *University, Inc.* Jennifer Washburn explores research universities' increasing emphasis on revenue streams generated from corporate funding and patents developed in faculty laboratories.[46] The result is that the rush to capitalize on new discoveries and inventions has severely restricted the circulation of new knowledge in what Washburn refers to as "the disappearance of the knowledge commons."[47] Her examples of absurd court cases, such as a patent infringement suit through which a faculty member was barred from using his own inventions, highlights a system ruled by profit and uninterested in justice.[48] In something of a turn, however, she concludes:

> It would be too easy to blame the employees who toil away inside these university tech-transfer offices for this seemingly irrational behavior. Yet, to a large, extent, they are merely responding to the financial incentives and imperatives coming from other, more powerful quarters. For in recent years, nearly every university president, dean, or provost has felt enormous pressure from federal legislators, state governors, and regents to turn his or her institution into an engine of economic growth, capable of spawning the next Silicon Valley.

To look on administration, then, one is reminded of the concluding moment in the third act of Charles Dickens's *A Christmas Carol*, when the otherwise jolly specter of Christmas Present pulls back his robes to reveal "two children; wretched, abject, frightful, hideous, miserable." The spirit names them "Ignorance" and "Want" and instructs Scrooge, "Beware them both, and all of their degree!"[49] The point, of course, is not that administrators are quite so unpleasant to behold, but that we ascribe to them, often symbolically, all that we sense is wrong with an enterprise that seems also to be so noble. Like the Ghost of Christmas Present, universities project a benevolent, approachable mien, wrapped in the nostalgic aura of homecoming parades, students reclining on the quad, and fatherly or motherly faculty members who always have a spare moment to talk. Similarly, the truth of what lies beneath this guise may seem repulsive, even as it did to unsuspecting Ebenezer. Yet once the shock of the reveal passes, what meaning we should make of what has been exposed, and what action we should take in response, are the key questions.

Administrators are a convenient scapegoat for widespread frustration with the lack of defining identity, story, purpose, moral vision, and meaningful presence in the world that the university could be. Often higher education critics express these sentiments as they pine for a simpler time—a time when colleges were primarily faculty, students, and a benevolent old president, more father figure than administrator. Or we look back further: to the university of the Middle Ages, to the age of the free republic of scholars who gathered students not to credential, but to *learn*. As we argued in chapter one, however, this version of history is likely a mirage.

In one of his final books, W. H. Cowley systematically disavows the notion that postsecondary education flourished without administrative intervention.[50] Cowley observes that external oversight was and is a fact—and a necessary part—of university life and not an imposition of the modern age. Furthermore, he argues, there was never a time when the university flourished in its absence.

> The medieval universities, at various times in their history, found themselves beholden either to the students, the Church, or the monarchy. Professors in English universities, when they finally did manage to attain autonomy, found that it led to a deterioration of their institutions so serious as to warrant government intervention. German professors owed their appointments to the ministry of education and thus remained limited in their autonomy from that source. In short, "the free republic of scholars" has seldom existed; and when it has, as in England before 1850, it has needed the help of outside forces to counteract the deterioration that ensued.[51]

Taken in this light, the professional administrator is not primarily an external imposition, nor even a necessary evil. Rather, he or she is an organizational fact and necessity, but one that might still reflect and magnify some of the university's tendencies toward control, excess, manipulation, and institutional narcissism that are not among its more flattering attributes. The more helpful question and positive one that Cowley's injunction suggests is this: What does the professional administrator look like as a positive force in university life? Or more to the point of this book (and less to Cowley's): If the professional administrator is an integral and necessary part of an institution fragmented by sin, what is his or her role in proclaiming and bringing about its redemption and the nourishing of its soul? Furthermore, if this era of specialization and particularization has a virtue, it might be that interdependence replaces independence in the multiversity.

A redemptive view of this development might frame this almost extreme division of labor in terms of expressions of singular expertise and excellence coinhered through a shared vision of instruction for kingdom citizenship. In this regard, the Pauline analogy of the body of Christ that we use throughout this book reminds us that the kingdom is not a system of homogeny, but heterogeneity, where the eye, the hand, the foot, and other parts recognize and celebrate their interdependence. Chapter sixteen will outline a vision of academic leadership that seeks to embody this vision.

10

THE MULTIVERSITY'S RELIGION

The Unifying and Fragmenting Force of Athletics

...

*But what could have made them so numb and callous?
How could they have not been seized by revulsion after hearing
the reports of what was happening? How could they have not felt
a desire to expunge this from their athletic system?*

DAVID BROOKS

*Football will never again be placed ahead of educating,
nurturing, and protecting young people.*

MARK EMMERT

IN THE SPRING OF 2002, a set of email exchanges were put into motion that would eventually shake Pennsylvania State University to its core. Football coach Joe Paterno, athletic director Tim Curley, senior vice president for finance and business Gary Schultz, and president Graham Spanier were trying to determine how best to proceed in relation to a long-standing challenge with former defensive coordinator Jerry Sandusky. The mastermind behind Penn State's "Bend, Don't Break" defense and the one who cultivated its identity as "Linebacker U," Sandusky, along with his former boss in Paterno, had carved out an iconic place in the history of college football.

Perhaps Sandusky's crowning achievement came in a Fiesta Bowl game that decided the 1986 national championship. The University of Miami Hurricanes featured a list of All-Americans so deep that a team of comparable talent may never be seen again. Led by Heisman Trophy winner Vinnie Testaverde, the Hurricanes ran through opponents in ways comparable to a category-five rendition of their mascot.

Garnering a comparable measure of public attention to their on-field performance was the off-the-field behavior of Hurricane players. That season alone, "Miami players [were] accused of everything from shoplifting to assault to credit-card fraud to packing a pistol on campus."[1] Perhaps the defining pregame moment for that year's Fiesta Bowl happened

> when the Miami players arrived in Tempe [and] shocked everyone by getting off the plane dressed in combat fatigues. When asked about it, team leader Jerome Brown said, "This is war." Head coach Jimmy Johnson told the *Phoenix Gazette*, "That was a great idea. I wish I had thought of it."[2]

The contrasting image of Paterno and Sandusky's Nittany Lions as a team that not only played by the rules but also defined them made the seven-point underdogs the national favorite.

The game, however, was closer than oddsmakers had predicted. With eighteen seconds left, Sandusky's "Bend, Don't Break" defense found itself backed into a fourth-and-goal situation with the nation's leading offense on the Nittany Lion thirteen. Testaverde would drop back, throw over the middle to a receiver at the goal line, only to be intercepted by the very personification of "Linebacker U," Shane Conlan, who ran the ball back to his own twelve before dropping to his knees. Twelve seconds later, the Nittany Lions defeated the mighty Hurricanes and captured their second national championship.

Fifteen years later, Penn State found itself facing a very different enemy—itself. Rumors had quietly echoed for years that Sandusky, the coach who had left his position at Penn State to work full time with a charity he started that worked to meet the needs of at-risk children, was sexually violating many of the young men his organization was charged with protecting. Some of this predatory behavior reportedly even occurred in the locker room at

Penn State's football building when Sandusky would bring children to campus for visits.

Instead of notifying law enforcement or child protective services, Penn State administrators, led by Spanier, decided that a "humane and a reasonable way to proceed"[3] was to encourage Sandusky to get help. In emails dating from that spring, Spanier then went on to acknowledge that the downside in such a plan was the possibility that Sandusky might not accept that encouragement, and thus the university might be left vulnerable for not having reported these crimes. However, Spanier also concluded such a risk "can be assessed down the road."[4]

Approximately nine and a half years after those emails were exchanged, that road came to an end. Jerry Sandusky was arrested on November 11, 2011, and charged with fifty-two counts of various forms of sexual abuse. Four charges were dropped, but Sandusky was later convicted on forty-five of the forty-eight remaining counts. He will spend the rest of his life in prison.

Spanier, Schultz, Curley, and Paterno were all fired by the university. Paterno had served as a coach at Penn State for sixty-two years, serving as head coach for forty-six of those years. In addition to leading the Nittany Lions to national championships in 1982 and 1986, Paterno led Penn State to five perfect seasons and won more games than any other football coach in the history of college football. Stripped of those accolades, Paterno died of cancer that January. Spanier, Curley, and Schultz were left to negotiate the legal system. The real tragedy, however, is the damage Sandusky did to the young men he abused over the course of those years.

Joining with David Brooks of the *New York Times*,[5] the American public was left to wonder how such behavior could be tolerated. No easy answers came—even after four years, an independent report, a documentary, several books, and countless articles. All we know with certainty is the Penn State football brand was deemed too valuable to the university to risk tarnishing in comparison to protecting children in the cross hairs of a sexual predator. Penn State is not alone in terms of finding itself the focus of such rightful scrutiny.

More recently, in May of 2016 one of the largest Christian research universities in the world received national headlines for all the wrong reasons.[6] Baylor University's board of regents fired the university's football coach, removed its president, and suspended its athletic director. The basis for these headline-grabbing actions was the failure of the university "to implement Title IX of the Education Amendments of 1972 (Title IX) and Violence against Women Reauthorization Act of 2013 (VAWA)."[7]

These scandals, we contend, stem not simply from people making bad decisions (although that is one element). They also spring from multiversities with fragmented souls. When university leaders subdivide the institution's parts it leaves intercollegiate athletics "free" to pursue excellence on a bigger and more prominent national stage. Yet it also leaves athletics susceptible to becoming disconnected from the larger identity, story, and purposes of the university. Ironically, universities have now become slaves to their athletic programs, which are seen as indispensable to the university's reputation and thriving. Brands such as Penn State or Baylor football are deemed as critical to a university's success. However, athletic departments, like academic departments, can become fiefdoms unto themselves. Such university cultures allow the independent fiefdoms that the fragmented soul of the university produces to take on a life of their own. These fiefdoms become sources of quasi-religious sagas that attempt to dominate, and thus undermine, other parts of the multiversity. In the cases above, athletics undermined the moral and academic soul of the university.

Overall, the move to give athletic departments quasi-independent status separates them from significant academic and moral forms of accountability, not to mention the educational practices of cocurricular educators who focus on developing the whole person. One finds evidence of this fragmentation in the summary of findings relayed by the Baylor board of regents regarding the football program and its overall disciplinary processes. Instead of integrating athletics into the various parts of the university, the football program became an island unto itself. The report noted:

> Athletics personnel failed to recognize the conflict of interest in roles and risk to campus safety by insulating athletes from student conduct processes. Football coaches and staff took affirmative steps to maintain internal control over discipline of players and to actively divert cases from the student conduct or criminal processes. In some cases, football coaches and staff had inappropriate involvement in disciplinary and criminal matters or engaged in improper conduct that reinforced an overall perception that

football was above the rules, and that there was no culture of accountability for misconduct.[8]

Overall, the football program and its disciplinary processes had been fragmented from the rest of the university. The result for the approach to discipline was problematic and unsurprising.

> The football program also operates an internal system of discipline, separate from University processes. . . . The ad hoc internal system of discipline lacks protocols for consistency with University policy and is wholly undocumented. The football program's separate system of internal discipline reinforces the perception that rules applicable to other students are not applicable to football players, improperly insulates football players from appropriate disciplinary consequences, and puts students, the program, and the institution at risk of future misconduct.[9]

Most importantly, in multiversities with fragmented souls, athletics become disconnected from any larger story that gives insight into and guides leaders' views of human and communal flourishing.

Consequently university leadership often fails to provide guidance to student-athletes about how to pursue excellence beyond athletics or how to arrange one's loves in a way that does not prioritize the student's athletic identity. Indeed, athletics is probably the best example of a substitute religion in today's contemporary university. Football games, in particular, become the place where the whole university community comes together to "worship" and to rail against false gods (the weekly opponent). This chapter explores the role intercollegiate athletics played and continues to play in fragmenting the university and also, ironically, providing a substitute form of limited identity, narrative, and coherence—in other words it attempts to supply the university with a fragmented portion of soul.

The impetus for our focus on football in this chapter to the exclusion of the many other intercollegiate sports is twofold: first, college football operates on a larger scale as defined by almost any measure—number of players, number of fans, size of facilities, volume of revenue—than any other intercollegiate sport. Men's college basketball ranks second in terms of several of those measures. However, the recent spate of conference realignments and the breakup of powerful basketball conferences proved which sport was first and which was second.

Second, college football was first to capture the interests of collegians on a large scale. Schools started playing football as well as baseball shortly after the Civil War. However, football far outpaced baseball in terms of the interests of the media and fans. In addition, challenges plaguing the game of football, as we will see, led to the formation of the National Collegiate Athletic Association (NCAA).[10] As a result, the history of intercollegiate athletics is arguably tied more to the history of football than any other sport.[11]

What follows is an overview of how successive waves of media interest in football (and what we now refer to as big-time football or football played by the "Power Five" conferences) fostered the need for reforms that, to date, have proved incapable of even slowing the fragmentation of college athletics from the university at the same time that athletics takes its place as the new religion on campus.

For the sake of full disclosure, perhaps it is best before moving forward to also note that one of us is a Penn State graduate, and all three of us have professional affiliations with Baylor—two as tenured faculty members and one as a research fellow. Our hearts first and foremost go out to the victims of these tragic occurrences. The future health of these two institutions is, albeit secondary, of vital concern to us.

The Origins of Collegiate Athletic Power

As previously mentioned, a number of colleges and universities began playing a game that would eventually become what we formally refer to as football shortly after the Civil War. However, the impetus behind the game's advance into the public consciousness rests with three members of what would become the Ivy League in Harvard University, Yale University, and Princeton University. As the twentieth century approached, the game drew crowds of ten thousand, twenty thousand, thirty thousand, and more. Ronald A. Smith notes that with a capacity of 30,323, Harvard's "building of the first reinforced concrete stadium in 1903 indicated that the commercialized form of football was likely to be a permanent fixture of colleges in America."[12] In response, on November 21, 1914, Yale University opened its Yale Bowl for a game against Harvard with a capacity approaching seventy thousand.

Drawn to the events taking place in these massive structures, Smith goes on to note, "College athletics were covered intently by both newspapers and by periodicals of the time."[13] As the game progressed during that era, what began to garner the greatest amount of attention were the mounting injuries to players, many proving fatal. Such injuries were "not freak accidents as much as the inevitable toll of an activity that encouraged strong men to crash into each other, again and again, over the course of a long afternoon."[14] In fact, 1905 may just be the watershed year in terms of concern over those injuries, as "eighteen men died on college and high school gridirons."[15]

A debate emerged between two groups, Progressive Era activists and reformers, who argued about the future of the game. Activists believed the current state of the game ran contrary to the ideals defining a university, and many even sought to bring the game to an end. Although his university nurtured the game in its earliest years, Harvard's Charles Eliot was a leading activist, saying that "the game had become too risky and the public no longer believed that coaches could fix the problem."[16] In addition, Eliot believed "the public was part of the problem" as he compared them to crowds drawn to other events hosting gratuitous violence such as prizefights, cockfights, bullfights, and even matches between Roman gladiators.

In contrast, "Reformers typically hoped to remove the taint of commercialism without eliminating strenuous college sport."[17] A number of college presidents such as Stanford University's David Starr Jordan and the University of Chicago's William Rainey Harper headed this group along with the bully pulpit of a sitting United States president, Theodore Roosevelt. Although historians disagree over the significance of the president's role, John J. Miller goes so far as to argue, "It is possible to believe that without his presidential intervention, football might not even exist today."[18]

Others credit Roosevelt with creating contexts for conversations that led to more formal discussions about needed rules and the eventual rise of the Intercollegiate Athletic Association of the United States, or what we know today as the NCAA. In contrast to its present identity as a regulatory organization, the NCAA emerged as an organization "within which they [college officials] could meet, draw up standard rules, and contemplate how to increase their growing influence."[19] The early history of the formation of the NCAA reveals that allusions to a "Golden Era" for the game are simply not true. As Brian M. Ingrassia notes, "Big-time athletics represented modern universities' flawed attempt to maintain a connection to the public in an era of intellectual fragmentation and isolation."[20]

An important part of that connection to the public involved the media. Unlike other aspects of collegiate life, the media and the public invested in college athletics from the very beginning, pulling the game away from the university that brought it into existence. In other words, the media became a major influence behind fragmenting this portion of the university's soul. Although references to the media in relation to this period of time are limited to print media such as newspapers and magazines, individuals populating the electronic age should not underestimate the influence of these publications. Referring to the 1890s, Michael Oriard argued that "both the quantity and the quality of the football coverage in the daily papers in New York, Philadelphia, and Boston were staggering: front-page, full-page, several-page accounts of the big games, accompanied by sometimes dozens of often sensationalistic illustrations."[21] The period of time college football took to go from a mere campus matter to a public spectacle was short to say the least. Newspaper coverage of games was initially local in nature. Papers in Boston would, at most, cover games taking place between schools in New England. Rarely did the press in New York and Philadelphia reach beyond the mid-Atlantic states. These publications fed the American appetite for college football, and as time passed that appetite spread beyond those particular regions. As a result, "The late nineteenth-century daily newspaper 'created' college football to an even greater degree, transforming an extracurricular activity into a national spectacle."[22]

The point at which the influence of print media in relation to college football may have reached its peak was between 1919 and 1930. During that period, one that spanned the close of World War I and the outbreak of the Great Depression, the American public encountered an unprecedented rise in both personal income and leisure time. A wider culture of sports and college football, in particular, met rising demand. In *Heroes and Ballyhoo: How the Golden Age of the 1920s Transformed America*, Michael

K. Bohn argues that this "era profoundly affected individual sports and established today's enormous sports entertainment industry. The period was not about games; it was a cornerstone of modern American life."[23] Driving this industry in many ways were the individuals covering the football games and bringing them to life for ever-expanding sectors of the American public.

The most prominent example was Grantland Rice, "considered by many to be the greatest sportswriter of all time."[24] Rice penned some of the most iconic words in the history of college football in relation to a then little-known university in South Bend, Indiana. Unable to secure a consistent schedule of games with the region's Big Ten institutions due to anti-Catholic bias, the University of Notre Dame, first under Jesse Haper and then under Knute Rockne, took it upon itself to play whatever football powers were willing to play them. Forming what is arguably the first great cross-sectional rivalry in college football, however, the United States Military Academy accepted Notre Dame's challenge.

After Notre Dame's 1914 visit to New York and its 13-7 win over Army, Rice would write those iconic words in the October 18, 1914, edition of the *New York Herald Tribune*.

> Outlined against a blue-gray October sky, the Four Horsemen rode again. In dramatic lore they are known as Famine, Pestilence, Destruction and Death. These are only aliases. Their real names are Stuhldreher, Miller, Crowley and Layden. They formed the crest of the South Bend cyclone before which another fighting Army football team was swept over the precipice at the Polo Grounds yesterday afternoon as 55,000 spectators peered down on the bewildering panorama spread on the green plain below.[25]

Referring to Rice's article concerning the Four Horsemen of Notre Dame, Allen Barra of the *New York Times* argued in 1999, "In a few swift, polished sentences—and with an assist from a photograph—Rice changed his own life, his profession, the course of college football and the character of American leisure culture."[26] A photograph taken by a Notre Dame student back in South Bend shortly after the team returned by train from New York shows Stuhldreher, Miller, Crowley, and Layden straddling horses, helmets donned, and pigskins tucked under their arms. The power of those words and the accompanying image contributed to the generation of a football power in South Bend comparable to the full force of the conference that once shunned them.

Most universities came to develop an addiction to such press coverage, and Notre Dame's appreciation for such interest is perhaps most accurately described as a love/hate relationship. The coverage brought attention to the university and gave America's marginalized Catholic population a team for which they could cheer. As Murray Sperber notes in *Shake Down the Thunder: The Creation of Notre Dame Football*, university leaders also became concerned with the possibility that such pressure could undermine not only the academic character of the university but also its Catholic character. Other university leaders also "thought that mania about sports distorted people's values, mistakenly convincing students, alumni, and the public that the most important thing about a university was a winning football team."[27]

Failed Attempts to Rein in Athletics

One school, an early member of the Big Ten, simply turned its back on the rising interest in its football program.[28] Under the leadership of Robert Maynard Hutchins, the University of Chicago, earlier a voice for reform during the tenure of William Rainey Harper, recalibrated its relationship with football.[29] Such a decision came with an appreciable price as the coaching efforts of Amos Alonzo Stagg once made the Maroons one of college football's powerhouses. Hutchins, unlike his predecessor, believed football was contributing to an already rapidly fragmenting university. Fortunately for Hutchins, the proximity of Notre Dame and Northwestern eclipsed the Maroons as the city of Chicago's top football attraction.[30] As a result, the gridiron Maroons were not as successful as in the past, and the ground for reform was thus softened.

Turning to one of the print media outlets that had done so much to generate interest in college football, Hutchins published "Gate Receipts and Glory" in the December 3, 1938, issue of the *Saturday Evening Post*. Toward the beginning of his piece, Hutchins offered:

> This [football] has been going on for almost fifty years. It is called "overemphasis on athletics," and everybody deplores it. It has been the subject of scores

of reports, all of them shocking. It has been held to be crass professionalism, all the more shameful because it masquerades as higher education.[31]

After laying out the challenges, Hutchins offered his recommendations for the public to consider, such as limiting admission costs to games and granting coaches academic tenure so that their expectations would be influenced by practices defining the work of other educators on campus.

Although Hutchins's recommendations had little influence beyond Hyde Park, one year later the University of Chicago decided to "develop an elaborate program of intramural football—the answer Hutchins would have given down the years if his fellow sports writers, when he told them that football would always be an integral part of the Chicago program, had thought to ask him, 'What kind of football?'"[32]

Milton Mayer, in *Robert Maynard Hutchins: A Memoir*, notes that when made, the announcement "was published on the front pages, not of the sports sections but of the news sections, across the country."[33] The economically driven interests of print media were a challenge from the very beginning for universities in relation to college football. Some leaders, such as Hutchins, labored to resist them, while others, however, simply embraced them.

Print media was also just the beginning, as electronic forms of communication such as radio and television were just around the historical corner. First to arrive was obviously radio, with the first broadcast of a football game airing on October 8, 1921, when "Backyard Brawl" rival West Virginia visited Pittsburgh. Ironically, most of the immediate concerns related to radio broadcasts of college football games revolved around whether such efforts would affect ticket sales. In particular, would people prefer to stay home and listen to a free radio broadcast rather than pay to attend the game in person? Part of the reason for this concern was that universities usually did not ask for compensation from radio broadcasting, as they viewed the publicity they received as an even trade. "Free publicity was appreciated, and it remained that way well into the 1930s."[34] Gate sales at the time were still the primary source of direct revenue.

That logic changed: "As the Depression wore on and income from college gate receipts decreased, however, colleges began to see radio broadcasting as a possible revenue source."[35] For example, "Yale broke tradition in a big way in 1936 by signing an agreement with the Atlantic Refining Company that provided the school with $20,000 for broadcasting its football games."[36] A number of individual schools then began to negotiate their own contracts.

Like print media, radio also came to be dominated by large-scale personalities. For example, Graham McNamee, a singer by training, launched his career by announcing baseball games on the radio. In fact, his career "was thrown into the limelight"[37] when he and Grantland Rice announced the 1923 World Series between the New York Yankees and the Giants. By 1925, McNamee was calling the major intersectional football rivalries of the day, including the Notre Dame/Army and Chicago/Penn games along with the Rose Bowl. Part of McNamee's success came in his ability not only to communicate the details of the game but also to do so by weaving those details into a larger narrative full of personalities that became larger than life to the listener. "According to Red Barber, later considered one of the great radio announcers, McNamee was the 'greatest.'"[38]

Perhaps one of McNamee's few rivals in capturing the interest of the public was Ted Husing. Twelve years younger than McNamee, Husing got into the radio business with RCA after serving in World War I and by lying that he was a college graduate and had studied music. He would call critical games such as the Cornell versus Penn game in 1925. "Husing's biggest break though came when he joined the Columbia Phonograph Broadcasting System (later CBS), which had been formed in September 1927."[39] Husing in particular was credited with what came to be known as an annunciator board. Roughly speaking, such a device "had been developed so that [an] assistant had a separate keyboard with numbers that corresponded to names on a glass board."[40] Husing could then call off players by name without having to take his eyes off of the field. As a result, Ronald A. Smith argued Husing proved to be an even more efficient commentator than McNamee.

Whatever concerns were raised with the pressure applied by the rise of radio, the rise of television, in contrast, was an absolute game changer. According to Keith Dunnavant,

> Television has dramatically multiplied the number of people who care about it [college football], significantly enlarged the role it plays in their lives, and harnessed the result of all that collective passion for the benefit of the networks [television] and colleges. Television has also simultaneously raised the

stakes, heightening the tension in the historic struggle between higher education and commerce.[41]

That heightened tension began on September 30, 1939, when Waynesburg College traveled to New York to play Fordham University in the first locally televised game.[42] On September 29, 1951, Duke University then traveled to Pittsburgh to play the University of Pittsburgh in the first nationally televised game.

The same concerns in relation to declines in attendance that were focused on radio broadcasts returned with the advent of television. However, the possible increase in revenue that came from signing television contracts proved too profitable to resist to schools with access to such opportunities. "For example, schools such as Notre Dame and Penn which signed contracts [in the early 1950s] to televise their games found that TV could provide a lucrative stream of revenue."[43]

The response to the challenge posed by television initially came from a long-standing but relatively silent presence in college athletics in the NCAA. Since its founding in the first decade of the twentieth century, the NCAA served as an arena for discussion concerning how college sports were to be played, such as the increasingly dangerous game of football.[44] Slowly but surely over the course of the ensuing fifty years, growing calls for reform compelled the NCAA to evolve its perception of the role it played in intercollegiate athletics from a discussion-oriented group to one focused on regulation. Perhaps the key moment in this change of identity came on the heels of World War II with the adoption of what came to be known as the Purity or Sanity Code. Calls for reform were primarily focused on growing challenges stemming from recruiting practices and subsidization. When the Sanity Code passed at the 1948 NCAA convention, "the NCAA was given the power to enforce an amateur code."[45]

With this newfound perception of its identity, the NCAA now viewed itself as the body responsible for determining the course its members would take in the new era of the television. Schools with their own television contracts such as Notre Dame and Penn were forced to break them.[46] Also concerned about gate receipts, the NCAA would set into motion regulations concerning blackouts (or the understanding that the broadcast of a game in a local market could be prohibited if it were not sold out by a designated time prior to kickoff) along with the number and nature of televised games. The lure of the exposure and the revenue television made possible never sat well with college football's most influential institutions, and efforts were made on various fronts to establish greater autonomy for the schools and/or conferences.

Admittedly glossing over a number of considerable details, the decisive blow to the role the NCAA played in regulating television came on June 27, 1984, in the form of the United States Supreme Court's ruling in the *NCAA v. the Board of Regents of the University of Oklahoma*. After the court found that the NCAA's efforts to regulate how football was broadcast were in violation of the Sherman Antitrust Act of 1890, schools and conferences were free to negotiate their own contracts.[47] This freedom came just in time to ride the wave that came with the present era of cable and satellite television.

For example, the Entertainment and Sports Programming Network, or ESPN, was launched in 1979. By the time the Supreme Court announced this decision five years later, ESPN was in a prime position to even go beyond its original intentions, as noted by its founder, Bill Rasmussen, to "contract with the NCAA to do 400 to 500 sporting events annually with at least one every day for a year. For 24 hours of sports, we've worked out a plan to charge the cable operators just a penny a day."[48] One year after those words were printed, Rasmussen and his colleagues were free, depending on the sport, to negotiate with the schools, the conferences, or the NCAA. The Bowl Championship Series and the College Football Playoff, in particular, worked to ESPN's advantage in ways Rasmussen could not have dreamed at that time.[49]

Like the prior forms of media, television came with its own cast of personalities that created larger-than-life portraits of the drama that was college football for an ever-increasingly large viewing public. While print media had Grantland Rice and radio had Graham McNamee and Ted Husing, television's Keith Jackson arguably had no rival. A native of rural Georgia, Jackson "became the individual most closely identified with college football broadcasting."[50] Part of his enduring appeal came via his unique ability to weave the details of the game into a battery of folksy phrases such as his patented "Whoa, Nellie!" He thus made audience members feel as if he were just one of the gang, hanging out in their living rooms with them. In many ways, determining whether Keith Jackson was responsible for the rise of college football or college football was responsible for the rise of Keith Jackson is difficult at best. Regardless, his voice proved synonymous with the increasing demand for the televised version of the game. Overall, personalities such as Rice, McNamee, and Jackson become the preachers and priests of the new religion presented every weekend to the growing masses of university alumni hungry for good news from their alma mater.

Preserving Academic Excellence

As demand increased, a small but influential number of schools collectively decided to withdraw from participating in big-time college football with the advent of the televised age. Prior to the 1950s, the Ivy League was simply a loose reference to a group of historically influential educational institutions in the Northeast. However, in 1945 the presidents of Harvard University, Yale University, Princeton University, Dartmouth College, Brown University, Columbia University, Cornell University, and the University of Pennsylvania set in motion a decision that would not only constitute the formal establishment of the Ivy League as an athletic conference but also seek to protect the core educational practices of their institutions from the influence of ever-widening cycles of economically driven media interests. In essence, this group of presidents saw a fork in the road approaching: one path led toward the power of television, but they took a very different direction.

An understanding among the universities was reached in 1954 and then implemented in 1956. Among the details was a commitment that each school would play one another each year, athletes would receive no subsidization as a result of participation in a particular sport, and athletes would come through the standard admission process available to all students. John Sayle Watterson notes, "Viewed from one perspective, the Ivy League represented the most dramatic example of de-emphasis in college football's history— eight schools that agreed to play by strictly amateur standards and to allow their football to tumble into oblivion."[51] However, Watterson also notes, "At another level Harvard and Yale's de-emphasis of football, which led to the Ivy League, reflected a reaction to problems that afflicted other institutions in the era."[52] In essence, most—if not all—Ivy League members were not willing, despite their relative wealth, to invest the funds at a level needed by strong programs going into the future.

Writing for *The Crimson* on the day Harvard opened the 1956 season against Cornell in Ithaca, New York, Bernard M. Gwertzman captured the mixed feelings surrounding the decision when he wrote:

> Thus, a paradox has arisen in this Ivy League. On the one hand, there is the Presidents Agreement, affirming the amateurish quality of the League, and on the other hand there is the picture of the filled stadium, the well-organized alumni, and the vigorous publicity offices. To some, as we said before, this is pure hypocrisy on the Ivy League's part—trying to capitalize on the idealism of the Agreement and the materialism of the games themselves.[53]

On one level, individuals with loyalties to Ivy League institutions wanted to maintain the festive atmosphere football fostered on a fall Saturday. On another level, those same individuals wanted to protect the academic integrity of the institutions from an ever-encroaching array of media interests. When Harvard and Yale meet at the end of each season for "The Game," it is possible to imagine that academic and athletic excellence can both be celebrated. On other Saturdays, one is left to wonder if big-time football and the academic integrity of the institutions can coexist.

Media, Money, and the Unbridled Pursuit of Athletic Excellence

In contrast to the Ivy League, most Division I universities were recently pressured into the formation of the "Power Five" (Pacific Twelve, Big Ten, Big Twelve, Atlantic Coast, and Southeastern) conferences by the desire to remain as competitive as possible to obtain slots in the College Football Playoff. What cannot be separated from that festive atmosphere is that schools are left susceptible to the ever-widening cycles of economically driven media interests. While a search for celebrations of the current state of the game yields almost nothing for consideration, a search for criticisms of the game yields just the opposite as such titles are almost as numerous as the criticisms of higher education as a whole.[54] Part of the problem with those titles, however, is that they often leave audience members with the impression that the current challenges facing college football are relatively new, and we just need to return to those glory days of the past. As this chapter notes, a longer view of history points out that the fragmentation of the university leaves intercollegiate athletics in general, and big-time college football in particular, susceptible to ever-widening cycles of economically driven media interests. As a result, the glory days of the past are far more myth than reality. The current set of pressures facing college football—ever-increasing salaries for coaches, ever-increasing upgrades and expansion of facilities, and, on the horizon, stipends in some form for players—are just the symptoms of a deeper illness.

The illness stems from a reality captured more than seventy-five years ago by the education theorist Isaac Kandel. He wrote that there is

> one part of our educational system, secondary and higher, in which there is no compromise with standards, in which there is rigid selection both of instructors and students, in which there is no soft pedagogy, and in which training and sacrifice of the individual for common ends are accepted without question. I refer, of course, to the organization of athletics.[55]

We must recognize that one reason we have athletic scandals is that it remains the major place where there is a relentless demand from multiple constituencies for excellence. This demand is fueled extensively by a vast media system that rewards winners with attention, prestige, and money. Although demands for excellence and temptations to corruption also exist in academic departments, these departments do not compete on national television for fame and fortune. As a result, athletics is the place in the university that most needs its pursuit for excellence to be guided by a larger moral identity, narrative, and purpose. In other words, athletics needs a university with a soul that can tame and direct it.

At its worst, the pursuit of excellence in institutions with fragmented souls leads institutions, even institutions with supposed decades-long histories of doing things the right way, to make compromises in favor of their brand and its ongoing appeal. If it means betraying students, athletes, and children, that is the price to pay. For Penn State, the price was the innocence Jerry Sandusky stole from the children he sexually abused. At Baylor, the price was the failure to protect young women and to make sure they receive justice. One could thus argue that not only have the core purposes of the university become distinct from the core purposes of the football program but also that the core saga and the associated practices of the football program usurped the very identity and purpose of the university. No lecture, play, concert, or gallery opening on campus could rival the thousands of people who make their way into Penn State's Beaver Stadium or Baylor University's new McLane Stadium for every football game. None of those events would consistently draw the interest of national forms of print and electronic media coverage. Implicitly, football becomes the most important saga on many campuses. Could a university with a unified soul prevent the moral corruption found in intercollegiate athletics in general, and college football in particular, when athletics is set free from a larger identity, story, and purpose? Our own experience at Baylor University, a university known for its "quality with soul,"[56] occasionally leaves us doubtful.[57] Our hope for a different vision springs from what we describe in part three, the occasions when we see the implementation of a more robust vision for a university with soul.

11

THE CONSEQUENCES OF MULTIVERSITIES WITH FRAGMENTED SOULS

Online and For-Profit Higher Education

...

But why . . . should a student waste his time upon studies which have no immediate connection with his future profession? . . . In answer to this, it may be observed that there is no science which does not contribute its aid to professional skill. "Every thing throws light upon every thing."

JEREMIAH DAY

THE PREVIOUSLY MENTIONED PROJECT MINERVA, launched in 2012, defies the standard criticisms of online and for-profit education, even though it is most certainly both of these. For-profit providers such as the University of Phoenix typically make around 90 percent of their revenue from federal student aid;[1] Project Minerva does not accept federal student aid. Many online learning opportunities increase the isolation of students who sit alone with their computers at home; Project Minerva brings students together from around the world for a live-in but online living and learning experience that makes its temporary home in a different major city each semester (Berlin, London, Buenos Aires, Mumbai, Hong Kong, and others are projected). For-profit providers are criticized for offering only narrow skills with limited market value; first-year students with Project Minerva focus on developing foundational skills and concepts that cultivate habits of the mind (critical thinking, reflection, analysis, and others), before focusing on one of five major choices (arts and humanities, social sciences, computational sciences, natural sciences, or business). Of course, all this innovation comes at a cost: no buildings clad in ivy, no football team to root for, and no tenure or honors bestowed on faculty (who are hired out from top universities around the world).

Even though Project Minerva hosted only thirty-three students in its inaugural academic year, this hybrid upstart has aspirations of undercutting, if not making obsolete, the elite universities of the early twenty-first century. One commentator's response carries with it a distinct tone of inevitability: "The idea that college will in two decades look exactly as it does today increasingly sounds like the forlorn, fingers-crossed hope of a higher-education dinosaur that retirement comes before extinction."[2] The ideals that result in innovations such as Project Minerva may represent either, or both, a best-case scenario and a worst-case scenario for the future of online/for-profit higher education and for higher education generally.

The rise of online and for-profit universities might appear to be natural outgrowth of multiversities with fragmented souls. Developing universities that focus on profit would appear to be the ultimate attempt to gain the material world at the expense of some higher identity, narrative, and purpose. Yet we believe we also need to understand parts of this emerging segment as an attempt to respond to the multiversity's fragmented soul (or perhaps its lack of any soul). In some ways, online and for-profit universities are merely a response to multiversities where professors' primary concern is their research, the curriculum has no coherence, cocurricular educators have less clarity regarding and concern with whole-person development, administrators simply focus on the bottom line, legal counsel sets policy and tends reputation, and the football team soaks up money while trying to avoid scandal and meet minimal academic requirements. Certainly multiversities have given up on the grand project of what Hugh of St. Victor described as the restoration of our divine image through the whole variety of arts. Online and for-profit universities address these developments. If multiversities try to do many things and have many purposes (but not the holistic development of students), online and for-profit universities focus on fewer and narrower ends. They seek to survive or profit by helping students gain the personal credentials for their professional lives.

In this chapter, our focus is on three aspects of the relationship between traditional colleges and universities (TCUs) and online/for-profit higher education that highlight some of the underlying ideals in need of critical examination, reflective of, and in some cases the products of, the fragmented university. The focus in particular centers on failed curricular attempts to link together what are commonly known as the liberal arts versus the more practical mechanical arts. First, we briefly review one early theologically informed proposal for including the practical arts. Although limited in its scope, it provides an example of how the liberal and manual arts could fit together in a Christian vision of education.

Second, we examine the historic and ongoing discomfort of TCUs with manual and technical training. We argue that this unease is due in part to commitments to particular forms of knowledge and related social capital that have made regard for technical and vocational training (much less offering it) frequently unattractive. The development of an approach to higher education in America emphasizing student formation, however laudable, has taken on the additional baggage of conferring social prestige, thereby further devaluing education focused explicitly on practical skills development. Consequently, rather than capitalizing on opportunities to improve the useful arts as an enterprise that increases workers' skills and capacity to serve their local communities, the inclination of universities to seek and generate prestige, either as a specific objective or an indirect output, has led instead to forms of exploitation. In this regard, the fragmentation of the university has manifested as a fragmentation between the university and its immediate community. As a result, these types of education have often been taken up by proprietary providers and through distance education, the progenitor of online education. The manual arts have thus been subject to either disregard for not contributing to institutional status or to manipulation in an attempt to refashion them to function more effectively as tools for individuals and institutional status.

Third, simultaneously, and despite these qualms, TCUs (and, in particular, research universities) have exhibited aggressive environmental opportunism in which online delivery and for-profit partnerships have become avenues for revenue generation and market-share expansion. In this sense, both the purpose and the functional areas of universities have accreted, expanding without plan or coherence. As we explore throughout this chapter, the historic and contemporary interplay between online/for-profit higher education and TCUs highlights some of the temptations to excess and commodification that TCUs continue to face, which reflect the ideals that have predominated in the absence of the theological foundation discussed in prior chapters. As a result, these two forms of postsecondary education (traditional liberal arts and vocational or professional education, often the focus of online/for-profit education) struggle to coexist without a larger guiding narrative about human flourishing provided by a soul.

Merging the Liberal and Mechanical Arts: A Medieval Model

In contemporary America, generalizations about "ivory tower eggheads" who cannot translate lofty ideas into practical knowledge are joined by stereotypes about penny-pinching bureaucrats more concerned with the bottom line than with the ideals that inspire people to greatness. Similarly, the university, with its lineage beginning in medieval Europe, is frequently described as a museum of knowledge, removed from practical applications. In the words of Thomas Hearn, "The university preserves and interprets the best of what human intelligence has created and written."[3]

However, the actual vision and aim of some early European educational leaders at times included education in the practical or mechanical arts as well as knowledge generation and preservation. Consider Hugh of St. Victor's original blueprint for the university curriculum discussed in chapter one. Among the twenty-one arts Hugh mentioned were the seven mechanical arts, which he placed within philosophy. The mechanical arts involved anything having to do with making human constructions. Just as

198

God created nature, humans made in the image of God create what is "imitative of nature," such as clothes, buildings for shelter, devices for hunting, and medicine.[4] Hugh included the study of such practices in his curriculum, although he did elevate the study of the liberal arts over the mechanical arts since the ancients believed "anyone who had been thoroughly schooled in them might afterward come to a knowledge of the others by his own inquiry and effort rather than by listening to a teacher."[5] Whether Hugh should have believed the ancients on this matter is something that will underlie much of the historical conflict we discuss.

The pattern Hugh outlined persisted with the founding of the first universities. Harold Shapiro maintained that in the centuries following the founding of Europe's first universities, such as Bologna and Paris, the liberal arts were actually the poor sisters of what Hugh labeled the theoretical art of theology, the mechanical art of medicine, and the practical art of law.[6] All three of these academic fields of study were connected to practical vocations. Still, one entered these fields of study by first engaging in the study of the liberal arts.

A History of Conflicted American Responses to "Useful" Higher Education

Higher education in the American colonies, however, consisted solely of liberal arts. As a result, they left behind this vocationally focused part of education since, unlike European universities, American educational institutions did not found separate faculties of theology, law, and medicine. The College of William and Mary in Virginia, chartered by the British crown in 1693, claimed as its founding purposes

> a seminary of ministers of the gospel . . . that the youth may be piously educated in good letters and manners, and that the Christian faith may be propagated amongst the Western Indians . . . to make, found and establish a certain place of universal study, or perpetual College of Divinity, Philosophy, Languages, and other good Arts and Sciences.[7]

The theology faculty (which never actually materialized) was intended to buttress the supply of clergy in the colony and affect religious conversion among the indigenous population.

Since American universities did not establish vocationally focused graduate programs until the latter part of the nineteenth century, students in American colleges primarily received a basic liberal arts education. The curricular core of the trivium (grammar, logic, and rhetoric) and quadrivium (arithmetic, geometry, astronomy, and music) employed passages from early Greek texts, but they were used primarily to introduce grammatical forms. The *Graeca Majora*, a popular summary textbook of the early to mid-nineteenth century, contained snippets from Greek masters such as Homer, Sappho, and Euripides that students would memorize and recite.[8] The goal was not to learn language per se, nor was it to become a scholar of ancient history. Rather, the process of studying the classics was thought to instill mental discipline, recitations developed skills of oration, and the content of these masterworks equipped young men with phrases and concepts as useful in debate as in graceful conversation.[9] Although Hugh would have agreed that the liberal arts should be the beginning, he would have found the absence of a theology faculty and the other mechanical arts limiting.

As a result of the liberal arts emphasis and the lack of vocational focus, the end of education became associated with a broader, nonvocational identity. In George Eliot's 1860 novel *The Mill on the Floss*, Phillip, the aristocratic father, puts forth the value of the classical curriculum to his wayward son, Tom, in these terms: "It's part of the education of a gentleman . . . all gentlemen learn the same things."[10] The broader importance of this brief interjection is twofold: first, that men of the times saw great pragmatic value in the dull and repetitious classical education they promoted. As mentioned in the epigraph to this chapter, Jeremiah Day argued passionately in the Yale Report of 1828 for the importance of the classical curriculum and viewed it as a foundation for all pursuits: "The course of instruction which is given to the undergraduates in the college, is not designed to include professional studies. Our object is not to teach that which is peculiar to any one of the professions; but to lay the foundation which is common to them all."[11] Others have argued that the classical curriculum of the early American colleges was, in a sense, vocational, in that their "vocation" was to be men of the world (gentlemen), and the concepts and dispositions stressed through the study of Greek and Latin were indicative of that world.[12]

Second, despite arguments for applicability, Eliot's story illustrates that the students of the day disputed whether the educational form put upon them was of any particular utility at all. In fact, it was this argument that gradually resulted in a fundamental shift from teaching the classics as a process whereby discipline would be developed to teaching classics as a means for inspiring youths through the adventures and virtues of the ancients. As historian Caroline Winterer succinctly phrases it, it was a transition "from *words* to *worlds*."[13]

Together, the earnestness for classical education and youthful resistance to it highlight an ongoing tension in the history of higher education that besets us yet today: educational forms that produce the general skills and dispositions that many traditional universities put forward as essential for adult life, for public engagement, and for professional aptitude are often quite different from the specific professional training many students desire that appears to directly prepare them for a particular profession. Returning to Day, the shift in educational emphases is apparent between the medieval university, where the focus included professional preparation, and the Antebellum college of his time.

> As our course of instruction is not intended to complete an education, in theological, medical, or legal science; neither does it include all the minute details of mercantile, mechanical, or agricultural concerns. These can never be effectually learned except in the very circumstances in which they are to be practised.[14]

Ironically, several decades later, universities would be called on to provide exactly this sort of education through the provisions of the Morrill Acts. The Morrill Acts marked a crucial turning point toward the massification of American higher education in large part due to programs of study intended to train students in pragmatic as well as theoretical areas of focus. However, several precursor movements toward manual and technical education frame the preexisting tension between this sort of education and society at large that influenced the advent and form of the Morrill Acts. Ultimately these developments would unwittingly spawn rival forms of postsecondary education.

Forays into Technical Education

At least two historical educational approaches of the eighteenth and nineteenth centuries attempted to unite practical and traditional learning: the manual labor movement and the "useful knowledge" movement. The manual labor movement merged training in agricultural and mechanical pursuits with traditional educational studies. Imported from Europe, manual labor institutes in the United States were based on Phillip Emanuel von Fellenberg's school reforms for orphaned and low-income boys.[15] Schools were established in Connecticut (1819), Maine (1821), Massachusetts (1824), New York (1824), and New Jersey (1830). The Oneida Manual Labor Institute in Whitesboro, New York, reflected the pattern of instruction and also the fate many similar institutions experienced. Students spent part of their days working in the shops and fields to sustain the institution through labor and income and, in the process, to develop technical knowledge and skills. The rest of the day was dedicated to the classroom, where students focused on traditional forms of instruction. Despite the apparent attractiveness of this model, the general public was largely ambivalent, and by the Civil War nearly all manual labor schools had closed, forestalling formal technical education by nearly half a century.[16]

The useful knowledge movement emerged in the late 1700s, born of Francis Bacon's scientific empiricism in Europe and championed by Benjamin Franklin in the newly formed United States of America. This movement was an attempt to infuse every activity with scientific principles, to reduce speculative truths to practice, to ground theories in experimentation, and to apply "science to the improvement of agriculture, commerce, and 'the common purposes of life.'"[17] Historian Joseph Kett argues that Thomas Jefferson at least flirted with incorporating the "useful arts" within the curriculum at his new institution in Charlottesville: "For a brief period . . . Jefferson envisioned organizing the curriculum of what would become the University of Virginia around professions and vocations, including even a school of 'technical philosophy' for mariners, soap makers, tanners, carpenters, and wrights of every sort."[18]

Popular postcolonial republican ideology further propelled interest in the useful arts. Citizens were inspired to infuse the virtues needed to sustain the new nation into traditional and emerging professions, from law to navigation to architecture. Historian Roger Geiger argues, however, that the chasm between the ideal and its collegiate implementation was not easily bridged: "Republicanism embraced the Enlightenment ideal of 'useful knowledge' with little regard for the difficulties of incorporating practical subjects into the college course."[19]

By the latter half of the nineteenth century the idea of the useful arts as a component of collegiate learning had fallen dramatically out of fashion, but it received an unexpected boost from federal legislation. As previously mentioned, the Morrill Act of 1862 provided tracts of western lands to each state, the sale of which were to be used to fund a new institution or expand an existing one focused on agriculture, mechanical arts, military officer training, and the liberal arts.[20] Although states and institutional leaders were generally eager to receive the financial benefit that the act (and subsequent renewal in 1890) provided, neither they nor the public these land-grant institutions were to serve demonstrated all that much enthusiasm for the type of instruction anticipated. Rather, Joseph Kett argues, "In contrast to Justin Morrill, leading university presidents of the late nineteenth century saw practical utility and higher education as fundamentally incompatible."[21]

Student response, particularly to agricultural programs, proved tepid. Kett suggests this was so because preparation was first theoretical and then practical. More centrally, however, because the prevailing cultural mood at the time reflected Day's previous injunction that workers best acquired skills on the job. The lack of an informal apprenticeship system nationally also further fueled this inclination. Those few who received college degrees found themselves better equipped to enter the middle and upper rungs of the professional ladder than the skilled trades at the bottom. In summary, "The framers of the Morrill Act had envisioned an intimate relationship between theory and practice, between higher science and the ordinary trades, but by 1890 few educators shared their confidence."[22]

The Emergence of Distance and For-Profit Education

It was within this vacuum, a vacuum caused by the disregard of university leaders for skilled and technical training, that a "vast industry" of part-time vocational institutions developed in the United States.[23] Although junior colleges and secondary vocational training courses were offshoots of the same inclination, it was the resulting proliferation of proprietary commercial schools and correspondence schools that represented an ancestor of today's online and for-profit education. Enrollments in commercial schools grew exponentially, adding roughly 100,000 additional students every decade between 1871 and 1921.[24] Through the late 1800s, the idea of limited vocational training that would provide employment or employment advancement without the opportunity cost of full-time college attendance captured the attention and imagination of the American public. This rising interest was aided by an increase in state licensing requirements that were based, for tradesmen such as embalmers, plumbers, mine inspectors, and electricians, on knowledge needed to pass a test rather than a credential from an institution.[25] Primarily, patrons of courses in such technical skills such as bookkeeping, typing, penmanship, and stenography were adult learners rather than teenagers.[26] This new emphasis on adult technical education represented an important shift away from prior forms of adult education that stressed the acquisition of knowledge of preferred cultural forms, such as literature, the arts, and languages.[27]

With an almost complete absence of technical education available at traditional colleges and with an adult population clamoring for opportunity, a land rush of correspondence-learning opportunities sprang up at the turn of the twentieth century. In this moment of grand opportunity, some players were rather unexpected: for example, the Young Men's Christian Association, or YMCA (and to a lesser extent YWCA), founded evening law and mechanical schools in addition to a correspondence school in response to members' desire for self-improvement.[28] TCUs, although at first slow to recognize the importance of this cultural shift, would soon respond and do so in ways that infused the ideals of the university into manual education.

Tensions over the Purposes of Higher Education

The point that emerges from the accumulated evidence thus far suggests that despite the inclusion of the practical arts in the early idea of the university, higher education in America developed in a way that emphasized college as preparation for entry into a typically high or higher status that made it both ill-suited for and uninterested in "useful" or skills-based education. The Christian theology that led Hugh of St. Victor to include the mechanical arts in a course of educational study no longer existed in the university, and other justifications for including it did not emerge. Even with the influence and structure of the Morrill Acts, entrenched preferences for theoretical exploration over practical application meant that a segment of the population that desired workforce development had few formal educational structures available to them. As interest in commercial and correspondence schools grew, however, traditional institutions did respond.[29]

In the latter decades of the nineteenth century, American higher education innovators such as William Rainey Harper at the University of Chicago sought to accommodate rising interest in skill-based and adult education. He established one of the first college-level for-credit correspondence courses by mail at the University of Chicago in 1892.[30] Foreshadowing the multiuniversity cooperative online ventures such as Fathom of the twenty-first century, in 1883 a group of thirty-two professors from top universities including Harvard, Johns Hopkins, Cornell, and Wisconsin formed Correspondence University.[31] This joint enterprise offered supplemental instruction to traditional classroom courses, much the way YouTube sensation Khan Academy does today. Individual universities across the nation responded as well. Minnesota, Iowa State, Baylor, California at Berkeley, and Penn State Universities soon established their own correspondence courses.[32]

The legacy of presidents at the University of Chicago illustrates American higher education's attempt to accommodate this increasing interest in vocational and adult education even while castigating the pressure to do so as beneath the lofty aims of the university. Twenty-three years after Harper's exit from the helm at the University of Chicago, another energetic and enigmatic visionary would take over its presidency. The previously mentioned Robert Maynard Hutchins, then age thirty-two, carried on the spirit of Harper's work. Under the so-called New Plan he inherited, Hutchins advanced a curricular structure in which the freshman and sophomore years were dedicated to general liberal arts. Perhaps echoing the structure of the medieval university as well as Jeremiah Day's desire to sequence the *discipline* (core knowledge and competencies) and *furniture* (topical knowledge) of the mind, a BA was awarded after the sophomore year, leaving the subsequent years for a specialized master's degree.[33]

Writing seven years into his eventual twenty-two-year presidency, Hutchins's contempt for the influence of mass access to higher education is clear.

> The universities are dependent on the people. The people love money and think that education is a way of getting it. They think too that democracy means that every child should be permitted to acquire the educational insignia that will be helpful in making money. They do not believe in the cultivation of the intellect for its own sake.[34]

Here, Hutchins derides "the people's" motives (money) as beneath the *real* purposes of the university ("the cultivation of the intellect for its own sake"). From his perspective, the university is a kind of holy ground where only the anointed should tread. Debasing it with utilitarian ends is tantamount to inviting the moneychangers to set up shop in the temple. What is missing from Hutchins that could be found in Hugh of St. Victor is a vision for human flourishing that could include the mechanical arts as more than a means for financial increase.

Even if the contemporary reader grants that Hutchins, in somewhat blunt terms, made a point that holds relevance today, Hutchins still managed to direct the reader's attention away from a crucial underlying point: that the university is a social and cultural gatekeeper through which status and entrée into social and economic advantage if not privilege is conferred, almost without respect to ability. Although most nineteenth-century colleges were not merely bastions for and of the social and economic elite (indeed, for the sake of steady enrollments they could not afford to be), increasingly in the 1900s, traditional four-year institutions discovered the tools of admissions selectivity and solidified their tacit role as conveyers of economic, social, and cultural forms of capital. Economic capital (via one's ability to find a well-paying job) is a clear-enough outcome. Colleges and universities gradually also facilitated students' acquisition of social capital (the development of advantageous interpersonal networks) and cultural capital (knowledge of preferred expressions of social class) that sociologist Pierre Bourdieu argued served to perpetuate rather than alleviate social inequality.[35]

In the context of this discussion it is to the advantage of selective colleges and institutions to be perceived as highly desirable forms of education not simply because they will successfully certify otherwise unskilled youths for well-paying professional employment, but because they create a social environment where networks (social capital) and valued formed of knowledge and behavior (cultural capital) can be passed on. The irony of Hutchins's distress, captured in the quote above, is that it may indicate how successful the University of Chicago had become at signaling to the public that economic capital was a dependable outcome of institutional association, which had certainly not been the case in prior centuries. Hutchins's consternation perhaps indicates that he prioritized the cultivation of what we might now call cultural capital (obtaining knowledge of literature, arts, sciences, and others) ostensibly for its "own sake" but most definitely to the benefit of both institution and student. Related, and far less opaque, was George Eliot's insight, via Phillip, that "all gentlemen learn the same things."

In short, then, it has been the university's emerging role as guardian and purveyor of culturally valued knowledge and hence opportunity that has helped to ensconce it as a desirable experience and investment in the minds of the general public. This was particularly true through the twentieth century. Furthermore, this institutional function has made the university wary, as Hutchins so clearly stated it, that the same public that now finds attendance so desirable does so for the wrong reasons. Very easily, then, those who understand that the advantages of higher education are also but not merely economic (that is, those who possessed cultural capital) are typically from families of a social status in harmony with that of the institution. Those without this "good breeding" (genetic or otherwise) are easily dismissed as desiring entry for the wrong reasons. As Andrew Delbanco (himself a Harvard grad) suggests in his analysis of elite universities: "We are too quick to assume that students with lesser preparation are unfit for education in this larger sense." His observation may also help to explain why at some top-tier institutions where low- and middle-income students can attend tuition-free, Pell Grant–eligible (a proxy for low-income status) students make up only slightly more than 10 percent of each entering class.[36]

Additionally, even among those who gain entry, their experiences are not equivalent. Although prestigious institutions have preferred to project the appearance that virtually by entry alone (and hard work, of course) a young person will gain all associated advantages, those from high-socioeconomic-status (SES) families are socialized to make different use of the same college access than those from low-socioeconomic-status families, resulting in less advantageous future opportunities.[37] For example, low-SES students tend to seek employment to help pay for school; higher-SES students are more likely to take on loans (if they need them at all) and use that time to build social connections with faculty and peers that pay off later in terms of graduate school recommendations and professional opportunities. Thus fragmentation occurred and occurs along not only curricular lines but also in terms of who profits from higher education, and how.

Status and Technical Education

In a conversation about the uneasy relationship between TCUs and online and for-profit education, this focus on social reproduction further clarifies TCUs' frequent and historical discomfort with technical and skills-focused education, reflected currently in a major segment of online and for-profit education. In this regard, TCUs have long struggled to recognize and honor the dignity of the practical or mechanical arts without either desiring to "transform" them into a higher-status activity or attempting to "inspire" those engaging in them with the desire to abandon them in favor of "higher" stations. TCUs have developed social functions with associated ontological and epistemological ideals that tacitly assign symbolic importance to some forms of knowledge (intellectual and scientific knowledge, primarily) and frequently devalue vocational, skills-based, and technical knowledge, except in cases when they contribute to preparation for high-status professions. Reflecting this tendency, Kett notes how the mechanical training emphasis in the Morrill Act was quickly co-opted by university faculty to instead prepare students for careers as engineers, a role with much greater social standing than a mechanical tradesperson might otherwise hold.[38]

Philosopher, farmer, and social prophet Wendell Berry also perceives that land-grant institutions drifted from the aims outlined in the Morrill Act. He argues that the vision of the Morrill Act legislation was to provide practical education to improve practice, and liberal education to improve service to one's community. However, Berry contrasts Thomas Jefferson, who viewed farmers as "the most valuable citizens" who were only in need of education to prepare them for public service and local leadership, with Morrill, the son of a blacksmith, who sought to exalt farming and other labors to the level of professions, less to increase their quality of work and life and more to attain a place of "higher consideration" or recognized social standing.[39] Thus it may be that from the start, America's most comprehensive plan to link together the resources of postsecondary education and the utility of agricultural and mechanical trade confused increased *utility* with increased *status*. According to Berry:

> The land-grant colleges have, in fact, been very little—and have been less and less—concerned "to promote the liberal and practical education of the industrial classes" [a quote from the Morrill Act legislation] or of any other classes. Their history has been largely that of the whittling down of this aim—from education in the broad, "liberal" sense to "practical" preparation for earning a living to various "programs" for certification. They first reduced "liberal and practical" to "practical," and then for "practical" they substituted "specialized." And the standard of their purpose has shifted from usefulness to careerism.[40]

By contrast, the dignity of the practical or mechanical arts has in some other historical moments been co-opted to reduce local leadership and agency. Berry notes that land grants used the opportunity of the Morrill Act to bolster institutional resources and prestige at a cost to the student. Presidents and faculty shifted institutional foci from pursuing efforts that would improve conditions locally to pursuing opportunities that would increase individual and institutional prestige in the eyes of guilds and peers. In recent years scholars have identified this institutional tendency to pursue perceived prestige through incremental shifts in institutional focus, describing it as mission "creep," mission "drift," and more recently as institutional "accretion," or the tendency of institutions to take on more and more organizational functions and facets that have little or no relationship to one another.[41] Thus research universities want to be elite research universities, comprehensive universities want to become research universities, and community colleges want to become four-year institutions. Although some students benefit from this transition, typically those who are less academically prepared and more likely to be seeking technical education are left out of the equation.

Seeding the Contemporary For-Profit University

It is no small wonder, then, that those who do not fit the traditional ideal of a four-year-degree-seeking student might sense that traditional colleges and universities are not *for* them and pursue educational opportunity through other means. In fact, in a very direct way it was this culture of exclusion and status seeking that led to the founding of one of TCUs' most prominent competitors: the University of Phoenix. John Sperling, who founded what would become the world's largest online for-profit university in 1976, was born into a poor farming family in the Missouri Ozarks in 1921. Raised with no concept of postsecondary education, he ended up serving in the merchant marine, then completing some community college courses, and after World War II, a bachelor's degree at prestigious Reed College (by his admission, almost by chance), followed by a PhD in history at the University of California, Berkeley. His attempts to unionize faculty as a professor at San Jose State failed miserably, but the experience taught him that one should always "ignore your detractors" and cemented his dislike for the higher education establishment.[42]

Later Sperling founded the Institute for Professional Development (IPD), the forerunner of the University of Phoenix, and secured contracts with struggling four-year colleges to deliver educational services—and students. The regional higher education accrediting body, however, attempted to limit his activities, claiming he was giving too much academic credit for work experience and generating excess profits. Charges that he was running a diploma mill further embedded his distrust of traditional institutions.

> The battles fought by IPD . . . against the educational establishment were, in a formal sense, regulatory battles, but they were largely proxies for cultural battles between defenders of 800 years of (largely religious) educational tradition, and an innovation that was based on values of the marketplace—transparency, efficiency, productivity, and accountability. To me, the defenders of academic traditions were protecting undeserved middle-class entitlements.[43]

It is certainly unfair to implicate the whole of American higher education with these charges. The great strength of our system has been in its diversity of aims, methods, structures, and intended outcomes. And yet as this narrative highlights, in aggregate, fostering and bestowing prestige has become a tacit if not explicit purpose of colleges and universities varying primarily by scale but seldom by intention.

If for-profit higher education is a source of crisis for traditional higher education, Sperling's quote identifies the battlefield of divergent values and priorities that fuel the conflict. The business orientation of for-profit universities challenges the legitimacy of the assumptions that have guided most sectors of higher education for the past few centuries. Sperling then implicates TCUs not (or not only) on the grounds that "tradition" is an outmoded organizational strategy but also on the grounds that these venerated traditions have been used to protect entitled students and, by extension, reduce opportunity for those not similarly advantaged. Expanding the implications of this claim, one could argue that serving entitled students is a byproduct of a system of entitlement protection in which market-driven utilitarian education, whether correspondence courses of the late nineteenth century or online education of the early twenty-first century, has little place. Sperling's argument is reminiscent of Bourdieu's claim that education is a tool of social reproduction. In this sense, the marketplace presence of alternative models (in this case for-profit universities) serves to illuminate and therefore question the systemic normalcy that Bourdieu describes as necessary for disadvantaged groups to accept the unequal treatment they receive.

The fallout has been the general disenfranchisement of adult learners, those seeking specifically technical or vocational training, and often those whose primary and secondary educational experiences did not socialize them into the sorts of ideals and behaviors valued by TCUs. Grant Venn, in a chapter now nearly half a century old, outlines the factors that further debase their ends and thus encourage "good" students to seek opportunities elsewhere.

> The problems in vocational and technical education are compounded by the present program's low prestige. Its students too often are the dropouts or castoffs of the academic curriculum. Its teachers, often less academically oriented, enjoy relatively low status within the teaching profession in many states. Its buildings are often the oldest, its facilities frequently the poorest, its extracurricular programs usually the weakest. Its subject matter suffers from the general debasement of manual and blue-collar occupations in contemporary social values.[44]

Venn's injunction on one hand describes the persistent low regard of universities for technical education, though this is certainly not the case in all quarters. However, he also frames the problem as a matter of prestige and the associated resources and advantages related to it. In an organizational context that values high-visibility faculty, high-dollar grants, and high-ability students, programs otherwise oriented naturally settle to the bottom.

And yet, in other ways a number of TCUs have been very active in embracing new technologies and using innovative delivery methods to increase educational opportunity for underrepresented and nontraditional students. In the next section of this chapter, we examine the advent of these innovations and the insights they provide regarding the ideals and concerns that motivate them.

Doing the Right Things for the Wrong Reasons

In 2012, Sebastian Thrun and Peter Norvig, two artificial intelligence researchers from Stanford University, decided to offer their graduate-level course free online and had 160,000 enrollees by the first day of class. Although this was not the first instance of faculty opening their class to the public for free, the idea of higher education unshackled from the bonds of traditional organizational structures and geographic confines seemed like a dream nearly achieved.[45] Massive online open courses (or MOOCs) promise access to some of the world's top faculty for eager learners who might otherwise be limited financially, geographically, politically, and even intellectually. MOOC clearinghouse websites such as Udemy link potential students to tens of thousands of college-level courses, many at no cost to the learner.

Within months of Stanford's MOOC launch, universities including Harvard, MIT, Michigan, and Princeton had committed tens of millions of dollars in venture capital to develop MOOCs of their own. Importantly, Thrun and Norvig's course did not award academic credit; the 23,000 students who completed the course (that is, 14 percent of students who originally enrolled) instead received a carefully worded "statement of accomplishment." Handing out credentials for free is hardly a sustainable business practice, even for nonprofit colleges and universities. The question has been, can these and other open-course ventures survive without generating income? As journalist and author Jeffery Salingo notes, "For that kind of money, you would think that these wealthy, respected universities had discovered the magic bullet solution to the future of higher education. But none of them have a plan for making money."[46] Instead these universities adopted an entrepreneurial perspective, holding that if enough people are attracted to something, a way of making money from it will be found. Gradually, for-profit ventures appeared as the pursuit of revenue intensified. Often these secondary parties acted as educational brokers, for a price. EdX, Coursera, and others added for-credit options but with enrollment fees. EdX even partnered with Arizona State University to offer the first year of a bachelor's degree completely online for only $8,000.[47]

Preferring to focus on extolling the virtues of access through online education and for-profit partnerships, TCUs have often been reluctant to claim revenue generation as an aim of these innovative forms of education delivery. A decade prior to the launch of the Stanford MOOC, a national survey of multisector distance education (which included online and other forms) found that institutional leaders were hesitant to identify generating revenue as a central motivation for distance-learning initiatives. In the survey, 92 percent of institutions claimed that "increased access" was the primary motivating factor in adopting or developing such programs.[48] Through distance education, two- and four-year institutions could offer coursework to students in challenging personal and geographic circumstances, such as those in extreme rural areas, homebound students, and employed students who would not be able to schedule their lives around "brick and mortar" classes. Only 56.4 percent of respondents agreed that generating new forms of revenue through new distance-program development was a primary concern. In his conclusions, Gary Berg presses that point.

> One needs to separate the rhetoric from the reality when assessing this data. . . . While strictly speaking the hypothesis [that increasing revenue was a primary driver] was disproved by direct questioning, the more general connection of distance learning to the commercialization of higher education is strongly indicated.[49]

Berg notes that among institution types in the study, research universities were far more likely to be oriented toward generating revenue from distance-education courses than were two-year and comprehensive colleges. The point here is not that institutional leaders at research universities are therefore unscrupulous connivers or that charging tuition and increasing access are necessarily antithetical. Berg's terminology choice is vital to this point. He links institutional motivation for distance learning not simply to a desire to generate revenue but to the ever-increasing "commercialization of higher education." That is, TCUs, whether in an effort to expand market share or simply remain financially viable, have increasingly viewed their educational offerings as a commodity to be marketed to results-oriented "consumers" (students).

In this regard, both institutions and students are complicit. Arthur Levine, former president of Teachers College, Columbia University, argues that "students increasingly are bringing to higher education exactly the same consumer expectations they have for every other commercial establishment with which they deal."[50] Evidence appears to support this point. In 1967, 79.1 percent of first-year college students surveyed considered it essential or very important to develop a meaningful philosophy of life.[51] Throughout the past three decades the percentage continued to decline, so that by 2014 it had dropped to 44.6 percent.[52] In contrast, the percentage of first-year students who prioritize "being very well-off financially" has risen from 54.2 percent to 82.4 percent during that same time.

In this context, students, and particularly those who have not been socialized to the intangible benefits of higher education, are unlikely to know to seek its higher goods. "The millions of first-generation undergraduates now in mass-market institutions have had little to no exposure to the power of thought within the liberal arts. They have no great interest in the life of the mind."[53] Fortunately, many students will learn this value through their undergraduate experience, whether they set out intending to or not. However, the danger is that in the rush to capitalize on new opportunities that may yield new revenue streams and increased market visibility, some of higher education's greatest virtues (increased access, but also issues of character development, human purpose, and civic participation) are being pushed aside in favor of vocationally focused curricula, particularly for the less well-prepared and more career-minded online student.

It is worth understanding that the opportunities and temptations of distance and for-profit higher education experienced by colleges and universities today are mirrored in its origins. As we discussed earlier in this chapter, TCUs were at first reluctant to embrace distance education. Opportunistic for-profit ventures and empathetic nonprofit entities (such as the YMCA) seized on this unmet need and developed popular courses of study that favored skills development for young adult learners.[54] By the turn of the twentieth century, TCUs expanded distance offerings from initial undergraduate academic coursework to doctoral degrees. By 1900 some forty-eight institutions made doctorates available through correspondence courses. Some of these degrees were of such dubious quality that it tainted the reputation of distance learning for decades.[55] Much like our current context, in a historical moment when many campuses had tight budgets and meager physical resources, the allure of paying students who would not require housing or local services was powerful. Writing of colleges in the early 1900s, David Portman argues that "the possibility of additional income from non-residential students must have been a great attraction to more than one beleaguered president who was continually hustling for cash, books, and buildings to keep his institution alive."[56]

Thus online learning and for-profit ventures and partnerships offer the possibility of expanded access to higher education, though the motivations for such enterprises merit scrutiny. We now turn to a second feature of the rise of online and for-profit higher education that requires critical reflection: the inherent limitations and opportunities of the content-delivery structures and how they shape the nature of educational outcomes.

Beyond Access: Online Learning, Educational Justice, and Human Purpose

Assuming that these emerging technologies and delivery forms are increasing access (and there is evidence that suggests they may not be[57]), questions of educational equity and justice still remain. Although burdened by its own tendencies to excess, critical theory helps to reveal the assumptions, tacit purposes, and implicit values of distance-education providers.[58] Although increasing access to higher education can seem like an unequivocally positive development, making an educational system available to a wider pool of people does not necessarily make the system fair.[59] In his study of distance education, Berg concludes his book by pressing this question: in the light of the rapid expansion of distance learning, "is the access given by distance learning meaningful?"[60] Following this argument, others propose that when institutions are too focused on clearing the bar of access and do not sufficiently attend to the quality of experience and achievement of ends beyond mere information exchange, distance learning fails to create learning environments where deep and genuine dialogue reflects the ideal of the self-directed learner empowered to create, rather than simply consume, education.[61]

Forms of distance education that rely on one-way communication (mail, radio, film, but also web) may reinforce educational subservience and reduce agency, particularly among first-generation students and those from underrepresented groups. Even the most successful free web-based applications may be subject to this critique. For example, the previously mentioned Khan Academy, a massive catalog of short instructional videos showing only a black tablet for illustrations, the voice of the instructor (founder Salman Khan), and his otherwise disembodied hand, has become the gold standard of free online instruction. Heralded widely for delivering easy-to-comprehend explanations of technical math and science topics, Khan Academy videos nevertheless venerate the instructor as expert and can convey that education is reducible to the mastery of skills.[62] Thus, similar to the throngs of adult learners who enrolled in correspondence courses to improve their vocational prospects a century ago, eager students from across the globe call up Khan's free online videos to prepare for credentialing tests, to clarify concepts they may not have understood in a traditional classroom, or to complete an assignment as part of another online or hybrid for-credit program. Khan's videos, though often a wonderful resource as a supplement to traditional courses, still only offer content explanation, largely focusing on topics where technical mastery can be removed from philosophical and theological issues. Although on one hand this may seem completely appropriate, the outcome at least tacitly suggests that issues of scientific fact and mathematical calculation are and perhaps should be separate from larger questions about the meaning of life, work, and the good life as well as more specific considerations of professional ethics.

An emphasis on equity and justice in a conversation about higher education delivery methods might seem extraneous. If colleges and universities are not merely education providers but also gatekeepers of social opportunity, then critically evaluating disparities in access takes on moral significance in two regards. First, justice generally is a biblical concern. The lineage of scriptural expectations that those at the margins of society (by citizenship, gender, class, or other factors) should receive special regard extends from Levitical injunctions not to oppress the "foreigner in your land" (Ex 22:21), from prophetic condemnations leveled at Israel for exploiting the powerless (Jer 22:3, 17), from Jesus' persistent alignment of his ministerial purpose with the outcast (Lk 4:18), and from New Testament directives that faith be expressed through care of the marginalized (Jas 1:27; 5:1).

Second, justice matters because a kingdom imagination for systems of higher education calls for Christians to facilitate the growth and flourishing of all people reflective of their divine gifting rather than their social and economic standing. Educational systems that attempt to track, trap, or "cool out" students who are perceived to be of lesser status or ability fall short of contributing to a meaningful vision of human purpose and flourishing. In this regard, then, the nature of distance education, whether a service of for-profit ventures or TCUs, is a platform susceptible to abuse where vulnerable students, rather than being enabled to fulfill their God-given potential, are treated as a revenue stream.

The Opposite of One Truth Is Another Truth

The astute reader may sense that we have been advancing two seemingly incongruous arguments in this chapter. On one hand, we have argued that historically TCUs have struggled to take manual, technical, and vocational training seriously, in part because a liberal education was gradually inter-twined with institutional and individual prestige that in turn conveyed social, cultural, and economic capital to the privileged. In the process, universities have taken on more and more functions with less and less internal coherence as the lure of market forces entices leaders to invest in new educational technologies. On the other hand, we have argued that online/for-profit partnerships and proprietary universities have, in the name of efficiency and market responsiveness, tended to deliver a product that may suppress rather than advance questions of meaning and purpose that a liberal education traditionally sought to instill.

Although these two arguments may arrive at opposing conclusions, taken together they point to the temptations of excess and misdirection that reflect the fallen nature of higher education as a system and the ideals that tempt each segment toward their own respective abuses of otherwise good educational functions. The rise of online/for-profit higher education has in part been a product of the university's development as a creator and dispenser of prestige and the costs and inefficiencies that have accompanied that model.[63] Distance education came into flower in the absence of a place for vocational training within the traditional college model in the late 1800s. Similarly, the University of Phoenix, a direct descendent of distance education, came to prominence in an era dominated by the research-oriented multiversity. In both contexts, environmental opportunity was a product of a status orientation that disregarded practical education for a largely nontraditional population.

The excesses of online/for-profit education are more familiar, as part of a culture-wide battle for the future of higher education.[64] Low retention rates, high loan-default rates, and accusations of predatory admissions practices have dogged for-profit institutions and may be indicative of the source of control (proprietary), the typical content (vocational), the delivery (impersonal), and the student type (frequently first-generation or low socioeconomic status).[65] Questions remain about the intentions and the viability of TCUs' investment in and partnerships with this sector, though some dramatic examples of failure are still fairly fresh.[66] In either case, the conversation has shifted from the viability of these market segments to acknowledgement that the future of higher education will include a widening rather than constricting range of educational forms, including a complex array of hybridized offerings that blend residential, online, private, and for-profit elements.[67] The distinctions between these categories of education providers will become increasingly muddied in the process. Regardless, the tendencies to excess, nested in ideals of prestige and culture preservation on one hand and efficiency and marketization on the other, are likely to continue to be the focus of critique and controversy when exclusion and exploitation result.

In this regard, Project Minerva, introduced at the start of the chapter, is a prototype and archetype. As a best-case scenario it unifies the resources of a liberal education with the expedience, efficiency, and utility that are the strengths of many online programs. As a worst-case scenario, Project

Minerva combines the marketization and careerism of the for-profit sector with the elitism and class reproduction of top private colleges and universities. Observing how these and other hybrid forms develop will reveal which of these sets of ideals are more reflective of the essential qualities of the university of the twenty-first century.

Finally, as an archetype, Project Minerva reflects an attempt to recover the coherence clearly missing from the multiversity by reducing the number of curricular and cocurricular options for students and focusing on intellectual-capacity building. The dizzying array of options universities offer may accentuate the appearance of fragmentation in comparison to the few offered by this hybrid higher education provider. Yet Project Minerva shares with the multiversity the temptation to replace the soul of a university containing a vision of human flourishing with the hollow core of a university understood primarily as a mechanism for gaining personal fulfillment and prestige. The resulting output may be fragmented individuals, even if the institution that produces them appears structurally unified.

Can Christian universities save the online and for-profit model? Two are certainly trying: Grand Canyon University (GCU), founded by Southern Baptists in 1949, was nearly 16 million dollars in debt and faced closure by 2003. In 2008, GCU went public and as of 2015 was the only for-profit four-year Christian liberal arts college in the nation, boasting an enrollment of around 60,000 students, 8,000 of whom are residential.[68] Similarly, Liberty University had made a massive investment in online education, boasting that as of fall 2012 it was the seventh-largest private, four-year, nonprofit university in the United States, with 77,778 students, 65,825 of whom were nonresidential.[69] Like Project Minerva, GCU dodges many of the typical criticisms of the segment: it costs less than half of what most Christian colleges and universities charge, even to its residential students, and it includes some focus on moral and spiritual formation often missing in the skills-transfer focus of many online providers. Still, we believe that in order to save the multiversity, leaders of Christian universities must do more than adopt the latest response to the fragmentation of the university. They need to rethink their vision for repairing the soul of the university.

PART THREE

RESTORING THE SOUL OF THE UNIVERSITY

...

ONE AIM OF PART TWO was to help Christians in universities (both secular and Christian) understand the forces behind the fragmentation of the multiversities' soul and the consequences. Only after understanding the consequences can Christians begin to formulate a response. Again, we do not want to ignore the fact that in some cases the postmodernism outlook that has produced this fragmentation has had some positive outcomes. For Christians in liberal democracies, the recognition of competing identities, narratives, and purposes—the tournament of souls—can reinforce and strengthen the validity of taking explicitly Christian approaches to teaching and scholarship and uniquely coherent visions of a university as one among many approaches to the university.

Yet the postmodern turn has also had the odd effect of reducing pluralism. Today there is the expectation that all universities must increasingly look alike (and that the federal government must increasingly be used to enforce this unity). As a result the multiversity with a fragmented soul has now become the norm and even the model that all universities in a liberal democracy are expected to follow. If Christians wish to resist this trend, they need to think in whole new ways about how to envision, create, and structure universities and the academic vocation of a university with a soul. Yet we must realize that creating a university with a soul, as we define the word—a university with a coherent identity, story, and purpose—can be undertaken by a whole variety of groups.

In part three we attempt to describe a university with soul from a distinctly Christian perspective. What first characterizes a Christian university with soul, we maintain in chapter twelve, is that theology is central to the university. It is the lifeblood of the university body. Since it is the lifeblood, it must flow into every area of the university in some way. In this respect, we need to rethink how theology can serve the university. Again, what also makes theology unique is that it is the only field of study that worships what it studies—God. Every other discipline and every other part of the university must learn how to seek excellence without idolatry, and it can only do this with the help of theology.

The need for theology starts with our understanding of the academic vocation. In chapter thirteen, we maintain that what characterizes the Christian academic vocation is not simply ethics but a particular theological way of thinking and living. Thinking and living in the light of God and God's story can also foster an integrated relationship for teaching, scholarship, and service as well as an integrated identity and life purpose. As image bearers of God, we must faithfully pursue a coinherence reflected in the Trinity.

Understanding the curriculum in light of the Christian story and theology also proves unifying and transformative. We contend in chapter fourteen that Christians must recognize there is nothing magical about a liberal arts education. Indeed, a liberal arts education can be quite corrupting. Still, we must not abandon the liberal arts for a narrowly specialized education. Instead, we must realize that the liberal arts must be preceded by the liberating arts in order to be truly liberating.

In the cocurricular realm, the subject of chapter fifteen, theology also then proves important. We contend we should seek to create a greenhouse community that nurtures what it means for students to grow as image bearers of God. Since we understand students as made in God's image, it is vital that we know God in order to understand what it means to be a fully developed human being.

Finally, in the last chapter we contend that Christian administrators must reimagine the university as an extension of God's kingdom in times that reflect the exilic experience of God's people in the book of Jeremiah. Although much of a Christian university's function may mirror that of its secular counterparts, an exilic perspective may help stakeholders reenvision ways and areas where a redemptive and prophetic voice can reflect a very different university soul.

12

WHEN THEOLOGY SERVES THE
SOUL OF THE UNIVERSITY

...

Theologians in the modern university bear the burden of proof,
which turns out to be very good for theology, because if you are
a theologian you need to know what your colleagues in other
disciplines know but they do not have to know what you know.

STANLEY HAUERWAS

THE RATE AT WHICH Friedrich Nietzsche is quoted is quite possibly equal
to the rate he is misunderstood. Perhaps this claim proves to be most true in
relation to the assertion that "God is dead."[1] T-shirts, bumper stickers, and
even posters are emblazoned with these words. At times such references are
simply attributed to Nietzsche. At other times the references are then followed up with the words "Nietzsche is Dead," which is then attributed to God.
The irony in these dialectically opposed exchanges is that they both miss the
point. Perhaps the would-be fourth-generation Lutheran minister has something more to offer us than a simple pronouncement of God's demise.

The passage bearing this claim is found in Nietzsche's collection of philosophical fragments known as *The Gay Science*. Published in 1882, this particular fragment begins with an individual referred to as a "madman"
running into a crowd gathered in a marketplace and shouting that he seeks
God. The villagers then respond by mocking God's pursuer and then dive

into a rather long and arguably melodramatic offering best summarized by the claim that *"we have killed him* [God]—you and I. All of us are his murderers."[2] God thus did not die of his own accord but was the victim of a form of intellectual homicide committed by those God loved.

As with most of Nietzsche's prose, more questions immediately emerge than answers. For example, who is the madman? In addition, who are these individuals gathered in the village marketplace? Finally, in what way is God dead? Quite possibly Nietzsche painted himself into this fragment as the madman. He himself was on a quest for truth, was raised to find truth in the Christian tradition, and yet was unable to accept it. If we follow that possibility, perhaps the villagers are Nietzsche's intellectual contemporaries. It is worth noting here that Nietzsche's first published work was a criticism of David Friedrich Strauss's *The Life of Jesus, Critically Examined.* In that work, Strauss applied the emerging historical-critical methods of his day to the life of Christ and the sacred Scripture Christ's life inspired. There is no doubt Nietzsche found the work of Strauss, and others like Strauss, to be disconcerting due to its power to undermine faith and reduce talk about the triune God to a mere intellectual exercise. Overall Nietzsche's parable raises the possibility that God's death could be ruled a homicide facilitated by an intellectual climate undermining knowledge of and belief in God.

Theology is usually defined as the study of God and God's relation to the world. Perhaps God was considered dead for no other reason than people in Nietzsche's age first dethroned and then largely "killed" theology. When theology began to be reduced to historical or literary study of the Bible, as it began to be during Nietzsche's time, theologians increasingly failed to offer additional knowledge about the subject of their study, God. University faculty and students no longer looked to the wisdom about God and God's creation found through theology to shape the lives of individuals or make sense out of the whole of creation. Consequently what was formerly known as the queen of the sciences was reduced to one discipline among many and in many public institutions was removed altogether. Freed from theology's claims, as previous chapters have related, an emerging cast of academic disciplines then sought unsuccessfully to replace theology. In this chapter, we point out that theology in Christian universities and certain secular ones is not dead. Instead, it is tamed and caged within narrow disciplinary boundaries. The contemporary post-Christian context, we contend, provides a wonderful opportunity for theology to be set free to fulfill a much grander role—being a servant that can nourish the soul of the university.

Caging and Taming Theology

In the Middle Ages it was quite understandable to use royal language to refer to the study of God as the queen of the sciences. In the age after Nietzsche, we think it might be more appropriate to use a different metaphor: theology as the frightening lion in the academic jungle. Universities from Nietzsche's time on either tried to dispense with theology, or they attempted something just as horrific: they sought to cage theology, because taking theology seriously can result in frightening consequences, ideological as well as physical. After all, as the previous chapters demonstrated, since the so-called Enlightenment, letting theologians argue about the important questions in life has been considered too dangerous (and usually some reference to religious wars is thrown in for good measure). Consequently practitioners of the other disciplines still no longer look to and no longer want theology to pull everything together to make sense of the world. For them, caging and taming theology allows them to roam free in the university jungle.

Of course, as is always the case when the dominant discipline is vanquished, various academic disciplines vie for the privilege of making sense out of the whole of creation. Lacking the wisdom that comes from theology's grand view of the universe and the university, those disciplines can at best only describe the details of smaller and smaller slices of our existence. Interestingly, the reality that secular ideological disagreement, or letting the other beasts in the academic jungle roam free, produces even more violence is a story that is often overlooked.[3] Today's multiversity has become an institution where faculty members in one discipline often no longer want to, or perhaps even are able to, speak to colleagues in another discipline. When students wander from one intellectual kingdom of the modern university to the next, they may rightly wonder if anything can bring peace and unity to our fragmented intellectual jungle.

The harsh reality is that no one single discipline can reconstitute this broken whole. Scientists tried, and continue to try, by imposing their methodological preference for empiricism and theoretical outlooks on all other domains of knowing.[4] Social scientists have tried by parading as scientists that can solve societal problems. Humanists promise that exposure to an enlightened culture and the best that humanity has to offer will provide meaning.[5] However, no one discipline, or even one discipline in league with its closest allies, could cultivate the wisdom that appropriately arcs across and calibrates all other ways of knowing.

Theology's replacement, religion—or more appropriately stated, religious studies, as it has come to be known in recent years—has attempted to gain legitimacy by poaching methods from other disciplines in order to study the behavior of religious people or the objects such people produce. For example, in her essay titled "Religious Studies Versus Theology," Denise Cush argues that theology "does still retain its overtones of confessionalism."[6] Instead, she prefers religious studies, which would not preference a particular religious tradition such as Christianity "but as one 'religion' among many."[7] A practicing Christian, Hindu, or Muslim could serve as a religious studies scholar, but they would need to find a way to bracket their beliefs from their motivation, means, and outcomes of scholarly practice. Although religious studies is thus a definable discipline suitable for inclusion in the academy, the focus of its scholars looks something more like the psychological or sociological study of religious peoples or perhaps even the study of religious texts as defined by those same people groups. They also reveal confusion about the discipline's identity. History professors try to teach people how to be historians, philosophy professors try to teach students how to think like philosophers, but religious studies professors do not try to teach students to be religious. In the end, they have reduced religion to a mere intellectual exercise. Theology professors, however, seek to teach their students how to be theologians.

The creation of a separate theology faculty, however, introduces a difficulty. Connecting one's scholarly endeavors to God and the Christian story is no longer something everyone must do. As we made clear, though, starting with chapter one, this problem with sequestering or taming theology began at the beginning of the university with the creation of theology faculty. It would continue for hundreds of years. In chapter three we noted that while John Henry Newman sought to save theology in the university, he primarily argued for its marginalized status as one discipline within the university to be preserved. In contrast, we contend that theology, when properly understood, cannot rest easily within the confines of a singular faculty. In fact, by its very nature, theology knows of no boundary between God, God's revelation, and every dimension of the created order. We should note that having those who specialize in theology is not necessarily anathema to sustaining its pervasiveness. Having educational specialists does not preclude all faculty from taking the craft of teaching seriously. Indeed, as we will outline below, theological specialists in the Christian tradition should be the best of academic servants.

What we want to emphasize is that, in contrast to every other discipline that operates with an impulse to reduce matters to their smallest possible unit of understanding, the practice of theology should help us cultivate the wisdom needed to draw all creation back to God. For example, when a theologian reads the Bible, he or she does not read it as a text that merely records history or was crafted in particular literary genres. Reading Scripture as a person of faith is an act of relationship that also has a formative effect—an effect that calls the reader to find his or her place in God's story. To read the narrative of Christ's crucifixion is not only an inquiry into history but more importantly a confrontation with the realization our sin compelled Christ to submit himself in such a way. Theologians cannot nor should they even try to bracket themselves out of that experience, as modern scientists were taught to do when undertaking experiments. The wisdom that comes from contemplating God and viewing creation and its various dimensions in their proper order would be lost if this were an academic exercise only. As a result, the only way theology can be what it is called to be is for us to give up the wrong-headed desire to make it *primarily* one elevated academic discipline among others. Fortunately, our current post-Christian setting allows theologians to cast off the restraints required to be a respectable professional disciple according to some deformed cultural standard and can encourage theologians to be free to do other more important tasks, such as helping the contemporary church, Christian university, and different disciplinary practitioners love and worship God.

The Consequences of Setting Theology Free

In the Middle Ages, theology became sequestered within one room of the academic palace. In the modern age, it was dethroned as the queen and sometimes even placed in the dungeon of the academic castle. We believe we must try to recapture the transdisciplinary nature of theology practiced by Hugh of St. Victor and envisioned by Peter Ramus and William Ames. If we are to set theology free from being primarily a marginal professional discipline within academia and reenvision it as a transdisciplinary endeavor that serves the academy and the church, we believe theologians must knock again at the door of the university, the various disciplinary rooms, and offer to serve. As Stanley Hauerwas writes, "Theology is only a 'queen' of the sciences if humility determines her work."[8] In other words, theologians must act like Christ, live among the disciplines, and learn how to be servants. Or to change the analogy, we contend that theology should strengthen the soul of the university by helping to nourish every academic discipline and every part of the cocurriculum.

What exactly can theologians then offer? First, theologians can help make sense of our fundamental human desire to worship. Indeed, theologians are the only ones who can truly love the subject of their discipline with the highest love without becoming slaves. Although other professors studying their disciplines can learn from that love, they cannot share it. In other words, the danger they face is idolatry; loving their discipline and the subject of their study over and above God. If so, they enter the dangerous zone Paul describes in Romans 1:25: "They exchanged the truth about God for a lie, and worshiped and served created things rather than the Creator—who is forever praised. Amen."

Indeed, some practitioners have turned their discipline into a functional religion. For example, Christian Smith writes about how American sociology has become a substitute religion for many of its practitioners. The end result of those who practice sociology in this way, according to Smith, is that sociologists become dishonest about the goals of sociology: the discipline becomes filled with internal self-contradictions (e.g., claiming to value equality while being as status conscious as any discipline), sociologists become slaves to standardized thinking and myopic socio-logic, the peer-reviewed process becomes corrupted, and other sociologists are alienated.[9]

Academic disciplines are not the only parts of the university subject to this temptation. Athletics, as we noted in chapter eleven, also serves as a substitute religion when it is separated from the larger purposes of the university. It becomes an arena for the pursuit of excellence unhinged from any standards of idolatry. Indeed, it becomes a substitute way to celebrate communal solidarity apart from God. Theology provides us the wisdom and the guidance needed to pursue wholeness and excellence without idolatry. With regard to athletics, we need theologians to help us understand the religious impulse they unleash, to teach us how to love God and sports in the right order, and to be prophetic voices who can alert Christian universities when their athletic devotion veers into idolatry.

Second, with regard to wholeness, theology can help us understand the way Christ can help us overcome disciplinary divisions to find wholeness again. As Oliver Crisp, Gavin D'Costa, Mervyn Davies, and Peter Hampson write, Christ's incarnation reveals "that the entire created world was the arena of redemption and the whole person was involved: the biological, the economic, the artistic, the literary, the political and so on."[10] Or as Colossians 1:17 reminds us, "He is before all things, and in him all things hold together." What this means for Christian universities is that our learning needs "to be underpinned by love, awe, and worship, not just be instrumental control over the created world, which all too often included control and reduction of the human."[11] Wisdom, as Proverbs reminds us, requires worship.[12]

With regard to excellence, every discipline of study needs theology since it offers the possibility of freedom from the slavery that results from loving and worshiping one's own created discipline or endeavor first and treating it as a sacred project. It can help faculty, students, and staff love God and their discipline or field in a way that results in excellence without an enslaving or corrupting idolatry. Ultimately it offers the freedom to worship God and love one's discipline without making it an object of sacred devotion.

Theology can only offer this freedom, however, if theologians free themselves from judging their performance solely by the standards of excellence determined by the academy. The corruption of theology is not that it has become a sacred project. After all, unlike any other discipline it can be a

231

unique kind of sacred project in that one can and should worship the focus of one's study in theology. Theology today becomes corrupted when it no longer *is* a sacred project, and theologians no longer serve God and God's whole creation. Theologians become content with theology being an academic discipline that provides them gainful employment, particularly in an academic setting where they may not be subject to church administrators and fickle denominations. When this happens, theology serves narrow sorts of masters such as one's self, the theology guild, book publishers, journal editors, and university interests. It also ends up serving originality instead of the Christian tradition. Provocative theology ends up selling books, increasing one's reputation, advancing one's career, and drawing attention to the university (which is what the university likes).

In contrast, imagine a sacred theology faculty whose goal is to deepen the worship and love of God through advanced academic study in every discipline. Honestly, it is hard for us to imagine. We do not know of a theology department that explicitly states that end as its mission, although we do know theologians and ethicists who do. Stanley Hauerwas and Samuel Wells maintain, "One of the tasks of Christian theology is to explore how Christians may get their worship of God wrong and as a result fail to witness to the God whose love moves the sun and the other stars."[13] Indeed, one of the ways theology departments become corrupted is when the mission of most theology departments in universities is thought to be the same as other academic departments in the university. The higher the publication rating, the more prestige brought to the university, and the more students they attract (and thus resources they acquire), the more prestigious and powerful they become. What the other disciplines can offer theology is a call for theology to be different and to retain its sacred calling. Admittedly, it is not clear how one can do a tenure or annual review for a theology faculty member based on the goal of how well he or she has advanced the worship and love of God in various academic contexts. Perhaps the reason we cannot imagine such a review is that we lack contemporary models.

In fact, one sometimes hears from religious studies faculty that other faculty should leave some of these matters of faith and learning to the professionals. Although their professional pride is understandable, reflecting on a medical analogy in this instance is helpful. We all cannot be medical doctors, but we all are called to steward the health of our body as best we can. At times, of course, we do need the service of a medical professional who ideally should be there to serve the patient. Similarly, every faculty member must engage in the worship of God in the practice of his or her discipline, but at times they need the service of those with expertise in delving into the primary study of God. Perhaps what other disciplines outside of theology need are more theologians who can think creatively with other academic specialists to relate theology to their area of specialization.

A second way that the medical analogy helps us not place too much trust in the professional theologian can be illuminated by considering the patient-doctor relationship. The patient knows his or her body the best. Indeed, each specific body should be the medical doctor's field of study. The ideal doctors are not simply bringing their knowledge to this body, they are also learning from the patient's body. Theologians must acknowledge that those who study God's creation, whether human or divine, provide them with greater insight into the Creator. Theologians cannot truly be theologians unless they are learning from the entire body of faculty in the university. After all, the theologian's realm of study is every discipline created by God.

A Set of Practical Proposals

Practically speaking, we think our outlook means that Christian universities need to provide structures that allow theologians to serve the university and the church instead of being slaves to their professional societies. Christian universities need to help provide the structures that allow theologians to serve. In this regard, we want to make three specific proposals.

First, Christian universities should allow theologians to choose the degree to which they may be judged by their academic publications for the professional societies, by their interdisciplinary work with other academic departments, or their popular publications meant to serve the church. Ideally they could hire a separate theologian who would work in partnership with one of four general areas—sciences, social sciences, humanities, and professions. At the very least, we would suggest that Christian universities should hire at least one if not more faculty members trained in theology whose job is not to advance their scholarly agenda within the professional fields of the discipline. Instead, they should serve more as a clinical theologian who would focus on learning from the rest of the faculty. In service, they could help faculty and students learn how to speak and think theologically, but they should also see it as their job to learn from the whole university. This might perhaps be similar to current vice presidents for the advancement of mission that one finds at Catholic universities but different in that these university theologians would seek to free theology from its professional confines and bring it back to the whole university.

At the same time, they would recognize that theology must also learn from other fields in order to know more about God. In other words, their job would be to serve and learn from the university. They would likely publish with scholarly Christian presses, and their focus would be on stimulating the conversation among their fellow academics about issues related to the animation of faith and learning. One could argue that a number of these centers with associated faculty already exist on various Christian campuses (e.g., Baylor, Pepperdine, Georgetown), although we find it noteworthy that in our experience they are not led by theologians who seek to offer their service to the university or to gather new insights from faculty across the university. Instead they are usually led by philosophers. In addition, the leaders are usually tasked more with leading a faculty conversation than initiating joint scholarly projects that place theology and other disciplines in dialogue.

Second, we would propose that Christian universities need more doctoral programs that combine theology and other academic discipline programs in a way that would not only allow doctoral students in theology to actually find jobs in a shrinking job market but that might also take their theological training into another academic sphere of the university. These dual-trained academics would model a form of defragmentation to those in other disciplines while also helping those outside theology.

Third, we contend that at a Christian university general education should not simply place a couple of Bible or theology courses into the curricular mix as if that actually helps students obtain a coherent understanding of how the rest of the curriculum fits into God's story. Unfortunately, few required theology or Bible courses help students make sense of the whole university or life as a whole outside the disciplinary concerns of those in religious studies departments.[14] Theology still largely functions as an upper palace room instead of a foundation in today's Christian university. We need faculty and students to learn how to speak theologically both about the university as a whole and about their particular discipline, and how what they learn might fit into the good life as a whole. Theologians can help.

Free to Worship

If theologians wish to serve the other disciplines, they can start by helping with something they specifically can provide. They can help us learn how to reintegrate our lives. As Hauerwas and Wells observe:

> So often it appears that lay Christians have a thriving life of personal devotion, an active life within a worshiping community, and an engaged life fulfilling a range of professional and public roles in the workplace, neighborhood, and family, but comparatively seldom do lay Christians have an equally developed way of bringing these three parts of their life together.[15]

What can bring together the disparate parts of our lives? Hauerwas and Wells suggest that worship provides the key. By worship, they mean more than singing worship songs and listening to preaching. They point out the variety of ways that a rich liturgy offers Christians the opportunity to do a number of essential things: (1) meet God and one another, (2) reencounter the Christian story, (3) experience being embodied in that story, (4) reenact the story, and (5) be commissioned to reenact the story in the world. As part of this process, one is invited to engage in

> a series of ordered practices that shape the character and assumptions of Christians, and suggest habits and models that inform every aspect of corporate life—meeting people, acknowledging fault and failure, celebrating, thanking, reading, speaking with authority, reflecting on wisdom, naming truth, registering need, bringing about reconciliation, sharing food, renewing purpose.[16]

Although Hauerwas and Wells are writing in particular about the discipline of Christian ethics, we believe this vision could be articulated for every discipline. Such a project is beyond the scope of this book, so we will focus on what we see as the foundational practice that might help academics in other disciplines encounter God and the Christian story, experience being embodied in that story, and reenact the story in their discipline. It is also the practice that was perhaps best exemplified by William Ames, whom we discussed in chapter two.

First and foremost, if academics are going to reenact the Christian story, they must learn to speak and live theologically. Christianity, in this sense, involves incarnating oneself in a story and culture and learning the language and practices of that story and culture. We do not ask a native English speaker in history to produce a thoughtful history of China in Chinese. In the same way, we must be realistic about the speaking ability of professors from other disciplines who have been immersed in thinking and speaking sociologically, psychologically, economically, and so on, but have little training to speak theologically about their discipline. Of course, the good news is that many practitioners of disciplines have at least a fundamental grasp of basic conversational theology. The problem is that they often do not know how to employ this basic conversational speaking ability to the specifics of their discipline. Here is where theologians can be helpful. Although theologians wrestle with being corrupted by many academic forces, they hopefully at least know how to speak theologically (however, in some cases they too only speak historically, or scientifically, or anthropologically).

Unfortunately, theologians have a long history of not wanting to share their language learning practices. Crisp, D'Costa, Davies, and Hampson note "that for large periods of history theology as an academic discipline was done in careful isolation from other disciplines and these other disciplines, as in the University of Paris, were forbidden to trespass upon the subject matter of theology: God."[17] It is thus possible that by protecting their own disciplinary boundaries, which we chronicled in the first chapters of this book, theologians sowed the seeds of autonomy that continue to take hold today. After all, autonomy is born in some measure when a discipline or subdiscipline establishes a set of scholarly practices and a language uniquely its own. Some more cynical observers may go so far as to argue that the more arcane the practices and the more esoteric the language, the greater the level of autonomy. This drive for autonomy that builds a language one does not share undermines the quest for transcendent wisdom and thus produces the inability to see across disciplinary lines. Today, as Crisp and company observe, formal conversations concerning the nature of theology and, in particular, its place among other academic disciplines, are generally limited. For example, a search of recent titles dealing with this particular topic yielded only a handful.[18] Yet, as two of us who experienced graduate theological training but currently work in other disciplines can attest, it helps for theologians to be forced to think in complex ways about other disciplines outside of theology.

The faculty and graduate students in every discipline will have to be apprenticed to think, speak, and practice their disciplines in this unique manner. At the very least, Christian professors must read particular canonical works in their discipline that integrate theology and disciplinary insights. In fact, we continually find it amazing that some presidents, provosts, and administrators at some Christian universities have also not read widely about what it means to lead a Christian university in this area. As a result, they tend to speak the language of administration and management that is no different from that spoken by other administrators at secular institutions. Part of the problem may be that they have not been provided with or found themselves a full range of scholars who read widely in what it means to practice their particular scholarly vocation as a Christian. As any person who has achieved excellence in a field knows, they could not do so without models and mentors to help them. Theologians can and should help in this area.

At the very least, every Christian professor at a Christian university should have a basic knowledge of a standard set of works addressing the relationship of Christianity with their discipline and the Christian university as a whole. An example of a set of tutoring works is the two-volume work by Oliver Crisp (Fuller Seminary), Mervyn Davies (Sarum College), Gavin D'Costa (University of Bristol), and Peter Hampson (Blackfriars Hall, Oxford), which we have been citing in this chapter. One goal the authors articulate is to seek to "facilitate a critical and positive relationship between Christianity and the wide variety of intellectual disciplines."[19] They believe that fostering this kind of relationship would produce a "Christian culture": "This would entail fresh developments and continuing research cultures within the natural, human and creative sciences that would, in the long term, help human flourishing as well as create an environment where the gospel would penetrate all aspects of human existence."[20] To achieve this goal, the editors asked their contributing authors to explore two questions, which would be the source of helpful discussion with professors of any discipline and theologians seeking to serve that discipline:

> Methodologically, what shifts might occur in your subject and the study of your subject if Christianity were taken as true? Substantively, what transformations might be seen in your subject area if the truth of Christianity were to penetrate those like yourselves who study and engage with the subject?[21]

The editors recognize that theologians and experts in the various disciplines can offer various tools for accomplishing these goals. In other words, they understand that all the disciplines within the church need each other. For example, in another volume they point to how philosophy "helps theology with the formal tasks of developing coherence, logical rigour, intelligibility and rhetorical elegance—among other things."[22] Philosophy then "helps theology in providing complex and sophisticated systems of conceptuality that have been employed to address a huge variety of questions."[23] In order to accomplish these kinds of creative interdisciplinary projects, they recognize that some deconstruction has to take place first. They assume that "some of the university disciplines have developed methodological assumptions that initially compel them to be at odds with the Christian faith" and that "Christians working within those disciplines have the responsibility to uncover those methodological assumptions."[24]

Overall, by asking theology to become a servant leader and help other disciplines outside of its own field, theology once again has the possibility of making the university just that—the university. In essence, the university once again has the possibility of demonstrating a unified understanding of knowledge and the world it claims to study. Professors in other disciplines will also have a better understanding of how to pursue excellence without idolatry, or said more positively, faithful excellence (a topic discussed in more detail in the next chapter).

Practicing Theology in the University

In 1938, William Adams Brown wrote a short book titled *The Case for Theology in the University*. In the final chapter, where he set forth his case for how to restore theology to a place of prominence in the future American university, he characterized what he thought theology had to offer: "Our concern is with the training of the mind, and we can make a central place for theology among the many interests which compete for a place in the attention of our students only as we can show that it has a distinctive contribution to make to the formation of sound intellectual habits."[25] Brown's approach offered a traditional view of theology, which saw it largely as an intellectual endeavor instead of a holistic enterprise. Although we have discussed the importance of learning to think and speak theologically, we want to emphasize that we believe theology in the university must be understood as more than "sound intellectual habits." As James K. A. Smith has argued, although education does concern itself with intellectual habits, if it hopes to be successful it forms the whole person.[26] The same would prove true for theology. In this regard, we believe a definition of theology's task, such as Karl Barth's understanding of theology as "the scientific self-examination of the Christian Church with respect to the content of its distinctive talk about God"[27] remains too small in many ways. Theology involves more than critical examination of talk.

Rightly practiced theology, we suggest, fundamentally (but not exclusively) involves a set of Christian practices associated with worship. According to this understanding, theology is not simply additional cognitive perspectives that one adds to one's work in another discipline. It also recognizes that every professor will engage in the practice of worship. Since Christian professors outside of theology must resist worshiping their discipline, they must necessarily practice worship of God from within their discipline. This combination involves what we have labeled faithful scholarship that pursues excellence without idolatry.

A helpful model of faithful scholarship again comes from Hauerwas and Wells in their edited volume *The Blackwell Companion to Christian Ethics*. In the volume, they approach the particular discipline of ethics through the lens of Christian worship. They do so by looking through the lens of multiple practices that Christian faith traditions use in worship.

239

Table 4. List of worship practices

Meeting God and One Another	Reencountering the Story	Being Embodied	Reenacting the Story	Being Commissioned
gathering greeting naming the risen Lord being reconciled praising in song collecting praise	reading the Scriptures listening proclaiming deliberating discerning confessing the faith	praying interceding being baptized becoming one body becoming one flesh sharing peace	offering participating remembering invoking breaking bread receiving Communion sharing Communion eating together being silent being thankful washing feet	being blessed bearing fruit being sent

Source: Hauerwas and Wells, "Christian Ethics as Informed Prayer," table of contents.

What is helpful about such an approach is that it expands our limited views of what worship involves (e.g., going to chapel, singing, and hearing a speaker). As they model in their book, we would suggest that these practices also occur within the context of one's discipline. In other words, rightly practiced theology is not something only done by professionals in an academic discipline. It is something in which everyone in the body of Christ must be tutored.

What might this endeavor look like in the context of different academic practices? In our own work, we have discovered that Christian professors often perceive the distinctive nature of their work as involving a variety of endeavors, some focused on their own activities and others focused on how students are shaped. For example, table 5 outlines what we found in a study of over 2,300 Christian professors at forty-six different institutions.[28]

Table 5. Ways of integrating one's faith tradition in the classroom

Activities of the Teacher	Student Focused
1. Introduce scriptural connections	5. Cultivate personal spiritual growth and practices
2. Employ specific interpretive views	6. Integrate a Christian worldview
3. Make distinctive curricular choices	7. Understand and utilize theological traditions
4. Use unique methodological approaches	8. Develop ethical thinking or behavior

We would suggest that activities one, two, six, and seven all involve to some degree what we refer to as learning to speak theologically. Here is one example from a professor:

> I believe that we are all fallen sinners, but that we can all be redeemed. Those that come to saving faith in Christ are gifted to serve Him. All of us need to be held accountable to give a good and honest effort to tasks that are presented to us. As faculty members, we need to see the potential in each student and do all that we can to help our students grow in faith as well as in our academic discipline and in the ability to use their gifts more fully for Christ's service.

An approach that incorporated rightly practiced theology would have implications for bringing all of these categories together. After all, the danger of approaches five and eight, as will be discussed in more depth in the next chapter, is that they are sometimes then thought of as separate from the content of the class or from the Christian story. Perhaps one prays before class (number five) or seeks to model or teach humility or servanthood (number eight) (e.g., "In many courses, we conduct service-learning projects serving the poor and homeless").

For instance, we can teach students about an extended version of baptism, as this professor did:

> It is very important to me that my students have a broad understanding of Christian history, in particular the Anabaptist insights—as these views have been frequently eclipsed by louder more strident voices. . . . Therefore my objectives often read something like: Students will grasp the complex and textured historical purposes of baptism; or students will gain a broader understanding of salvation—not as simply a moment in time, but an ongoing stepping into discipleship that accompanies one's putting on Christ.

Although this example comes from theology, realizing that other disciplines also create worship structures helps clarify the role of baptism in other disciplines. Baptism, after all, is a ritual that only makes sense in a larger story that signals an identity change. Through taking on the identity of Christ, one now views knowledge and the world differently. Christians simply cannot be objective observers of the world. They participate in worship of the Creator of the world.

Moreover, "Worship challenges assumptions about what goodness, truth and beauty mean in the light of the gospel."[29] Although such an approach involves adopting what in the past might have been referred to as a "Christian worldview," the implications for this identity change are much broader. If one switches from being a boxer to a gymnast, a soldier to a diplomat, or a violinist to a conductor, one simply does not adopt a different worldview. One adopts a whole different set of practices that inform how one understands one's endeavors.

For example, in an academic world defined by a proper modern distinction between subject and object, prayer would serve no reasonable function. The process of knowing begins with the subject as it positions itself in relation to an object that the subject defines. In contrast, the willingness to practice prayer on the part of educators in an academic community is a recognition of one's unique identity and the fact that the knowing subject needs redefinition. In *Theology and the Public Square*, Gavin D'Costa argues:

> Since the object of theology is the Truth which is the living God and his plan for salvation in Jesus Christ, the theologian is called to deepen his own life of faith and continuously unite his scientific research with prayer. In this way, he will become more open to "the supernatural sense of faith" upon which he depends, and it will appear to him as a sure rule for guiding his reflections and helping him assess the correctness of his conclusions.[30]

In order for scholars to be in proper relation to God in this context, they must submit themselves to the wisdom that can only come from God.

Stanley Hauerwas, in commenting on D'Costa's claim, says, "D'Costa's argument for the recovery of prayer for theology is not a pious gesture, but rather his attempt to name the condition necessary for theology to be recognized as knowledge."[31] In order for theology to locate its rightful place in the university, it must first accept it is not a discipline like all of the others. By doing so and placing a practice such as prayer in the center of its work, it redefines the subject-object relationship and, in turn, now holds the potential to redeem the fragmented nature in which all of the other disciplines exist.

The villagers in Nietzsche's "madman" fragment knew of no such value for prayer. The loss of an ability to know and appreciate God brought on the demise of God in their eyes. In their world, only a madman would then seek God. If such an interpretation of this famed fragment is remotely accurate, what then are the ramifications for scholars who teach theology? Or, more appropriately stated, scholars who teach any discipline? If theology is simply another discipline, theologians will leave the public they serve to wonder about its wider value. Theology would then only be of value in a self-constructed and self-concealed private world. However, it will never rise to the level of its created potential. In addition, scholars in any other discipline will be "set free" to worship their own discipline. In reality, those scholars simply become peddlers of ever-reductionistic views of the world and, if honest with themselves, join the chorus in asking, "How shall we comfort ourselves, the murderers of all murderers? What was holiest and mightiest of all that the world has yet owned has bled to death under our knives: who will wipe this blood off us?"[32]

REIMAGINING
THE ACADEMIC VOCATION

...

We are a university; that is, we are all members of a body dedicated
to a single cause. There must be among us distinctions of function,
but there can be no division of purpose.

PETER SALOVEY

THE ACADEMIC VOCATION as understood in the contemporary research
university is defined by the practices of teaching, service, and scholarship,
although others might add additional duties.[1] As described in chapter six,
the standards of excellence for each practice are usually determined by unrelated criteria, which often mean each task is addressed separately in faculty
development books.[2] Unhinged from one another, a hierarchy has emerged
over time with research at the top. Disconnected from one another and thus
valued in a hierarchical order, the academic practices have become tools for
building sets of individual stories with no interconnecting narrative. Research garners the greatest prestige and is measured by criteria held loosely
and inconsistently among professional peers who judge relevance to the
defining scholarly questions of the moment, no matter how arcane to those
outside the field or discipline. Teaching is most frequently measured by a
different kind of "review": by the feedback faculty members receive from
student evaluations. Although momentum is building for faculty members
to also receive peer evaluations, a mix of political and practical realities

holds such efforts back from reaching a systemic level of acceptance. Finally, service is not only ill-defined but also the most frequently neglected leg of the so-called stool.[3]

Motivating professors to seek excellence in all three aspects requires more than calls to simply do one's academic duty.[4] Moral motivation usually requires a more compelling narrative.[5] Although professors draw on many such narratives, whether feminism, Marxism, liberalism, environmentalism, or sexual identity, the question we wish to explore is what Christians have to offer. Mark Schwehn provides an example of how to place the academic vocation within a larger Christian narrative by noting that "all academics are exiles from Eden."[6] In other words, all academics fall short of the ideals we share for the academic vocation. What can help us save it? Schwehn makes the following proposal for how to reorient the academic calling:

> First, teaching . . . becomes the activity in terms of which all others—publication, collegiality, research, consultation, advising—are to be understood, interpreted and appraised. Second, the cultivation of those spiritual virtues that make genuine teaching and learning possible becomes a vitally important aspect of pedagogy. Finally, both charity and *philia* [friendship/familial love] . . . become once again central to its self-conception and to its overall mission in the world.[7]

Schwehn argues that this conception is perhaps most at home and best sustained in religious communities, although he believes that those outside the Christian tradition can appropriate the virtues on which this vision rests.

Although we agree with the importance of practicing virtue in the academic calling, we contend that any approach to integrating virtue must not prioritize teaching over scholarship or service but should instead prioritize the role of the triune God and God's theological story in defining, directing, and empowering the virtues that sustain excellence in these practices and help promote flourishing academic communities. We doubt broadly defined virtues on which we all agree can sufficiently reorient the academic vocation. After all, professors need a compelling identity and story that will motivate them to acquire certain virtues. Instead, Christians must think about virtues such as faith, hope, and love, as well as other fruits of the Spirit, in the light of a theological narrative and realities that usually do not enter standard secular reasoning.

Our biblical example for the necessity of understanding virtues such as faith within a narrative context is the story of Abraham. Faith for Abraham is only a virtue when directed toward God. By faith, Abraham moved his entire family from the land they knew and in which they prospered to a land they had yet to see. Later, God had given Isaac to Abraham and Sarah in their advanced age—an age at which the common earthly narrative dictated conception was incomprehensible. Yet this same God also commanded Abraham to sacrifice the gift of that child. By faith, Abraham embraced an even more challenging request from God. Accordingly, as Søren Kierkegaard notes in *Fear and Trembling*, "Abraham had faith and did not doubt, he believed the preposterous."[8] The act of sacrificing one's child, a child long promised to Abraham and Sarah, is only exceeded in its "unethical" qualities by the crucifixion of the innocent Christ centuries later. Such a request appears unethical by the set of standards we might utilize if reasoning in a world without God. In other words, Abraham's obedience only makes sense in the light of reasoning within a larger theological story. Or as the author of Hebrews writes, "Abraham reasoned that God could even raise the dead, and so in a manner of speaking he did receive Isaac back from death" (Heb 11:19). This kind of faithful reasoning frees one to consider possibilities never before considered by those enslaved to narrow cultural expectations about the divided practices of one's vocation. Christian scholars are not bound by the cultural standards of their profession or the teaching evaluations of their students. Faithful Christian scholars enjoy a different range of ontological awareness.

Faithful Teaching, Scholarship, and Service

In the light of the above example, we find it unsurprising that one of the common though helpful ways of reenvisioning the academic vocation that scholars have employed is placing an emphasis on faithfulness to God.[9] Christian academics should pursue excellence without idolatry, or said more positively, faithful excellence. What pursuing faithful excellence means likely consists of numerous elements and will vary depending on the particular practice (teaching, scholarship, and service).

Two types of books have been written about the vocation of the faithful Christian scholar that can help with these matters. One kind has tended to focus on specific academic practices such as scholarship[10] or teaching.[11] A second type of book has sought to focus on faculty development and covered how Christian professors might address all three areas.[12] All of these books provide helpful guidance about what it means to pursue faithful excellence in the various areas of the academic vocation.

What we want to outline here, though, is a way of thinking about the academic vocation that can help us resist the fragmentation of our academic selves. This approach sets forth a theological way of connecting all three of these elements as well as connecting how we think about the academic vocation to our lives as a whole. Although we find much to admire in Ernest Boyer's approach outlined in chapter six, we believe any full conception of the academic vocation requires further linguistic help from theology. We need to draw on what we know about God and God's work in the world to speak theologically and truthfully about the vocation of a Christian professor.

To start, finding coherence means that we cannot talk about what it means to be a good professor without talking about what it means to be a good human being made in God's image. Fragmentation begins when we fragment our identity as a professor or staff member from our other identities or when a Christian university fragments the life of a professor or staff member so that it is only concerned with academic goals and productivity.

Professors who fragment their identity from the other parts of themselves often make their career identity their fundamental identity. If one fails to make tenure, gets passed over for an administrative position, or feels alienated from the future direction of the university, then one's sense of self becomes eroded. Coming up short in one's career means coming up short in life. Gary Burge observes that one of the keys to a successful professor in the last stage of his or her career is a pervasively integrated identity and purpose. Burge thus maintains, "We must find a meaningful involvement that *does not* tie itself entirely to the welfare of the college. This means we can take it with us even after we leave the college."[13] We must also find a purpose and identity that is more than the titles attached to our academic community.

Christian universities play an important role in shaping professors to be whole persons. A Christian university will have failed if it contains outstanding professors and staff according to the criteria of professional societies and the world but they have lost their purpose, their marriages, their children, their churches, and their character. Anton Chekov's short story "The Black Monk" contains a masterful description of the price a young scholar named Korvin paid for his academic work.

> He thought of the high toll life takes for the insignificant or very ordinary blessings it bestows on man. For instance to have to have a chair by the time you are forty, to be an ordinary professor, to explain ordinary thoughts, and other people's at that, in sluggish, boring, heavy language—in short to attain the position of a mediocre scholar—he, Korvin, had had to study for fifteen years, to work day and night, to suffer a grave mental illness, to live through an unsuccessful marriage, and to do all sorts of stupid and unfair things, which it would be more pleasant not to remember.[14]

We do not mean to suggest that the Christian university is somehow responsible for the other portions of a professor's life. Professors make their own choices, and they also need their families, communities, and first and foremost the church. Nonetheless, the university can be responsible for communicating that, while it prizes and seeks to nourish the excellent professor, the excellent professor, in its eyes, must be interpreted in the context of the larger Christian story of faithful excellence.

We found thus this chilling story from Burge a helpful example of unhealthy fragmentation:

> Many years ago I lived through a rough patch in my own personal life. . . . Since I was in a Christian college, I assumed that an important administrator would be empathetic, supportive and wise in his counsel. Instead, after I told him what was going on, he told me some very strange story about how military sergeants don't really want to know about how the troops feel—they just want to make sure they can fight the war. He then rocked back in his chair with hands folded behind his head and stared at me. It was one of those moments you don't forget.[15]

Excellence requires sacrifice, but it does not and should not require one's mental health, marriage, or worship. Again, one of the defining marks of

Christians and Christian universities should be that they seek excellence without idolatry. After all, that is what faithful excellence would entail. Such faithfulness may cost reputation in *US News and World Report* rankings, but in the kingdom of God, we should play by different rules. A caring Christian university will also demand excellence, but it should be through standards of excellence specified by God's kingdom.

Thankfully we can also tell positive, personal stories about this matter. The weekend before my first sabbatical I (Perry) had to take my wife to the hospital because she lacked feeling in her arms and legs. She ended up being diagnosed with a condition called Guillain-Barre syndrome. Consequently, she spent much of the next year in bed as I sought to care for a first grader and three-year-old while also fulfilling my academic duties. At times, making my son's lunches for school each night felt like an overwhelming burden since I was spiritually, mentally, and emotionally exhausted at the end of the day. Fortunately, at every turn I found supportive colleagues and administrators (as well as a supportive Sunday school class that brought meals to our house for the entire year). At no time was I ever asked to be a good soldier and not let the sergeant know what was going on. My colleagues understood that there was more to the good life than simply completing talks associated with a narrow understanding of the university's mission. The ultimate fragmentation is to treat the university's faculty, staff, and students as merely university faculty, staff, and students, and not human beings made in the image of God.

Understanding ourselves as made in the image of God also brings coherence and vital motivation to the overall understanding of the academic vocation. One of the joys of being a professor is being able to exercise those qualities that God also modeled to us and thus fulfill our divine purpose. Just as the triune God has done, we can create and disciple others. We create the products of scholarship such as books, articles, music, computer programs, art, films, and more. We have the privilege (and not just the duty) of discipling young adults in how to also engage in these creative endeavors to be Christian chemists, architects, filmmakers, and philosophers. We are then given the privilege of being servant-leaders and giving of ourselves, our time, and our talents to serve those who perhaps have not received the same intellectual gifts from God and who need our wisdom (while we also need them to remind us of the limits of those gifts).

Unfortunately, we find that the Christian communities in which students grow up often tend to emphasize the value of only a specific set of redemptive tasks (usually being a pastor or missionary) while failing to teach about the importance of what it means to be made in God's image and how to bear that image in the multiple arenas of creation. We can recall few teachings that helped place the full range of vocations for which college prepares students within the context of a theological story and perspective. Part of what many churches—and many universities—fail to convey is a theology in which work as worship makes sense. The great commission and the mandate to make disciples is understood narrowly as making Christian converts and teaching them various practices related to personal Christian piety. Much less emphasis is placed on discipling individuals in more complex creative endeavors such as what it means to be a Christian artist, writer, musician, engineer, chemist, and more. The result is that these other callings appear second-rate.

Resisting and Transforming Fragmentation

Thinking about the academic vocation in the light of God and God's story also resolves two problems with the fragmentation or distortion of teaching, scholarship, and service described earlier. First, there are those who perceive that one leg of the academic stool is prized in ways that delegitimizes the gifting and roles of all others. We know of one university where tenured faculty were told of a new distinction that was going to be made between those who would focus on teaching and those who would be engaged in both teaching and research. Many older faculty were insulted. Although such divides are common in the university (between lecturers and tenured faculty), in this case faculty interpreted the new divide as being driven by different values regarding teaching and scholarship (with scholarship being the more valued role). While we did not believe this was the case, the negative reaction could have been tempered by setting forth a view similar to that of 1 Corinthians 12 that acknowledges that different types of professors, in many ways, function similarly to the church in that it is a body with many parts. Each professor may have gifts in one particular area more than others, and the Christian university should seek to maximize the use of a professor's gifting. We need to recognize that all professors may not be equally outstanding in scholarship, teaching, and service. Yet the Christian university should make it clear that striving for faithful excellence in all three is ideal, and the failure to achieve excellence in one of the three areas becomes problematic.

Often, at Christian universities this pursuit of excellence in all three areas becomes unbalanced. Susan VanZanten makes a helpful critique of most Christian universities with regard to scholarship.

> Rather, in a kind of reverse elitism, [Christian college faculty] sometimes suspect those who conduct research and publish extensively as perhaps not being the best teachers. Formal reward structures may reflect this bias; how many institutions that honor a "Teacher of the Year" also honor a "Scholar of the Year"? While the research institution tends to overemphasize research as the cost of their teaching mission, mission-driven institutions can overemphasize teaching and service at the cost of their responsibility to produce scholarship.[16]

In contrast, in the university where two of us work, professors at all levels can receive awards for scholarship, teaching, and service, although we should note one interesting oddity: the number of teaching awards teaching faculty or lecturers can win is actually limited in order to reserve space for tenure-track faculty. Still, most faculty-development opportunities, such as summer faculty institutes, retreats, and other professional options, are open for the full range of faculty and concentrate on all areas. Faithful excellence in every domain is rewarded and praised.

Besides rewarding and valuing excellence in all three arenas, Christian universities should also do their best to help professors lead less fragmented lives when it comes to their research, teaching, and service. Although scholars of faculty life have suggested pragmatic reasons for such a connection, such as its efficiency, one of our former colleagues, Charles Talbert, has made the argument based on the concept of *coinherence* (defined as "inhere together"), a term used to describe the Cappadocian Fathers' approach to the Trinity.[17] Talbert uses the term to talk about the ideal way to think about the interface between teaching, research, and service. In Talbert's view, one should not simply *balance* teaching, research, and service;

251

rather, one must have one's teaching, research, and service "coinhere." In other words, while each of these tasks requires one to perform different functions, professors can and should seek to draw connections between the three. For instance, one of us is currently involved in a research project regarding academic honesty, teaches a course to student life personnel that addresses moral development, and serves on the honor council of the university. For obvious reasons, this kind of combination is helpful for finding coinherence in all three areas. The research helps inform insights offered in teaching and service. For instance, some of the literature regarding academic honesty explains what professors can do to create a better learning environment that minimizes cheating (insights that are then applied to classes). In addition, the service illuminates the teaching and research. Service on the honor council gives firsthand experience of the topics and themes discussed in the literature as some of the barriers to change—the tremendous commitment of time and resources, as well as emotional energy, it takes to enforce the rules associated with academic honesty. Consequently, the proposals made in research papers for addressing this problem can be informed by both research findings and firsthand experience.

The even more challenging yet all the more critical need for encouraging coinherence is the development of suitable assessment materials to be employed in relation to faculty promotion. The most standard approach seeks to quantify a faculty member's teaching performance, scholarly productivity, and contributions to some community, whether a local community or the university community.[18] In contrast, an integrative assessment tool would find ways to evaluate how well faculty members weave these practices together. For example, efforts such as service-learning and undergraduate research, when well implemented, would help faculty members foster the ability to weave the practices of teaching, scholarship, and service together into coherent, educational efforts. Both examples also create opportunities for the narrative of the gospel to permeate the experiences shared by faculty members, students, and the members of a particular community with which they interact. An educational imagination defined by such a narrative would undoubtedly yield assessment tools capable of reflecting the highest of ideals that define the Christian scholar.

Faithful Excellence Without Idolatry:
Academic Virtues and Practices

In the literature about what it means to practice faithful research, teaching, and service, two different elements tend to be emphasized—virtues and practices.[19] In fact, sometimes these are understood as one and the same (e.g., hospitality). For instance, just as Hugh of St. Victor noted, Christian writers today observe the importance of exercising humility with regard to scholarship, teaching, and service.[20] One obvious reason is that pride is often the vice of academics. We know a professor who while teaching a seminar replied to a student's question, "I don't know the answer." One senior then exclaimed, "I've never heard a professor say those words!"

Although we agree with much of this scholarship about virtues and practices, any emphasis on these two elements alone can succumb to the danger of fragmentation if they are not continually given context within the larger Christian identity and story. After all, why should we exercise humility as a primary academic virtue? Although positive psychology may appeal to the fact that the exercise of certain virtues may lead to human flourishing,[21] it is not always clear that certain virtues (particularly humility) lead to the advancement of one's academic career. In fact, you could argue that the lack of humility often seems to benefit faculty (e.g., shameless self-promotion).

Again, we think it is helpful to return to Hugh of St. Victor and continually connect our understanding of virtues and practices to the triune God and God's story. As Christians made in God's image, we fully bear that image when we bear God's virtues. We understand and come to know God's virtues by learning about God's story and then imitating the triune God's virtues. Moreover, we need the Holy Spirit to help us recognize when we fail to exhibit those virtues and to demonstrate them (e.g., the virtues specified in Gal 5:22-23). The important theological line for Christian professors is the one between trying to be God and bearing God's image. The temptation to be God is usually an attempt to manipulate and control, which demonstrates a futile grasp at omnipotence, which only God has.

This particular understanding of Christian virtue means that certain virtues will be prioritized. Faith, hope, and love, as Paul specifies, are primary for Christians, and they should be primary for Christian scholars. The redemptive virtues we are specifically told by Christ and the apostles to imitate are also vital.[22] We suggest that they are redemptive because they usually require reversing the fall through some kind of sacrifice or suffering. These virtues include humility, servanthood, forgiveness, and submission. These redemptive Christian virtues will not always make the top of secular lists of virtues. For instance, over half the states have laws mandating or encouraging public schools to teach children virtues. There is little agreement among the lists of virtues, which altogether include sixty-four character qualities. Faith, hope, and charity, unsurprisingly, are missing from any state's list of virtues, and humility, submission, and servanthood are nowhere to be found. Forgiveness is taught only in Arizona.[23]

In contrast, the teacher's Christian identity shapes the virtues he or she considers using and prioritizing for his or her scholarship, teaching, and service. For instance, in our research on Christian professors, one described how particular theologically informed practices guided the process of dealing with a student who cheated.

> When I have discovered a student who has copied a classmate's paper, I will ask both students for a private meeting. In the context of that meeting, I will show the student the evidence for the act, and ask for his/her explanation. Typically, a student will confess right away. Occasionally, a student may make excuses, and I gently but firmly encourage them to acknowledge their error. When they have done so, I explain the consequences for their act, but also offer forgiveness and a plan for the future to avoid such acts. If the student has used another's paper without their permission, I encourage him/her to seek the forgiveness of the classmate. In a few cases, I have also worked with the victim of plagiarism to help him/her work through the sense of betrayal and anger towards a fellow student.

For this professor, the specific emphasis on the virtue of forgiveness and involving various parties in a reconciliation process emerged from the Christian story. Of course, we are not implying that other non-Christian professors might not apply some of the same virtues, but it is clear they would do so for different reasons and possibly through a different process.

This kind of virtue and practice formed by God and God's story can and should influence every dimension of research, teaching, and service. We know of a professor on a search committee who wanted things to go a certain way. Yet he realized that this longing to reach a certain outcome, which in his mind would advance the Christian mission of the university, still needed to be formed by the Christian story in several ways. First, he recognized that a fair process should come before getting one's way and that he should not try to manipulate the system since it is basically a fair system. Second, while he thought he had good reasons for wanting a certain outcome, he also realized that a presumption existed on his part about what the future held and what he thought would be best. At that moment, he realized that what needed to happen was a movement of his heart toward God's will; that he may not really know what would be best for his department or institution. Danny Morris and Charles Olsen, in their work on decision-making processes for Christian organizations, use the Quaker concept of "indifference" to describe a posture in which an individual has discarded interest to all but God's will.[24] This does not mean that one has or even can shed preferences, biases, and perspectives, but that hearing God's will is prioritized and sought above any of these. The future always plays out in mysterious ways. As a result of these reflections, he gave the situation over to God. Then he planned to argue his case. Ironically, that evening he received an email that revealed a change in the job-applicant pool. He would not need to argue his case at all since the candidate he preferred was now the only one. Although such a "happy ending" is not always the case, it was the practice of faith in God (and not simply an undirected and nebulous faith) that freed him from the temptation to manipulate and control. The integration of faith and learning in a search committee means one does not need to be consumed with conniving, stage-managing, and manipulating. One can focus on integrity by sustaining a relationship and faith in God and not merely by virtue talk (e.g., "I should be humble here").

The Christian academic vocation is first and foremost defined by thinking about and living one's vocation in the light of the triune God and God's story of the world. These elements not only nourish the university's soul but should also define professors' fundamental identities and direct them to engage in certain story-formed virtues and practices that shape their vocations in unique ways. Thinking and living in the light of God and God's story can also foster an integrated relationship for teaching, scholarship, and service as well as an integrated identity and life purpose. As image bearers of God we can then pursue a coinherence reflected in the Trinity. The vocation of the Christian scholar is defined by a different story, identity, and purpose. As a result, the Christian scholar is free to fulfill his or her calling without having one's soul fragmented by it.

14

REIMAGINING
THE ACADEMIC DISCIPLINES

...

*I fear too often university curriculums make it
impossible for anyone, Christian and non-Christian alike,
to make sense of the world in which we find ourselves.*

STANLEY HAUERWAS

*I remember very well the time I was captured
by the dream of unified learning.*

EDWARD O. WILSON

THE NUMBER OF ACADEMIC DISCIPLINES the contemporary university creates and sustains keeps expanding. Today there are over 1,500 academic majors from which students can choose, an increase of 25 percent from a decade ago.[1] Although particular universities offer only a small percentage of these majors, how universities organize the increasingly complex and diverse array of disciplines will continue to be a challenge. The challenge presents itself in two ways. First, how do you help faculty make sure they do not become isolated in their disciplinary silos, so that they have some vision for doing more than building their personal research empire? Second, how do you help students make sense of the vast array of knowledge and the different ways the disciplines approach it? As outlined in chapter seven, these challenges prove to be increasingly challenging in a multiversity with a fragmented soul. Without a larger identity and coherent identity narrative, curricular choices often become little more than an agreement about how to divide up the academic spoils among self-interested departments searching for resources, power, and influence.

Many university leaders settle on the trend outlined in chapter seven of setting forth rather broad distribution requirements and allowing students to choose from a wide variety of courses on the curricular buffet. A minority of dissenting university leaders require a more strictly defined core curriculum as they view it as the university's responsibility to try to help students organize the courses they take into some sort of semicoherent whole. Do Christian universities have anything better to offer?

Two Proposals

Christian thinkers are just as divided regarding how to help students make sense of the curriculum as universities. Gilbert Meilaender appears to be ready to give in to the multiversity and the existence of the curricular buffet. Too often, he claims, "educational traditionalists and defenders of the liberal arts all too easily turn to commending the need for core curricula and to bemoaning the rise of specialization among faculty."[2] Instead, he wants to offer students the freedom to explore (at least outside of one's specialization). Meilaender claims, "What we need is not core curricula but fewer general education requirements."[3] Consequently, he suggests that students should look for a school that leaves them "free to find their own way into the conversation about the meaning of our humanity that is at the heart of the liberal arts."[4] In other words, students do not need some sort of authoritative academic nanny from the university making sure students eat a well-rounded, coherent curricular meal.

Despite his desire for curricular freedom, Meilaender's aim is not to facilitate a self-motivated holistic educational experience. He goes so far as to claim, "We should not seek to produce well-rounded students. Rather, our aim should be to form people who care and know about our humanity from within a particular discipline."[5] Meilaender points out that today's liberal education tries to make a student a little bit of a psychologist, sociologist, economist, and so on. Of course, we cannot expect one course to make one good in any of these fields: "No one's knowledge is narrower than that of the non-specialist, who knows a very little about a very lot."[6] In other words, there is nothing more dangerous than the friend who has taken one or two psychology courses beginning to offer advice about mental health or human flourishing.

One reason Meilaender offers for reducing general education requirements has to do with the realities found in universities. Students have little patience for or interest in required courses outside their area of interest. Plus, those courses tend to be taught by the adjuncts or assistant professors with little teaching experience. Consequently, for students, "these general education requirements tend to stifle rather than liberate the *eros* that draws them in search of wisdom."[7] Overall, Meilaender appears refreshingly realistic about the difficulties with general education. Yet he is also surprisingly optimistic about the benefits of specialization. He is convinced that students can discover human-enhancing capabilities and skills through learning one particular discipline.

Certainly one only achieves excellence by trying to become a first-rate specialist in a particular practice, although one can still learn about various kinds of educational excellence without participation in the actual practices. Furthermore, it is within disciplines that students encounter the guides who provide the wisdom by which they can then become a good biologist, accountant, teacher, engineer, sociologist, and so on. Yet required courses within one's major can also have the same influence as required general education courses. Required courses, whether within a major or outside of it, may not attract students who are passionate about the subject, although an excellent teacher can later inspire that kind of passion. Moreover, Meilaender also fails to note that the specialist can be quite dangerous. Only the student who has taken courses in other disciplines will understand the narrow focus they receive from looking at a subject through one particular disciplinary lens. The student needs something that can provide a cross-disciplinary perspective regarding big questions.

One finds an argument for this kind of approach in Parker Palmer and Arthur Zajonc's *The Heart of Higher Education*, where they offer a vision for integrative education. The authors note that in the early history of the university an integrative education helped build "the good and perfect man" who could make a spiritual journey toward God. Palmer and Zajonc give up on a theologically informed and guided integrated education. Instead, they suggest that contemporary integrative education "engages students in the systematic exploration of the relationship between their studies of the 'objective' world and the purpose, meaning, limits and aspirations of their lives."[8] For Palmer and Zajonc, higher education should not focus merely on creating professionals or even good citizens but on what Wendell Berry describes as "human beings in the fullest sense of those words."[9] In contrast to Meilaender, they suggest, "We should attend to the cultivation of our students' humanity at least as much as we instruct them in the content of our fields."[10]

Although they do not turn to theology for help with integration, Palmer and Zajonc propose what can be called a spiritually friendly vision of integrative education that attempts to be palatable to the whole higher education community. Overcoming our fragmented approach to education, they contend, involves "expanding our ontology to embrace the interconnectedness of reality and its multiple dimensions," "extending our epistemology to include contemplative, aesthetic, and moral knowing," and "recognizing the ethical dimensions of our way of knowing."[11] We can do these things, they believe, through conversations with colleagues, something that goes against the grain of the privatized, busy, and fractured university faculty culture. Such conversations, they suggest, start with storytelling about our personal journeys. These narratives necessarily reveal how we order and make sense of our lives. They suggest that such stories should be followed up with open, honest questions, which then move into discussions about ideas.

While Palmer and Zajonc's proposal is appealing in its generality, it becomes unclear how it works when one descends to the level of specificity. This awkwardness becomes apparent when Palmer does try to get specific. He provides as an example the Indians of the Six Nations' response to representatives from Maryland and Virginia when negotiating a 1774 treaty that involved higher education. The colonial representatives invited the Native Americans to send their boys to William and Mary. The tribal elders responded:

We know that you highly esteem the kind of learning taught in those Colleges, and that the Maintenance of our young Men, while with you, would be very expensive to you. We are convinced that you mean to do us Good by your Proposal; and we thank you heartily. But you, who are wise must know that different Nations have different Conceptions of things and you will therefore not take it amiss, if our ideas of this kind of Education happen not to be the same as yours. We have had some Experience of it. Several of our young People were formerly brought up at the Colleges of the Northern Provinces: they were instructed in all your Sciences; but, when they came back to us, they were bad Runners, ignorant of every means of living in the woods . . . neither fit for Hunters, Warriors, nor Counsellors, they were totally good for nothing. We are, however, not the less oblig'd by your kind offer, tho' we decline accepting it; and, to show our grateful Sense of it, if the Gentlemen of Virginia will send us a Dozen of their Sons, we will take Care of their Education, instruct them in all we know, and make Men of them.[12]

Interestingly, despite what would appear to be an exchange between two contrasting, competing, and focused visions of the best curriculum and what it means to be fully human, Palmer claims,

Here we are, two and a half centuries later, wanting the same thing these tribal elders wanted, in principle if not in detail: an education that embraces every dimension of what it means to be human, that honors the varieties of human experience, looks at us and our world through a variety of cultural lenses, and educates our young people in ways that enable them to face the challenges of our time.[13]

We would argue that Palmer misinterprets this story. Neither group's vision of education embraced every dimension of what it means to be human. The colonialists' curriculum omitted certain things the Native Americans wanted taught, and the Native Americans' understanding of how to "make Men" omitted certain things taught at William and Mary.

We would agree, though, with the Native Americans' underlying argument that different intellectual traditions have competing visions of what makes a person fully human. Reenvisioning an integrative curriculum, we believe, requires drawing on a particular metanarrative about the universe and humans' place in it that may not encompass every outlook. Like the tribal-education example, the resulting story does not seek to explain or

261

locate everything—only those elements thought to be essential to fulfilling a complete picture of human creational potential.

If this is true, Meilaender is correct that we cannot look to a general education focused on equipping students with broad capacities to provide unity and integration. Currently the unity general education provides is an attempt to develop particular human capacities that might extend to all humans (e.g., critical thinking) or a brief exposure of all students to certain capacities as understood within a vocational identity (e.g., the research skills of a historian, the observational skills of a scientist). General education does not provide an integrative education. It provides a way to acquire particular kinds of human capacities a particular university deems important. Although we would not expect a state university to attempt something broader, a Christian university can attempt to recover something of the lost idea of curricular unity that Hugh of St. Victor proposed. Even better, they can attempt to correct the sequestering of theology that occurred in those initial visions.

A Christian Vision of the Disciplines

A Christian vision must begin with the type of specificity that might be offensive to many contemporaries. The reason is that our understanding of what constitutes a successful education stems from our different overarching narrative that includes what it means to be fully human. We would also suggest that Christians in America should be careful not to equate this kind of education with a liberal arts education. Although a liberal arts education has been historically defined as the education for a free person, a Christian vision of a liberal arts education must begin and end with the Christian theological narrative that reminds us who we were created to be, what it means to be a slave, and the liberating arts that help one become free. Only when a person experiences those particular liberating arts can he or she properly understand and benefit from the traditional kind of liberal arts education.

This distinction between the liberating arts and the liberal arts proves vitally important. We should not expect the liberal arts found in a liberal arts college to liberate us. Meilaender, in contrast, suggests that a liberal arts education can perhaps help with this liberation.

262

> The liberal arts should help us to understand the truth about our lives—
> which means, in part, the truth of our contingency and neediness, and,
> ultimately, our dependence on the divine. . . . It seeks not power but
> wisdom, not to change the world but to know it in truth. And to know the
> world truly is to know it as creation, as a gift that invites our gratitude more
> than our mastery.[14]

While we would like to hope that Meilaender is right, we are doubtful that secular liberal arts education in American institutions can produce this result. If secular liberal arts professors seek to point out our contingency and neediness, they often do so to attach students to other ideological and political agendas and not to help them understand their dependence on the divine. Students often willingly comply.

We should realize this reality is not new. Augustine provides a helpful historical example of someone who experienced this distorting education. He famously recalls how his early liberal arts education merely amplified his enslavement. He wrote about his teaching from ages nineteen to twenty-eight in the *Confessions*: "We were seduced and we seduced others, deceived and deceiving by various desires, both openly by the so-called liberal arts and secretly in the name of a false religion, proud in the one, superstitious in the other, and everywhere vain."[15] "So called" accurately describes these liberal arts. In this situation, the supposed liberal arts are powerful instruments for enhancing misdirected desires that result in pride, envy, lust, and more. Seeking knowledge for its own sake can become an idol. Intellectual virtues developed for a career can serve an individual's interest in power and prestige. Even moral virtues, as Augustine wisely observed, become corrupted by pride when one believes they are achieved through one's own efforts. In particular, Augustine lamented his lack of gratitude to God for the ability to be able to understand the various arts.

> Whatever was written in any of the fields of rhetoric or logic, geometry, music,
> or arithmetic, I could understand without any great difficulty and without the
> instruction of another man. All this thou knowest, O Lord my God, because
> both quickness in understanding and acuteness in insight are thy gifts. Yet for
> such gifts I made no thank offering to thee. Therefore, my abilities served not
> my profit but rather my loss.[16]

As Augustine found, acquiring expertise in the so-called liberal arts can merely amplify our pride, ingratitude, and enslavement.

An education for the free person must for Christians rest on a particular understanding of freedom and personhood that does not descend into vague generalities about human capacities. The liberal arts cease to be liberal if they do not help humans cultivate and expand our understanding, experience, and imitation of the triune God, especially God's wisdom, holiness, and grace, Christ's humility and redemptive love, and the fruits of the Spirit. A Christian understanding of the liberal arts, therefore, must begin with a theology that teaches the core of what liberates—the truth about Christ as well as the overarching Christian story.

This story reveals that we are made as free, dependent human beings in the image of God. God created us with the potential to obtain God's intellectual and moral virtues, including God's love and wisdom. Although our sin kept us from growing this fruit through patient cultivation, through Christ we can become free from sin—what it truly means to be a free person. In and through Christ and through God's Spirit, we can bear the triune God's image and demonstrate holiness, wisdom, love, patience, servanthood, forgiveness, and humility.

The Liberating Arts

To develop in this manner, we need the liberating arts. Our acknowledgment of and trust in Christ's redemptive work on our behalf leads to the first and most fundamental liberating art. Although we suggest Meilaender is perhaps too hopeful about what the unaided liberal arts can provide us, he does recognize the importance of the fundamental liberating art for cultivating the gratitude that Augustine mentions. He suggests, "This gratitude can be cultivated not only in the liberal arts but also and most especially in the words and actions of worship."[17] We would suggest that this gratitude is cultivated first and foremost through worship. There is a reason the Proverbs state, "The fear of the LORD is the beginning of wisdom" (Prov 9:10). Reverence for God, a form of rightly directed worship, is the first liberating art that leads to wisdom.

Said differently, the fundamental basis for a Christian education should be *excellence without idolatry*. By idolatry, we simply mean the worship of any

264

created thing. When our pursuit of excellence in any field or the development of any human capacity becomes an object of worship, it enslaves us. The education we pursue to obtain excellence then transforms into slavish education. This understanding of a Christian education recognizes that every developed human capacity can be used for fallen ends, and only when we pursue excellence in the liberating art of worship can someone properly undertake an education for the free person. The second liberating art emerges from worship and involves following the example of Christ and demonstrating humility. It should be no surprise that Proverbs states that "with humility comes wisdom" (Prov 11:2). Part of this humility extends to recognizing that an education in the liberating arts is much more important than an education in the liberal arts.

If the liberating arts do not come first, distortions follow. Indeed, the liberal arts graduate may more easily demonstrate pride (e.g., placing too much confidence in their newly acquired abilities to understand, manipulate, and control the world). In contrast, as Paul admonishes us:

In your relationships with one another, have the same mindset as Christ Jesus:

Who, being in very nature God,
   did not consider equality with God something to be used to his own advantage;
rather, he made himself nothing
   by taking the very nature of a servant,
   being made in human likeness.
And being found in appearance as a man,
   he humbled himself
   by becoming obedient to death—
      even death on a cross! (Phil 2:5-8)

If an understanding of the triune God's story and the practice of the liberating arts of worship and humility liberate us through Christ, they prepare us for an education proper for a free person.

A Christian View of the Disciplines

Once Christians experience the liberating arts, they are now truly free and ready to engage in a broader education for a free person. Augustine famously argued that "all the branches of pagan learning" contain "studies for the liberated mind." In other words, once the mind is freed by the liberating arts, the liberal arts become helpful. The question is, helpful for what? The Christian justification for this education should not depend on pragmatic appeals to the well-being of the democratic nation-state or its economy. Instead, we can draw on Hugh's of St. Victor's purpose of education:

> To restore within us the divine likeness, a likeness which to us is a form but to God is his nature. The more we are conformed to the divine nature, the more do we possess Wisdom, for then there begins to shine forth again in us what has forever existed in the divine Idea or Pattern, coming and going in us but standing changeless in God.[18]

Education is one of God's gifts for amplifying our God-given capacities to restore us to our original purpose—to be image bearers of God. The random development of our capacities without attention to God's story and our identity and purpose within that story cannot be a true education.

Professors and academic disciplines. This approach also provides a coherent understanding of how university leaders should envision the disciplines. If we are made in God's image, we can only understand our humanity and human development in the light of God's nature and character. Wolfhart Pannenberg provides helpful guidance about what this means.

> Talk about God has to deal with God the creator of the world. Otherwise it would come to nothing. To deal with the creator or the world, however, requires us to consider everything to be a creature of that God, and that requires [us] to clarify whether each single reality can be understood and has to be understood to be a creature of that God. Thus, a doctrine of God touches upon everything else. Therefore, it is necessary to explore every field of knowledge in order to speak of God reasonably.[19]

The mind of the church, which means Christian universities, must seek to study the whole of creation to understand God and what it means to be made in God's image. As mentioned earlier, a Christian university should seek *manifold excellence without idolatry*. We explore every field using every known tool in our effort to understand God and God's creation so that we may love God and others more deeply. This mission provides the ground for curricular coherence for the overall university project.

Christian universities must be the church's experimental communities, where we figure out new ways to understand God and God's creation. We are to steward and use our human capacities to expand God's creative and redemptive work. For particular kinds of creative and redemptive work, one needs mathematics to build and create, biology to help heal, physics to design and explore, psychology to redeem our mind and bodies, languages to communicate our love deeply, movingly, and self-sacrificially, and more.

The core danger facing this vision of the disciplines is that found in the body imagery in 1 Corinthians 12. One may love one's discipline too much or believe others do not love it enough. Quite simply, the discipline becomes an object of worship. The idolatrous devotion of one's discipline or its particular method of knowing then limits the knowledge one can discover. Modernism, with its devotion to the quantitative and supposedly objective, became problematic for the university in a number of ways. As a result, the university now recognizes the need for qualitative forms of knowing.

The triune God, the church, and the discipline of theology become crucial within this understanding of the disciplines because they remind us that we must keep God and God's larger story in mind in order to properly understand the larger goal of overall human flourishing. For Christians, an understanding of our common humanity comes from God and our story with God—it is fundamentally about theology (the study of God), but it also involves every aspect of God's creation. Theology provides substance, cohesion, and a primary story of development. However, we should not expect this theology to be uniform in light of God's diverse creation. Like the four Gospels, we should expect people's experience of the triune God to focus on different aspects of God and God's creation.

God and the study of God, theology, also provides a common perspective from which to evaluate the growth of the disciplines and specialization. To think about the growth of specialized disciplines and how to critically evaluate them, one needs a standpoint and a story. It helps us make sure that in the sciences, for example, we do not focus on what America needs, but we focus on what humanity needs. Theology provides a much wider perspective. It helps us consider the moral components of the discipline using a common narrative and moral language (and prevents incommensurability of disciplines). How do you critique a discipline, particularly its moral components and codes? You need a larger narrative, a concept of human flourishing and metavirtues, such as an understanding of love derived from the triune God's example. Theology is necessary to be able to set forth a larger vision for a discipline and to be able to critique it. Of course, theology needs the disciplines to inform and critique theology, as the practice of theology may also become arrogant, stale, or idolatrous without insights from other disciplines.

What this view means is that faculty and administrators must encourage interdisciplinary work within a theological story and framework. Interdisciplinary work is incredibly hard due to established power structures embedded in defined disciplinary boundaries. For many faculty, a good chair or dean is one who defends your discipline, gathers scarce and contested resources, and expands your department or college. Presidents and provosts try to communicate the big picture, but an academic dean, chair, or individual faculty member does not always have significant incentive to look out for the body (especially when attempting to obtain resources).

Establishing centralized incentives for faculty to engage in interdisciplinary research projects, courses, and service becomes vital in a Christian university. Such projects could focus on common identities and associated practices linked to the good life (e.g., teaching, fatherhood/motherhood) or even a larger conversation about "putting together a good life" that goes beyond the disciplinary conversation about what it means to be a good historian, accountant, chemist, or artist.

Students. For the individual student, the Christian university can and should offer ways to develop the full range of the students' identities and the associated capacities necessary for excellence in those identities. Not every student can gain the specialized expertise, and the college should not try. Today general education courses attempt to function both as quick tours of the field in hopes of producing well-rounded students.[20] One of us recently interviewed a nonreligious student at a Lutheran liberal arts college who had developed this capacity through advanced work with a chemistry professor. The professor saw the student's passion and vision: "Even though this is very theoretical work, she sees a grand sort of application to which she sees that this work, given time, will make life better for other people in either appreciable or non-appreciable ways. That was something that I think was a revelation to me." Interestingly, while this student grew up Methodist, he had not seen how his passion for chemistry might fit into a larger purpose and story.

> Before I kind of saw work as a necessary thing to do in order to continue to basically live with the whole purpose of life was to serve God, so if you weren't called to kind of a full-time indication of ministry then the work was a necessary distraction from whatever your personal ministry would be, and that the work was somehow lower than that higher calling.

An introductory course in chemistry will also be less likely to produce this revelation, although it is possible for a professor to convey this understanding in some ways. Learning what it takes to achieve excellence without idolatry in a particular profession requires immersion with practitioners and not dabbling.

Meilaender is wrong, however, to suggest that colleges and universities should not seek to produce well-rounded students. We merely need to correct our idea of what a flourishing, well-rounded student is. A flourishing student is one who not only seeks vocational excellence without idolatry but also thinks deeply about and has some initial practice with attaining excellence in the various identities of his her or her life. The major problem with specialization is that to learn how to think within the context of one aspect of our human identity does not always carry over to other identities. Being a great specialist enhances our humanity when it comes to learning how to acquire intellectual and moral virtues through the hard work of practice and submitting to a mentor. Yet many great professionals may not experience human flourishing because they do not know how to cultivate their other identities beyond their work identity. In other words, they pursued specialized excellence but not excellence without idolatry and certainly not *manifold excellence without idolatry.*

A Christian liberal arts education should enhance our practice not only of work-related forms of excellence but also of other forms of human excellence unrelated to vocations for which one earns a living. They should provide students, the church, and humanity insight into what it means to be a good Christian, neighbor, enemy, son/daughter, spouse, citizen, steward of culture (especially money) and nature, woman or man, and much more.[21] These are essential aspects of our human identity. We all must acquire God's wisdom about how to create and redeem in these areas. At this point, a basic exposure to sociology can help one become a good neighbor, and learning developmental psychology can help one be a good parent. The problem with most general education courses is that they fail to connect the knowledge they provide to improving one's capacities in ways that develop excellence within students' fundamental identities, what elsewhere we have called the "great identities."[22] General education should help one live the good life in every aspect of one's life, though its purposes should also extend to less pragmatic goals, such as simply relishing and enjoying the complexity and beauty of God's creation.

Moreover, the common moral dilemmas most of us face are not figuring out what it means to be a good engineer, nurse, lawyer, or accountant, or even what it means to be a good citizen. Although we certainly face some of those issues as we pursue excellence without idolatry within a particular specialization, our major life dilemmas, as the Christian tradition has long taught, involve figuring how to order our loves and identities. How do we balance a good professional life with being a good parent, spouse, son or daughter, citizen, friend, neighbor, member of the human race, and lover of God? What do we do when our efforts to be a good friend conflict with our efforts to be a good spouse? Or what happens when being a lover of God conflicts with what the culture tells us the good citizen or good professional should do? The Christian university should provide students the type of critical thinking to help them with these identity conflicts that one will be engaged in throughout life. Balancing excellence without idolatry in multiple identities requires God's wisdom.

The job of the Christian university should be to offer an education for the whole person and thus provide students wisdom about how to order our overall loves and identities. We would suggest that Christian institutions provide students with a "Great Lives and Communities" course that actually helps students look at such lives and communities as a whole. If we study the best experts when learning what it means to be a great historian, social worker, biologist, or philosopher, we should also study those exemplars, both individual and communal, who sought to put together a good life as a whole. These are indirect mentors and experts who can help nurture a true, good, and beautiful life.

Overall, a Christian approach to the disciplines must start with learning the liberating arts of worship and humility that nurture loving gratitude and obedience to Jesus. This foundation provides an education for the free person—the pursuit of manifold excellence without idolatry not only in a particular academic vocation but also in all the other vocations where we seek to be image bearers of God. Developing this particular capacity for this specific identity is indeed an education for a free person.

15

REIMAGINING THE COCURRICULAR

Transforming the Bubble to a Greenhouse

...

The righteous will flourish like a palm tree,
they will grow like a cedar of Lebanon;
planted in the house of the LORD,
they will flourish in the courts of our God.
They will still bear fruit in old age,
they will stay fresh and green,
proclaiming, "The LORD is upright;
he is my Rock, and there is no wickedness in him."

PSALM 92:12-15

Trees, of all things, are not cultivated overnight.

DAVID I. SMITH AND SUSAN M. FELCH

IF PROFESSORS ARE SOMETIMES critiqued for living in an ivory tower where they produce irrelevant scholarship and teach esoteric concepts, residential college students themselves will talk about living in a "bubble." The idea of living in a bubble is usually not considered a good thing. For instance, at the institutional home for two of us, if one simply types "Baylor bubble" into a search engine, you'll find articles such as "Get Out of the Baylor Bubble," "Break Through the Baylor Bubble," "Popping the Baylor Bubble," and "Life Beyond the Baylor Bubble." Usually one does not want to live in a bubble, since it's seen as inhibiting one's growth and discovery instead of nurturing one's progress toward maturity. To a college student eager to experience the apparent freedom of adulthood, the bubble suggests confinement and separation from the "real" world. These kinds of critiques provide helpful insight into how the ideals we hold for the residential community of the university relate to the soul of the university, how the realities may fall short of those ideals, and how we go about redeeming them.

As mentioned in chapter eight, the cocurricular is set apart by its emphasis on the whole student. Traditionally this view has been understood in two senses. First, cocurricular educators are concerned with more than a narrow range of *capacities*, such as the intellectual development of students. A holistic concept of student development helps students consider what their intellectual development has to do with their emotional, physical, behavioral, and other capacities. Second, cocurricular educators are more likely to focus on a wider range of different student *identities*. They focus not only on what it means to be a good student or a good historian, biologist, accountant, social worker, and so on, but they also help students explore what it means to be a good neighbor, friend, man or woman, community member, citizen, and so on. The challenge, though, is how a university or an individual student within a university can bring coherence to these capacities and identities. As chapter eight demonstrated, multiversities with fragmented souls will have greater difficulty with this task. We cannot figure out how to think in a holistic way about the capacities and identities of students without first figuring out who both we and they are. This chapter sets forth a guiding vision for universities with a singular soul.

Who Are We?

As illustrated by the bubble critique, there is some confusion over what kind of group environment the university provides or how we should understand the cocurricular dimension of the university. Similar to critiques of the bubble, one of us knows a cocurricular student leader who likes to point out that the environment they are creating is not another youth camp. If we do not want to create a bubble or a youth camp, what images can help us think about the campus environment? A couple common metaphors often tossed around the university are "family" or "nation." Indeed, we find it interesting that universities often use the term "family" when they are a certain size and then "nation" when they become much larger (and use the latter with regard to the marketing of intercollegiate athletics).[1] The problem with the former is that while the university was perhaps once thought of as a substitute family in which student life staff functioned in loco parentis, that is no longer the case. Indeed, residential colleges at universities are not homes in the sense that students have long-term bonds and identity connections that elicit moral demands in the same way a family does. At most, they are short-term neighbors and roommates—identity designations that carry moral weight (particularly for Christians) but that must be understood differently (as we will discuss below).

To refer to a university as a nation, of course, is perhaps appropriate when one considers the politics of many universities today. Indeed, much of what increasingly guides the structure and environment of university life are federal policies, such as Title IX. In this respect, the university is indeed becoming like the nation in that the federal government influences and sometimes even dictates how university life functions. "Nation" language may also be a way to make the multiversity a coherent whole, like the United States, with multiple governing bodies, is considered a whole.[2] It is perhaps also a metaphor used to make alumni feel part of an institution, such as when a university advertises to its alumni, as one of ours recently did, at homecoming: "Welcome home, Baylor nation."

Still, most cocurricular educators and other authors will find such metaphors problematic. Wendell Berry contends that "education has become increasingly useless as it has become increasingly public."[3] He contrasts "public," which is perhaps close to "nation," with the word "community" and notes, "A community, unlike a public, has to do first of all with belonging to a group of people who belong to one another and to their place. We would say, 'We belong to our community,' but never 'We belong to our public.'"[4] Communities have specific locations and histories associated with those locations and often elicit different moral expectations. To be a neighbor is to live in community with someone.

To understand the difference between a university that is merely a public space and one that attempts to embody elements of a community, it may help to consider two research universities one of us recently visited in quick succession. The two campuses are within a few miles of one another. One campus is laid out in grids with buildings, hallways, and classrooms that are more often than not numbered. Although orderly, the design and presentation of space on the first campus resisted the imprint of history by maintaining a sterile, uniform, and anonymous mien. In contrast, the other campus is laid out in a more organic or, to some, haphazard manner that emerged over the course of a long history. Regardless, almost every venue on that haphazard campus of any significance bears the name of a prominent alum, administrator, educator, or benefactor. In addition, the identification with names runs so deep in the campus culture that students are often aware of the names and reputations of previous generations of individuals who once occupied their respective rooms in the residence halls. New generations of students are then invited to inscribe their identity onto their rooms. However, the process goes both ways. Not only being at a place physically but also the *mode* of presence, or what we call "dwelling successfully" within a community, opens the student up to having the institutional patterns and lessons of the past also inscribed on him or her. The second campus, far more than the first, is a place that had leveraged spaces and what Burton Clark called "organizational saga" or stories of success and survival that shape and animate present identity and purposes of a community.[5]

Communities also exhibit certain virtues in their personal relationships. As Berry observes:

> A community . . . exists by proximity, by neighborhood, it knows face to face, and it trusts as it knows. It learns, in the course of time and experience, what and who can be trusted. . . . If the word *community* is to mean or amount to anything, it must refer to a place (in its natural integrity) and its people.

To expect a student to inhabit a community and not a "nation" or public institution creates two different types of expectations, as Berry notes:

> A young person, coming of age in a healthy household and community, will understand her or his life in terms of membership and service. But in a public increasingly disaffected and turned away from community, it is clear that individuals must be increasingly disinclined to identify themselves in such a way.[6]

275

In general, using the word *community* or *neighbor* provides a third approach to understanding the cocurricular environment of the university that recognizes the importance of place and virtue. Berry even uses a place metaphor to describe it: "A healthy community is like an ecosystem, and it includes—or it makes itself harmoniously a part of—its local ecosystem."[7] Berry then goes on to use an even more coherent and situated description that we are also using: "And to extend Saint Paul's famous metaphor by only a little, a healthy community is like a body, for its members mutually support and serve one another."[8] An ideal community, in other words, mirrors the kingdom of God, which should ideally be reflected in the church.

Yet the university is not the full church, and we would suggest it is also not a complete community. In other words, we believe the claim that the university is a community needs to be qualified in light of the realities of university life for students. After all, for students, the university "community" is transient, requires very little commitment, is generationally homogenous, and is filled with people just beginning to care for themselves fully. To use Arthur Chickering's developmental terms, they are more frequently developing autonomy than interdependence.[9] Moreover, its leaders want its members to leave. The new members that change continuously often know little about the community's history and have limited experience with performing acts of self-giving, gift-oriented functions that a communal body requires. The college community may contain worship opportunities, but it is not meant to be a long-term, multigenerational worshiping body of believers for all as is the church. In this respect, the kind of community Berry has in mind is beyond the reach of a university. Moreover, all of these limitations feed into the popular language often used to describe the university as a bubble. Consider this commentary regarding student life experience in Catholic higher education:

> Conventional wisdom in Catholic colleges and universities is that as a result of excellent liturgical experiences on campus, students after graduation often become disengaged with what parishes have to offer them and frequently disengage from parish life. Part of what makes liturgy so compelling at a Catholic university is that it usually brings together hundreds of young students all of approximately the same age and with similar interests. It is perhaps one of the most homogeneous but stimulating religious experiences students

have in their young lives, since most liturgies in the postuniversity environment have participants who are much more diverse in age, socioeconomic status, and interests.[10]

Clearly there are strengths and weaknesses to be acknowledged by the unique type of "community" experience in college. We believe Christians should be clear about the type of limited but important community the university provides.

As opposed to the negative critique of the university as a bubble, we believe Berry provides some insight into a more positive metaphor that can reframe the nature of the undergraduate experience. The university provides what we call a greenhouse community. A greenhouse is a place where young plants are nurtured within a protected environment marked by consistent temperature, ready access to nourishment, and attentive care from those skilled in fostering the transition from seedling to stable plant. Few people would critique a greenhouse for failing to provide a "real world" experience. Indeed, that it does not is exactly the point. However, in many cases it is intended to be a temporary arrangement that prepares fragile plants to then be transplanted into stable and often long-term locations where the natural elements can be endured with success. Similarly, the university creates what it hopes to be the ideal conditions for growth by providing resources for the holistic development of a certain age demographic. It does, however, want the student to eventually leave the protective and nurturing greenhouse community and not become dependent on it. It also needs to discourage students from viewing the "greenhouse" period of life as an ideal state to be sought again after departure. The university is not meant to be a long-term community of students, nor one they should venerate.

A Biblical Example of Protective and Nurturing Community Building

Although the whole biblical narrative contains insight about learning to build a healthy community from a broken one, for the sake of our discussion, we are going to draw most heavily from the call God issued to Nehemiah. One of the reasons is that Nehemiah sought to build what we consider a certain kind of protected and nurturing community, one in which a fragile group of people needed extra protection and a particular type of environment for growth. Again, we should note, however, that Nehemiah was building a more permanent community that is quite different from the greenhouse community of the university for students. Still, we believe the story provides important insights.

Nehemiah was among the people of Judah taken captive and enslaved in service to the Babylonians. He indicates at the end of Nehemiah 1 that he was cupbearer to the king. At the beginning of the chapter, Nehemiah reports that he encounters one of his brothers, Hanani, who came with a group of men from Nehemiah's home. Eager for news about those who remained, Nehemiah

> questioned them about the Jewish remnant that had survived the exile, and also about Jerusalem.
>
> They said to me, "Those who survived the exile and are back in the province are in great trouble and disgrace. The wall of Jerusalem is broken down, and its gates have been burned with fire." (Neh 1:2-3)

Upon hearing this news, Nehemiah "sat down and wept. For some days I mourned and fasted and prayed before the God of heaven" (Neh 1:4). His people, the people whom he loved, were experiencing the brokenness of their community. Nehemiah's first redemptive action to repair a broken community was to engage in set of spiritual practices.

First, Nehemiah starts with what we call a liberating art—confession. He publicly acknowledges the moral and religious failings of his community, and more pointedly himself, seeking reconciliation. He opens by acknowledging the essence of God's character as exhibited to God's chosen people. In particular, he notes that while God demands that the people of Judah keep the commandments, God also is eager to welcome them back into right relationship on certain conditions. As a result, Nehemiah realizes that the first thing he and others must do to restore community is turn to God and repent. He thus says, "I confess the sins we Israelites, including myself and my father's family, have committed against you. We have acted very wickedly toward you. We have not obeyed the commands, decrees and laws you gave your servant Moses" (Neh 1:6-7).

Now that Nehemiah has repented for his sins and the sins of his family, he continues with another liberating art—petitionary prayer. He makes a plea to God concerning what he believes he is now called to do to build his community. He thus asks, "Lord, let your ear be attentive to the prayer of this your servant and to the prayer of your servants who delight in revering your name. Give your servant success today by granting him favor in the presence of this man!" (Neh 1:11). Nehemiah knows that his calling is to build protections so his community can prosper. He has turned to God and pledged his repentance and the repentance of his people. With a clear sense of calling and God's grace in his favor, Nehemiah now approaches the king of Babylon with a request to return home and meet one of the most basic needs of his community, their safety. Nehemiah thus asks, "If it pleases the king and if your servant has found favor in his sight, let him send me to the city in Judah where my ancestors are buried so that I can rebuild it" (Neh 2:5).

The next ten chapters of Nehemiah tell the dramatic story of how this repentant son of God led his people through the process of rebuilding the walls of Jerusalem and, thus, their way of life. On the day the walls were dedicated, Nehemiah says, "They [the people of Judah] offered great sacrifices, rejoicing because God had given them great joy. The women and children also rejoiced. The sound of rejoicing in Jerusalem could be heard far away" (Neh 12:43). Providing a safe space for the growth of the people of God is certainly a noble task to which student life staff can relate. Many cocurricular educators are in charge of maintaining what we have called the greenhouse environment on campus. As part of this task, their job is to ensure that students remain safe and healthy. Student leaders and first-year students are often barraged with a whole host of talks about safety, sexual assault, alcohol and drug abuse, and more. All of it is meant to help keep students safe in the greenhouse.

The story of Nehemiah, however, does not end with the dedication of the city wall, as building the wall was not an end but simply a means to a greater communal good. The wall simply provided protection for the people so that they could once again dwell as God had called them. As a result, immediately after Nehemiah describes the festivities that defined the day the city walls were dedicated, he describes the installation of persons to serve in various posts as acts of worship to God—another liberating art.

At that time men were appointed to be in charge of the storerooms for the contributions, firstfruits and tithes. From the fields around the towns they were to bring into the storerooms the portions required by the Law for the priests and the Levites, for Judah was pleased with the ministering priests and Levites. They performed the service of their God and the service of purification, as did also the musicians and gatekeepers, according to the commands of David and his son Solomon. (Neh 12:44-45)

With the city wall in place, the people of Judah were now able to turn to higher forms of human flourishing, starting with offering praise and worship of God. The people were not called to build the wall and simply live as they had in recent years minus the challenges imposed by their surrounding neighbors. They were called to become a set-apart worshiping community with particular standards for communal life.

With the walls again in place and the people able to dedicate their lives to the praise and worship of God, Nehemiah then led Israel through the process of determining the particular qualities that define their life together. Similar to a greenhouse, he had created a protected physical space that could nurture growth. He was then able to turn to questions of how to build a flourishing community within the walls. In particular, he wrestled with questions such as: What kind of relations should the people of Judah share with individuals of foreign descent? Should indiscretions by members of the priesthood be overlooked? What was the nature of Sabbath practices? Would mixed marriages with nonbelievers be allowed to continue?

Whether or not Nehemiah's decisions reflect priorities we might hold, what is ultimately important is the fact that he led the people through a process of discernment concerning what standards and ideals would define their community. That conversation did not end once the wall went up and the temple was opened. In contrast, it was an ongoing discussion guided by God's Word and prayerful discernment.

Similarly, whether cocurricular educators serve as residence directors, coaches, career counselors, or orientation leaders, all contribute in their own unique ways to an understanding of how people of faith prepare inside the "walls" for what awaits outside. Some campuses may be defined on the perimeter by a wall of brick or stone. However, the physical nature of the wall, which in this time is primarily of symbolic importance, is not as significant as its metaphorical meaning. Physical environments play a crucial role in reinforcing community identity by linking historically significant persons, places, and events to the dilemmas of our time, just as the wall in Nehemiah's day was both a historic artifact and a contemporary manifestation of set-apartness. The structures, interactions, and programming cocurricular educators offer are at their most potent when they leverage space, time, and accumulated institutional identity, story, and purpose in ways that seek to create a greenhouse community.

What Are We Trying to Grow?

Cocurricular educators cannot know what students should become unless they know who they are and who they are meant to be. This identity provides a key to understanding our divinely established purpose. When a cocurricular educator knows the fundamental human purpose, they can focus on more comprehensive ways to foster human development. Much of contemporary student life education, as mentioned in chapter eight, sets forth only a limited range of human ideals because it lacks more extensive agreement about what a flourishing person looks like. Although a variety of psychological[11] and sociological[12] attempts have been made to begin the task of identifying the virtues or capacities of a flourishing human being, Christians have the advantage of beginning with the soul of the matter. In other words, we can begin with a theologically informed understanding of our identity, story, and larger purpose.

The most beautiful reality, although some in the contemporary university will tell us differently, is that we do not define everything about ourselves. God, our Creator, defines who we are. If we wish to foster students' development, we need to remind them of who they are in God's eyes. Only when cocurricular educators and students have an understanding of this story we inhabit and our identity within it can they understand the ends or purposes of their overall endeavor. We can begin this process by drawing on the biblical narrative.

The Bible starts by revealing to us that God created humanity "in his own image" (Gen 1:27). It is on this identity that Christian educators must build any effort to engage in student development. They should seek to help them, as Hugh of St. Victor admonished, more fully become image bearers of the

281

triune God. In this regard, a Christian approach changes how cocurricular educators think about developing student capacities and identities in important ways. In other words, instead of understanding students' development as a process that cultivates disparate threads of human capacities and identity, it insists that we must start with a fundamental identity that helps us bring all those disparate capacities and identities together and helps us order and reconcile them. What does it mean to be made in God's image? Scholars have identified at least two important elements.[13]

First, being made in God's image, according to the biblical contexts, means we share a special connection and relationship with God. It is important to recognize that this status is true of all people, no matter their sinfulness and no matter whether they have certain human excellences such as reasoning ability. After the fall, God still pointed to this theological reality as a basis for justice:

> Whoever sheds human blood,
>> by humans shall their blood be shed;
> for in the image of God
>> has God made mankind. (Gen 9:6)

Interestingly, similar to what it means to be "in Christ" and fully reconciled to God, being made in God's image is something given by and dependent on God's grace.

For cocurricular educators this claim supports the view that, like the Trinity, every person has equal dignity, intrinsic worth, and unique gifts. When talking about the reason to respect and value every student, the core reason stems from the theological reality that every person is made in God's image. Consequently, we should treat all students, including those who are different, as intrinsically valuable. After all, science or political states cannot provide us with human dignity. As Thomas Jefferson noted, we are endowed with dignity and rights by our Creator. Only God can do that.

From this basis we can move to the second important implication of being made in God's image. God *intends* for us to reflect God in many ways. Another interpretation of this phrase indicates that all human beings are meant to be the physical representations of God here on earth.[14] This part of the image is the potential. We can grow into a beautiful tree filled with fruit.

Yet, like a seed, we do not see the full image of the large tree, which the seed is capable of producing.

How do we get a sense of the final creation? We start with the Creator. In other words, *if we are made in God's image to reflect him, we cannot fully understand what it means to be a whole person without knowing God.* Reflecting God's image involves developing and exercising the various aspects of our capacities that reflect God's already existing capacities.[15] We will merely touch on three particular aspects of God's capacities and character qualities that we are to reflect: (1) Demonstrating loving relationships with the triune God, others, and creation; (2) exercising God-given capacities (e.g., unique creating capacities and royal stewarding capacities); (3) embodying specific social identities.

First, to be made in God's image means we are relational beings who are meant to commune with and depend on God and relate to others and creation. As Stanley Grenz observers, "The image of God does not lie in the individual per se but in the relationality of persons in community. The relational life of the God who is triune comes to representation in the communal fellowship of the participants in the new humanity."[16] The most important standard of excellence by which we are to judge these relationships is the virtue that God continually expresses with all of them—love. Again, as Grenz states, "The biblical imperative to love is an anticipated outworking of the principle that the ultimate foundation for human relationships resides in the eternal dynamic of the triune God. Thus humans fulfill their purpose as destined to be the *imago dei* by loving after the manner of the triune God."[17] If cocurricular educators fail to teach students to love God, others, and creation, they have failed to develop students made in the image of God.

Recently, Bill Gates hosted a video contest asking entrants to answer the question, "What does it mean to be human?" The winner, selected by a group of teachers and students, was an eighteen-year-old freshman who explained that what makes humans more evolved than ducks and elephants is that they can extend compassion beyond their own immediate circle to "all of humankind," thus sharing "an infinite circle of compassion" and demonstrating "a responsibility to ourselves, to our planet, and to each other."[18] It is no wonder she won. Extending love to all of creation is what God does.

It is also the pinnacle of what makes us human. Of course, the Trinity also demonstrates other virtues in relationship that we will discuss further below.

Second, we must recognize that humans are endowed with creative and royal stewarding capacities. If there is anything we know about God from Genesis 1, it is that God is a Creator. Thus it would make sense that humans are also designed to create. Indeed, we are given the honor of creating culture (essentially the human creations added to God's creation). We name animals and people just as God endowed us with identity. We create languages and symbols. We create tools, music, and even build cities (all things described in Genesis 4). Humans are called to create civilizations and all that it entails. It is no accident that the Bible begins with a garden and ends with a city, the new Jerusalem, into which "the kings of the earth will bring their splendor" (Rev 21:24). Consequently, cocurricular educators must encourage a whole range of student creativity. For instance, Christian campuses should foster a whole range of student groups where students are given leadership and creative responsibilities. Student cultural productions, sports, music, theater, and more should all have a place on a college campus. Indeed, cocurricular educators should look for every opportunity to help students express their creativity.

Moreover, as image bearers of God we are not merely to exercise our creative capacities without regard for God's creation. In fact, being made in the image of God makes us different from the rest of creation. Just as God takes care of his whole creation, we are to be stewards of it as well. As biblical scholar J. Richard Middleton states, "The *imago Dei* designates the royal office or calling of human beings as God's representatives and agents in the world, granted authorized power to share in God's rule or administration of the earth's resources and creatures."[19] We are to steward God's creation. God says let them rule over the fish of the sea and the birds of the air, and over all the creatures on the earth (Gen 1:26). One of the essential elements of student life must be teaching students how to steward their creations. After all, we all know that student creativity can be used for ignoble and noble ends.

This stewardship education extends to a whole range of responsibilities. Separated from parents and various other structured forms of eating and activities, students likely need to be taught how to steward their bodies. On their own, they need to be taught how to steward their money and possessions. College is one of the most important places they begin to steward their talents and gifts. They also continue to learn what it means to steward their identities.

Third, in Genesis 2 God imbues us with unique identities and also gives us the capacity to take on ourselves other created identities. In other words, one of the other aspects of being human involves the social identities we inherit or create and take upon ourselves. Similarly, Scripture continually reveals God to us through these social roles and images. God's character is revealed through the role of particular professions (e.g., potter, shepherd, teacher). God is also presented to us as a king, parent, friend, father, and husband. Of course, these images do not at all capture the whole of God, just as we cannot be reduced to our human roles.

Still, with humans, our identity also becomes intertwined with these social roles. We inherit roles such as that of being a member of a particular family, ethnicity, and nation. We take upon ourselves other identities, such as being a member of a certain profession, a member of various social groups, and more. While these identities do not define us completely, they constitute an essential part of who we are. A component of our divine calling is to fulfill those roles creatively, to steward them to the best of our ability, and to pursue excellence within them. What does it mean to be a good or excellent student, neighbor, citizen, son/daughter, and more?

The Secondary but Fundamental Role of Rules

One of the most important things to help students understand is the secondary and fundamental role of rules in regard to the social identities we are able to embody. Just as one cannot play a game or sport without having rules, you cannot have a social identity without rules. Figure skating ceases to be figure skating without a rule requiring the use of skates. For those who want to become college students, they must also abide by certain rules because a violation of those rules undermines the very identity of their community. Indeed, agreeing to abide by rules is what endows you with an identity.

Students do not like rules. One reason is that they exclude people from the social practice associated with an identity. Yet we must face this reality.

The academic greenhouse community must be honest that it will not admit some members into its greenhouse community for reasons having to do not with their spiritual views but with their capabilities and ability to abide by the rules related to being a good student or good neighbor. It also may exclude members from the academic community for this reason. Nehemiah also made difficult decisions about the composition of the community with the ends in mind (Neh 13:23-27). Those who might undermine the community's commitment to worshiping God were excluded.

Another reason students do not like rules, though, likely pertains to something they know and adults often forget. Rules should never be the focus. They preserve identity, but they do not produce identity excellence. When educational leaders focus merely on making sure students do not break the rules, they miss the chance to educate students about the high ideals communicated through God's story. The focus turns to making sure students do not engage in premarital sex, underage drinking, or certain kinds of technology use, rather than understanding sex, alcohol, and technology as all part of God's good creation (or human creation that reflect being made in God's image) that must be faithfully appreciated for their proper created ends.

Still, rules cannot be neglected in a fallen world (e.g., Mark 10). One rule that proves particularly important in a university context relates to our creative capacities. This is because universities in particular are meant to enhance and help students' creative capacities. In order to fully understand how to develop our creative capacities, however, it is important to recognize that these capacities can also be corrupted when humans worship the creation or their own creations. In other words, the capacities mentioned can only be properly fulfilled when undertaken in the context of worshiping and glorifying God first. Otherwise, they become idolatrous objects of devotion, and we lose ourselves in the process. This is why God placed a clear restriction on our creative capacities: "You shall not make for yourself an image in the form of anything in heaven above or on the earth beneath or in the waters below" (Ex 20:4). The restriction is not simply on making images. It pertains to making images for certain purposes related to the previous command, "You shall have no other gods before me" (Ex 20:3), and the command immediately following the creation restriction, "You shall not bow down to them or worship them" (Ex 20:5). Adhering to this restriction is the toughest job of the university, which is in the business of creating. After all, humans, and particularly universities, are always creating potential objects of idolatry.

Idol worship, in whatever form, diminishes our full humanity. God does not worship us, and we are not to worship the things we create. Kings in the Near East, such as Nebuchadnezzar, set up statues of themselves as a symbol of their rule (Dan 3:1). The Bible, by contrast, reveals we are all image bearers of the King here on earth. Creating and worshiping idols is wrong, not only because it tries to imbue something physical with divine power, but also because it diminishes the honor of the idol worshipers themselves. By creating and worshiping idols we give up our own status as the representatives of the divine.

Students, faculty, and alumni are incredibly creative, and they can be incredibly creative idol producers. Students on one of our campuses will spend large parts of a whole semester, and sometimes neglect other parts of their life, in order to perfect a seven-minute singing production they have created. Alumni and educational leaders will sacrifice a tremendous amount of money, capital, and sometimes even their principles for winning athletic teams. These things are all wonderful products of our creation that are incredibly dangerous as well when they become objects of worship.

Growing Excellence in the Academic Greenhouse

When cocurricular educators and students focus on excellence within our identities and the way to achieve excellence, they should also focus on at least six particular elements required for such growth: virtue, wisdom, mentors, practice, imagination, and models.

The first element is *virtue*. Virtue is a foremost focus because the language of virtue is one of the primary forms of language used to depict God, who is described as "compassionate and gracious . . . slow to anger, abounding in love and faithfulness" (Ex 34:6-7).[20] Moreover, just as we are called to create as God created, we are also commanded to image God by demonstrating God's virtues. In other words, just as God is holy, we are to be holy. A central New Testament motif is that Christians should imitate Christ, particularly his self-sacrificial love, but also his forgiveness, servant leadership, humility, and acceptance.[21] If universities in the Christian tradition seek to develop students to their highest capacities, they must help students cultivate particular virtues, especially love that is properly ordered to the highest truth—the triune God.

As illustrated in chapter eight, various campuses often focus on one particular virtue such as justice or service, although a few may focus on virtues in general.[22] Helping students acquire and practice virtues is vitally important, but we can only identify, define, and prioritize virtues in the light of the overarching story mentioned above. The story matters. When communities enforce certain virtues without a story, they may be criticized for what the famous moral educator Lawrence Kohlberg called the "bag of virtues" approach to moral education.[23] Kohlberg mistakenly thought the various bags of virtues chosen by communities were often arbitrary. In actuality, they must be grounded in a true metanarrative that provides a clear understanding of the end of life as a whole.[24] Only then can a community agree on the virtues necessary for the flourishing of that particular role or of life as a whole.[25]

The second element, *wisdom*, often considered a virtue, is uniquely important in academic settings. It is the knowledge that comes from excellent practice. This kind of expert knowledge is the kind acquired by someone who has observed and practiced in the field (e.g., think of Solomon's Wisdom literature in the Old Testament). Unfortunately, humans often do not want to make the effort to acquire this wisdom. Philip Cary suggests this is what was wrong with Adam and Eve's eating the fruit from the tree of knowledge of good and evil. They sought a shortcut to wisdom. They did not wait for the seed to grow. Yet he observes:

> If wisdom is to be ours, it must grow in us slowly like a tree—a tree of life—and at the end of the long growing we have its ripe fruit, sweet to the taste, which is the knowledge of good and evil—the kind of knowledge by which a king may rule well, and any of us may govern our lives well. But wisdom does take time.[26]

We must remind students that they can attain wisdom only by the hard work of becoming excellent in their various identities. The third element is *mentors*. We expect mentors to possess this type of wisdom. If one examines the autobiographies of those who have achieved excellence in various fields, they often had mentors, teachers, or coaches who could provide them with the wisdom to perfect their practice.

This reality is why it is important for cocurricular educators to make sure they do not view autonomy as the goal for their students. Instead, their students must learn to be disciples of the triune God who depend on a mentor for help. Sometimes these mentors may come from unlikely sources. Nehemiah likely learned how to lead a community by serving under a pagan king. Still, he also looked to God for ultimate wisdom and mentoring. Just as Nehemiah's first response to building a community for Israel was an expression of dependence, the same should be true for cocurricular educators.

The fourth important element is that students have to *practice* under a mentor to develop the virtues and gain wisdom. The benefits of what are called "deliberate practice" for excellence are well known.[27] One of the things that Nehemiah did was formulate the types of practices the community needed in order to flourish, such as the public reading of Scripture, prayer, fasting, and keeping the Sabbath. Of course, these practices only make sense in the light of a metanarrative. Nehemiah took great effort to enforce the practice of the Sabbath in the walled city, but he did so with the end of the worship of God in mind (Neh 13:15-22). For Nehemiah, building a wall was also a practice that made sense in the light of a metanarrative that involved God's redemptive purposes for the people of Israel. Nehemiah did not simply build the wall to protect the people (although that played a role). The protection helped the more important ends. Nehemiah built the wall so that Israel could be a redeemed worshiping community. In this regard, the story brings coherence to our different practices.

Similarly, we must always understand the practices we promote in light of this larger identity, story, and purpose. One of our cocurricular colleagues shared a story with one of us over breakfast about an effort to hold a prayer service for the victims of an earthquake in Nepal. Initiated out of a heartache being experienced by a group of Nepali graduate students, the event attracted over 150 students as well as members of the local Nepali community in town. Yet this colleague also noted that the event had its detractors. One student wrote on Facebook about pictures of students gathered to pray for those affected by the Nepali earthquake: "Hope they did something useful as well." Unfortunately this student clearly had not grasped the place of "faith" in a faith-based university. Prayer becomes a meaningless practice if one does not believe God exists and still moves in our current story.

Through practice and the exercise of wisdom we build the capability to exercise the fifth element—increased moral and theological *imagination*. Cocurricular educators should be the expert practitioners who are able to see new and creative ways to enhance the greenhouse community development occurring on a college campus. Like an expert gardener, they can use the creative imagination they've acquired over years of practice to offer advice about creating the best environment for cultivating fruit-bearing trees of life.[28]

Finally, there are those who have achieved excellence in practice, what we might call *models* (or *heroes* or *saints*): those who incarnate the best of all of these elements. It might be helpful to consider another practice when contemplating how all these elements must work together. A couple of positive psychologists tell the story of Greg Manning, whose wife Lauren was engulfed by flames after the first plane struck the World Trade Towers on 9/11.[29] She said that she initially prayed to die, but her love for her son and husband helped her fight for life. After she was placed in a drug-induced coma,

> Greg ignored Lauren's unconscious state, reading poetry to her and playing her favorite CDs, all the while reassuring her that she was loved, that he would take care of her, that everything would be okay. During his home shifts, he took Tyler to birthday parties and play dates, read and sang to him, and documented his development on videotape for Lauren's future viewing.[30]

In the end, doctors had to replace more than 80 percent of Laura's skin. As the chroniclers of their ordeal recount:

> Exactly 3 months after admission to the hospital, Lauren saw her new, scarred face for the first time. The predictable shock and sadness were tempered by the fact that her husband had prepared her through repeated reminders that she always had been and always would be his soul mate, and in his eyes was as beautiful as ever.[31]

Notice how all the above elements work together in a modeling situation. Greg exemplified wisdom in the midst of a trial that required expert knowledge of how to love Lauren. He engaged in various practices and virtues and followed the rules of marriage. As this story also illustrates, models prove vitally important because they capture the emotional aspect of the good life in ways that instruction using commands, general virtues, mentoring, or practices can never do. They inspire.

A helpful model of someone who focused on the unique nature of a Christian greenhouse community and the importance of our embodied Christian identity for realizing it is Dietrich Bonhoeffer. As many know, Bonhoeffer's opposition to Adolf Hitler's regime cost him his life. The professed pacifist was so appalled by the oppression the Nazis were unleashing across Europe that he participated in an attempt to kill Hitler and other party leaders. His efforts were uncovered and thus thwarted. With the Allies driving further into the heart of Europe, Bonhoeffer was put to death in Flossenberg on April 9, 1945. V-E Day, May 8, 1945, occurred just less than one month later. Bonhoeffer, however, left behind not only an example of what it means to wrestle with the complexities of the gospel in the face of one of the greatest evils human civilization has known but also a battery of writings that provide an ongoing witness to the commitments he held most dear.

Life Together was one of those writings. Prior to agreeing to participate in the plot to kill Hitler, Bonhoeffer committed himself to the training of young pastors for the Confessing Church through a clandestine seminary in Pomerania.[32] Standing in opposition to the Third Reich, the Confessing Church was thus not state supported but, like the early church, worked at the margins. At the time of writing, Bonhoeffer moved "to Finkenstein near Strettin, where he shared a common life in emergency-built houses with twenty-five vicars. This was life together, the life of Christian community."[33]

Drawing from Zechariah and Deuteronomy while also reflecting the spirit of his age, Bonhoeffer argued Christian community is defined by both "its curse and its promise. God's people must dwell in far countries among the unbelievers, but it will be the seed of the Kingdom of God in all the world."[34] For Bonhoeffer, any wall that can be built to help the people dwell will be more metaphoric than literal. As a result, the bulk of Bonhoeffer's text thus takes off from where the book of Nehemiah ends—wrestling with the details of what it means to build a flourishing Christian community. He explored the development of wisdom and the role of common practices such as singing, prayer, devotions, fellowship over meals, and more.

According to Bonhoeffer, the need to be in community, to dwell, and to do so well in the company of others is also woven into the very nature of what it means to be human. As a result, he claimed: "Man was created a body, the Son of God appeared on earth in the body, he was raised in the body, in the sacrament the believer receives the Lord Christ in the body, and the resurrection of the dead will bring about the perfected fellowship of God's spiritual-physical creatures."[35]

In all phases of our existence, we humans are meant to exist in a certain kind of virtuous community and be in right relationship with our God. Such an effort is not made possible by our own efforts. In contrast, the "message of the justification of man through grace alone; this alone is the basis of the longing of Christians for one another."[36] God and God alone through the sacrifice of the Son makes such community possible.

Ordering and Connecting Disparate Identities

God has created a complex world. By seeking multifaceted forms of identity excellence, we can avoid truncated forms of education that focus only on one or two moral components and avoid other essential parts. Identities, narratives, and ends are the most important components. Rules or virtue can only be effectively established by greenhouse communities that conceptualize a specific human end derived from particular narratives. Based on this conception of human flourishing, greenhouse communities can then seek to establish certain rules and embody, prioritize, and exemplify particular virtues. Only with a common identity, narrative, and end can we find agreement about what it means to be a good friend, neighbor, citizen, and more.

Christians also recognize that our attempts to achieve these goods will always face conflict due to the fall. Moral conflict continually occurs in our lives in multiple forms. First, we face the challenge of pursuing excellence within a particular practice and with particular moral elements of the practice (e.g., Will I show self-control and study for the test? Will I violate a moral rule by cheating on the test? Do I study only for my own self-esteem and glory?). This type of moral conflict occurs between our two most fundamental identities as humans made in God's image and as sinners. As Paul outlines in Romans 7, we fight among our identities about what to do: "For

I do not do the good I want to do, but the evil I do not want to do—this I keep on doing" (Rom 7:19). Paul Bloom from Yale argues, "An evolving approach to the science of pleasure suggests that each of us contains multiple selves—all with different desires, and all fighting for control."[37] The new science is merely old theology. As Paul writes, "Now if I do what I do not want to do, it is no longer I who do it, but it is sin living in me that does it" (Rom 7:20). At the end of this verse, Paul recognizes that an alien identity has entered humanity, and it is killing us.

Second, we must realize that merely because we think we have controlled this alien identity in one area, those moral achievements will transfer to another identity area. We may be honest at church but dishonest at school. We may be courageous at work but cowards when interacting with our neighbors. We must consider what psychologists have "discovered" and most people recognize. Behavior does not exhibit "cross-situational stability."[38] Christians simply confess, as Paul does, that we are sinners and hypocrites. This should be no surprise. God created identity excellence to be complex in that we must always learn and acquire virtues in particular identity role contexts, and it is not easy to transfer the virtues between roles. Jumping in basketball and ice skating are both jumping, but they are quite different. In addition, we may have experienced both creative and redemptive growth in one area but not another. The fall must be addressed in multidimensional ways. I may be quite creative in my professional job, but I may lack creativity when thinking about how to celebrate my spouse's birthday. Such multidimensional forms of development require both practice and mentors with expertise, as well as the ultimate guide—the Spirit of God.

Finally, we need to realize that we may also face conflicts between competing forms of identity excellence (e.g., Should I be a good student and study for the exam or be a good friend and listen to my best friend's relationship struggles?). We face this issue every day. Should I be a good professional and work more on this lecture for work or spend time with my wife and kids? We are constantly faced with the question of how we integrate all of these competing selves, desires, and loves. Unfortunately, higher education sometimes creates an environment where students may ironically reduce themselves to being less than made in God's image. For instance, though being an athlete, an honors student, a musician, or student government organization leader are important roles, they are only threads of a larger identity. Cocurricular educators need to cultivate opportunities by which students view themselves as something more than any one strand or even the subtotal of forms of human identity. Students must learn to order their loves and figure out how to prioritize their identities. What Jesus identified as the greatest commands of loving God and loving one's neighbor are the obvious way that Christians start to order their loves. The problem, of course, is that we cannot do it alone.

Here we must fall back to our most fundamental identity. If one reads through the New Testament with a focus on identity, one finds that it emerges as a major theme to virtually every book. The Gospels center on the question of Jesus' identity as the Christ who can save us from our sins. After Paul discusses his frustration with the alien identity that leads him to sin, he asks, "Who will rescue me from this body of death?" The answer is, "Thanks be to God through Jesus Christ our Lord" (Rom 7:24-25 NRSV).

The importance of Christ's identity has profound implications for our identity and the motivation driving our moral lives. This is why the writers of the epistles usually spend the first half or more of their letters, as in Romans, Galatians, Ephesians, and others, helping us understanding our own identity in the light of God's story and particularly what Christ has done for us. Only then do they start to give ethical commands. Unlike the civility code at Harvard mentioned in chapter eight, the biblical writers recognize that we need to understand God's metanarrative, our identity, and the rationale for rules, virtues, and wisdom before we can be persuaded to engage in its demands. When one of our sons engaged in the practice of basketball as a child, he always asked, "Dad, what team are you going to be?" He wanted to place the practice of basketball in an already existing story to give it excitement, drama, and meaning. He pretended we were competing in the NBA championship. In this example, a metanarrative provided one of the most important elements for engaging in formative practices. Indeed, understanding ourselves as living within a divine story becomes a powerful instrument for energizing and shaping our loves and desires. While we find much to agree with in the current literature about the importance of practice for shaping our loves,[39] we would insist that encountering the emotive and motivating power of stories is the first essential element to providing a context and motivation for practice. Throughout the New Testament, Christian motivation stems from encountering the story of God's love, grace, and mercy. This story is what awakens our desire to engage in the hard work of worship that forms us to be saints. It shapes our affections. Moreover, the story reminds us that we need the triune God's help to empower and mentor us as we seek to practice living the good life. Christ's loving sacrifice then provides for us the ultimate model of God's love and, therefore, the ultimate model (recall Eph 5:1), and God's Spirit empowers us to acquire the virtues we need to follow that model.[40]

If cocurricular (as well as curricular) educators wish to be excellent mentors in the good life, they themselves must be experienced identifiers with and imitators of Christ. There is a reason most great teachers have themselves engaged extensively in practice. In sum, the question is thus not whether cocurricular efforts are integrated into curricular efforts on campus. If anything, the question is whether cocurricular efforts are designed, implemented, and assessed in such a way that they cultivate a fertile yet temporary "greenhouse" community where not only students but all members are capable of dwelling in a manner reflective of the created potential that God invested in each of us as image bearers.

16

REIMAGINING ACADEMIC LEADERSHIP

...

This is what the LORD says:
"Let not the wise boast of their wisdom
or the strong boast of their strength
or the rich boast of their riches,
but let the one who boasts boast about this:
that they have the understanding to know me,
that I am the LORD, who exercises kindness,
justice and righteousness on earth,
for in these I delight,"
declares the LORD.

JEREMIAH 9:23-24

FOR CHRISTIANS WHO ARE most comfortable with cultural presumptions that match their own religious commitments, these are strange and estranging times. "All sorts of Christians are waking up and realizing that it is no longer 'our world'—if it ever was."[1] This seismic shift is not all that new in higher education, and for some not that surprising. Yet, just as moving to a new and unfamiliar country is accompanied by rational expectations that things will be different, the accumulating and disorienting weight of what seem to be extraneous cultural eccentricities gradually coalesces into a

296

troubling sense that they all emanate from some unspoken whole or system of thought to which you are not privy but with which you are expected to comply. We have written this book in the hopes of helping students, faculty, and educational leaders identify and understand the dominant culture that has emerged due to these shifts.[2] We have sought to outline the consequences that occur when the university's soul breaks apart, and we have also sought to give guidance regarding how a university with a singular Christian soul could be nourished.

Along with some other writers, we believe this turn is an opportunity for Christians, the church, and Christian educational leaders.[3] Freed from the burden of tending the cultural majority, Christians are now able to focus on life as a faithful, alternative, and perhaps even radical presence in a post-Christendom age.[4] Like the loss that Israel experienced upon entering exile, Christians may now be able to realize that the kingdom they seek is not something in the past. One must bring the kingdom of God into the future by locating it in the context of our times—as they are, not as we would prefer them to be. In this chapter we argue that the sense we make of the times— what we name them—is central to how we make sense of the task of academic administration and our efforts to mend the fragmented soul of the university. We suggest that ideas for invigorating educational leaders in this new setting could be found in old revelations from God.

Situating the University Prophetically

Swept along by fast-flowing cultural waters, American colleges and universities have from the beginning both reflected and directed religio-cultural sense making, as we have argued in various ways throughout this book. In this regard, higher education has been one of the frontline institutions in the shift toward a secular, pluralistic society.[5] In the light of this gradual recognition by churches and colleges alike that there is likely no returning to the era of Christian cultural dominance, we argue that we need a new set of tools (e.g., symbols, narratives, metaphors) or, perhaps more accurately, to newly engage an old set of tools that better reflect our contemporary context— tools that can help Christians relocate the institutions we oversee and re-envision the pursuit of faithfulness within them as well.

Among the scholars who can help us begin to conceptualize how followers of Christ should live in these uncertain times is Old Testament scholar Walter Brueggemann. Brueggemann appropriates Jeremiah's prophetic pronouncements against Jerusalem in the days preceding Babylonian exile and redirects them toward the excesses of our hypermodern/postmodern age. He argues that faithfulness in these times requires "the assertion of critical reality in the face of an ideology of chosenness, voiced grief in the face of denial, and buoyant hope as a counter to despair."[6] In a recent talk, Brueggemann adapted this prophetic message to the context of the higher education, aligning the context of preexilic Jerusalem with the contemporary university.

> It was very late for the ancient city of Jerusalem because the city was being devoured by greedy corruption of which the poet Jeremiah could say, "From the least to the greatest, everyone is greedy for unjust gain, they have treated the wound of my people carelessly, saying: Peace! Peace! When there is no peace."[7]

Brueggemann weaves together two functions of the prophetic tradition: a critique of the systems, powers, and ideals, both manifest and latent, that give shape to higher education in our times, and elements of a vision for the enterprise nested in an alternative conceptualization of collective identity and purpose.

The literary and poetic fulcrum of his talk is Jeremiah's entreaty for humility and reconciliation, situated in the midst of his prediction of death, destruction, and exile.

> This is what the LORD says:

> "Let not the wise boast of their wisdom
>   or the strong boast of their strength
>   or the rich boast of their riches,
> but let the one who boasts boast about this:
>   that they have the understanding to know me,
> that I am the Lord, who exercises kindness,
>   justice and righteousness on earth,
>   for in these I delight,"
>   declares the LORD. (Jer 9:23-24)

From this passage, Brueggemann derives two central elements: the "triad of control" (might, wealth, and wisdom) and, in contrast, the "triad of fidelity" (love, justice, and righteousness). The university, he claims, has benefited greatly from collusion with the triad of control. And although both triads are "compelling" and "indispensable," "the triad of control has carried the day in our society without much critical reflection, it may be the great tilt of the university to give privilege and priority to the triad of fidelity that has nearly disappeared from the public face of our society, as it disappeared from the ancient city of Jerusalem."[8] The preponderance of the address he then dedicates to the intersection of the two triads, each representing a different account of "wisdom," that in their fullness "yield two very different worlds" as well. The resulting forms he titles "fast wisdom" and "slow wisdom," naming seven contrasts (see table 6) that elucidate the nature of their difference.

Table 6. Brueggemann's triads and associated contrasting wisdoms

Triad of Fidelity (Love, Justice, Righteousness)	Triad of Control (Might, Wisdom, Wealth)
Slow Wisdom Characteristics	*Fast Wisdom Characteristics*
body	abstraction
the neighborhood	the club
pain	numbness
dreams	present possession
imagination	explanation
vocation	career
commandments (Torah)	gold/honey

Brueggemann concludes with three thoughts: that the "slow" mystery of God requires a relational integrity that appears as steadfast love, justice, and righteousness. Education is the disputatious reflection of those wisdoms. Second, that slow wisdom calls us to sustain and evoke relational identity for the common good. Third, that Jeremiah's poetry is profoundly contemporary.

> As in our time, as in that ancient city, time is very short. We, like that ancient city, are now an anxious society in which everyone is greedy for unjust gain. We, like that ancient city, are now a society against which comes an enduring nation which language we do not know. We, like that ancient city, are now a society deeply at risk. The poetic response to that risky circumstance seems to me to be completely pertinent now as then.[9]

When Brueggemann gave this talk at one of our universities, he was asked by an administrator in the question-and-answer time, "What can institutions who are committed to slow wisdom and formation do to more effectively resist consumptive practice?" He answered, "That is a hard, complex question to which I have no answers." Although he then did propose several approaches of response, the urgency for application and the candor of his answer highlighted how pressing and difficult charting a way forward can be. Given all the changes we have surveyed in this text—expansion of university functions, diversification of fields and disciplines, cultural dominance of intercollegiate athletics, proliferation of student consumerism (among others)—articulating and pursuing an alternate vision for academic leadership in this environment is no small feat.

We therefore put this dilemma to ten current and former college and university provosts and presidents who serve or served at Christian institutions.[10] In particular, one of us asked them: Does Brueggemann's conceptualization of the times as "late" match with how they make sense of their institutional environment? What aspects of Brueggemann's prophetic vision do you find compelling, challenging, unrealistic, or hopeful? Are there actions, initiatives, or ways of reconceptualizing your institution that answer the call for "slow wisdom" and the triad of fidelity? What might academic leadership look like in the context of this conversation? In the following sections, we explore the administrators' aggregated responses and what they suggest about a vision for a kingdom view of higher education in times that are "late," "very late," or perhaps "too late."

It's Getting "Late": Signs of the Times for Higher Education

As noted in the prologue, critical voices writing missives declaring the demise of the university have become something of a cottage industry.[11] These authors typically herald the end of times with apocalyptic language, at least for higher education. Initially, Walter Brueggemann's injunction that it is "late" appears to add little to this crowded marketplace. However, his prophetic analogy does have the advantage of hindsight: for Israel, it really *was* late and in fact too late, at least in the sense that the national political arrangement they had known would not continue unabated. Using the scale

Brueggemann suggests of "late," "very late," and "too late" by historical analogy provides a more complex analytic perspective lacking from those who simply decry "the end."

Late. In Jeremiah's text, lateness had a clear antecedent: Brueggemann points to greedy corruption and the link the prophet draws between it and the coming geopolitical threat. Posing this analogy to the collection of participant presidents and provosts, the hallmarks of "late" and the accompanying troubles they identified reflect some of the same emphases found in the popular press. Some divergent themes emerged as well. Fundamentally, the ills of the university they noted fit within the tripartite elements of might, wealth, and wisdom that Brueggemann names the "triad of control." In many cases their examples fit two or more of these categories.

Most of the examples offered by the participants emphasized wealth in some combination with might and wisdom. Concerns about the commodification of higher education as a market good and the financial and related educational implications were the most common themes. Robert, a former provost, described the fiscal pressures since the financial collapse in 2007 and the level of attention to debt and income that has resulted. He wondered, "Where is the line where responsible attention to fiscal issues . . . becomes kind of an unmitigated focus on wealth?" Other administrators named specific issues, such as employee pay disparity and the student debt, tuition, and aid model as practices indicative of a system from which extrication is difficult, if not impossible. Jennifer, a college president, expanded on these points and redirected them to an observation about how the university's credibility and function is perceived as a result.

> The university has usually been thought of as maybe a little odd or maybe as an ivory tower, but it's doing important things. The university now, rather than being viewed as something for the social good is either viewed as for . . . consumer or private benefit, or it is viewed as itself almost a consumer of public good in ways that are not necessarily responsible or defensible.

Participants intimated that one function of the university in late times is that it is both complicit in fueling student careerism and consumerism, and that, perhaps worse yet, it has taken to modeling that behavior for its students. Athletics, technology transfer, admissions, and student aid are all university functions where wealth can be converted to power, and vice versa, but at high cost. Students can become commodities to the university just as students seek to "commodify" their college experience.

As Brueggemann noted, wisdom can seem out of place in the triad of control. One participant quibbled, arguing that he should have substituted "knowledge" for "wisdom." Greg, a provost, pointed to the European Bologna Accords[12] and the shift from education for the common good to education for technical competency that drives national workforce needs and individual economic ends as problematic. This, he suggested, is what happens when wisdom becomes a consumer good and is redefined in accordance with expedient outcomes reflective of "fast wisdom." Wesley described this mindset as an outcome of cultural pluralism as well. Rather than seeking to understand truth as coherent, the tendency is instead "to say there is no truth; there is simply knowledge and there are the ways in which knowledge gets configured." Kevin, a college president, suggested that wisdom is still greatly desired tacitly, but culturally we have lost a clear sense of what wisdom is and what it is for.

> I think society is crying out for wisdom. But it's pretty hard for society to even understand what it is asking for given most of society has been educated, if it's been educated at all, with a different kind of knowledge being important. You know, I'm not even sure they know how to ask the wisdom question anymore.

Very late. Several participants made the case that what makes the times not just late but "very late" is how completely enveloping the pressures for institutional conformity have become. Austin, a provost, reflected, "I do think that universities like ours have either intentionally or unintentionally allowed the surrounding culture to set the terms of the discussion for the value of higher education." Worse still may be the loss of a sense of agency—that change to this system is possible. Christian, a provost, redefined "late" as "deep," describing the ubiquity of an enterprise that is both vast and disorienting.

> From my perspective, the feeling is that we're in so deep in the system and the system is deep within another system it's hard to figure out what can be done. . . . It's really complicated to figure out how to challenge that triad with

anything, particularly love, justice, and righteousness—given the environment in which we operate.

He later suggested that the line between "late" and "very late" or even "too late" is crossed when we lose our imagination for and will to pursue other paths: "My feeling at least is that the cycles that entrap us are getting more difficult to escape." The price paid to "play the game," as many participants phrased it, and whether that price was unacceptably high, was an ongoing theme throughout the interviews.

Too late. Several participants raised the possibility that the times may in fact be "too late" and referenced the implications of that chronological or eschatological position. Jennifer used that phrase to question whether the opportunity to recover a voice of vision in society had already passed, largely because of systemic participation and compromise.

> So, is it too late for Christian higher education to be independent enough to be prophetic? That would be one thing. Is it too late, given the social and cultural critique of higher education right now, is it too late for Christian higher education to be seen as relevant? And that could all be summed up in, is it too late for Christian higher education to be a credible critic of the very system of which we are so complicit?

Joseph, a provost, interpreted this loss of voice similarly, though emphasizing the undesirable transition from a social institution that questions the status quo to one that tacitly perpetuates it: "The university is in danger of losing its creative redemptive role in society by giving in too much to the power elite structures of its day and really becoming a tool that kind of supports those ongoing structures rather than challenging those."

Christian pointed to the example of the young King Josiah as a way to suggest the implications of the current conditions. Judges 22 records how, upon finding the book of the law during temple repairs after years of neglect and hearing it read for the first time, Josiah deeply lamented Israel's unfaithfulness and inquired what could be done to stay the anger of the Lord. Christian explained, with a bit of narrative license, what happened next:

> And [Josiah] goes through the process . . . let's find out if it's too late . . . if we can renew the covenant and if it's too late. And it came back, it was kind of a hush story, but the word comes back, and "Oh, good for you that you care,

that you're interested, that you're going to buck your immediate forefathers, that you're going back, but yep, it's too late." Then Josiah gathers all the people and reads to them their history and says basically, "It's late, it's too late, but we're going to do this anyway; we're going to renew the covenant." So, that's the thing that was, to me, what I kept thinking about, "so what if it's too late?" if Josiah found out it was too late and he still attempted to be faithful.

Taken in this way, "late" has a new ring to it. If "late" is a warning to right the ship, if it is a call to action, then mobilization is aimed at fixing what is broken while there is still time. This is the version of "late" that Robert suggested, using God's mercy on Nineveh as an example. But if our times are "late" in the sense of the context in this passage and the Jeremiah reference Brueggemann was working from, then the word primarily implies that the time is short before the inevitable consequences of chronic unfaithfulness come to pass. In this "too late" context, living faithfully, as Josiah committed to do, is firmly an "end" and not a means to a different preferred end. Living faithfully for Josiah was in essence preparation for living in exile.

As much as the times may be "late" for higher education generally to recover or return to the position of social prominence it once held, using this literary device to examine the Christian university may be insufficient. Christians are, as we have discussed, coming to accept the fact that the age of Christian cultural dominance in the United States has ended. In that sense, it really is "too late." A more helpful analogy that a few participants entertain is that of the Christian university in exile.

Living in exile. If a central goal of the Christian university is fostering a prophetic voice in the marketplace, then it may indeed be too late, according to several participants. James, a provost, described his struggle with how to administrate counterculturally when so much of his job required him to respond to aspects of the triad of control.

And so how do you opt out of competition? [That] is to me one of the biggest questions in a Christian institution. How do I opt out of that, all the cultural assumptions that are made about successful institutions that translate into marketing campaigns, that translate into students willing to come and spend the money for your services? You can simply say, "We don't care about them coming and their money," but that's incoherent because you have to, to make the institution work. So, it's really a paradox to know how to present yourself in a way that will still be understandable and attractive to people.

Christian also argued that the alternative is difficult if not impossible to pursue, and that is how we know how "late" it has become.

> Maybe one way to think about it is like this: the "too late" line, perhaps, is drawn when the only way we can do what we believe is faithful and right and just is so perilous that it's almost irresponsible to do it. So, I mean, just one example, if you take salaries, do we think it's right for there to be the disparity that we have within our institutions on salaries? Does anybody think that's right? The only way you can think that's right is by indexing it to what other places are doing and if you don't index it, it's hard to do business.

This overriding systemic normativity would seem to surpass an expectation of conformity. That is, not only do institutions tend to mimic successful peers in times of uncertainty, but failure to fall in line has severe marketplace credibility repercussions.[13] In Christian's example above, could an institution attract faculty and administrators if it paid everyone a similar wage? How faithful Christian administrators should respond in times both uncertain and highly prescribed is a question interview participants asked rhetorically as much as they answered. Nevertheless, our conversations brought to light three approaches, each with its own philosophical, ontological, and theological assumptions.

How Then Shall We Live?
Separation as Preferred Narrative

Brueggemann's use of the phrases "late," "very late," and "too late" to establish the context for the triads of control and fidelity has the advantage of suggesting that distinctively independent and faithful operation is possible. So long as Israel remained a geopolitical entity, establishing a system-wide counternarrative was possible. Indeed, Josiah's renewal of the covenant reestablished this very reality. The countercultural approach sets a purposefully divergent path from that of the externally normative but internally corruptive powers of might, wisdom, and wealth. It is the city on the hill: obtuse by design. As Greg suggested, pursuing a countercultural path is a clear way to establish a strong position of identity and alternative reality.

I think it's absolutely critical for you to understand the way in which many of the norms and patterns in mainstream higher ed can in fact be crushing and can work against community, can work against the flourishing of people on your campus. [You must] determine that you're going to not simply follow those patterns because somebody says that is the way to excellence. Say: "We are going to . . . by God's grace try to find and embody a more excellent way, if possible."

By setting up a series of contrasts (control/fidelity; fast/slow wisdom), Brueggemann effectively demarcates the boundary lines for an alternative community where the operational norms contrast dramatically with those of the corrupter/oppressor. The features that guide this paradigm—love, justice, and righteousness—find expressive form through the seven contrasts Brueggemann draws (table 6). Of them, many participants found *neighborhood versus club* to be one of the most compelling contrasts and indicative of a radically different set of priorities. In short, the "neighborhood" is a place where all may be known, and welcome is extended to all who choose to live there. It is a sphere of mutual regard, exchange, and diversity—an open block, not a gated community. The "club" by contrast is a system of membership and exclusion: of privilege and fickle judgment. Austin described how his own thinking about institutional mission had shifted as he realized that institutional regionalism had "neighborhood" value.

> Most of our students come from west [state] and frankly [laughs] their highest goal in life is to stay in west [state], which funny, growing up in [metropolitan area] and moving around, I used to see this as a limitation. The more that I understand what Brueggemann and others are saying, the more I see that as really kind of a strength that we have as an institution or an opportunity for us rather than something to overcome. I think I used to in my earlier years, tended to see someone who stays in their own community their whole life or goes back to where they grew up after college as somewhat of a failure, frankly. I've come to, I guess, change my thinking on that and say if we can prepare someone to more intentionally and fully live out faithfulness in the community that they grew up in, love, and want to be in, that's a good thing. It's not a bad thing. It took me a while to kind of recognize that.

The subtext of Austin's remarks is that the club values prestige, aspiration, and mobility. The neighborhood, in this case a person's place of origin, is either a source of embarrassment or a locus of identity, purpose, and relationship, depending on one's orientation. The club, as Kevin noted, is about creating systems that excuse homogenization, often in the name of excellence. Contextualizing, he reflected on places where this may be manifest at his own institution: "So, yeah, one of the things that this conversation is making me think about is our honors program. [It should be] 24 percent Pell eligible [to match the general student population]. If it's not, why not? It should be. If it's only 4 percent Pell eligible, then it's a club."

Despite valuing aspects of the separation modality, most if not all participants found Brueggemann's implicit countercultural approach to be an unrealistic vision for higher education, if desirable at all. James summarized this response, pointing to the obligations to which institutional leaders must answer simply to remain operational.

> So as a Christian college we are unavoidably intertwined with the academy's understanding of knowledge and the academy's understanding of standards for what it means to be an academic institution. . . . So you think okay, that's "in but not of the world." How do we maintain some sort of countercultural or different paradigm when we, by definition, have bought into various outside agencies we are accountable to? So, that's a challenge. So we have to serve the ends and goals and assumptions of these legitimizers of our existence.

Cooperative Subversion: The Example of Daniel

Despite his constructions of contrasts and dichotomies, it is unlikely that Brueggemann views participation in one triadic system as completely antithetical to participation in the other. His example of Daniel and his apparent navigation of this slippery middle ground suggests that a faithful way forward through and not in complete isolation from the triad of control is possible. Toward this end, the next two approaches attempt to redefine the obligations that come with participation in the triad of control and fast wisdom.

In his discussion of the seven contrastive examples of slow and fast wisdom, Brueggemann invokes the story of Daniel to illustrate the seventh, "vocation versus career." Leading up to his discussion of Daniel, he highlights the tension embedded in the university between its employment and status-certification functions and its identity and purpose-development functions.

> The pressure in higher education now is all about career and practical study in order to make a good living. The university, moreover, must justify itself in terms of earning power. But of course, the university at its best is not just about making a living, but about making a life that is deeper and more serious than the next advancement in might and wealth.[14]

Nearly every story of young Daniel's activities ends with a note about another imperial promotion. Brueggemann lauds Daniel as proof that "one can live amid the regime of might, wisdom, and wealth but still be a practitioner of love, justice, and righteousness."[15] This is about as much of a compromise position as Brueggemann makes, and it is quite a lot. The weight of his analysis of Daniel is instead placed on his three companions, known foremost in the book of Daniel by their given imperial names (Shadrach, Meshach, and Abednego) and not their Jewish names (Hananiah, Mishael, and Azariah) (see Dan 1:6-7). Brueggemann wonders: Did they maintain their Jewish names, or were they consumed by their "career" names? He concludes ominously that "the names to which we answer are determined by the triad in which we are situated."[16] But does "situated" mean our cultural location or our religio-cultural allegiance? The difference is vital. In exile, the latter may be chosen, at cost, but the former likely not.

In addition to the tacit suggestion that faithful living might be possible within the triad of control (so long as one follows the advice of many parents to "remember who you are and where you came from"), something else important has happened here: Brueggemann has shifted contexts from a preexilic Israel where the triad of control marks corruption, to exilic Babylon where might, wisdom, and wealth are culturally and functionally normative. This second environment would seem to align more fully, by analogy, with experiences of participant administrators who view their work as spanning two worlds or, in Brueggemann's language, two triads.

Austin's comments about the growth and maturing of the Christian university mirrors Brueggemann's commentary above about the challenges of the university's dual functions.

I think that this is something that a lot of our Christian institutions are getting a better handle on, that we're not, for one, we're emphasizing career preparation more than we used to because you have to. That's kind of the name of the game nowadays. But also, I think we're getting a better sense of how we do that differently than a secular university would. Our emphasis needs to be on vocation and students developing a sense of calling and that fidelity, faithfulness to that calling is . . . their success in life, not having a lucrative or a secure career.

Thus, at the risk of mixing analogies, it might be that the hour is "late," "very late," or "too late" for higher education at the societal level because the compromises made in the name of attracting and satiating students have come at the price of institutional focus and integrity. It might also be that for Christian higher education, acquiescence to market demands has come at the additional cost of a prophetic voice within the field of higher education.

However, given the prevalence of secular and consumerist thinking within the culture at large, the analogy of exile suggested by the Daniel example may be more apropos. A perspectival shift from recovering the lost university to living in the exilic university requires the difficult first step of accepting a foreign (and mostly, though not wholly, objectionable) set of values as the new normal. This done, we are freed from the burden of cultural transformation (in the sense of exercising dominion over it) to search for places and times where God's redemptive purpose can be unleashed in creative and unexpected ways that functionally and symbolically testify to the coming of Christ's kingdom.

Living Faithfully in Babylon: Two Additional Approaches

In addition to Brueggemann's countercultural approach, two overlapping but distinct ways of parsing out faithful institutional living in a strange land arose in conversation with administrators. Both emerged in part through the example of Daniel, as administrators processed the lessons that might be inherent in that story. In the first, which we title the *redemptive approach*, participants expressed resistance to Brueggemann's penchant for dichotomizing and his apparent condemnation of the triad of control and its accompanying expressions within fast wisdom. Wesley connected this perspective to his interpretation of Brueggemann's take on Daniel's significance.

It is funny to me that part of Brueggemann, he gives examples like Daniel's rise to power, but it's almost dismissive of the redemptive way that Joseph or Daniel or other key Old Testament leaders redeemed the positions of influence they were in. He's almost dismissive of that in the way he talks of them. Or wants to almost, he doesn't suggest it but he almost suggests that that they got co-opted by that.

In many cases these perspectives were nested in theological commitments that tend to emphasize transformation of systems rather than rejection of them. Greg asserted that his theological orientation (Calvinist) informed his view of grace and redemption.

So, yeah I guess my tradition and my own personal makeup is more reform-minded than it is radical alternative-minded. Although I see the need for doing things, creating communities that are alternatives, but not, should we say, totally sealed off ones. I believe in God's providence, I believe in God's working through unredeemed people and flawed institutions to work good things. So, I'm not willing to just say that for sake of the gospel and righteousness compels me to throw it all out and to say it's all irredeemably evil. I think each of us in our everyday experience see the goodness and usefulness of much of it that we've learned. Right, so, I get a little impatient with prophetic posturing sometimes because I think a lot of it throws the baby out with the bathwater.

Kevin responded similarly, objecting to Brueggemann's seeming rejection of the triad of control, arguing, "He seems to err on the side of viewing all three of these things [might, wisdom, wealth] as mostly corruptible. He doesn't hold up a lot of examples of them being redeemed." The redemptive approach largely rejects the implicit condemnation seated in the strong contrasts Brueggemann constructs. Instead, participants suggested that the triad of fidelity could operate as a transformational mechanism on the triad of control. Participants that advanced this approach were cautious about the temptations of power abuse but still advocated for the positive outcomes available through faithful engagement. Wesley pressed this point.

I think the thing that it still misses is if all we give [students] is an understanding of steadfast love and righteousness as Brueggemann has described it, there's no sense that when you go into this place, are you able to bring a redemptive aspect to what you do? Are you able to be a redemptive agent at

IBM, at Citibank, at the Defense Department, at the CIA? Are you able, in a sense, to bring a humanizing aspect to it?

The themes emphasized here are strongly indicative of Reformed theological perspectives rooted in a positive view of God's redemptive power in and through systems corrupted by sin.[17] Optimism that engagement with the powers can result in their transformation in substance and outcome reduces fear of the "other" and insularity. It might also result, as Brueggemann hinted in his use of the example of Daniel's associates and their imperial names, in willingness to compromise in an effort to be seen as legitimate at the cost of one's kingdom identity.

The second approach, which we call the *prophetic margin*, takes a more cautious tone toward the triad of control and fast wisdom, positioning them as facts on the ground that one must navigate successfully. They are not, however, by their presence alone terminal to expressions of love, justice, righteousness, and slow wisdom. Greg called on the Daniel narrative in a slightly different way than Austin (above) did, emphasizing, rather than systemic redemption, demonstration that the true things of Yahweh, despite their seeming unconventionality, were still true even in a foreign land.

> One of my favorite passages in the Bible is Daniel 1–2, where these young Hebrew lads who are chosen for leadership development say, "We're going to do it a different way, look at us and see how we fare," and so I think Christian institutions ought to be willing to say that, too, and say . . . "We think we have a more excellent way and check out our results."

Jennifer brought up the Daniel narrative as well; although her use of it positioned students, rather than the institution, as the Daniel figure, able to thrive by drawing on a fundamentally different identity and self-understanding and with a foundationally different sense of purpose: "You want Daniel to have this inner type of identity that will allow him to not lose a sense of who he is even while he is being successful in Nebuchadnezzar's court. That's the kind of preparation that we need to be giving to young people in Christian higher education these days." The prophetic margin approach seeks to identify practices, behaviors, and modes of being and may draw from both redemptive and countercultural approaches in that process.

311

Compared with the other two approaches, the difference is in the tactical nature of sense making. The *countercultural* approach would view the prophetic margin as concessionist; the redemptive approach, as not sufficiently bold. The implication administrators gave is that doing the procedural stuff (securing accreditation, for example) that Babylon requires provides space to deliver the prophetic word, the alternative perspective, or the distinctive practice. Christian articulated this perspective as well, both acknowledging the weight of the system and searching for the margin that remains where transformation can occur: "If Brueggemann is right, then it makes it even more difficult for us to find the prophetic space, because the larger system is one of control, and expresses itself at so many levels."

In contrast to those who conceptualized the structures of postsecondary legitimacy as obstacles or hurdles to be navigated (as above), other administrators described them as counterparts that administrators must learn to fit together somehow. As James suggested: "I think we're stuck with more of the both/and, and maybe my thesis would be that we shouldn't see those, the power against the fidelity in the either/or, that you can't have power without fidelity and you can't have fidelity without power."

As part of the search for the prophetic margin, administrators reacted with little uniformity to what they perceived as the implications of pursuing slow wisdom in a fast-wisdom world. The contrasts constructed by Brueggemann (table 6) seem to leave little room for compromise or transformation: slow wisdom *is* the faithful and countercultural position; fast wisdom *is* the corrupted and conformist position. Joseph was among those who objected to the fast/slow-wisdom contrast. He claimed instead that the university is by its nature oriented to slow wisdom: "We have a lot of need in society for fast, I'm not against fast, but the unique contribution of the university is it is intended to be spacious. So, given that, I'm not sure that I would buy that the university has sort of caved into fast wisdom, I don't see much evidence of that."

Other participants were quicker to identify ways that fast wisdom has infiltrated university functioning in negative ways. Still, the idea that some areas of university life might operate better through a fast-wisdom paradigm received support. Robert supplied an example objection to the slow/fast contrast, making a distinction between those areas of the university that can rightly benefit from fast wisdom and those that do not.

> I'll give you a terrific example of good change in the university and that was outsourcing grounds work. . . . Well, it was one of the best things that we ever did, to outsource campus maintenance because we were able to contract out a particular service that didn't require university expertise whatsoever. . . . Now, there is nothing to draw from that example regarding the core of the university. I would not want to outsource the teaching function or the faculty function in any way. That is a core activity of the university, not to be outsourced, that is our expertise, that's our excellence. Dining service, yeah, outsource that. I see no reason why the university personnel should be in charge of dining.

Robert's example suggests that slow-wisdom parts of the university (instruction, primarily) can or should be separated from fast-wisdom functions. Other aspects, such as housing, may be less obviously placed. Christian also discussed maintenance and campus grounds workers, but used the example to show how he pursued slow wisdom as a college president.

> Every August, you know, I would meet for an hour and a half, I'd have the physical plant, the facilities people, over to the president's house for lunch—and so we'd eat and then we'd spend an hour where they were giving their best ideas for ways to strengthen the university—and then part of that hour was celebrating all the things that they had suggested from the year before that were implemented. Sometimes their suggestions were within their domains of their work, but sometimes they went beyond it and in that respect they are providing leadership to the university, and then helping them recognize that. And so when a parent would talk about a campus visit where somebody from custodial staff, for example, was so helpful and so attentive and what an influence that had on a parent's perception of the university, you know, I don't think that happens if their sense is that "our job is to clean up after the faculty." You know, so, that's one puny example of that, but I think that it requires some intention to soften the hierarchy.

This small example opens a window into two different ways of thinking about faithful living in Babylon. No direct harm may come from outsourcing facilities or other functions—fast wisdom might increase efficiency, reduce costs, and even improve performance.

The harm may come when facilities ceases to be an area where slow wisdom is imagined to do anything but impede expedience. Having a well-run physical plant and grounds that prospective students find attractive may be part of the cost of doing business. It may even be an opportunity. Having the imagination, as Christian did, to reject the "club" of administrative hierarchy in favor of a neighborhood where everyone has something of value to contribute—not as tokenism, but really something otherwise inaccessible—embraces slow wisdom as a normative community value. Wesley described how this tendency toward following peers results not only in a great deal of time spent chasing the priorities of other kinds of institutions but ultimately in a lost focus on those aspects of institutional identity that deeply ground it.

> So, I think that's what happens a lot, I mean I see it a lot because we work with private Christian colleges, we work with private schools, we work with public [institutions] and its interesting, there's almost amongst some Christian schools a constant chasing after the things that they see to be important at the major privates and major publics, Harvard, Yale, Michigan, Berkeley and rather than saying, "let's be true to who we are," this is: "we're rooted in something constant and we can do everything that they do but we can do more and we can do better because it's rooted in this way."

Academic Leadership for Exilic Times

However much we prefer the vision of living in the Promised Land, the Christian experience in early twenty-first-century America is more accurately reflected in the analogy of Israel in exile.[18] Christian cultural influence has waned and is waning. Unbelief has become normative and secularity prevalent.[19] Describing the advantages of an exilic life perspective, Mark Labberton argues,

> It means choosing to give ourselves to those around us with fewer and different expectations, not as settlers but as guests and visitors. We don't whine about the world being the world. We are instead called to love it out of the integrity of our lives, without making our love dependent on its changing.[20]

Others have similarly advanced the case that this sea change, desired or not, is an opportunity for the church to cease centuries of grasping for cultural control and adjust to life as strangers in a strange land.[21] Embracing exilic life means accepting that the rules of the higher-education game are set largely outside of the control of Christian higher education. Consequently demonstrating competence if not excellence will mean jumping through the hoops of accreditation, federal policy, and marketplace credibility that are required to establish legitimacy.

Once we acknowledge that most of what Christian administrators do will be nearly the same as what their secular peers do, where then is the space for transformation to occur? It is instructive to recall that before the *nation* of Israel, the *people* of Israel spent nearly five hundred years enslaved to the Egyptians. This time of oppression, though different in some important ways, mirrored the Babylonian exile as an experience that extensively threatened the collective consciousness of God's people. Some lessons learned in this first captivity translated to Israel's exile and, by analogy, our times as well. Writing about this context elsewhere, Brueggemann argues that three elements embedded in the exodus story became and remained influential and formative throughout Israel's existence: a critique of the dominant ideology, public processing of pain, and the release of a new social imagination.[22] These three elements provide additional insight in our attempt to reenvision academic leadership in the exilic university as well.

1. A critique of the dominant ideology. A group enslaved for hundreds of years might begin to assume that the power of Pharaoh/Babylon is absolute, just as it might be tempting to cede ontological permanence to secular humanism. However, the Hebrews developed and maintained an identity apart from that power through names, rituals, and stories. In doing so, they called into question the narrative of dominance of Pharaoh, rejecting his power as legitimate, identifying it as a contrivance that would not last, and naming the dismantler: Yahweh. The existence and persistence of the people of Israel was a rejection of a system that legitimated oppression and attempted to normalize enslavement.

Critique of the dominant ideology for the academic administrator may take a variety of forms. We suggest two general categories under which a variety of expressions may be pursued. Critique may be implicit in programs and structures. For example, developing hiring and personnel practices that value rest and growth as equal goods to productivity reminds all parties that our work and its flourishing belong to the Lord. This prioritizing rejects cultural pressure for perpetual output. Critique may also be explicit in programs and structures: using faculty seminars or retreats to discuss topics such as the effect of student consumerism on curriculum or embedding cross-curricular themes grounded in Christian perspectives such as justice and reconciliation, hospitality, and sacrifice may challenge faculty and students to critically reflect on the subtle ways kingdom priorities are displaced by alternative cultural messages.

2. Public processing of pain. Not only did Israel reject this dominant ideology, but they did so in part by loudly and communally crying out to God against it. Brueggemann argues, "The cry of pain begins the formation of a counter-community around an alternative perception of reality."[23] This is not simply a dislike of enslavement but collectively claiming that the world ought to be different, and Yahweh will set it right. We are most familiar with these practices in situations of campus violence. However, there are other sorts of pain that university administrators are often less forthright about—the pain of a junior faculty member denied tenure, the pain of a student who dropped out for lack of funds, the pain of student and even employee impropriety. Some of these occurrences could be defended as realities of organizational life. Others may not be spoken about publicly for legal or political reasons. Both reasons, at times, can be valid. Nevertheless, much like our prior example of outsourcing grounds crews, each of these circumstances also represents an opportunity to be reminded that organizations operate through webs of relationships in which commitments to a common cause binds disparate members together. Participating in higher education means participating in systems that hurt people. One function of the "cry of pain" in this context is to publicly acknowledge that removal from institutional life (not receiving promotion, dropping out, and so on) is painful, embarrassing, and disorienting, particularly in a culture that so highly values academic success as a means to economic and identity security. The cry of pain emanates from a legitimate longing for belonging—one that organizational membership cannot fulfill.

As we discussed in the academic administration chapter, the cry of pain may also be self-inflicted, requiring institutional confession. When administrators are able to acknowledge mistakes of policy or leadership that unjustly hurt or fail to protect faculty, staff, or students from harm, the cry of pain becomes a countercultural act that simultaneously rejects the tendency to suppress unflattering details and embraces the need for God's grace and forgiveness.

3. *The release of a new social imagination.* Flowing from the first two, the release of a new social imagination heralds the possibility of an order not yet realized. Yahweh's power that liberated the Hebrews and legitimated both their cry and critique established a vision for a political and confessional community that operated on a different set of rules: those of the Sabbath rest and the Year of Jubilee, when debts were forgiven, lives redeemed, and the destitute restored to their place in society.

What does this reimagination look like for the academic administrator? We suggest three avenues, though this list is not exhaustive. First, however restricted or restrictive compiling data, meeting donors, attending cabinet meetings, or distributing policy memos might be, the knowledge of what one is contributing to—the collective enterprise—can fundamentally change that which otherwise appears procedural. Authors such as David I. Smith and James K. A. Smith, Etienne Wenger, and Alasdair MacIntyre argue that developing and maintaining an imagination for the value and coherence of the larger ends invigorates and gives purpose to procedural tasks.[24]

Second, the difference between a Christian administrative perspective and a secular one will not be whether administrators spend the majority of their time concerned with the political and procedural. The difference is found, in part, in what they do with the time that is left. Anthony, a former provost at a research university, highlighted the importance of this alternative orientation.

> One thing is the universities today are primarily run by the administrators. And what are administrators interested in? They're interested in success of a particular kind. They want enrollment, they want revenue, and they want visibility. They are not asking themselves what can we do to prepare our students for wisdom. That's not what they're thinking about. . . . I would get at it this way: 80 percent of an administrator's time should be spent on these issues,

20 percent of the time should be spent on the mission. You know, emoting the mission and talking about it. And that's where such matters as wisdom and the like would always be front and center.

In the story of Daniel and his companions, it is instructive that they refused to eat the king's food but were still measured against those who followed the king's preferred regimen (Dan 1:11-16). Most students arrive at college expecting that, having been chosen like Daniel and his friends "showing aptitude for every kind of learning, well informed, quick to understand, and qualified to serve in the king's palace" (Dan 1:4) (at least in the best of cases), they will be fed the metaphorical "king's food." That "meal plan" is the reward they expect to receive for their diligent practice at conforming to systemic expectations up to that point.

Subversion of these expectations occurs at two levels: first, Christian educators envision the process of preparing for the test of the marketplace as an opportunity to undermine the values of the marketplace. Educators have a few short years to convince students preparing to serve in the "king's court" that this skill set is best acquired and executed through the virtues of love, justice, and righteousness. Christian articulated this desired shift in priorities in this way: "We want [students] to fall in love with the triad of fidelity, but they at least need to learn to operate in the triad of control." Replacing the dream of eating the food from the king's table is difficult but possible. Participants described campus programs for students and faculty that introduce yearly virtues themes (e.g., gratitude, hope, hospitality), study-abroad programs that focus on living among the people of developing countries, STEM programs that feature service applications, worship and learning unified through Christian practices and habits, and topics of reconciliation pursued across the curriculum and cocurriculum. In and through these pursuits, the campus community assembles both marketplace competence and kingdom imagination. Jennifer hinted at the joys and struggles of this process when she commented, "One of the hardest things to do in preserving the triad of fidelity is to make it seem practical to people who are shaped primarily by the triad of control."

The second aspect of subversion occurs when Christian educators convince those who are already adopting the social status derived from this royal tutelage to separate their "imperial" functioning from their kingdom identity. The Daniel narrative identifies the young men's Jewish names and their Babylonian names and, in doing so, establishes how unabashedly pervasive the imperial influence was intended to be. Taking the best of Israel's royal youth to be renamed and retrained in the service of the empire is a pinnacle achievement of national obliteration. Similarly, the triad of control in our own times seeks total allegiance. "Good" employees give their lives to the company, the state, the family, and in doing so perpetuate the mythology that the claims of centrality each makes are self-evident. But Daniel never confused his identity with his work for the emperor, no matter how many promotions he received. It is noteworthy that in an era when "faith integration" has become such a pervasive aspect of Christian work life, thought, and behavior,[25] *dis-integrating* work and identity is an essential part of faithfulness in Babylon. In fact, it was Daniel's insistence on maintaining this dichotomy that landed him in a cave of lions and his friends in a massive bonfire. God's miraculous intervention in both cases should not divert attention from the fact that in both instances these young Hebrews were willing to "throw away a perfectly good career" (as the parental critique might go) in defense of their kingdom identity. Much like the first form of identity maintenance Israel pursued (critiquing the dominant ideology), these young men took pains to critique the presumed ideals of the empire in which they were also highly successful participants.

This is precisely the dilemma that faces not just students but institutions as well. Jennifer outlined the real potential for hazard in the current environment.

> Talking with other Christian college presidents, this is something we've talked quite a bit about, because if Christian colleges are put in the position because of some of the current church/state discussions. . . . If all of that comes crashing down, then the question is, Do you in fact pursue accreditation at all costs? Do you pursue the ability to obtain government funding at all costs if those are in fact requirements to carry on your mission to actually effect student's lives?

Those living in exile should expect that insistence on a kingdom identity might occasionally result in brushes with calamity, just as it did for Daniel.

Let the One Who Boasts

This is what the LORD says:

"Let not the wise boast of their wisdom
or the strong boast of their strength
or the rich boast of their riches,
but let the one who boasts boast about this:
that they have the understanding to know me,
that I am the LORD, who exercises kindness,
justice and righteousness on earth,
for in these I delight,"
declares the LORD. (Jer 9:23-24)

Reviewing again Jeremiah's appeal for prioritization in the context of exilic organizational life, the call issued forth can be read sympathetically for the higher-education administrator in the early twenty-first century. *Having* wisdom, strength, or riches is not condemned by the prophet. One could even argue that condemning those who boast about having wisdom, strength, or riches misses his point. Rather, the directive of the Lord is a positive injunction: to celebrate ("boast of") knowledge of the Almighty, the one who "exercises kindness, justice and righteousness on earth." This reorientation rejects the institutional idolatry and self-glorification that has become the stock-in-trade of the American university. It refocuses organizational priorities on rejoicing in the acts of a loving, just, and righteous God who calls institutions and individuals alike to reflect these kingdom priorities even under the shadow of an opposing empire. In this context, just as the cry of pain is a subversive act, so boasting in the Lord is a similarly countercultural act of community building and extending. Reconceptualizing the Christian university with soul as exilic honors both the magnitude of the resistance Christian administrators face and the deep reliance on the sustaining power of our Redeemer God required to walk faithfully in a foreign land.

CONCLUSION

Can a University with a Singular Soul Exist?

...

One cannot be religious in general . . . one must speak . . .
from a particular religious tradition. As it happens, that tradition
tends to construe the world, including the part of it discussed here
as "higher education," as good but systemically flawed, as animated
by a range of noble ideals and aspirations but unable fully
to realize them, as simultaneously graced and disgraced.

MARK SCHWEHN

IN A POST-CHRISTIAN CULTURE, Christians in higher education must recognize that pursuing academic coherence and excellence without idolatry requires increased intentionality, courage, and wisdom. It will require more intentionality since the standards of excellence in the broader culture for various academic practices will more and more undermine the pursuit of faithful excellence for Christians. Increasingly we will not share the same identity, story, purposes, virtues, principles, practices, mentors, and models as institutions considered "elite." We will then need to find the courage and wisdom to rethink every aspect of the academic endeavor in light of distinctly Christian approaches to these matters. Mending and nourishing the university's soul will take incredible fortitude and Spirit-filled grace and power.

Yet we can and should look for creative ways to find common ground. As we have argued, one of the ways we believe we can find agreements about what the university should or should not be concerns the complaints about the university. As we mentioned in the introduction, there are always students, faculty, administrators, alumni, and other commentators grousing about the university. Although it sometimes requires a great deal of patience to listen to these complaints, we believe the complaints often contain something else, in addition to an opportunity to practice virtue. They speak to our longings for what the university should be. The ideals driving our grievances often stem from a deep longing and desire that is not simply the product of our culture. Our desire for the university to embody an institution with a soul—one with a clear identity, story, and purpose—stems from our longings as creatures made in God's image for God and the kingdom of God.

Unfortunately the contemporary multiversity in a post-Christian culture, we have argued, is developing in such a way that it downplays and frustrates the fulfillment of these longings and reinforces fragmentation and even schizophrenia regarding the knowledge of what is true, good, and beautiful. We hope we have provided some ideas for ways Christian universities, as well as Christian faculty in secular contexts, can approach this situation. Although we have tended to emphasize the hazards of this development, we think it is important to close by recognizing one dangerous way academic and political elites have attempted to produce more coherence in a postmodern culture. The outcome of this false coherence can be a unique form of idolatry.

Often we want to force a university to have a soul. As a result, university systems throughout the world are becoming much more centralized, with federal governments playing a much greater role in assessing, accrediting, and generally controlling the type of universities that exist. We contend that Christians should be concerned about this trend and not welcome it as a way to bring about artificial forms of coherence and resistance to fragmentation. A dangerous form of centralization of educational authority and thinking often develops in response to a fear of ideological differences. As our history of the university revealed, when political authorities attempt to reduce ideological diversity among universities in the name of some overarching religious or political ideology, blood may run in the streets. The fear of sectarianism is what motivated the early American founders who called for a national university. Entrusting political authorities with the task of preventing academic fragmentation and bringing coherence often leads to the enslavement and death of universities. Whether in revolutionary France, the former Soviet Union and Communist Eastern Europe, Communist China, or repressive state regimes in Africa and Latin America, Christians in the university and Christian universities have always suffered and sometimes have been killed under these new political masters promising coherence and the end to fragmentation.[1] If there is one major entity that has the potential for enslaving the university across the world today to various identities, a coherent story, and corrupting purposes, it is the contemporary nation-state. Creating a system that allows universities with soul requires a university system that allows universities with an overarching identity and meta-narrative to exist in a variety of forms.

Consequently we need to recognize an important difference between our God-given longing for coherence and unity in knowledge; a healthy respect for the pluralism of ideas, individuals, and communities; and the danger of the fragmentation resulting from the proliferation of the multiversity. We need to acknowledge that in order to affirm the first two while avoiding the latter, we must encourage political elites to create pluralistic systems of higher education that allow coherent higher-education institutions to exist and live out their different visions. Within this system, we must recognize the need for institutions that can set forth a more coherent approach to wisdom and learning and more pluralistic state-funded institutions that recognize and show justice toward the diversity of students and citizens that exist in a nation. In other words, we need a system of higher education that allows for both individual freedom and institutional freedom. Overall, instead of fearing theological and philosophical conflict, we need a system of higher education that allows civil and deep intellectual debate and exchange among institutions where professors attempt to develop a coherent vision of truth, goodness, and beauty. When giving freedom to such universities, we may actually discover what a free university with a soul is.

Yet we also wish to be realistic about the fulfillment of the longings we have discussed. A university with soul will never be fully embodied on this earth. Like all ideals, humans can only approximate it. Moreover, our understanding of a university with soul will always be partial, and therefore our approximation of our developing understanding of it will always be inexact this side of eternity. Yet, as with most of life, what matters is not the fulfillment of the ideal but the degree to which one can approximate it. One of us often tells our students, "Yes every country, family, and university is fallen, but you would rather live in, grow up in, or attend some more than others." Of course, some of those choices depend merely on power, prestige, and financial resources, but other reasons stem from the story, wisdom, virtues, and practices manifest in those contexts. Wisdom requires learning how to discern the degrees of redemption happening in our lives and the lives of our institutions. Living among a redeemed community with a mission to fully image God in communal academic life makes an important difference. We long for it. We pray, as Christ commanded us, for it to come.

NOTES

INTRODUCTION: CAN THE SOUL OF THE UNIVERSITY BE SAVED?

[1]"World University Rankings," *Times Higher Education*, www.timeshighereducation .com/world-university-rankings (accessed August 3, 2016).

[2]"The World's 50 Wealthiest Universities," Nonprofit Colleges Online, www.nonprofit collegesonline.com/wealthiest-universities-in-the-world/ (accessed August 3, 2016); "The 100 Richest Universities: Their Generosity and Commitment to Research," The Best Schools, www.thebestschools.org/features/richest-universities -endowments-generosity-research/ (accessed August 3, 2016).

[3]"World's Top 100 Universities for Producing Millionaires," *Times Higher Education*, November 4, 2013, www.timeshighereducation.com/news/worlds-top-100-universities -for-producing-millionaires/2008749.article.

[4]Scholars at Risk Network, http://scholarsatrisk.nyu.edu/ (accessed August 3, 2016).

[5]Bill Readings, *The University in Ruins* (Cambridge, MA: Harvard University Press, 1997); C. John Sommerville, *The Decline of the Secular University* (New York: Oxford University Press, 2006); Mark Taylor, *Crisis on Campus: A Bold Plan for Reforming Our Colleges and Universities* (New York: Knopf, 2010); Bruce Wilshire, *The Moral Collapse of the University: Professionalism, Purity and Alienation* (Albany: State University of New York Press, 1990).

[6]Andrew Delbanco, *College: What It Was, Is, and Should Be* (Princeton, NJ: Princeton University Press, 2013), 150.

[7]Harry Lewis, *Excellence Without a Soul: Does Liberal Education Have a Future?* (New York: PublicAffairs, 2007).

[8]Ibid., xi.

[9]Ibid., xiv.

[10]For a recent example, see Delbanco, *College*, 25.

[11]Clark Kerr, *The Uses of the University*, 5th ed. (Cambridge, MA: Harvard University Press, 2001), 1.

[12]Ibid., 14.

[13]Ibid.

[14]Ibid., 7.

[15]Ibid., 15.

[16]Ibid.

[17]James W. Wagner, "Multiversity or University? Pursuing Competing Goods Simultaneously," *The Intellectual Community* 9, no. 4 (February/March 2007), www.emory.edu/ACAD_EXCHANGE/2007/febmar/wagneressay.html.

[18]Ibid.

[19]Ibid.

[20]Ibid.

[21]Robert Maynard Hutchins, *The Higher Learning in America* (1936; repr., New Haven, CT: Yale University Press, 1999), 95.

[22]Ibid., 96.

[23]Gene Edward Veith and Andrew Kern, *Classical Education: The Movement Sweeping America* (Washington, DC: Capital Research Center, 2015).

[24]Hutchins, *Higher Learning in America*, 97.

[25]Julie Reuben, *The Making of the Modern University: Intellectual Transformation and the Marginalization of Morality* (Chicago: University of Chicago Press, 1996).

[26]James W. McClendon, *Ethics* (Nashville: Abingdon, 1986), 143.

[27]Christian Smith, *What Is a Person?* (Chicago: University of Chicago Press, 2010), 4.

[28]Burton R. Clark, "The Organizational Saga in Higher Education," *Administrative Science Quarterly* 17, no. 2 (1972): 178-84.

[29]Ibid., 178.

[30]Frank Donoghue, *The Last Professor: The Corporate University and the Fate of the Humanities* (New York: Fordham University Press, 2008).

[31]Readings, *University in Ruins*.

[32]Derek Bok, *Our Underachieving Colleges: A Candid Look at How Much Students Learn and Why They Should Be Learning More* (Princeton, NJ: Princeton University Press, 2006), 8.

[33]Andrew Hacker and Claudia Dreifus, *Higher Education? How Colleges Are Wasting Our Money and Failing Our Kids—And What We Can Do About It* (New York: Times Books, 2010), 8-9.

[34]See Anthony Kronman, *Education's End: Why Our Colleges and Universities Have Given Up on the Meaning of Life* (New Haven, CT: Yale University Press, 2007); and Hacker and Dreifus, "Triumph of Training," 95-112 in *Higher Education*.

[35]Taylor, *Crisis on Campus*, 4.

[36]Robert Benne, *Quality with Soul: How Six Premier Colleges and Universities Keep Faith with Their Religious Traditions* (Grand Rapids: Eerdmans, 2002).

[37]One of the leaders of this conversation is Rod Dreher, who advocates "the Benedict Option." See his author page at *The American Conservative*, www.theamericanconservative.com/author/rod-dreher/ (accessed August 3, 2016).

[38]Melanie M. Morey and John J. Piderit, *Catholic Higher Education: A Culture in Crisis* (New York: Oxford University Press, 2006).

[39]David I. Smith and Susan M. Felch, *Teaching and Christian Imagination* (Grand Rapids: Eerdmans, 2016), 16.

[40]Most recently in *Ex Corde Ecclesiae* Pope John Paul II wrote about the university as being "born from the heart of the Church." *Apostolic Constitution of the Supreme Pontiff John Paul II on Catholic Universities*, Vatican website, 1990, http://w2.vatican.va/content/john-paul-ii/en/apost_constitutions/documents/hf_jp-ii _apc_15081990_ex-corde-ecclesiae.html.

PART ONE: BUILDING THE UNIVERSITY

[1]See, e.g., John Amos Comenius, *The Labyrinth of the World and the Paradise of the Heart*, trans. Howard Louthan and Andrea Sterk, Classics of Western Spirituality (Mahwah, NJ: Paulist Press, 1998), 165-71.

1 CREATING THE ORIGINAL BLUEPRINT OF A UNIVERSITY

Epigraphs: Hugh of St. Victor, *De arca Noe morali* 4.1 (Patrologia Latina 176.663B), quoted in Jerome Taylor, introduction to *The Didascalicon of Hugh of St. Victor: A Medieval Guide to the Arts*, trans. Jerome Taylor (New York: Columbia University Press, 1991), 171n132; *Didascalicon of Hugh of St. Victor*, 61, 87.

[1]The earliest European universities are generally considered to include the University of Bologna, the University of Paris, and the Universities of Oxford and Cambridge (end of twelfth and early thirteenth centuries). *A History of the University in Europe*, vol. 1, *Universities in the Middle Ages*, ed. Hilde de Ridder-Symoens (Cambridge: Cambridge University Press, 1992). The oldest university in South America is generally considered to be the University of San Marcos in Peru (1551). See "Galeria de Fotos," Universidad Nacional Mayor de San Marcos website, www.unmsm.edu.pe/galerias/. The first university in Asia is generally considered the University of Santo Tomas in the Philippines (1611). See the Pontifical and Royal University of Santo Tomas website, www.ust.edu.ph/.

[2]Andrew Delbanco, *College: What It Was, Is, and Should Be* (Princeton, NJ: Princeton University Press, 2013); Michael S. Roth, *Beyond the University: Why Liberal Education Matters* (New Haven, CT: Yale University Press, 2014); Harold Shapiro, *A Larger Sense of Purpose* (Princeton, NJ: Princeton University Press, 2005).

[3]*Didascalicon of Hugh of St. Victor*, 101. Also see Paul Rorem, *Hugh of St. Victor* (New York: Oxford University Press, 2009).

[4]Ian P. Wei, *Intellectual Culture in Medieval Paris: Theologians and the University, c. 1100–1330* (New York: Cambridge University Press, 2012), 75-76.

[5]Jim Halverson, "Restored Through Learning: Hugh of St. Victor's Vision for Higher Education," *Christian Scholar's Review* 2011, 37.

[6]Ibid.

[7]Jerome Taylor, introduction to *Didascalicon of Hugh of St. Victor*.

[8]Ibid.

[9]Some scholars have mistakenly interpreted Hugh of St. Victor as inheriting Augustine's view of the liberal arts. E.g., G. R. Evans, *Old Arts and New Theology: The Beginnings of Theology as an Academic Discipline* (Oxford: Clarendon, 1980), 34.

[10]We should note that some scholarly disagreement exists regarding Hugh's relationship to Augustine. For more see Halverson, "Restored Through Learning," 35-50.

[11]Evans, *Old Arts and New Theology*, 15-16; *Didascalicon of Hugh of St. Victor*, 61.

[12]*Didascalicon of Hugh of St. Victor*, 61.

[13]Ibid.

[14]Ibid., 46.

[15]Ibid., 48.

[16]Rodney Stark, *For the Glory of God: How Monotheism Led to Reformations, Science, Witch-Hunts, and the End of Slavery* (Princeton, NJ: Princeton University Press, 2003).

[17]*Didascalicon of Hugh of St. Victor*, 52.

[18]Taylor, introduction, 29.

[19]John Howard Yoder, *The Politics of Jesus* (Grand Rapids: Eerdmans, 1972).

[20]*Didascalicon of Hugh of St. Victor*, 54-55.

[21]Taylor, introduction, 32.

[22]Hugh of St. Victor, *De arca Noe morali* 4.1 (PL 176.663B), quoted in Taylor, introduction, 171n132.

[23]Taylor, introduction, 29.

[24]*Didascalicon of Hugh of St. Victor*, 48.

[25]Wei, *Intellectual Culture in Medieval Paris*, 85.

[26]Ibid., 61.

[27]Bruce A. Kimball, *Orators and Philosophers: A History of the Idea of Liberal Education* (New York: The College Board, 1995), 12-42.

[28]Charles Haskins, *The Renaissance of the Twelfth Century* (Cambridge, MA: Harvard University Press, 1971), 356-57.

[29]Evans, *Old Arts and New Theology*, 34.

[30]Ibid.

[31]Ibid., 28-32.

[32]*Didascalicon of Hugh of St. Victor*, 63.

[33]Ibid., 69.

[34]Thomas Albert Howard, *Protestant Theology and the Making of the Modern German University* (New York: Oxford University Press, 2006), 56-57.

[35]Evans, *Old Arts and New Theology*, 35.

[36]Hugh of St. Victor, *Expositio in Hierarchiam coelestem* 1.1 (PL 175.927A), quoted by Jerome Taylor, introduction, 35.

[37]*Didascalicon of Hugh of St. Victor*, 89.

[38]Ibid., 101.

[39]Ibid., 100.

[40]Ibid., 94-95.

[41]Ibid., 92-93.

[42]Ibid., 132.

[43]Stephen C. Ferruolo, *The Origins of the University: The Schools of Paris and Their Critics, 1100–1215* (Stanford: Stanford University Press, 1985), 27-44; Michael Higton, *A Theology of Higher Education* (New York: Oxford University Press, 2013), 16-24.

[44]Ferruolo, *Origins of the University*, 28.

[45]Higton, *A Theology of Higher Education*, 40-41.

[46]Ferruolo, *Origins of the University*, 306-7.

[47]Monika Asztalos, "The Faculty of Theology," in Ridder-Symoens, *Universities in the Middle Ages*, 409-12.

[48]Evans, *Old Arts and New Theology*, 11.

[49]Howard, *Protestant Theology*, 56.

[50]Ibid., 57.

[51]Hastings Rashdall, *The Universities of Europe in the Middle Ages*, ed. F. M. Powicke and A. B. Emden, vol. 1 (New York: Oxford University Press, 1936).

[52]Higton, *A Theology of Higher Education*, 13.

[53]Ibid., 28.

[54]Ibid., 31.

[55]Ibid., 36.

[56]Ibid., 14-18; Paolo Nardi, "Relations with Authority," in Ridder-Symoens, *Universities in the Middle Ages*, 81-82.

[57]Nardi, "Relations with Authority," 81-82.

[58]Jacques Verger, "Patterns," in Ridder-Symoens, *Universities in the Middle Ages*, 35-67; Nardi, "Relations with Authority." See also Wei, *Intellectual Culture in Medieval Paris*, 49.

[59]Nardi, "Relations with Authority," 81-86; Ferruolo, *Origins of the University*, 288-95.

[60]W. J. Hoye, "The Religious Roots of Academic Freedom," *Theological Studies* 58 (1997): 415.

[61]Ibid., 414-19. See also Nardi, "Relations with Authority."

[62]"A propos de la naisance de l'universite de Paris: contexte social, enjeu politique, portee intellectuelle," in *Schulen und Studium*, as quoted by Walter Rüegg, "Themes," in Ridder-Symoens, *Universities in the Middle Ages*, 15.

[63]Hugh of St. Victor, *Expositio in Hierarchiam coelestem* 1.1 (PL 175.923-28), quoted by Jerome Taylor, introduction, 35.

[64]Ibid.

[65]Alasdair MacIntyre, *God, Philosophy, Universities: A Selective History of the Catholic Philosophical Tradition* (Lanham, MD: Rowman & Littlefield, 2009), 95.

[66]Ibid., 95.

[67]Ibid., 76. See also 93-95.

[68]We should note that although Aquinas distinguishes between reason and faith, and between the natural and the supernatural, according to Frederick Bauerschmidt these are distinctions that he was "constantly blurring in practice" (142). Frederick Christian Bauerschmidt, *Thomas Aquinas: Faith, Reason, and Following Christ*, Christian Theology in Context (Oxford: Oxford University Press, 2013).

[69]We discovered this picture in David I. Smith and Susan M. Felch, *Teaching and Christian Imagination* (Grand Rapids: Eerdmans, 2016), 170. The source of this picture is Wikiwand, "Margarita Philosophica," www.wikiwand.com/de/Margarita_Philosophica (accessed August 4, 2016).

[70]Augustine, *Confessions*, trans. John Ryan (New York: Image, 1960), 93.

[71]Ibid., 111.

[72]Ibid.

[73]Melanie M. Morey and John J. Piderit, *Catholic Higher Education: A Culture in Crisis* (New York: Oxford University Press, 2006), 106.

2 A CRACKED PINNACLE AND SHIFTING FOUNDATION: ATTEMPTING TO REPAIR THE UNIVERSITY (1517–1800)

Epigraphs: Peter Ramus, *Pro philosophica parisiensis academiae disciplina oratio* (Paris, 1557), quoted in Walter Rüegg, "Themes," in *A History of the University in Europe*, ed. Walter Rüegg, vol. 2, *Universities in Early Modern Europe, 1500-1800*, ed. Hilde de Ridder-Symoens (Cambridge: Cambridge University Press, 1996), 12; Alasdair MacIntyre, *God, Philosophy, and Universities: A Selective History of the Catholic Philosophical Tradition* (Lanham, MD: Rowman & Littlefield, 2009), 16.

[1]Alfred North Whitehead, *Science and the Modern World* (New York: Macmillan, 1925), 17.

[2]For an explanation of these reasons, see Perry L. Glanzer and Konstantin Petrenko, "Resurrecting the Russian University's Soul: The Emergence of Eastern Orthodox Universities and Their Distinctive Approaches to Keeping Faith with Their Religious Tradition," *Christian Scholar's Review* 36 (2007): 263-84.

[3]Wilhelm Schmidt-Biggemann, "New Structures of Knowledge," in Ridder-Symoens, *Universities in Early Modern Europe (1500-1800)*, 489.

[4]Geoffrey Treasure, *The Huguenots* (New Haven, CT: Yale University Press, 2013), 173.

[5]See James Veazie Skalnik, *Ramus and Reform: University and Church at the End of the Renaissance* (Kirksville, MO: Truman State University Press, 2002), 27, for a summary of the debate.

[6]Ibid., 1.

[7]Walter J. Ong, title page to *Ramus: Method and the Decay of Dialogue: From the Art of Discourse to the Art of Reason* (Cambridge, MA: Harvard University Press, 1958).

[8]Skalnik, *Ramus and Reform*, 65.

[9]Steven Reid and Emma Wilson, *Ramus, Pedagogy and the Liberal Arts: Ramism in Britain and the Wider World* (Farnham, UK: Ashgate, 2011), 230.

[10]As quoted in Ong, *Ramus*, 19.

[11]Ibid., 133. In 1362, for example, one list of professors at the University of Paris listed 25 theology, 11 law, 27 medicine, and 449 liberal arts professors.

[12]Schmidt-Biggemann, "New Structures of Knowledge," 489.

[13]Alasdair MacIntyre, *God, Philosophy, Universities: A Selective History of the Catholic Philosophical Tradition* (Lanham, MD: Rowman & Littlefield, 2009), 76.

[14]Ong, *Ramus*, 134.

[15]Ibid., 37-41.

[16]Ibid., 54.

[17]Skalnik, *Ramus and Reform*, 48-52.

[18]As cited in Mordechai Feingold, "English Ramism: A Reinterpretation," in *The Influence of Petrus Ramus*, ed. Mordechai Feingold, Joseph S. Freedman, and Wolfgang Rother (Basel: Schwabe, 2001), 154.

[19]Skalnik, *Ramus and Reform*, 41.

[20]Ibid., 60-63.

[21]Ibid., 92-93.

[22]Peter Ramus, *Commentariorium de Religione* (Frankfurt, 1577), quoted by Keith L. Sprunger, *The Learned Doctor William Ames: Dutch Backgrounds of English and American Puritanism* (Urbana, IL: University of Illinois Press, 1972), 132.

[23]Ibid., 133.

[24]Sprunger, *Learned Doctor William Ames*, 135.

[25]Skalnik, *Ramus and Reform*, 158.

[26]Sprunger, *Learned Doctor William Ames*, 109.

[27]Ibid., 15.

[28]Ibid., 9-15.

[29]Ibid., 109.

[30]Ibid., 105-6.

[31]Ibid., 116.

[32]Ibid.

[33]Ibid., 113.

[34]Norman Fiering, *Moral Philosophy at Seventeenth-Century Harvard* (Chapel Hill: University of North Carolina Press, 1981), 26.

[35]John D. Eusden, introduction to William Ames, *The Marrow of Theology*, trans. and ed. John D. Eusden (Durham, NC: Labyrinth, 1968), 2.

[36]Sprunger, *Learned Doctor William Ames*, 118.

[37]Ibid.

[38]Ames, *Marrow of Theology*, 226-27.

[39]Sprunger, *Learned Doctor William Ames*, 141.

[40]Ibid., 144.

[41]Ames, *Marrow of Theology*, 78.

[42]Sprunger, *Learned Doctor William Ames*, 127.

[43]John Cotton, "An Apologetical Preface for the Reader of Mr. Norton's Book," quoted by John Norton, *The Answer to a Whole Set of Questions of the Celebrated Mr. William Apollonius*, trans. Douglas Horton (Cambridge, MA: Harvard University Press, 1958), 17.

[44]Sprunger, *Learned Doctor William Ames*, 127.

[45]Ibid.

[46]Ibid., 137.

[47]Ibid., 140.

[48]Ibid., 137.

[49]Ibid., 138.

[50]Fiering, *Moral Philosophy*.

[51]Willem Frijhoff, "Patterns," in Ridder-Symoens, *Universities in Early Modern Europe (1500–1800)*, 43-113.

[52]Ibid.

[53]Brad S. Gregory, *The Unintended Reformation: How a Religious Revolution Secularized Society* (Cambridge, MA: Belknap Press of Harvard University Press, 2012).

[54]Schmidt-Biggemann, "New Structures of Knowledge," 507.

[55]Ibid., 512.

[56]Fiering, *Moral Philosophy*, 26.

[57]Schmidt-Biggemann, "New Structures of Knowledge," 511-12.

[58]Ibid., 529.

[59]Jeffrey H. Morrison, *John Witherspoon and the Founding of the American Republic* (Notre Dame: University of Notre Dame Press, 2005), 7.

[60]Fiering, *Moral Philosophy*.

[61]Garry Wills, *Explaining America: The Federalist* (Garden City, NY: Doubleday, 1981), 18.

[62]Varnum Lansing Collins, introduction to John Witherspoon, *Lectures on Moral Philosophy* (Princeton, NJ: Princeton University Press, 1912), xxi.

[63]John Witherspoon, *The Selected Writings of John Witherspoon*, ed. Thomas Miller (Carbondale: Southern Illinois University Press, 1990), 153.

[64]Ibid.

[65]Ibid., 154.

[66]Ibid.

[67]D. G. Hart summarizes Witherspoon's departure from the previous Puritan orthodoxy. Witherspoon, he claims, "denied that human depravity fundamentally impeded the ability of reason to formulate natural virtue, understood the achievements of the scientific study of nature to stem from natural powers of observation rather than the conformity of human intellect to the divine mind, and regarded God in a more remote fashion, as the one who designed the world but now stood back from the outworkings of creation." Hart, *The University Gets Religion* (Baltimore: Johns Hopkins University Press, 1999), 28.

[68]Morrison, *John Witherspoon,* 51.

[69]Mark Noll, *Princeton and the Republic, 1768–1822* (Princeton, NJ: Princeton University Press, 1989), 36.

[70]Witherspoon, *Selected Writings*, 13.

[71]Morrison, *John Witherspoon*, 2.

[72]John Witherspoon, *Works*, 3:79, 85, as quoted by Mark Noll, *Princeton and the Republic, 1768–1822* (Princeton, NJ: Princeton University Press, 1989), 81.

[73]Julie Reuben, *The Making of the Modern University: Intellectual Transformation and the Marginalization of Morality* (Chicago: University of Chicago Press, 1996), 19-23.

[74]Frederick Rudolph, *Curriculum: A History of the American Undergraduate Course of Study Since 1636* (San Francisco: Jossey-Bass, 1977), 42.

[75]Fiering, *Moral Philosophy*, 62.

[76]Donald H. Meyer, *The Instructed Conscience: The Shaping of the American National Ethic* (Philadelphia: University of Pennsylvania Press, 1972), 161.

[77]Perry L. Glanzer and Todd Ream, *Christianity and Moral Identity in Higher Education* (New York: Palgrave Macmillan, 2009).

[78]Schmidt-Biggemann, "New Structures of Knowledge," 517.

[79]Ibid.

3 THE STATE TAKES OVER THE ACADEMIC PALACE IN EUROPE (1770–1870)

Epigraph: R. D. Anderson, *European Universities from the Enlightenment to 1914* (New York: Oxford University Press, 2004), 20.

[1]John W. O'Malley, SJ, *The Jesuits: A History from Ignatius to the Present* (Lanham, MD: Rowman & Littlefield, 2014), 83. Another source claims the network included over eight hundred institutions. George W. Traub, ed., *A Jesuit Education Reader* (Chicago: Loyola Press, 2008), 44.

[2]Philip Caraman, *The Lost Paradise: The Jesuit Republic in South America* (New York: Seabury, 1976), 11.

[3]Quoted in ibid., 12.

[4]As quoted in Caraman, *Lost Paradise*, 242.

[5]*The Mission*, directed by Roland Joffé (Burbank, CA: Warner Bros., 1986).

[6]We are using Michael Walzer's definition of "civil society" as "the space of unco-erced human association and also the set of relational networks—formed for the sake of the family, faith, interest, and ideology—that fill this space." Michael Walzer, "The Idea of Civil Society," *Dissent* 38 (Spring 1991): 270.

[7]Jonathan Wright, "The Suppression and Restoration," in *The Cambridge Companion to the Jesuits*, ed. Thomas Worcester (New York: Cambridge University Press, 2008), 263-77.

[8]Charles Stephen Dessain, ed., *The Letters and Diaries of John Henry Newman* (London: T. Nelson, 1961), 12:117.

[9]R. D. Anderson, *European Universities from the Enlightenment to 1914* (New York: Oxford University Press, 2004), 23-34.

[10]Ibid.

[11]Walter Rüegg, "Themes," in *A History of the University in Europe*, vol. 3, *Universities in the Nineteenth and Early Twentieth Centuries (1800–1945)*, ed. Walter Rüegg (Cambridge: Cambridge University Press, 1996), 3.

[12]Ibid.

[13]Notker Hammerstein, "Epilogue: The Enlightenment," in *A History of the University in Europe*, ed. Walter Rüegg, vol. 2, *Universities in Early Modern Europe (1500–1800)*, ed. Hilde de Ridder-Symoens (Cambridge: Cambridge University Press, 1996), 632. See also Anderson, *European Universities*, 51; Thomas Albert Howard, *Protestant Theology and the Making of the Modern German University* (New York: Oxford University Press, 2006), chap. 2.

[14]Anderson, *European Universities*, 39. It should be noted that some scholars do not view this control as positive. Notker Hammerstein claims, "In France of the eight-eenth century, the university ceased to have any marked influence on the intel-lectual life of French society and the course of enlightened discussion there. The faculties of arts under the influence of the Jesuitical Counter-Reformation, had been reduced to being nothing more than diploma-granting institutions." Ham-merstein, "Epilogue: The Enlightenment," 631.

[15]Edmund Burke, *Reflection on the Revolution in France*, ed. Frank M. Turner (New Haven, CT: Yale University Press, 2003).

[16]Ibid., 41.

[17]Fritz K. Ringer, *Education and Society in Modern Europe* (Bloomington: Indiana University Press, 1979), 114.

[18]Anderson, *European Universities*, 45.

[19]Ringer, *Education and Society*, 114.

[20]Ibid., 47-48. See also Howard, *Protestant Theology*, 1-3.

[21]Immanuel Kant, *The Conflict of the Faculties*, trans. M. J. Gregor (New York: Abaris, 1979), 19.

[22]Ibid., 25.

[23]Ibid.

[24]Ibid., 27.

[25]Ibid.

[26]Ibid., 28.

[27]Mike Higton, *A Theology of Higher Education* (Oxford: Oxford University Press, 2012), 67.

[28]Howard, *Protestant Theology*, 22.

[29]Ibid., 225-26.

[30]Anderson, *European Universities*, 54-55.

[31]Heinrich Steffens, *The Idea of the University*, trans. Gordon Walmsley, *Copenhagen Review* 2 (2008): 4, www.copenhagenreview.com/backissues1-5/two/the%20university.pdf.

[32]Ibid., 346, quoted by Higton, *A Theology of Higher Education*, 68.

[33]Anderson, *European Universities*, 54.

[34]Johann Gottlieb Fichte, *Addresses to the German Nation*, trans. Bela Kapossy, Isaac Nakhimovsky, and Keith Tribe (Indianapolis: Hackett, 2013), 47.

[35]Ibid., 4.

[36]Higton, *A Theology of Higher Education*, 77.

[37]Ibid., 66-72. Higton provides examples of how all the major German thinkers associated with the founding of the University of Berlin thought in similar ways about the relationship between the state and the university.

[38]Thomas Albert Howard, *Protestant Theology*, 131.

[39]Ibid., 130.

[40]Anderson, *European Universities*, 57.

[41]Ibid., 58.

[42]Ibid., 52.

[43]Friedrich Schleiermacher, *Gelegentliche Gedanken über Universitäten im deutschen Sinn: Nebst einem Anhang über eine neu zu errichtende* (Berlin, 1808), quoted in Rüegg, "Themes," 5.

[44]Wilhelm Weischedel, *Idee und Wirklichkeit einer Universität: Dokumente Zur Geschichte Der Friedrich-Wilhelms-Universität zu Berlin* (Berlin: Walter de Gruyter, 1960), as quoted in Anderson, *European Universities*, 57.

[45]Rüegg, "Themes," 17.

[46]Politically speaking, we are referring only to England (including Wales) and not the kingdom of Great Britain (originating in 1707). Scotland, another part of the kingdom, actually had four universities at this time: Andrews (1410), Glasgow (1451), Aberdeen (1495), and Edinburgh (1582) that were "essentially secular but

with a broad framework of Christian culture." Anderson, *European Universities*, 94.

[47]Ibid.

[48]V. H. H. Green, *Religion at Oxford and Cambridge* (London: SCM Press, 1964), 153.

[49]Negley Harte, *The University of London 1836–1986* (London: Athlone, 1986), 64.

[50]Ibid.

[51]Ibid., 73.

[52]Ibid., 65, 67.

[53]Ibid., 110.

[54]Ibid., 96.

[55]Ibid., 98.

[56]Anderson, *European Universities*, 65-66.

[57]Rainer A. Müller, "Student Education, Student Life," in Ridder-Symoens, *Universities in Early Modern Europe*, 331-33.

[58]Paul Gerbod, "Relations with Authority," in Rüegg, *Universities in the Nineteenth and Early Twentieth Centuries*, 83-100; Anderson, *European Universities*.

[59]Müller, "Student Education, Student Life," 326.

[60]Hammerstein, "Epilogue: The Enlightenment," 623.

[61]Ibid.; Rüegg, "Themes."

[62]Müller, "Student Education, Student Life"; Anderson, *European Universities*, 13.

[63]Hammerstein, "Epilogue: The Enlightenment," 624-26.

[64]Ibid., 628.

[65]Ibid., 625.

[66]Ibid., 626; Anderson, *European Universities*, 89.

[67]Anderson, *European Universities*, 89.

[68]Rüegg, "Themes," in *A History of the University in Europe*, vol. 2 and vol. 3. For example, Frijhoff observes, "In eighteenth-century Poland, for example, virtually all theology teaching was done outside the university, either at Jesuit schools or at Episcopal seminaries." Willem Frijhoff, "Patterns," in Ridder-Symoens, *Universities in Early Modern Europe*, 63.

[69]Anderson, *European Universities from the Enlightenment to 1914*, 20-38.

[70]Müller, "Student Education, Student Life," 327.

[71]Anderson, European Universities, 29.

[72]Ibid., 88.

[73]Ibid., 90-91.

[74]James Arthur, *Faith and Secularisation in Religious Colleges and Universities* (New York: Routledge, 2006), 18.

[75]Hugh McLeod, *Secularisation in Western Europe, 1848–1914* (New York: St. Martin's Press, 2000).

[76]Anderson, *European Universities*, 102.

[77]Ibid., 39.

[78]John Henry Newman, *The Idea of a University* (Notre Dame: University of Notre Dame Press, 1960), 31.

[79]Ibid., 31-32.

[80]Ibid., 46.

[81]Ibid., 49-50.

[82]Ibid., 52-53.

[83]Ibid., 33.

[84]Ibid., 54.

[85]Ibid.

[86]Ibid., 55.

[87]Ibid., 73.

[88]Ibid., 74.

[89]For the rise of the importance of the law faculty, see Wilhelm Schmidt-Biggemann, "New Structures of Knowledge," in Ridder-Symoens, *Universities in Early Modern Europe*, 489-530.

[90]Alasdair MacIntyre, *God, Philosophy, Universities: A Selective History of the Catholic Philosophical Tradition* (Lanham, MD: Rowman & Littlefield, 2009), 135.

4 THE AMERICAN IDEA OF THE UNIVERSITY:
FREEDOM WITHIN THE BOUNDS OF SCIENCE (1825–1900)

Epigraphs: John Henry Newman, *The Idea of a University* (Notre Dame: University of Notre Dame Press, 1960), 74; Daniel C. Gilman, *The First Annual Report of The Johns Hopkins University* (Baltimore: William K. Boyle and Son, 1876), 63-64.

[1]Francis Wayland, *A Discourse Delivered at the Dedication of Manning Hall, the Chapel and Library of Brown University, February 4, 1835* (Providence, 1835), 20-21, as quoted in Richard Hofstadter and Wilson Smith, eds., *American Higher Education: A Documentary History* (Chicago: University of Chicago Press, 1961), 1:242-43.

[2]US Department of Education, "Degrees Conferred by Degree-Granting Institutions, By Level of Degree and Sex of Student: Selected Years, 1869–70 Through 2021–22," in *Digest of Educational Statistics* (Washington, DC: US Department of Education, 2012), table 310.448.

[3]William Adams Brown, *The Case for Theology in the University* (Chicago: University of Chicago Press, 1938).

[4]Alasdair MacIntyre, *Three Rival Versions of Moral Enquiry: Encyclopaedia, Geneology, and Tradition* (Notre Dame: University of Notre Dame Press, 1990), 216-36.

[5]Julie Reuben, *The Making of the Modern University: Intellectual Transformation and the Marginalization of Morality* (Chicago: University of Chicago Press, 1996).

[6]Ibid.; George Marsden, *The Soul of the American University: From Protestant Establishment to Established Nonbelief* (New York: Oxford University Press, 1994).

[7]Marsden, *Soul of the American University.*

[8]Benjamin Rush, "To Friends of the Federal Government: A Plan for a Federal University," quoted in L. H. Butterfield, ed., *Letters of Benjamin Rush* (Princeton, NJ: Princeton University Press, 1951), 491.

[9]Ibid.

[10]Ibid.

[11]Ibid.

[12]Ibid.

[13]Edgar B. Wesley, *Proposed: The University of the United States* (Minneapolis: University of Minnesota Press, 1936), 5-12.

[14]John C. Fitzpatrick, ed., *Writings of George Washington, 1745-1799* (Washington, DC: Government Printing Office, 1940), 35:316-17.

[15]James Madison, State of the Union address, December 5, 1810, http://history central.com/documents/NEWNATION/Madison2.htm.

[16]James Madison to Edward Everett, March 19, 1823, in *The Writings of James Madison*, vol. 9, *1819-1836*, ed. Gaillard Hunt (New York: Putnam & Sons, 1910), 124.

[17]R. D. Anderson, *European Universities from the Enlightenment to 1914* (New York: Oxford University Press, 2004), 91.

[18]Richard Hofstadter and Wilson Smith, eds., *American Higher Education: A Documentary History* (Chicago: University of Chicago Press, 1961), 1:198.

[19]University of Virginia Board of Commissioners, *Report of the Board of Commissioners for the University of Virginia to the Virginia General Assembly*, August 4, 1818, http://founders.archives.gov/documents/Madison/04-01-02-0289.

[20]Rex Bowman and Carlos Santos, *Rot, Riot and Rebellion: Mr. Jefferson's Struggle to Save the University That Changed America* (Charlottesville: University of Virginia Press, 2013), 2.

[21]Ibid., 33-34.

[22]Charles E. McClelland, *State, Society and University in Germany 1700-1914* (New York: Cambridge University Press, 1980), 141.

[23]William C. Ringenberg, *The Christian College: A History of Protestant Higher Education in America*, 2nd ed. (Grand Rapids: Baker Academic, 2006), 59.

[24]Donald G. Tewksbury, *The Founding of American Colleges and Universities Before the Civil War* (New York: Teacher College Press, 1932), 90.

[25]Peter Onuf, "Degrees of Freedom: Higher Education in America," interview by *BackStory*, September 26, 2014, http://backstoryradio.org/shows/degrees-of -freedom-3/.

[26]Ibid.

[27]Hofstadter and Smith, *American Higher Education*, 1:232-50.

[28]Philip Lindsley, *The Works of Philip Lindsley*, ed. L. J. Hasley (Philadelphia, 1866), quoted in Hofstadter and Smith, *American Higher Education*, 1:233.

[29]Douglas Sloan, "The Teaching of Ethics in the American Undergraduate Curriculum, 1876–1976," in *Ethics Teaching in Higher Education*, ed. Daniel Callahan and Sissela Bok (New York: Plenum, 1980), 1-57.

[30]Norman Fiering, *Moral Philosophy at Seventeenth-Century Harvard* (Chapel Hill: University of North Carolina Press, 1981), 62.

[31]Sloan, "Teaching of Ethics," 7.

[32]*Report of the Commissioner of Education Made to the Secretary of the Interior for the Year 1870* (Washington, DC: Government Printing Office, 1870), 418.

[33]Theodore Dwight Jr., *President Dwight's Decisions of Questions Discussed by the Senior Class in Yale College, in 1813 and 1814* (New York: Jonathan Leavitt, 1833).

[34]Francesco Cordasco, *The Shaping of American Graduate Education: Daniel Coit Gilman and the Protean Ph.D.* (Totowa, NJ: Rowman & Littlefield, 1973), 16.

[35]John C. French, *A History of the University Founded by Johns Hopkins* (Baltimore: Johns Hopkins University Press, 1946), 4.

[36]George Tickner to Thomas Jefferson, Göttingen, March 15, 1816, Jefferson Manuscripts, Vol. CCVI, Library of Congress, quoted in Hofstadter and Smith, *American Higher Education*, 1:257-58.

[37]Charles F. Thwing, *The American and the German University* (New York: Macmillan, 1928), 40-44.

[38]Ibid.

[39]Charles McClelland, *State, Society and University in Germany, 1700-1914* (New York: Cambridge University Press, 1980), 156-57.

[40]Walter Rüegg, "Themes," in *A History of the University in Europe*, vol. 3, *Universities in the Nineteenth and Early Twentieth Centuries (1800–1945)*, ed. Walter Rüegg (Cambridge: Cambridge University Press, 1996), 4-5.

[41]"Gilman's Inaugural Address," Johns Hopkins University, www.jhu.edu/about/history/gilman-address/.

[42]Daniel Coit Gilman, *The Launching of Johns Hopkins University*, 41-43, quoted in Hofstadter and Smith, *American Higher Education*, 2:755.

[43]The power and freedom Gilman gave to faculty was claimed to be the primary German influence. See D. G. Hart, "Faith and Learning in the Age of the University: The Academic Ministry of Daniel Coit Gilman," in *The Secularization of the Academy*, ed. George Marsden and Bradley Longfield (New York: Oxford University Press, 1992), 114.

[44]Daniel C. Gilman, "The Johns Hopkins University," in *History of Education in Maryland*, ed. Bernard O. Steiner (Washington, DC: Government Printing Office, 1894), 149.

[45]Laurence Veysey, *The Emergence of the American University* (Chicago: University of Chicago Press, 1970).

[46]Gilman, "The Johns Hopkins University," 149.

[47]Hugh Hawkins, *Pioneer: A History of the Johns Hopkins University, 1874–1889* (Ithaca, NY: Cornell University Press, 1960), 41.

[48]D. G. Hart, *The University Gets Religion: Religious Studies in American Higher Education* (Baltimore: Johns Hopkins University Press, 1999), 44.

[49]Ibid., 36.

[50]"Gilman's Inaugural Address."

[51]Ibid.

[52]Ibid.

[53]Perry L. Glanzer and Todd C. Ream, *Christianity and Moral Identity in Higher Education* (New York: Palgrave Macmillan, 2009).

[54]Hart, *University Gets Religion*, 31.

[55]Ibid., 34.

[56]Ibid., 35.

[57]Reuben, *Making of the Modern University*, 88-89.

[58]John Dewey, "The Influence of Darwinism on Philosophy" (1909), in *James and Dewey on Belief and Experience,* ed. John M. Capps and Donald Capps (Chicago: University of Illinois Press, 2005), 179.

[59]Reuben, *The Making of the Modern University*, 45.

[60]Lawrence Kohlberg and Rochelle Mayer, "Development as the Aim of Education," *Harvard Educational Review* 42 (1972): 449–96.

[61]Charles S. Peirce, "The Marriage of Religion and Science," *Open Court* 1 (1893): 3559.

[62]Reuben, *Making of the Modern University*, 49.

[63]Ibid.

[64]Marsden, *Soul of the American University*, 56.

[65]Ibid., 156.

[66]Reuben, *Making of the Modern University*, 89. For Hall's religious background and struggles see Marsden, *Soul of the American University*, 159-64.

[67]Reuben, *Making of the Modern University*, 51.

[68]Ibid., 60.

[69]Ibid.

[70]Ibid.

[71]Ibid.

[72]John Dewey and James Tufts, *Ethics* (New York: Holt, Rinehart, and Winston, 1908).

[73]Reuben, *Making of the Modern University*, 186-87.

[74] Anne Colby, Thomas Ehrlich, Elizabeth Beaumont, and Jason Stephens, *Educating Citizens: Preparing America's Undergraduates for Lives of Moral Responsibility* (San Francisco: Jossey-Bass, 2003); Reuben, *Making of the Modern University*; Derek Bok, *Beyond the Ivory Tower: Social Responsibilities of the Modern University* (Cambridge, MA: Harvard University Press, 1984); Sloan, "Teaching of Ethics"; Hastings Center, *Ethics Teaching in Higher Education* (New York: Plenum, 1980).

[75] Reuben, *Making of the Modern University*, chapters 5 and 6.

[76] Sloan, "Teaching of Ethics."

[77] Abraham Flexner, *Universities: American, English, German* (New York: Oxford University Press, 1930), 42.

5 FRACTURING THE SOUL: THE CREATION OF THE AMERICAN MULTIVERSITY (1869–1969)

Epigraph: Clark Kerr, *The Uses of the University*, 5th ed. (Cambridge, MA: Harvard University Press, 2001), 1.

[1] Several biographical studies of Eliot's life and educational thought fortunately exist. Perhaps the most comprehensive biographical effort is Henry James's two-volume *Charles W. Eliot: President of Harvard University, 1869–1909* (Cambridge, MA: Houghton Mifflin, 1930). Other important biographical sketches of Eliot include Hugh Hawkins, *Between Harvard and America: The Educational Leadership of Charles W. Eliot* (New York: Oxford University Press, 1972); Henry Hallam Saunderson, *Charles W. Eliot: Puritan Liberal* (New York: Harper and Brothers, 1928); Edward H. Cotton, *The Life of Charles W. Eliot* (Boston: Small, Maynard, 1926); Eugen Kuehenemanns, *Charles W. Eliot: President of Harvard University, May 19, 1869–May 19, 1909* (Boston: Houghton Mifflin, 1909); William Allan Neilson, *Charles W. Eliot: The Man and His Beliefs*, 2 vols. (New York: Harper and Brothers, 1926), is a collection of many of Eliot's most important writings.

[2] Henry James, *Charles W. Eliot: President of Harvard University, 1869–1909* (Cambridge, MA: Houghton Mifflin Company, 1930).

[3] Charles W. Eliot, *Addresses at the Inauguration of Charles William Eliot as President of Harvard College* (Cambridge, MA: Sever and Francis, 1869), 30.

[4] Ibid., 34.

[5] Ibid., 35-36.

[6] Hawkins, *Between Harvard and America*, 71.

[7] Charles W. Eliot, *The Religion of the Future* (Boston: John W. Luce, 1909), 3.

[8] Ibid., 7.

[9] Charles Taylor, *A Secular Age* (Cambridge, MA: Belknap Press of Harvard University Press, 2007), 472.

[10] Ibid., 219.

[11] Ibid., 232.

[12] Hawkins, *Between Harvard and America*, 71.

[13]Ibid.; Caroline Winterer, "The Humanist Revolution in America, 1820–1860: Classical Antiquity in the Colleges," *History of Higher Education Annual* 18 (1998): 111-30.

[14]Charles W. Eliot, "Inaugural Address as President of Harvard, 1869," in *American Higher Education: A Documentary History*, ed. Richard Hofstadter and Wilson Smith (Chicago: University of Chicago Press, 1961), 2:609.

[15]Ibid., 2:608.

[16]Ibid., 2:609-10.

[17]Charles W. Eliot, *Educational Reform: Essays and Addresses* (New York: Century, 1898), 128-29.

[18]Ibid., 129.

[19]Ibid., 609.

[20]"Charles Eliot Expounds the Elective System as 'Liberty in Education' 1885," in Hofstadter and Smith, *American Higher Education*, 2:701.

[21]Ibid., 2:713.

[22]Ibid.

[23]Ibid.

[24]Julie Reuben, *The Making of the Modern University: Intellectual Transformation and the Marginalization of Morality* (Chicago: University of Chicago Press, 1996), chap. 8.

[25]Samuel Eliot Morison, *Three Centuries of Harvard, 1636–1936* (Cambridge, MA: Belknap Press of Harvard University Press, 1986), 403.

[26]Ibid.

[27]Ibid.

[28]Charles W. Eliot, "The Religion of the Future," *Harvard Theological Review* 2, no. 4 (1909): 391.

[29]Ibid.

[30]Ibid.

[31]Ibid., 393.

[32]Ibid.

[33]Ibid., 395-96.

[34]Robert Maynard Hutchins, *The Higher Learning in America* (New Haven, CT: Yale University Press, 1936), 1.

[35]Ibid., 19.

[36]Ibid., 70-71.

[37]Ibid., 21.

[38]In addition to his numerous books on this topic, please see the autobiographical works by Mortimer J. Adler, *Philosopher at Large: An Intellectual Biography* (New York: Macmillan, 1977); and Adler, *A Second Look in the Rearview Mirror: Further*

Autobiographical Reflections of a Philosopher at Large (New York: Macmillan, 1992).

[39]Hutchins, *Higher Learning in America*, 78.

[40]Ibid., 79.

[41]Robert M. Hutchins, *The University of Utopia* (Chicago: University of Chicago Press, 1953).

[42]Ibid., 49.

[43]Ibid., 99.

[44]Ibid.

[45]Ibid., 100.

[46]Neil Postman, *The End of Education: Redefining the Value of School* (New York: Knopf, 1995).

[47]A fascinating insight into Hutchins's concerns about the fate of the university and intellectual culture in the West is evident in *Zuckerkandl!* A work of biting satire, Hutchins crafts a conversation he supposedly shared with Alexander Zuckerkandl, the most successful of all of Sigmund Freud's disciples. Originally delivered with the air of nonfiction as a lecture at Brandeis University, Hutchins sought to slice through the polarizing air of his age as defined by what he saw as militarized right and a sentimentalized left. A cartoon version was produced by John Hubley and is available for viewing at *Zuckerkandl by John and Faith Hubley (1968)*, YouTube video, 15:20, posted by "Lost Animations," December 12, 2015, www.youtube.com/watch?v=7UTnOaqkQ2s. Robert M. Hutchins, *Zuckerkandl!* (New York: Grove, 1968).

[48]Clark Kerr, *The Great Transformation in Higher Education: 1960–1980* (Albany: State University of New York Press, 1991), 81.

[49]Clark Kerr, *The Uses of the University*, 4th ed. (Cambridge, MA: Harvard University Press, 1995), xiii.

[50]Ibid.

[51]Clark Kerr, *The Blue and the Gold: A Personal Memoir of the University of California*, vol. 1, *Academic Triumphs* (Berkeley: University of California Press, 2001), 267-68.

[52]Ibid., 268.

[53]Kerr, *Uses of the University*, 7.

[54]Clark Kerr, *The Blue and the Gold: A Personal Memoir of the University of California*, vol. 2, *Political Turmoil* (Berkeley: University of California Press, 2001), 267-68.

[55]Kerr, *Uses of the University*, 5.

[56]Ibid., 31.

[57]Ibid., 31-32.

[58]Ibid., 32.

[59]Mario Savio, from a speech given on the steps of Sproul Hall on December 2, 1964, quoted by Robert Cohen, *Freedom's Orator: Mario Savio and the Radical Legacy of the 1960s* (New York: Oxford University Press, 2009), 178-79.

PART TWO: THE FRAGMENTATION OF THE MULTIVERSITY

[1]Clark Kerr, *The Uses of the University*, 4th ed. (Cambridge, MA: Harvard University Press, 1995).

[2]Jean-François Lyotard, *The Postmodern Condition: A Report on Knowledge*, trans. Geoff Bennington and Brian Massumi (Minneapolis: University of Minnesota Press, 1993), xxiv.

[3]Stephen V. Monsma and J. Christopher Soper, *The Challenge of Pluralism: Church and State in Five Democracies*, 2nd ed. (Lanham, MD: Rowman & Littlefield, 2009).

[4]Robert Maynard Hutchins, *The Higher Learning in America* (New Haven, CT: Yale University Press, 1936).

[5]Charles Taylor, in *A Secular Age* (Cambridge, MA: Belknap Press of Harvard University Press, 2007), argues that "the presumption of unbelief has become dominant" (p. 12). As a result, Christians increasingly find themselves forced to the margins of society and influence, notes Philip Eaton in *Engaging the Culture, Changing the World: The Christian University in a Post-Christian World* (Downers Grove, IL: IVP Academic, 2011).

6 THE FRAGMENTED SOUL OF THE PROFESSOR

Epigraph: *A Beautiful Mind*, directed by Ron Howard (Universal City, CA: Universal Pictures, 2001), DVD.

[1]*A Beautiful Mind*, directed by Ron Howard (Universal City, CA: Universal Pictures, 2001), DVD.

[2]Ibid.

[3]Ibid.

[4]Ibid.

[5]Ibid.

[6]See Jacques Verger, "Teachers," in *A History of the University in Europe*, vol. 1, *Universities in the Middle Ages*, ed. Hilde de Ridder-Symoens (Cambridge: Cambridge University Press, 1992), 144, 162.

[7]Ibid., 162-63.

[8]Ibid., 163.

[9]Ibid., 155-68. See also Peter A. Vandermeersch, "Teachers," in *A History of the University in Europe*, vol. 2, *Universities in Early Modern Europe (1500–1800)*, ed. Hilde de Ridder-Symoens (Cambridge: Cambridge University Press, 1996), 214-18.

[10]As cited in Jacques Verger, "Teachers," 164.

[11]Ibid., 165.

[12] Ibid., 156.

[13] As cited in ibid., 165.

[14] Desiderius Erasmus, *The Praise of Folly* (Princeton, NJ: Princeton University Press, 2015).

[15] Ibid., 73.

[16] Ibid., 73-74.

[17] Ibid., 74.

[18] Ibid., 214-18.

[19] Ibid., 223-24; Matti Klinge, "Teachers," in *A History of the University in Europe*, vol. 3, *Universities in the Nineteenth and Early Twentieth Centuries*, ed. Walter Rüegg (Cambridge: Cambridge University Press, 2004), 123-62; George Marsden, *The Soul of the American University* (New York: Oxford University Press, 1994).

[20] See Perry L. Glanzer, "Will the Parent Abandon the Child? The Birth, Secularization and Survival of Christian Higher Education in Western Europe," in *Christian Higher Education: A Global Reconnaissance* (Grand Rapids: Eerdmans, 2014), 134-62.

[21] Vandermeersch, "Teachers," 224.

[22] Talcott Parsons, "Professions," in *The International Encyclopedia of the Social Sciences*, ed. David L. Sills (New York: Macmillan and Free Press, 1969), 12:536.

[23] Thomas L. Haskell, *The Emergence of Professional Social Science: The American Social Science Association and the Nineteenth-Century Crisis of Authority* (Urbana: University of Chicago Press, 1977).

[24] Klinge, "Teachers."

[25] Haskell, *Emergence of Professional Social Science*, 47.

[26] Ibid., 89.

[27] Carl L. Prieber, "The Authority of Collegiality: The History of University Faculty and the Dialectic in the Recognition of Higher Knowledge" (PhD diss., State University of New York at Buffalo, 1991).

[28] Ibid., 68.

[29] Ibid., 91.

[30] Ibid.

[31] Haskell, *Emergence of Professional Social Science*, 240.

[32] Roger L. Geiger, *To Advance Knowledge: The Growth of American Research Universities, 1900–1940* (New York: Oxford University Press, 1986), 72.

[33] Ibid.

[34] R. Eugene Rice, "The Academic Profession in Transition: Toward a New Social Fiction," *Teaching Sociology* 14, no. 1 (1986): 12-23.

[35] Max Weber, "The Vocation of Science," in *The Essential Weber: A Reader*, ed. Sam Whimster (New York: Routledge, 2004), 270.

[36] Ibid., 282.

[37]Ibid., 283. Part of the reason for Weber's position, it should be noted, pertained to the fact that professors might abuse their power when teaching a captive audience. Weber noted of this situation, "It is far too easy for him to demonstrate the courage of his convictions where those present, who perhaps think differently, are condemned to silence." Ibid.

[38]Ibid., 285.

[39]Mark R. Schwehn, *Exiles from Eden: Religion and the Academic Vocation in America* (New York: Oxford University Press, 1993), 4.

[40]Ibid., 5.

[41]Richard A. Posner, *Public Intellectuals: A Study in Decline* (Cambridge, MA: Harvard University Press, 2002).

[42]Ibid., 388-89.

[43]Roger L. Geiger, *Research and Relevant Knowledge: American Research Universities Since World War II* (New Brunswick, NJ: Transaction, 2004), 35.

[44]Ibid., 34.

[45]Parker J. Palmer, *To Know as We Are Known: Education as a Spiritual Journey* (San Francisco: HarperSanFrancisco, 1993), 74.

[46]Ibid.

[47]Robert B. Barr and John Tagg, "From Teaching to Learning: A New Paradigm for Undergraduate Education," *Change* 27, no. 6 (1995): 13.

[48]Kenneth Prewitt, "Who Should Do What?," in *Envisioning Doctoral Education*, ed. Chris M. Golde and George E. Walker (San Francisco: Jossey-Bass, 2006), 26.

[49]George E. Walker et al., *The Formation of Scholars: Rethinking Doctoral Education for the Twenty-First Century* (San Francisco: Jossey-Bass, 2008), 67.

[50]Ibid., 69.

[51]Ibid.

[52]Ibid., 149.

[53]Ibid.

[54]Colleen Flaherty, "Flawed Evaluations," *Inside Higher Ed*, June 10, 2015, www.insidehighered.com/news/2015/06/10/aaup-committee-survey-data-raise -questions-effectiveness-student-teaching.

[55]Derek Bok, *Higher Education in America* (Princeton, NJ: Princeton University Press, 2013), 329.

[56]Burton R. Clark, *The Academic Life: Small Worlds, Different Worlds* (Princeton, NJ: Carnegie Foundation for the Advancement of Teaching, 1987), 98-99.

[57]Ibid., 330.

[58]Nittish Kulkarni, "Professor Takes on Jargon in the Sciences," *The Stanford Daily*, October 25, 2012, www.stanforddaily.com/2012/10/25/professor-takes-on-jargon -in-the-sciences/#comment-696184245.

[59]Ibid.

[60]Ibid.

[61]Mark C. Taylor, *Crisis on Campus: A Bold Plan for Reforming Our Colleges and Universities* (New York: Knopf, 2010), 45.

[62]Ibid.

[63]Ibid.

[64]Donald Kennedy, *Academic Duty* (Cambridge, MA: Harvard University Press, 1997), v.

[65]Todd C. Ream and John M. Braxton, "Inspiring Hope," in *Ernest L. Boyer: Hope for Today's Universities*, ed. Todd C. Ream and John M. Braxton (Albany: State University of New York Press, 2015), 246.

[66]Ernest L. Boyer, *Scholarship Reconsidered: Priorities of the Professoriate* (Princeton, NJ: The Carnegie Foundation for the Advancement of Teaching, 1990), 1.

[67]Ibid., 15.

[68]Ibid., 17.

[69]Ibid.

[70]Ibid., 18.

[71]Ibid., 22.

[72]Ibid.

7 Falling to Pieces: Declaring Independence from Curricular Coherence

Epigraph: Naomi Schaefer Riley, "It's Not Just Athletes—College Screws Everyone," *New York Post*, April 12, 2014, http://nypost.com/2014/04/12/its-not-just-athletes-college-screws-everyone/.

[1]Graeme Wood, "The Future of College?," *The Atlantic*, September 2014, 54.

[2]Ellen Gamerman, "Everybody's a Curator," *Wall Street Journal*, October 24, 2014, D1.

[3]Ibid.

[4]Ibid.

[5]Mark C. Taylor, *Crisis on Campus: A Bold Plan for Reforming Our Colleges and Universities* (New York: Knopf, 2010), 5.

[6]Ibid., 4.

[7]G. R. Evans, *Old Arts and New Theology: The Beginnings of Theology as an Academic Discipline* (Oxford: Clarendon, 1980).

[8]*The Didascalicon of Hugh of St. Victor: A Medieval Guide to the Arts*, trans. Jerome Taylor (New York: Columbia University Press, 1991), 89.

[9]Ibid., 61.

[10]Ibid.

[11]Gordon Leff, "The *Trivium* and the Three Philosophies," in *A History of the University in Europe*, vol. 1, *Universities in the Middle Ages*, ed. Hilde de Ridder-Symoens (Cambridge: Cambridge University Press, 1992), 308.

[12]Lawrence Brockliss, "Curricula," in *A History of the University in Europe*, vol. 2, *Universities in Early Modern Europe, 1500-1800*, ed. Hilde De Ridder-Symoens (Cambridge: Cambridge University Press, 1996), 575.

[13]Lawrence Brockliss, "Curricula," 565.

[14]John S. Brubacher and Willis Rudy, *Higher Education in Transition: A History of American Colleges and Universities*, 4th ed. (New Brunswick, NJ: Transaction, 1997), 12.

[15]Ibid., 13.

[16]Perry L. Glanzer and Todd C. Ream, *Christianity and Identity in Higher Education: Becoming Fully Human* (New York: Palgrave Macmillan, 2009).

[17]William Adams Brown, *The Case for Theology in the University* (Chicago: University of Chicago Press, 1938), 35.

[18]George Marsden, *The Soul of the American University: From Protestant Establishment to Established Nonbelief* (New York: Oxford University Press, 1994), 99.

[19]*Reports on the Course of Instruction in Yale College by a Committee of the Corporation, and the Academic Faculty* (New Haven, CT: Hezekiah Howe, 1828), 15.

[20]Ibid., 8.

[21]Ibid.

[22]Ibid.

[23]Ibid., 9.

[24]Richard Hofstadter and Wilson Smith, "The Development of the Elective System," in *American Higher Education: A Documentary History*, ed. Richard Hofstadter and Wilson Smith (Chicago: University of Chicago Press, 1961), 2:697.

[25]"James McCosh Attacks the New Departure and President Eliot, 1885," in Hofstadter and Smith, *American Higher Education*, 2:717.

[26]Ibid., 2:721.

[27]Ibid., 2:720-21.

[28]Ibid., 2:725-26.

[29]Ibid., 2:728.

[30]Marion LeRoy Burton, "The President's Report," in *The President's Report for the Year 1921–22* (Ann Arbor: University of Michigan, 1923), 184-85.

[31]Ibid.

[32]Marion LeRoy Burton, "The Undergraduate Course" (educational suppl.), *New Republic*, October 25, 1922, 2.

[33]Ibid.

[34]Lawrence A. Lowell, "President's Report for 1908–1909," in *Reports of the President and Treasurer of Harvard College, 1908–09* (Cambridge, MA: Harvard University Press), 15.

[35]Julie Reuben, *The Making of the Modern University: Intellectual Transformation and the Marginalization of Morality* (Chicago: University of Chicago Press, 1996), 234.

[36]Woodrow Wilson, "Position and Importance of the Arts Course as Distinct from the Professional and Semi-Professional Courses," *Proceedings of the Annual Conference, Association of American Universities* 11 (1910): 75. http://catalog.hathitrust .org/Record/000521549.

[37]Ibid., 76.

[38]Brown, *Case for Theology in the University*, 40.

[39]Douglas Sloan, *Faith and Knowledge: Mainline Protestantism and American Higher Education* (Louisville: Westminster John Knox, 1994), 213.

[40]David Sloan Wilson, "Evolution for Everyone," *New York Times*, April 8, 2007.

[41]Parker Palmer and Arthur Zajonc, with Megan Scribner, *The Heart of Higher Education: A Call to Renewal* (San Francisco: Jossey-Bass, 2010), 2.

[42]Michael S. Roth, *Beyond the University: Why Liberal Education Matters* (New Haven, CT: Yale University Press, 2014), 3.

[43]Ibid., 183.

[44]Ibid.

[45]Ibid., 186.

[46]Ibid., 189.

[47]Ibid.

[48]Ibid.

[49]Ibid.

[50]Alasdair MacIntyre, *Three Rival Versions of Moral Enquiry: Encyclopaedia, Genealogy, and Tradition* (Notre Dame: University of Notre Dame Press, 1990), 171.

[51]Martin Smith, "What Universities Have in Common with Record Labels," *Quartz*, July 6, 2014, http://qz.com/223771/universities-are-the-record-labels-of -education/.

[52]Derek Newton, "Higher Education Is Not a Mixtape," *The Atlantic*, January 2015, www.theatlantic.com/education/archive/2015/01/higher-education-is-not-a -mixtape/384845/.

8 FRAGMENTING STUDENTS: THE CURRICULAR/COCURRICULAR DIVISION

Epigraph: C. John Sommerville, *The Decline of the Secular University* (New York: Oxford University Press, 2006), 8.

[1]We would suggest that this idea stems from the Christian roots of the American university system.

[2]Ray Franke et al., *Findings from the 2009 Administration of the College Senior Survey (CSS): National Aggregates* (Los Angeles: Higher Education Research Institute, UCLA, 2010), 4.

[3]Marcia B. Baxter Magolda, *Making Their Own Way: Narratives for Transforming Higher Education to Promote Self-Development* (Sterling, VA: Stylus, 2001);

Magolda, *Creating Contexts for Learning and Self-Authorship: Constructive-Developmental Pedagogy* (Nashville: Vanderbilt University Press, 1999); Marcia B. Baxter Magolda and Patricia M. King, *Theories and Models of Practice to Educate for Self-Authorship* (Sterling, VA: Stylus, 2004). See also Robert J. Nash and Michelle C. Murray, *Helping College Students Find Purpose: The Campus Guide to Meaning-Making* (San Francisco: Jossey-Bass, 2010).

[4]Perry L. Glanzer, Jonathan Hill, and Byron Johnson, *The Quest for Purpose: The Collegiate Search for a Meaningful Life* (Albany: State University of New York Press, forthcoming).

[5]Rod Dreher, *The Little Way of Ruthie Leming: A Southern Girl, a Small Town, and the Secret of a Good Life* (New York: Grand Central, 2013), 189.

[6]Though not until after students and para-university organizations had first taken on and pioneered responses to these needs, most notably under the auspices of the YMCA Student Associations between 1880 and 1920, when, due to size and re-source needs, universities gradually assumed responsibility for many of these functions and services. See Dorothy E. Finnegan and Nathan F. Alleman, "The YMCA and the Origins of American Freshman Orientation Programs," *Historical Studies in Education* 25, no. 1 (2013): 95-114.

[7]C. S. Yoakum, "Plan for a Personal Bureau in Educational Institutions," in *Student Affairs: A Heritage's Profession*, ed. Audrey L. Rentz (Lanham, MD: University Press of America, 1994), 5.

[8]Francis F. Bradshaw, "The Scope and Aim of a Personal Program," in Rentz, *Student Affairs*, 36.

[9]Julie Reuben, *The Making of the Modern University: Intellectual Transformation and the Marginalization of Morality* (Chicago: University of Chicago Press, 1996), 254.

[10]Even this term is a relatively new innovation advanced by the field of student affairs and some segments of the academy. *Cocurricular* is intended to replace *extracurricular* since the latter implies something outside of the curriculum. *Cocurricular* is thought to instill a greater sense of dignity and parallel importance to areas of learning and growth that are not traditionally part of a student's course requirements.

[11]W. H. Cowley, "The Nature of Student Personnel Work," in Rentz, *Student Affairs*, 43.

[12]American Council on Education, "The Student Personnel Point of View," in Rentz, *Student Affairs*, 68.

[13]Ibid.

[14]Herbert Stroup, "Theoretical Constructs in Student Personnel Work," *Journal of Higher Education* 28 (1957): 321.

[15]"The Student Personnel Point of View," *American Council on Education Studies*, first series, 1, no. 3 (1937): 1.

[16]Ibid., 3.

[17]Ibid., 4.

[18]E. G. Williamson et al., *The Student Personnel Point of View* (Washington, DC: American Council on Education, 1949), 2.

[19]Ibid.

[20]Ibid.

[21]Ibid.

[22]The Committee on the Student in Higher Education, *The Student in Higher Education* (New Haven, CT: The Haven Foundation, 1968), 9.

[23]Ibid., 58.

[24]Harry Lewis, "The Freshman Pledge," *Bits and Pieces* (blog), August 30, 2011, http://harry-lewis.blogspot.com/2011/08/freshman-pledge.html.

[25]Lawrence Kohlberg, *Essays on Moral Development*, vol. 1, *The Philosophy of Moral Development: Moral Stages and the Idea of Justice* (San Francisco: Harper & Row, 1981), 9.

[26]Ibid.

[27]Ibid.

[28]The six stages of moral reasoning are (1) the punishment and obedience orientation; (2) the instrumental relativist orientation; (3) the interpersonal concordance or "good boy–nice girl" orientation; (4) society maintaining orientation; (5) social contract orientation; and (6) the universal ethical principle orientation. Ibid., 17-19.

[29]Nancy J. Evans et al., *Student Development in College: Theory, Research, and Practice*, 2nd ed. (San Francisco: Jossey-Bass, 2010), 101.

[30]Ibid., 85.

[31]William G. Perry, *Forms of Intellectual and Ethical Development in the College Years: A Scheme* (San Francisco: Jossey-Bass, 1998), 238.

[32]Ibid.

[33]Perry L. Glanzer and Todd C. Ream, *Christianity and Moral Identity in Higher Education* (New York: Palgrave Macmillan, 2009).

[34]Ibid.

[35]For one example of what such an approach might look like, see Christian Smith, *What Is a Person? Rethinking Humanity, Social Life, and the Moral Good from the Ground Up* (Chicago: University of Chicago Press, 2010).

[36]See Richard P. Keeling, ed., *Learning Reconsidered: A Campus-Wide Focus on the Student Experience* (Washington, DC: National Association of Student Personnel Administrators/American College Personnel Association, 2004); Richard P. Keeling, *Learning Reconsidered 2: Implementing a Campus-Wide Focus on the Student Experience* (Washington, DC: American College Personnel Association

[ACPA], Association of College and University Housing Officers–International [ACUHO-I], Association of College Unions–International [ACUI], National Academic Advising Association [NACADA], National Association for Campus Activities [NACA], National Association of Student Personnel Administrators [NASPA], and National Intramural Recreational Sports Association [NIRSA], 2006).

[37] American College Personnel Association, "The Student Learning Imperative," 1996, 1, www.myacpa.org/sites/default/files/ACPA%27s%20Student%20Learning %20Imperative.pdf.

[38] Ibid.

[39] See Keeling, *Learning Reconsidered*; and Keeling, *Learning Reconsidered 2*.

[40] Daniel R. Kenney, Ricardo Dumont, and Ginger Kenney, *Mission and Place: Strengthening Learning and Community Through Campus Design* (Westport, CT: Praeger, 2005).

[41] Alex Duke, *Importing Oxbridge: English Residential Colleges and American Universities* (New Haven, CT: Yale University Press, 1996).

[42] "Residential Colleges Defined," Yale University, http://admissions.yale.edu/residential -colleges-defined (accessed June 15, 2015).

[43] Smith, *What Is a Person?*, 54.

9 CHIEF FRAGMENTATION OFFICER: THE ADVENT OF THE PROFESSIONAL ADMINISTRATOR

Epigraphs: E. P. Chase, "Research or Administration," *Journal of Higher Education* 1, no. 4 (1930): 216-19; Clark Kerr, *The Uses of the University*, 5th ed. (New York: Harper & Row, 1963), 21.

[1] Clark Kerr, *The Uses of the University*, 5th ed. (New York: Harper & Row, 1963), 90.

[2] Ibid.

[3] Samuel P. Capen, *The Registrar's Office a Barometer of Educational Tendencies* (Washington, DC: Proceedings of the Tenth Annual Meeting, American Association of Collegiate Registrars, 1920), 24, quoted in Earl James McGrath, "The Evolution of Administrative Offices in Institutions of Higher Education in the United States from 1860 to 1933" (PhD diss., University of Chicago, 1936), 1-2.

[4] McGrath, "Evolution of Administrative Offices."

[5] Ibid., 116.

[6] Christopher Newfield, *Ivy and Industry: Business and the Making of the American University, 1880–1980* (Durham, NC: Duke University Press, 2000).

[7] David F. Noble, *America by Design: Science, Technology, and the Rise of Corporate Capitalism* (New York: Knopf, 1977), 118.

[8] Kakar Sudhir, *Frederick Taylor: A Study in Personality and Innovation* (Cambridge, MA: MIT Press, 1970).

[9]William H. Cowley, *Presidents, Professors, and Trustees: The Evolution of American Academic Government* (San Francisco: Jossey-Bass, 1980).

[10]Ibid., 63.

[11]Ibid.

[12]Ibid.

[13]Charles H. Judd, "Lines of Study Suitable for College Registrars," Proceedings of the Twelfth National Meeting, American Association of Collegiate Registrars, 28, quoted by McGrath, "Evolution of Administrative Offices," 1.

[14]Newfield, *Ivy and Industry*, 75.

[15]John D. Burton, "The Harvard Tutor: The Beginnings of the Academic Profession," *History of Higher Education Annual* 16 (1996): 5-20.

[16]Thomas D. Snyder, *120 Years of American Education: A Statistical Report* (Washington, DC: National Center for Education Statistics, GPO, 1993), 63.

[17]Snyder, *120 Years of American Education*, 63.

[18]"The Ohio State University Annual Enrollment Total University 1873–1874 Through 1921–1922," Ohio State University Office of the Registrar/SERRS, http://oesar.osu .edu/pdf/student_enrollment/historical/1873_1922.pdf (accessed September 13, 2016); "UNC Enrollment and Tuition Data 1833–2013," courtesy of the UNC Chapel Hill Office of the University Registrar; University of Illinois historical enrollment data, courtesy of the Division of Management Information, University of Illinois at Urbana–Champaign, www.dmi.illinois.edu/stuenr/#historical (accessed August 8, 2016).

[19]Snyder, *120 Years of American Education*, 65.

[20]Ibid.

[21]This lack of prior socialization, a particular annoyance to other students, was soon addressed through a range of initiation rituals and practices and codified in student handbooks distributed to incoming students prior to their first semester. The YMCA Student Association men and women were particularly active in these pursuits. See Nathan F. Alleman and Dorothy E. Finnegan, "'Believe You Have a Mission in Life and Steadily Pursue It': Campus YMCAs Presage Student Development Theory, 1894–1939," *Higher Education in Review* 6 (2009): 11-45.

[22]John R. Thelin, *The History of Higher Education in America*, 2nd ed. (Baltimore: Johns Hopkins University Press, 2013), 198.

[23]Ibid.

[24]Alleman and Finnegan, "Believe You Have a Mission."

[25]J. Carleton Bell, "Mental Tests and College Freshmen," *Journal of Educational Psychology* 7 (1916): 387.

[26]J. Patrick Biddix and Robert A. Schwartz, "Walter Dill Scott and the Student Personnel Movement," *Journal of College Student Affairs Research and Practice* 49, no. 3 (2012): 285-98.

[27]Nicholas Lemann, *The Big Test: The Secret History of the American Meritocracy* (New York: Farrar, Straus and Giroux, 1999).

[28]"Frosh Receive First Taste of College in Week of Instruction," *The Campus*, September 29, 1922. Courtesy of the Rush Rhees Library Department of Rare Books and Special Collections, University of Rochester.

[29]Institutionalized by Maine President Clarence Cook Little in 1923 and transplanted with him in 1925 when he assumed the presidency of the University of Michigan, Freshman Week was a standard part of the new-student experience by the early 1930s. For a full exploration of its origins, including forerunner programs developed by the campus Student YMCA, see Dorothy E. Finnegan and Nathan F. Alleman, "The YMCA and the Origins of American Freshman Orientation Programs," *Historical Studies in Education* 25, no. 1 (2013): 95-114. The discussion of Freshman Week in this chapter leans heavily on the source scholarship of that paper.

[30]Biddix and Schwartz, "Walter Dill Scott," 287.

[31]Ibid., 298.

[32]Ibid.

[33]Vasti Torres and Jan Walbert, *Envisioning the Future of Student Affairs: Final Report of the Task Force on the Future of Student Affairs* (Washington, DC: NASPA and ACPA, 2010), 2.

[34]Donna M. Desrochers and Steven Hurlburt, *Trends in College Spending: 2001-2011, a Delta Data Update* (Washington, DC: American Institute for Research, 2014).

[35]Julie A. Reuben, *The Making of the Modern University: Intellectual Transformation and the Marginalization of Morality* (Chicago: University of Chicago Press, 1996).

[36]Thelin, *History of Higher Education*, 75.

[37]Keith W. Olson, *The G.I. Bill, the Veterans, and the Colleges* (Lexington: University of Kentucky Press, 1974).

[38]Thelin, *History of Higher Education*, 75.

[39]See Suzanne Mettler, *Soldier to Citizens: The G.I. Bill and the Making of the Greatest Generation* (New York: Oxford University Press, 2005), who argues that the GI Bill gave veterans a positive view of government, made them more likely to be involved in civic life, and increased social capital and democratic vibrancy reflective of the "greatest generation's" best features.

[40]Snyder, *120 Years of American Education*, 80.

[41]National Defense Education Act (NDEA), Pub. L. No. 85-864, 72 Stat. 1580-1605; Higher Education Act of 1965 (HEA), Pub. L. No. 89-329; Title IX of the Education Amendments of 1972 and its implementing regulation at 34 C.F.R. Part 106 (Title IX).

[42]Kerr, *Uses of the University*, 122.

[43]Ibid., 1.

[44]Todd C. Ream and Perry L. Glanzer, *The Idea of a Christian College: A Reexamination for Today's University* (Eugene, OR: Cascade, 2013).

[45]Laurence Veysey, *The Emergence of the American University* (Chicago: University of Chicago Press, 1970), 311.

[46]Jennifer Washburn, *University Inc.: The Corporate Corruption of Higher Education* (New York: Basic Books, 2006).

[47]Ibid., 145

[48]Ibid., 143.

[49]Charles Dickens, *A Christmas Carol* (New York: J. H. Heinemann, 1967), 102.

[50]William H. Cowley, *Presidents, Professors, and Trustees.*

[51]Ibid., 28.

10 THE MULTIVERSITY'S RELIGION: THE UNIFYING AND FRAGMENTING FORCE OF ATHLETICS

Epigraphs: Referring to the Penn State athletic scandal, David Brooks and Gail Collins, "The Horror Show at Penn State," *Opinionator* (blog), *New York Times*, November 9, 2011, http://opinionator.blogs.nytimes.com/2011/11/09/the-horror-show-at-penn-state/?_r=0; NCAA president Mark Emmert, announcing the Penn State sanctions, quoted in John U. Bacon, *Fourth and Long: The Fight for the Soul of College Football* (New York: Simon and Schuster, 2013), 2.

[1]Paul Domowitch, "Miami Hurricanes Are Glad to Be Bad," *Philadelphia Daily News*, December 30, 1986, http://articles.philly.com/1986-12-30/sports/26068056_1_bad-guys-hurricanes-second-best-party-school.

[2]"Greatest Penn State Football Upsets of All Time—The 1987 Fiesta Bowl," *Black Shoes Diaries*, September 9, 2010, www.blackshoediaries.com/2010/9/9/1677482/greatest-penn-state-upsets-of-all.

[3]Michael Sokolove, "The Trials of Graham Spanier; Penn State's Ousted President," *New York Times Magazine*, July 16, 2014, www.nytimes.com/2014/07/20/magazine/the-trials-of-graham-spanier-penn-states-ousted-president.html?_r=0.

[4]Ibid.

[5]David Brooks and Gail Collins, "The Horror Show at Penn State."

[6]See Mark Tracy, "Baylor Demotes President Kenneth Starr Over Handling of Sex Assault Cases," *New York Times*, May 26, 2016, www.nytimes.com/2016/05/27/sports/ncaafootball/baylor-art-briles-kenneth-starr-college-football.html; Matt Bonesteel and Nick Anderson, "Baylor to Fire Football Coach Art Briles, Demotes Kenneth Starr Amid Team's Sexual-Assault Allegations," *Washington Post*, May 26, 2016, www.washingtonpost.com/news/early-lead/wp/2016/05/26/baylor-reportedly-fires-football-coach-art-briles-amid-teams-sexual-assault-allegations/; Michelle Boorstein, "The Ken Starr–Baylor Story Shows How Religious Schools Struggle to

Deal with Sex Assault," *Washington Post*, May 25, 2016, www.washingtonpost.com /news/acts-of-faith/wp/2016/05/25/the-ken-starr-baylor-story-shows-the -struggle-of-religious-schools-to-deal-with-sex-assault; Paul Newberry (Associated Press), "Baylor Should Pull Plug on Its Athletic Program," *USA Today*, May 26, 2016, www.usatoday.com/story/sports/ncaaf/2016/05/26/column-baylor -should-pull-plug-on-its-athletic-program/84996974/; Andy Thomsen, "Baylor Demotes President and Moves to Fire Football Coach Amid Sex-Assault Controversy," *Chronicle of Higher Education*, May 26, 2016, http://chronicle.com/blogs /ticker/baylor-removes-president-fires-football-coach-amid-sex-assault-controversy /111629; Dana Farrington, "Baylor Removes Ken Starr as President Over University's Response to Sex Assault Cases," *The Two-Way* (blog), *NPR*, May 26, 2016, www.npr.org/sections/thetwo-way/2016/05/26/479614022/baylor-removes-ken -starr-as-president-over-universitys-response-to-sex-assault-c; Eric Kelderman and Robin Wilson, "'Fundamental Failure' on Sexual Assaults Brings Sweeping Change at Baylor," *Chronicle of Higher Education*, May 27, 2016, http://chronicle .com/article/Fundamental-Failure-on/236624; Fernanda Zamudio-Suaréz, "Five Damning Findings from the Baylor Investigation," *The Ticker* (blog), *Chronicle of Higher Education*, May 26, 2016, http://chronicle.com/blogs/ticker/5-damning -findings-from-the-baylor-investigation/111650; Jake New, "Consequences at Baylor," *Inside Higher Ed*, May 27, 2016, www.insidehighered.com/news/2016/05/27 /baylor-university-regents-fire-head-football-coach-ken-starr-steps-aside; Jake New, "Ken Starr to Step Down," *Inside Higher Ed*, May 25, 2016, www.inside highered.com/news/2016/05/25/baylor-university-prepares-fire-president-over -handling-assaults.

[7]"Baylor University Board of Regents Findings of Fact," Baylor University website, accessed June 8, 2016, www.baylor.edu/rtsv/doc.php/266596.pdf, 1.

[8]Ibid., 11.

[9]Ibid., 12.

[10]Despite the role the NCAA has played in intercollegiate athletics, only two histories appear to focus on it: Jack Falla, *NCAA: The Voice of College Sports— A Diamond Anniversary History, 1906–1981* (Mission, KS: National Collegiate Athletic Association, 1981); and Joseph N. Crawley, *In the Arena: The NCAA's First Century* (Indianapolis: National Collegiate Athletic Association, 2006). As is evident in these details, both books were produced by the NCAA, thus leaving a hole in the literature concerning intercollegiate athletics needing to be filled.

[11]For example, please see Dave Revsine, *The Opening Kickoff: The Tumultuous Birth of a Football Nation* (Guilford, CT: Lyons Press, 2014); and John Sayle Watterson, *College Football: History, Spectacle, Controversy* (Baltimore: Johns Hopkins University Press, 2000).

[12]Ronald A. Smith, *Pay for Play: A History of Big-Time College Athletic Reform* (Urbana: University of Illinois Press, 2011), 49.

[13]Ibid., 43.

[14]John J. Miller, *The Big Scrum: How Teddy Roosevelt Saved Football* (New York: HarperCollins, 2011), 11.

[15]Brian M. Ingrassia, *The Rise of Gridiron University: Higher Education's Uneasy Alliance with Big-Time Football* (Lawrence: University Press of Kansas, 2012), 56.

[16]Ibid., 47.

[17]Ibid., 53.

[18]Miller, *Big Scrum*, 13.

[19]Paul R. Lawrence, *Unsportsmanlike Conduct: The National Collegiate Athletic Association and the Business of College Football* (New York: Praeger, 1987), 12.

[20]Ingrassia, *Rise of Gridiron University*, 9.

[21]Michael Oriard, *Reading Football: How the Popular Press Created an American Spectacle* (Chapel Hill: University of North Carolina Press, 1993), 57.

[22]Ibid., 57-58.

[23]Michael K. Bohn, *Heroes and Ballyhoo: How the Golden Age of the 1920s Transformed American Sports* (Lincoln, NE: Potomac, 2009), 1.

[24]Revsine, *Opening Kickoff*, 150.

[25]Grantland Rice, "The Four Horsemen," *New York Herald Tribune*, October 18, 1924, http://archives.nd.edu/research/texts/rice.htm.

[26]Allen Barra, "The Sports Story That Changed America," *New York Times*, October 17, 1999, www.nytimes.com/1999/10/17/weekinreview/the-sports-story-that-changed-america.html.

[27]Julie Reuben, *The Making of the Modern University: Intellectual Transformation and the Marginalization of Morality* (Chicago: University of Chicago Press, 1996), 258.

[28]Murray Sperber, *Shake Down the Thunder: The Creation of Notre Dame Football* (New York: Henry Holt, 1993).

[29]For a detailed discussion of the differences between Harper's and Hutchins's views when it came to athletics, see Hal A. Lawson and Alan G. Ingham, "Conflicting Ideologies Concerning the University and Intercollegiate Athletics: Harper and Hutchins at Chicago, 1892–1940," *Journal of Sport History* 7, no. 3 (1980): 37-67.

[30]John Sayle Watterson, *College Football: History, Spectacle, Controversy* (Baltimore: Johns Hopkins University Press, 2000), 191.

[31]Robert Maynard Hutchins, "Gate Receipts and Glory," *Saturday Evening Post*, December 3, 1938, 23.

[32]Robert Milton Mayer, *Maynard Hutchins: A Memoir* (Berkeley: University of California Press, 1993), 145.

[33]Ibid.

[34] Ronald A. Smith, *Play-by-Play: Radio, Television, and Big-Time College Sports* (Baltimore: Johns Hopkins University Press, 2001), 29.

[35] Ibid.

[36] Ibid., 33.

[37] Ibid., 25.

[38] Ibid.

[39] Ibid., 27.

[40] Ibid.

[41] Keith Dunnavant, *The Fifty-Year Seduction: How Television Manipulated College Football, from the Birth of the Modern NCAA to the Creation of the BCS* (New York: St. Martin's Press, 2004), xv-xvi.

[42] Ibid., 51.

[43] Watterson, *College Football*, 265.

[44] Ronald A. Smith, *Sports and Freedom: The Rise of Big-Time College Athletics* (New York: Oxford University Press, 1988).

[45] Ibid., 96.

[46] Watterson, *College Football*, 267-68.

[47] Ibid., 180.

[48] Bill Rasmussen, *Sports Junkies Rejoice: The Birth of ESPN!* (Hartsdale, NY: QV, 1983), 115.

[49] For an articulate history of the move to the Bowl Championship Series (BCS), see Michael Oriard's *Bowled Over: Big-Time College Football from the Sixties to the BCS Era* (Chapel Hill: University of North Carolina Press, 2009). At the time of writing, the College Football Playoff had been in place only for one year. While no considerable assessment of its impact is available yet, ESPN secured a contract to air those games from 2014 to 2015. Rachel Bachman of the *Wall Street Journal* reported that "a person familiar with the negotiations said it is worth about $470 million annually or $5.64 billion for the duration of the contract." For more details, see Rachel Bachman, "ESPN Strikes Deal for College Football Playoff," *Wall Street Journal*, November 21, 2012, www.wsj.com/articles/SB10001424127887324851704578133223970790516.

[50] Smith, *Play-by-Play*, 128.

[51] Watterson, *College Football*, 253-54.

[52] Ibid., 254.

[53] Bernard M. Gwertzman, "Ivy League: Formalizing the Fact," *The Crimson*, October 13, 1956, www.thecrimson.com/article/1956/10/13/ivy-league-formalizing-the-fact-pthe/.

[54] To name only a few, see John U. Bacon, *Fourth and Long: The Fight for the Soul of College Football* (New York: Simon and Schuster, 2013); Jeff Benedict and Armen Keteyian, *The System: The Glory and Scandal of Big-Time College Football* (New York:

Doubleday, 2013); and Howard L. Nixon, *The Athletic Trap: How College Sports Corrupted the Academy* (Baltimore: Johns Hopkins University Press, 2014). Perhaps the most influential volume in this genre is Murray Sperber, *Beer and Circus: How Big-Time College Sports Is Crippling Undergraduate Education* (New York: Henry Holt, 2000). Walter Byers, Executive Director of the NCAA for thirty-six years, published *Unsportsmanlike Conduct: Exploiting College Athletes* (Ann Arbor: University of Michigan Press, 1995). Finally, William G. Bowen and Sarah A. Levin, *Reclaiming the Game: College Sports and Educational Values* (Princeton, NJ: Princeton University Press, 2003), may be among the most thoughtful of volumes on the topic.

[55]Isaac L. Kandel, *The Dilemma of Democracy* (Cambridge, MA: Harvard University Press, 1934), 71-72.

[56]Robert Benne, *Quality with Soul: How Six Premier Colleges and Universities Keep Faith with Their Religious Traditions* (Grand Rapids: Eerdmans, 2002).

[57]See Matt Sayman, *The Leftovers: Baylor, Betrayal and Beyond* (Maitland, FL: Xulon, 2013).

11 THE CONSEQUENCES OF MULTIVERSITIES WITH FRAGMENTED SOULS: ONLINE AND FOR-PROFIT HIGHER EDUCATION

Epigraph: Jeremiah Day, "The Yale Report of 1828," in *American Higher Education: A Documentary History*, ed. Richard Hofstradter and Wilson Smith (Chicago: University of Chicago Press, 1961), 1:282.

[1]Peter Glander, "The Unlikely Innovator," *Christianity Today* 58, no. 8 (2014): 63.

[2]Graeme Wood, "The Future of College?," *The Atlantic*, August 13, 2014, www .theatlantic.com/features/archive/2014/08/the-future-of-college/375071/.

[3]Thomas K. Hearn, "Leadership and Teaching in the American University," in *University Presidents as Moral Leaders*, ed. David Brown (Westport, CT: Praeger), 159-76.

[4]*The Didascalicon of Hugh of St. Victor: A Medieval Guide to the Arts*, trans. Jerome Taylor (New York: Columbia University Press, 1991), 16.

[5]Ibid., 86-87.

[6]Harold T. Shapiro, *A Larger Sense of Purpose: Higher Education and Society* (Princeton, NJ: Princeton University Press, 2005).

[7]Royal Charter Collection, Special Collections Research Center, Earl Gregg Swem Library, College of William and Mary.

[8]Caroline Winterer, "The Humanist Revolution, 1820–1860: Classical Antiquity in the Colleges," *History of Higher Education Annual* 18 (1998): 111-29.

[9]Ibid.

[10]George Eliot, *The Mill on the Floss* (1860; repr., Ware, UK: Wordsworth Editions, 1993), 152.

[11] Jeremiah Day, "The Yale Report of 1828," in *American Higher Education: A Documentary History*, ed. Richard Hofstadter and Wilson Smith (Chicago: University of Chicago Press, 1961), 1:281.

[12] James F. Davidson, "On Furniture, First Jobs, and Freedom," *Liberal Education* 49 (1963): 268.

[13] Winterer, "Humanist Revolution," 121.

[14] Day, "Yale Report," 282.

[15] Charles A. Bennett, *History of Manual and Industrial Education, 1870–1917* (Peoria, IL: Manual Arts Press, 1937).

[16] Will S. Monroe, "Manual Labor Institutions and the Manual Labor Society," in *Encyclopedia of Education*, ed. Paul Monroe (New York: Macmillan, 1911), 4:156-61; Herbert Galen Lull, *The Manual Labor Movement in the United States*, Bulletin of the University of Washington University Studies 8 (1914): 375-76.

[17] Joseph F. Kett, *The Pursuit of Knowledge Under Difficulties: From Self-Improvement to Adult Education in America, 1750–1990* (Stanford: Stanford University Press, 1994), 31.

[18] Ibid., 7.

[19] Roger L. Geiger, *The History of American Higher Education: Learning and Culture from the Founding to World War II* (Princeton, NJ: Princeton University Press, 2015), 92.

[20] The Morrill Act of 1862, Pub. L. No. 37-108, 12 Stat. 503 (1862).

[21] Kett, *Pursuit of Knowledge*, 229.

[22] Ibid., 234.

[23] Ibid.

[24] Janice Weiss, "Education for Clerical Work: The Nineteenth-Century Private Commercial School," *Journal of Social History* 14 (1981): 407-23.

[25] Kett, *Pursuit of Knowledge*, 236.

[26] Ibid.

[27] Ibid.

[28] For more on the topic and about the YMCA's founding of universities, see Dorothy E. Finnegan and Brian Cullaty, "Origins of the YMCA Universities: Organizational Adaptations in Urban Education," *History of Higher Education Annual* 21 (2001): 47-79; Dorothy E. Finnegan, "Raising and Leveling the Bar: Standards, Access, and the YMCA Evening Law Schools, 1890–1940," *Journal of Legal Education* 55, nos. 1-2 (2005): 208-33.

[29] Although we have narrowed our focus here to correspondence courses reflective of early distance-learning approaches, a forerunner of Harper's efforts at Chicago was the highly successful Chautauqua Literary and Scientific Circle, a series of residential summer lectures and correspondence courses geared to engage the common citizen in issues of high culture through instruction. In the late 1800s

universities were reaching out to their local communities as well through "extension" lectures, or talks given by faculty to interested citizens, and through various summer-school programs. These alternate opportunities are explored at length in David N. Portman, *The Universities and the Public: A History of Higher Adult Education in the United States* (Chicago: Nelson-Hall, 1978); and in Kett, *Pursuit of Knowledge.*

[30]Michael Simonson, Sharon Smaldino, and Susan Zvacek, *Teaching and Learning at a Distance: Foundations of Distance Education* (Upper Saddle River, NY: Prentice-Hall, 2000), 36.

[31]Ossian MacKenzie, Edward L. Christiansen, and Paul H. Rigby, *Correspondence Instruction in the United States* (New York: McGraw-Hill, 1968), 26.

[32]Gary A. Berg, *Why Distance Learning? Higher Education Administrative Practices* (Westport, CT: Oryx, 2002), 11.

[33]Thomas Wakefield Goodspeed, *A History of the University of Chicago* (Chicago: University of Chicago Press, 1972).

[34]Robert Maynard Hutchins, *The Higher Learning in America* (Piscataway, NJ: Transaction, 1999), 31.

[35]Pierre Bourdieu's concepts of social and cultural capital helpfully capture the invisible ways that college facilitates opportunity. *Social capital* describes interpersonal networks that reinforce norms and values and provide legitimacy and opportunity for those who (formally or informally) gain membership and acceptance by aligning themselves with these tacit norms. *Cultural capital* includes possession of and identification with culturally valued symbols that might include credentials that legally certify achievement and ability and knowledge of high-status expressions such as theater, art, and classical music. A simple example provides some orientation: social capital is what gains a person an invitation to an exclusive black-tie dinner party; cultural capital is then knowing what behaviors (where to sit, what to drink, which fork to use and when) are acceptable and convey symbolically that a person belongs.

Central to Bourdieu's aims is the idea of social reproduction, or the means by which those in privileged positions ensure that their progeny attain and maintain a similar social standing (and by extension, others do not). In this, the university plays an important part by reinforcing class differentiation and the status quo. Education can also serve social reproduction by assuring that those who are not a part of this social elite find their lot in life acceptable, or at least acceptable enough not to band together and demand change. Borrowing from Max Weber, Bourdieu suggests that the most effective form of constraint is the one imposed on oneself by oneself. This feat is accomplished through what Bourdieu terms "symbolic violence," or the imposition of systems of symbols and meanings in ways that are experienced by others as the natural and legitimate order of the world, and not a socially constructed system that privileges one group over another. For Bourdieu, formal education is one form of symbolic violence since it rewards those who acquiesce to its ideals and priorities, reinforcing their self-evident legitimacy. For more, see Pierre Bourdieu, "The Forms of Capital," in *Handbook of Theory and Research for the Sociology of Education*, ed. J. G. Richardson (New York: Greenwood, 1986); Pierre Bourdieu and Jean-Claude Passeron, *Reproduction: In Education, Society, and Culture* (London: Sage, 1977); for a helpful summary of Bourdieu in the context of higher education, see Jeffery P. Bieber, "Cultural Capital as an Interpretive Framework for Faculty Life," in *Higher Education: Handbook of Theory and Research*, ed. John C. Smart and William G. Tierney (London: Sage, 1999), 14:367-97.

[36] *US News and World Report*, "Economic Diversity Among the Top 25 Ranked Schools," 2015, http://colleges.usnews.rankingsandreviews.com/best-colleges /rankings/national-universities/economic-diversity-among-top-ranked-schools. Princeton University (12%), Yale University (13%), and the University of Virginia (13%) sit near the bottom; Harvard University (19%) occupies a middle position, and the University of California-Los Angeles (39%) enrolls the most Pell-eligible students.

[37] Marybeth Walpole, "Socioeconomic Status and College: How SES Affects College Experiences and Outcomes," *Review of Higher Education* 27, no. 1 (2003): 45-73.

[38] Kett, *Pursuit of Knowledge*, 103.

[39] Wendell Berry, *The Unsettling of America: Culture and Agriculture* (San Francisco: Sierra Club Books, 1986).

[40] Ibid., 147.

[41] Stephen F. Aldersley, "'Upward Drift' Is Alive and Well: Research/Doctoral Model Is Still Attractive to Institutions," *Change* 27, no. 4 (1995): 16-20; Christopher C. Morphew, "'A Rose by Any Other Name': Which Colleges Became Universities," *Review of Higher Education* 25, no. 2 (2002): 207-23; David Breneman, *Are We Losing Our Liberal Arts Colleges?* (Washington, DC: American Association of Higher Education, College Board Review, 1990); Joan Gilbert, "The Liberal Arts College—Is It Really an Endangered Species?," *Change* 27, no. 5 (1995): 36-38; Neil J. Smelser, *Dynamics of the Contemporary University: Growth, Accretion, and Conflict* (Berkeley: University of California Press, 2013), 13.

[42] John Sperling, *Rebel with a Cause: The Entrepreneur Who Created the University of Phoenix and the For-Profit Revolution* (New York: Wiley, 2000), 56.

[43] Ibid., 79.

[44] Grant Venn, *Man, Education and Work: Postsecondary Vocational and Technical Education* (Washington, DC: American Council on Education, 1964), 34.

[45] A more complete account of their massive online course is recounted in Jeffery J. Selingo, *College (Un)bound: The Future of Higher Education and What It Means for Students* (New York: Houghton Mifflin Harcourt, 2013).

[46]Ibid., 90.

[47]Dayna Catropa and Margaret Andrews, "This Way to the All-Star Degree?," *Inside Higher Ed*, April 30, 2015, www.insidehighered.com/blogs/stratedgy /way-all-star-degree.

[48]Berg, *Why Distance Learning?*, 68.

[49]Ibid., 145.

[50]Arthur Levine and Jeanette S. Cureton, "Collegiate Life: An Obituary," *Change*, 1998, 14.

[51]Robert J. Panos, Alexander W. Astin, and John A. Creager, *National Norms for Entering College Freshman—Fall 1967* (Los Angeles: American Council on Education, 1967), 18.

[52]Kevin Eagan et al., *The American Freshman: National Norms Fall 2014* (Los Angeles: Higher Education Research Institute, UCLA, 2014), 44.

[53]John A. Flower, *Downstairs, Upstairs: The Changed Spirit and Face of College Life in America* (Akron, OH: University of Akron Press, 2003), 174.

[54]Kett, *Pursuit of Knowledge*.

[55]David N. Portman, *The Universities and the Public: A History of Higher Adult Education in the United States* (Chicago: Nelson-Hall, 1978), 31.

[56]Ibid., 33-34.

[57]A study found that the majority of MOOC participants are advanced degree-holding adults who are currently employed, rather than undereducated persons from underrepresented groups. See Ezekiel J. Emanuel, "Online Education: MOOCs Taken by Educated Few," *Nature* 503 (November 20, 2013), www.nature .com/nature/journal/v503/n7476/full/503342a.html.

[58]See Brian Connelly, "Interpretations of Jürgen Habermas in Adult Education Writings," *Studies in the Education of Adults* 28, no. 2 (1996): 241-52; Jennifer Sumner, "Serving the System: A Critical History of Distance Education," *Open Learning* 15, no. 3 (2000): 267-85; Terry Evans and Daryl Nation, eds., *Reforming Open and Distance Education: Critical Reactions from Practice* (New York: St. Martin's Press, 1993); Mechthild U. Hart, *Working and Educating for Life: Feminist and International Perspectives on Adult Education* (London: Routledge, 1992).

[59]Rick Powell, Sharon McGuire, and Gail Crawford, "Convergence of Student Types: Issues for Distance Education," in *The Convergence of Distance and Conventional Education: Patterns of Flexibility for the Individual Learner*, ed. Alan Tait and Roger Mills (London: Routledge, 1999), 86-99.

[60]Berg, *Why Distance Learning?*, 161.

[61]Lee Herman and Alan Mandell, "On Access," in Tait and Mills, *Convergence of Distance and Conventional Education*, 36.

[62]The Khan Academy and its founder, Salman Khan, received Google's $2 million Global Impact Award, the Skoll Foundation's 2013 Economist Innovation Award,

the $250,000 Heinz Family Foundation Award (2014), and the 2014 David Packard Award, among many others.

[63] David W. Breneman, Brian B. Pusser, and Sarah E. Turner, *Earnings from Learning: The Rise of For-Profit Universities* (Albany: State University of New York Press, 2006).

[64] Michael W. Krist and Mitchell L. Stevens, *Remaking College: The Changing Ecology of Higher Education* (Redwood City, CA: Stanford University Press, 2015).

[65] As of 2014, 34 percent of University of Phoenix students graduated within 150 percent of the expected two-year time frame. The default rate at for-profit institutions nationally was 19.1 percent, compared to 12.9 percent at public institutions and 7.2 percent at private institutions. Bourree Lam, "For-Profit Colleges: Here to Stay," *The Atlantic Online*, April 3, 2015, www.theatlantic.com/business/archive /2015/04/for-profit-colleges-here-to-stay/389045/.

[66] Columbia University's Fathom project is perhaps the best example of a major investment in MOOC infrastructure and curricula that proved to be unsustainable. After three years and more than $25 million in investments, this for-profit venture closed in 2003. See Neil J. Smelser, *Dynamics of the Contemporary University: Growth, Accretion, and Conflict* (Berkeley: University of California Press, 2013).

[67] Krist and Stevens, *Remaking College*.

[68] Glader, "The Unlikely Innovator."

[69] "Liberty Ranks Number 7 in the Nation in Enrollment," *Liberty News*, May 25, 2012, www.liberty.edu/news/index.cfm?PID=18495&MID=56085.

12 WHEN THEOLOGY SERVES THE SOUL OF THE UNIVERSITY

Epigraph: Stanley Hauerwas, *The State of the University: Academic Knowledges and the Knowledge of God* (Malden, MA: Blackwell, 2007), 94.

[1] Friedrich Nietzsche, *The Gay Science*, trans. Walter Kauffman (New York: Vintage, 1974), 181.

[2] Ibid.

[3] William Cavanaugh, *The Myth of Religious Violence: Secular Ideology and the Roots of Modern Conflict* (New York: Oxford University Press, 2009).

[4] See, e.g., David Sloan Wilson, *Evolution for Everyone: How Darwin's Theory Can Change the Way We Think About Our Lives* (New York: Delacorte, 2007).

[5] Anthony T. Kronman, *Education's End: Why Our Colleges and Universities Have Given Up on the Meaning of Life* (New Haven, CT: Yale University Press, 2007).

[6] Denise Cush, "Religious Studies Versus Theology," in *Theology and Religious Studies in Higher Education: Global Perspectives*, ed. Darlene L. Bird and Simon G. Smith (New York: Continuum, 2009), 27.

[7] Ibid., 24.

[8] Hauerwas, *State of the University*, 31.

[9]Christian Smith, *The Sacred Project of American Sociology* (New York: Oxford University Press, 2014).

[10]Oliver D. Crisp et al., "Introduction: Theology and the Disciplines: Building a 'Christian Culture,'" in *Christianity and the Disciplines: The Transformation of the University*, ed. Oliver D. Crisp et al. (New York: T&T Clark, 2012), 3.

[11]Ibid.

[12]Douglas Sloan, *Faith and Knowledge: Mainline Protestantism and American Higher Education* (Louisville: Westminster John Knox Press, 1994), last chapter.

[13]Stanley Hauerwas and Samuel Wells, "How the Church Managed Before There Was Ethics," in *The Blackwell Companion to Christian Ethics*, ed. Stanley Hauerwas and Samuel Wells (Malden, MA: Blackwell, 2004), 41.

[14]See Perry L. Glanzer, Jonathan Hill, and Byron Johnson, *The Quest for Purpose: The Collegiate Search for a Meaningful Life* (Albany: State University of New York Press, forthcoming), chap. 8.

[15]Stanley Hauerwas and Samuel Wells, "Christian Ethics as Informed Prayer," in Hauerwas and Wells, *Blackwell Companion to Christian Ethics*, 4.

[16]Ibid., 7.

[17]Oliver D. Crisp et al., "Theology in Search of a Handmaiden: Reason and Philosophy," in *Theology and Philosophy: Faith and Reason*, ed. Oliver D. Crisp et al. (New York: T&T Clark, 2012), 2.

[18]Examples include the following: David Ray Griffin and Joseph C. Hough, eds., *Theology and the University: Essays in Honor of John B. Cobb, Jr.* (Albany: State University of New York Press, 1991); David F. Ford, Ben Quash, and Janet Martin Soskice, eds., *Fields of Faith: Theology and Religious Studies for the Twenty-First Century* (New York: Cambridge University Press, 2005); Darlene Bird and Simon G. Smith, eds., *Theology and Religious Studies in Higher Education: Global Perspectives* (New York: Continuum, 2009); Christopher Craig Brittain and Francesca Aran Murphy, eds., *Theology, University, Humanities: Intium Sapientiae Timor Domini* (Eugene, OR: Cascade, 2011); and Brian W. Hughes, *Saving Wisdom: Theology and the Christian University* (Eugene, OR: Pickwick, 2011).

[19]Untitled series description, in Crisp et al., *Theology and Philosophy*, page opposite title page.

[20]Ibid.

[21]Crisp et al., "Introduction," 3-4.

[22]Ibid., 2.

[23]Ibid.

[24]Ibid., page opposite title page.

[25]William Adams Brown, *The Case for Theology in the University* (Chicago: University of Chicago Press, 1938), 82.

[26]James K. A. Smith, *Desiring the Kingdom* (Grand Rapids: Baker Academic, 2009).

[27]Karl Barth, *Church Dogmatics*, vol. I/1, *The Doctrine of the Word of God*, ed. Geoffrey W. Bromiley and T. F. Torrance (Edinburgh: T&T Clark, 2009), 3.

[28]Nathan F. Alleman, Perry L. Glanzer, and David Guthrie, "The Integration of Christian Theological Traditions into the Classroom: A Survey of CCCU Faculty," *Christian Scholar's Review* 45, no. 2 (2016): 103-25.

[29]Hauerwas and Wells, "Christian Ethics as Informed Prayer," 5.

[30]Gavin D'Costa, *Theology in the Public Square: Church, Academy, and Nation* (Malden, MA: Wiley-Blackwell, 2005), 115.

[31]Hauerwas, *State of the University*, 183-84.

[32]Nietzsche, *The Gay Science*, 181.

13 REIMAGINING THE ACADEMIC VOCATION

Epigraph: Peter Salovey, "Inaugural Address: Our Educational Mission," Yale University, October 13, 2013, http://president.yale.edu/inaugural-address-our-educational-mission.

[1]Donald Kennedy, *Academic Duty* (Cambridge, MA: Harvard University Press, 1997), v.

[2]Robert Boice, *The New Faculty Member* (San Francisco: Jossey-Bass, 1992).

[3]See Janet Lawrence, Molly Ott, and Alli Bell, "Faculty Organizational Commitment and Citizenship," *Research in Higher Education* 53 (2012): 325-52.

[4]Kennedy, *Academic Duty*. See also Stanley Fish, *Save the World on Your Own Time* (New York: Oxford University Press, 2008).

[5]See Steven M. Cahn's introduction about his moral frustrations in his 25th anniversary edition of *Saints and Scamps: Ethics in Academia* (Lanham, MD: Rowman & Littlefield, 2011).

[6]Mark R. Schwehn, *Exiles from Eden: Religion and the Academic Vocation in America* (New York: Oxford University Press), 134.

[7]Ibid., 58-59.

[8]Søren Kierkegaard, *Fear and Trembling*, trans. Howard V. Hong and Edna H. Hong (Princeton, NJ: Princeton University Press, 1993), 20.

[9]Douglas V. Henry and Bob R. Agee, *Faithful Learning and the Christian Scholarly Vocation* (Grand Rapids: Eerdmans, 2003); Susan VanZanten, *Joining the Mission: A Guide for (Mainly) New College Faculty* (Grand Rapids: Eerdmans, 2011); Donald Opitz and Derek Melleby, *The Outrageous Idea of Academic Faithfulness* (Grand Rapids: Brazos, 2007); Patrick Allen and Kenneth Badley, *Faith and Learning: A Guide for Faculty* (Abilene, TX: Abilene Christian University Press, 2014); Nicholas Wolterstorff, *Educating for Shalom: Essays on Christian Higher Education*, ed. Clarence W. Joldersma and Gloria Goris Stronks (Grand Rapids: Eerdmans, 2004).

[10]George Marsden, *The Outrageous Idea of Christian Scholarship* (New York: Oxford University Press, 1996); William Lane Craig and Paul M. Gould, eds., *The Two Tasks of the Christian Scholar* (Wheaton, IL: Crossway, 2007); Douglas Jacobsen

and Rhonda Hustedt Jacobsen, *Scholarship and Christian Faith: Enlarging the Conversation* (New York: Oxford University Press, 2004).

[11]David I. Smith and Susan M. Felch, *Teaching and Christian Imagination* (Grand Rapids: Eerdmans, 2016); David I. Smith and James K. A. Smith, eds., *Teaching and Christian Practices* (Grand Rapids: Eerdmans, 2011).

[12]VanZanten, *Joining the Mission*; Allen and Badley, *Faith and Learning*.

[13]Gary M. Burge, *Mapping Your Academic Career: Charting the Course of a Professor's Life* (Downers Grove, IL: IVP Academic, 2015), 104.

[14]Anton Chekhov, "The Black Monk," in *Anton Chekhov: Short Stories*, trans. Richard Pevear and Larissa Volokhonsky (New York: Bantam, 2000), 250-51.

[15]Burge, *Mapping Your Academic Career*, 42.

[16]VanZanten, *Joining the Mission*, 136.

[17]Our source for this idea comes from a talk Charles Talbert would give to new faculty at Baylor University as well as the summer faculty institute.

[18]For an example see Azusa Pacific University's policy, www.apu.edu/faith integration/about (accessed August 10, 2016).

[19]See Smith and Smith, *Teaching and Christian Practices*; VanZanten, *Joining the Mission*, 97-158; Allen and Badley, *Faith and Learning*, 109-16, 130-33, 149-54.

[20]See for example Allen and Badley, *Faith and Learning*, 111-12, 151-53.

[21]Christopher Peterson and Martin Seligman, *Character Strengths and Virtues: A Handbook and Classification* (New York: Oxford University Press, 2004).

[22]John Howard Yoder, *The Politics of Jesus* (Grand Rapids: Eerdmans, 1972).

[23]Perry L. Glanzer and Andrew J. Milson, "Legislating the Good: A Survey and Evaluation of Contemporary Character Education Legislation," *Educational Policy* 20, no. 3 (2006): 525–50. Arizona requires public schools to teach students "sincerity." Alabama, Georgia, and South Carolina now require children to be taught "cleanliness" and "cheerfulness." Five states have mandated that children learn "punctuality" (AL, GA, SC, TX, and VA). Three states believe children must learn "attentiveness" (AZ, FL, and KY).

[24]Danny E. Morris and Charles M. Olsen, *Discerning God's Will Together: A Spiritual Practice for the Church* (Nashville: Upper Room, 1997).

14 REIMAGINING THE ACADEMIC DISCIPLINES

Epigraphs: Stanley Hauerwas, *The State of the University: Academic Knowledges and the Knowledge of God* (Malden, MA: Blackwell, 2007), 2; Edward O. Wilson, *Consilience: The Unity of Knowledge* (New York: Vintage, 1998), 3.

[1]Naomi Schaefer Riley, "It's Not Just Athletes—College Screws Everyone," *New York Post*, April 12, 2014, http://nypost.com/2014/04/12/its-not-just-athletes-college -screws-everyone/.

[2]Gilbert Meilaender, "Who Needs a Liberal Education?," *New Atlantis* 41 (Winter 2014): 101.

[3]Ibid.

[4]Ibid., 102.

[5]Ibid., 103.

[6]Ibid., 104.

[7]Ibid., 102.

[8]Parker Palmer and Arthur Zajonc, *The Heart of Higher Education: A Call to Renewal* (San Francisco: Jossey-Bass, 2010), 7, 10.

[9]Ibid., 13.

[10]Meilaender, "Who Needs a Liberal Education?," 102.

[11]Ibid., 122-23.

[12]Palmer and Zajonc, *The Heart of Higher Education*, 19.

[13]Ibid., 19-20.

[14]Meilaender, "Who Needs a Liberal Education?," 107.

[15]*The Confessions of St. Augustine*, trans. John K. Ryan (New York: Doubleday, 1960), 93.

[16]Ibid., 111.

[17]Meilaender, "Who Needs a Liberal Education?," 108.

[18]*The Didascalicon of Hugh of St. Victor: A Medieval Guide to the Arts*, trans. Jerome Taylor (New York: Columbia University Press, 1991), 61.

[19]Wolfhart Pannenberg, "An Intellectual Pilgrimage," *Dialog* 45, no. 2 (Summer 2006), 190.

[20]Meilaender, "Who Needs a Liberal Education?," 103.

[21]For curricular suggestions about how to accomplish this goal, see Perry L. Glanzer and Todd C. Ream, *Christianity and Moral Identity in Higher Education* (New York: Palgrave Macmillan, 2009), chaps. 9 and 10.

[22]Ibid.

15 REIMAGINING THE COCURRICULAR: TRANSFORMING THE BUBBLE TO A GREENHOUSE

Epigraph: David I. Smith and Susan M. Felch, with Barbara M. Carvill, Kurt C. Schaefer, Timothy H. Steele, and John D. Witvliet, *Teaching and Christian Imagination* (Grand Rapids: Eerdmans, 2016), 109.

[1]See, for example, the Baylor University website, www.baylor.edu/ (accessed August 10, 2015).

[2]We are grateful to Cara Allen for this insight.

[3]Wendell Berry, *Sex, Economy, Freedom, and Community* (New York: Pantheon, 1992), 123. We first came across these insights in Stanley Hauerwas, *The State of the University: Academic Knowledges and the Knowledge of God* (Malden, MA: Blackwell, 2007), 92-107.

[4]Berry, *Sex, Economy, Freedom, and Community*, 123, 147-48.

[5]Burton R. Clark, "The Organizational Saga in Higher Education," *Administrative Science Quarterly* 17, no. 2 (1972): 178-84.

[6]Berry, *Sex, Economy, Freedom, and Community*, 149.

[7]Ibid., 155.

[8]Ibid., 155.

[9]Arthur Chickering and Linda Reisser, *Education and Identity* (San Francisco: Jossey-Bass, 1993).

[10]Melanie M. Morey and John J. Piderit, SJ, *Catholic Higher Education: A Culture in Crisis* (New York: Oxford University Press, 2006), 367.

[11]Christopher Peterson and Martin Seligman, *Character Strengths and Virtues: A Handbook and Classification* (New York: Oxford University Press, 2004).

[12]Christian Smith, *What Is a Person? Rethinking Humanity, Social Life, and the Moral Good from the Ground Up* (Chicago: University of Chicago Press, 2010).

[13]See, e.g., John Frederic Kilner, *Dignity and Destiny: Humanity in the Image of God* (Grand Rapids: Eerdmans, 2015); J. Richard Middleton, *The Liberating Image: The Imago Dei in Genesis 1* (Grand Rapids: Brazos, 2005); and Stanley Grenz, *The Social God and the Relational Self: A Trinitarian Theology of the Imago Dei* (Louisville, KY: Westminster John Knox, 2001).

[14]Middleton, *Liberating Image*.

[15]As Stanley Grenz observes, what it means to be understood in the image of God has been interpreted in three broad ways throughout Christian history: (1) structurally, (2) relationally, and (3) as goal or telos. Historically the structural understanding of the *imago Dei* as reflecting certain God-like qualities or capacities has focused on two in particular—reason and will. As will be seen from our discussion, we found this focus too narrow. In the relational view, "image" is more of a verb than a noun. Humans have the ability to image God whenever they follow God's will. As will be seen from our discussion, we think this approach can easily be combined with the structural view. In other words, it is only when humans properly image God using the capacities we identify that they bear God's image. The third view sees the image as the goal to which humans are ultimately directed in the future. Again, we think this view can be combined with the other two. In other words, humans, using the capacities we described can image God at times, but they will never fully image God until the future eschaton. Grenz, *Social God and the Relational Self*, 141-82.

[16]Ibid., 305.

[17]Ibid., 320.

[18]"Watch the Winner of Our Video Contest," *Gatesnotes, The Blog of Bill Gates*, July 27, 2015, www.gatesnotes.com/Big-History.

[19]Middleton, *Liberating Image*, 27.

[20]The ability to demonstrate virtue that is God-imitating should not be reduced to the idea of moral agency (e.g., see Malcolm Jeeves, "The Emergence of Human Distinctiveness: The Story from Neuropsychology and Evolutionary

Psychology," in *Rethinking Human Nature: A Multidisciplinary Approach*, ed. Malcolm Jeeves [Grand Rapids: Eerdmans, 2011], 196-98). While moral agency is certainly a part of this ability, what is discussed in this section is the ability to use one's will to demonstrate to some degree a particular virtue in the way God would demonstrate it.

[21] For more about this emphasis, see John Howard Yoder, *The Politics of Jesus* (Grand Rapids: Eerdmans, 1972).

[22] Anne Colby et al., *Educating Citizens: Preparing America's Undergraduates for Lives of Moral and Civic Responsibility* (San Francisco: Jossey-Bass, 2003).

[23] Lawrence Kohlberg, *The Philosophy of Moral Development* (New York: Harper & Row, 1981).

[24] Perry Glanzer and Todd Ream, *Christianity and Moral Identity in Higher Education* (New York: Palgrave Macmillan, 2009).

[25] Alasdair MacIntyre, *After Virtue; A Study in Moral Theory* 3rd ed. (Notre Dame: University of Notre Dame Press, 2007).

[26] Philip Cary, "The Fruit of Wisdom," *First Things*, December 12, 2013, www .firstthings.com/blogs/firstthoughts/2013/12/the-fruit-of-wisdom.

[27] Geoff Colvin, *Talent Is Overrated: What Really Separates World-Class Performers from Everybody Else* (New York: Portfolio, 2008).

[28] James K. A. Smith, *Desiring the Kingdom: Worship, Worldview, and Cultural Formation* (Grand Rapids: Baker Academic, 2009).

[29] Peterson and Seligman, *Character Strengths and Virtues*, 303-4.

[30] Ibid., 303.

[31] Ibid., 304.

[32] John W. Doberstein, introduction to Dietrich Bonhoeffer, *Life Together: A Discussion of Christian Fellowship* (New York: Harper & Row, 1954), 10.

[33] Ibid., 10-11.

[34] Bonhoeffer, *Life Together*, 19.

[35] Ibid., 19-20.

[36] Ibid., 23.

[37] Paul Bloom, "First Person Plural," *The Atlantic*, November 2008, 90.

[38] Kwame Anthony Appiah, *Experiments in Ethics* (Cambridge, MA: Harvard University Press, 2010).

[39] Smith, *Desiring the Kingdom*.

[40] See also Mt 20:25-28; Mk 10:42-45; Lk 14:27-33; Jn 15:12, 20-21; Rom 6:6-11; 1 Cor 10:33–11:1; 2 Cor 1:5; 4:10; Gal 2:20; 5:24; Eph 5:1-2; Phil 1:29; 3:10-11; Col 1:24; 2:20–3:1; 2 Tim 3:12; Heb 11:1–12:5; 1 Pet 2:20-21; 3:14-18; 4:12-16; 1 Jn 2:6; 3:11-16; Rev 12:10-11. For additional writing about this issue see Richard B. Hays, *The Moral Vision of the New Testament* (San Francisco: HarperSanFrancisco, 1996).

16 REIMAGINING ACADEMIC LEADERSHIP

[1]Stanley Hauerwas and William H. Willimon, *Resident Aliens* (Nashville: Abingdon, 1990), 17.

[2]It is this transformation that thinkers such as Charles Taylor, James Davison Hunter, Christian Smith, and Stanley Hauerwas, among many others, have attempted to articulate in its substance and effect. Taylor, in particular, charts the complex shift from a Western cultural belief in transcendence seated in the collectivist theology of the Middle Ages to a presumption of unbelief in which the psychological self is the mediator of truth and reality. Charles Taylor, *A Secular Age* (Cambridge, MA: Belknap Press of Harvard University Press, 2007); James Davison Hunter, *To Change the World: The Irony, Tragedy, and Possibility of Christianity in the Late Modern World* (New York: Oxford University Press, 2010); Stanley Hauerwas, *After Christendom? How the Church Is to Behave if Freedom, Justice, and a Christian Nation Are Bad Ideas* (Nashville: Abingdon, 1991); Christian Smith, *Lost in Transition: The Dark Side of Emerging Adulthood* (New York: Oxford University Press, 2011).

[3]Hunter, *To Change the World*; Philip W. Eaton, *Engaging the Culture, Changing the World: The Christian University in a Post-Christian World* (Downers Grove: IVP Academic, 2011); J. Richard Middleton and Brian J. Walsh, *Truth Is Stranger Than It Used to Be: Biblical Faith in a Postmodern Age* (Downers Grove, IL: InterVarsity Press, 1995).

[4]Hauerwas, *After Christendom?*; Middleton and Walsh, *Truth Is Stranger Than It Used to Be*; Hauerwas and Willimon, *Resident Aliens*; Mark J. Labberton, *Called: Living as God's People in the World* (Downers Grove, IL: InterVarsity Press, 2014).

[5]George M. Marsden, *The Soul of the American University: From Protestant Establishment to Established Nonbelief* (New York: Oxford University Press, 1994); Julie A. Reuben, *The Making of the Modern University: Intellectual Transformation and the Marginalization of Morality* (Chicago: University of Chicago Press, 1996); James T. Burtchaell, *The Dying of the Light: The Disengagement of Colleges and Universities from their Christian Churches* (Grand Rapids: Eerdmans, 1998).

[6]Walter Brueggemann, *Reality, Grief, Hope: Three Urgent Prophetic Tasks* (Grand Rapids: Eerdmans, 2014), 3.

[7]Walter Brueggemann, "Slow Wisdom as a Sub-version of Reality" (lecture, Baylor University, Waco, TX, October 28, 2011), 2; a slightly revised version of his talk is published in *Educating for Wisdom in the Twenty-First Century*, ed. Darin H. Davis (South Bend, IN: St. Augustine's Press, forthcoming). Page numbers used to reference the talk in this chapter refer to the unpublished manuscript.

[8]Ibid., 6.

[9]Ibid., 3.

[10]We identified participants based on recommendations of experienced administrators and scholars who study and administrate Christian colleges and universities. Participants were selected based on their years of experience, their thoughtfulness as practitioners and scholars in their own right, and their recognized ability to articulate how their Christian faith informed their administrative practice. All names are pseudonyms. We asked participants if we could identify them and their institutions for purposes of this chapter. Several declined, so we have blinded the identities of all for consistency. Participants were asked to watch the video or read the transcript of Brueggemann's address and converse with us about it. Interviews typically lasted between forty-five and ninety minutes.

[11]For examples see Neil Postman, *The End of Education: Redefining the Value of School* (New York: Knopf, 1995); Anthony T. Kronman, *Education's End: Why Our Colleges and Universities Have Given Up on the Meaning of Life* (New Haven, CT: Yale University Press, 2007); Allan Bloom, *The Closing of the American Mind* (New York: Simon and Schuster, 1988); Richard Arum and Josipa Roksa, *Academically Adrift: Limited Learning on College Campuses* (Chicago: University of Chicago Press, 2011); Bruce Wilshire, *The Moral Collapse of the University: Professionalism, Purity, and Alienation* (Albany: State University of New York Press, 1990).

[12]The Bologna Process harmonized structures and curricula between universities in various European nations beginning in 2010. One result has been an increased emphasis on developing professional qualifications as part of the degree process. For more, see "The Bologna Process and the European Higher Education Area," European Commission, http://ec.europa.eu/education/policy/higher-education/bologna-process_en.

[13]Sociologists refer to this sort of institutional conformity as "mimetic isomorphism." See Paul J. Dimaggio and Walter W. Powell, "The Iron Cage Revisited: Institutional Isomorphism and Collective Rationality in Organizational Fields," *American Sociological Review* 48 (1983): 147-60; Mark S. Mizruchi and Lisa C. Fein, "The Social Construction of Organizational Knowledge: A Study of the Uses of Coercive, Mimetic, and Normative Isomorphism," *Administrative Science Quarterly* 44 (1999): 653-83.

[14]Brueggemann, "Slow Wisdom," 22.

[15]Ibid., 24.

[16]Ibid. 24-25.

[17]Richard T. Hughes, *How Christian Faith Can Sustain the Life of the Mind* (Grand Rapids: Eerdmans, 2001).

[18]Mark Labberton makes this point in his book *Called: Living as God's People in the World* (Downers Grove, IL: InterVarsity Press, 2014); and this concept is applied

to higher education in Philip W. Eaton's text, *Engaging the Culture, Changing the World.*

[19]For a full conversation see James K. A. Smith, *How (Not) to Be Secular: Reading Charles Taylor* (Grand Rapids: Eerdmans, 2014). This book is a companion to Taylor, *A Secular Age.* Also, the sociological work of Christian Smith identifies and expands on these trends and shifting cultural mindsets.

[20]Labberton, *Called*, 58.

[21]Hauerwas and Willimon, *Resident Aliens.*

[22]Walter Brueggemann, *Hope Within History* (Atlanta: Knox, 1987).

[23]Ibid., 17.

[24]David I. Smith and James K. A. Smith, *Teaching and Christian Practices: Reshaping Faith and Learning* (Grand Rapids: Eerdmans, 2011); Etienne Wenger, *Communities of Practice: Learning, Meaning, and Identity* (Cambridge: Cambridge University Press, 1999); Alasdair MacIntyre, *After Virtue*, 3rd ed. (Notre Dame: University of Notre Dame Press, 2007).

[25]Douglas V. Henry and Bob R. Agee, eds., *Faithful Learning and the Christian Scholarly Vocation* (Grand Rapids: Eerdmans, 2003); Nicholas Wolterstorff, *Educating for Shalom: Essays on Christian Higher Education*, ed. Clarence W. Joldersma and Gloria Goris Stronks (Grand Rapids: Eerdmans, 2004); Mark A. Noll, *The Scandal of the Evangelical Mind* (Grand Rapids: Eerdmans, 1994).

CONCLUSION: CAN A UNIVERSITY WITH A SINGULAR SOUL EXIST?

Epigraph: Mark R. Schwehn, *Exiles from Eden: Religion and the Academic Vocation in America* (New York: Oxford University Press), 136.

[1]See Joel Carpenter, Perry L. Glanzer, and Nicholas S. Lantinga, eds., *Christian Higher Education: A Global Reconnaissance* (Grand Rapids: Eerdmans, 2014).

SELECTED BIBLIOGRAPHY

Alleman, Nathan F., and Dorothy E. Finnegan. "'Believe You Have a Mission in Life and Steadily Pursue It': Campus YMCAs Presage Student Development Theory, 1894–1939." *Higher Education in Review* 6 (2009): 11-45.

Alleman, Nathan F., and Perry L. Glanzer. "Creating Confessional Colleges and Universities That Confess." *Journal of Education and Christian Belief* 18, no. 1 (2014): 13-28.

Alleman, Nathan F., Perry L. Glanzer, and David Guthrie. "The Integration of Christian Theological Traditions into the Classroom: A Survey of CCCU Faculty." *Christian Scholar's Review* 45, no. 2 (2016): 103-25.

Anderson, R. D. *European Universities from the Enlightenment to 1914.* New York: Oxford University Press, 2004.

Benne, Robert. *Quality with Soul: How Six Premier Colleges and Universities Keep Faith with Their Religious Traditions.* Grand Rapids: Eerdmans, 2002.

Berg, Gary A. *Why Distance Learning? Higher Education Administrative Practices.* Westport, CT: Oryx, 2002.

Berry, Wendell. *Sex, Economy, Freedom, and Community.* New York: Pantheon, 1992.

Biddix, Patrick J., and Robert A. Schwartz. "Walter Dill Scott and the Student Personnel Movement." *Journal of College Student Affairs Research and Practice* 49, no. 3 (2012): 285-98.

Bok, Derek. *Beyond the Ivory Tower: Social Responsibilities of the Modern University.* Cambridge, MA: Harvard University Press, 1984.

———. *Our Underachieving Colleges: A Candid Look at How Much Students Learn and Why They Should Be Learning More.* Princeton, NJ: Princeton University Press, 2006.

Bonhoeffer, Dietrich. *Life Together: A Discussion of Christian Fellowship.* Translated by John W. Doberstein. New York: Harper & Row, 1954.

Boyer, Ernest L. *Scholarship Reconsidered: Priorities of the Professoriate.* Princeton, NJ: Carnegie Foundation for the Advancement of Teaching, 1990.

Brueggemann, Walter. *Reality, Grief, Hope: Three Urgent Prophetic Tasks*. Grand Rapids: Eerdmans, 2014.

———. "Slow Wisdom as a Sub-Version of Reality." In *Educating for Wisdom in the Twenty-First Century*. Edited by Darin H. Davis. South Bend, IN: St. Augustine's Press, forthcoming.

Burtchaell, James T. *The Dying of the Light: The Disengagement of Colleges and Universities from their Christian Churches*. Grand Rapids: Eerdmans, 1998.

Carpenter, Joel, Perry L. Glanzer, and Nicholas S. Lantinga, eds. *Christian Higher Education: A Global Reconnaissance*. Grand Rapids: Eerdmans, 2014.

Cowley, William H. *Presidents, Professors, and Trustees: The Evolution of American Academic Government*. San Francisco: Jossey-Bass, 1980.

Crisp, Oliver D., Gavin D'Costa, Mervyn Davies, and Peter Hampson, eds. *Theology and Philosophy—Faith and Reason*. New York: T&T Clark, 2012.

Delbanco, Andrew. *College: What It Was, Is, and Should Be*. Princeton, NJ: Princeton University Press, 2013.

Eaton, Phil. *Engaging the Culture, Changing the World: The Christian University in a Post-Christian World*. Downer's Grove, IL: IVP Academic, 2011.

Evans, G. R. *Old Arts and New Theology: The Beginnings of Theology as an Academic Discipline*. Oxford: Clarendon, 1980.

Fiering, Norman. *Moral Philosophy at Seventeenth-Century Harvard*. Chapel Hill: University of North Carolina Press, 1981.

Finnegan, Dorothy E., and Nathan F. Alleman. "The YMCA and the Origins of American Freshman Orientation Programs." *Historical Studies in Education* 25, no. 1 (2013): 95-114.

Glanzer, Perry, and Todd Ream. *Christianity and Moral Identity in Higher Education*. New York: Palgrave Macmillan, 2009.

Hacker, Andrew, and Claudia Dreifus. *Higher Education? How Colleges Are Wasting Our Money and Failing Our Kids—And What We Can Do About It*. New York: Times Books, 2010.

Hart, D. G. *The University Gets Religion*. Baltimore: Johns Hopkins University Press, 1999.

Haskell, Thomas L. *The Emergence of Professional Social Science: The American Social Science Association and the Nineteenth-Century Crisis of Authority*. Chicago: University of Chicago Press, 1977.

Hauerwas, Stanley. *After Christendom? How the Church Is to Behave if Freedom, Justice, and a Christian Nation Are Bad Ideas*. Nashville: Abingdon, 1991.

———. *The State of the University: Academic Knowledges and the Knowledge of God*. Malden, MA: Blackwell, 2007.

Hauerwas, Stanley, and Samuel Wells, eds. *The Blackwell Companion to Christian Ethics*. Malden, MA: Blackwell, 2004.

Hauerwas, Stanley, and William H. Willimon. *Resident Aliens*. Nashville: Abingdon, 1990.

Hawkins, Hugh. *Between Harvard and Man: The Educational Leadership of Charles W. Eliot*. New York: Oxford University Press, 1972.

Higton, Michael. *A Theology of Higher Education*. New York: Oxford University Press, 2013.

Hofstadter, Richard, and Wilson Smith, eds. *American Higher Education: A Documentary History*. 2 vols. Chicago: University of Chicago Press, 1961.

Hugh of St. Victor. *The Didascalicon of Hugh of St. Victor: A Medieval Guide to the Arts*. Translated by Jerome Taylor. New York: Columbia University Press, 1991.

Hutchins, Robert Maynard. *The Higher Learning in America*. New Haven, CT: Yale University Press, 1936.

Ingrassia, Brian M. *The Rise of Gridiron University: Higher Education's Uneasy Alliance with Big-Time Football*. Lawrence, KS: University of Kansas Press, 2012.

James, Henry. *Charles W. Eliot: President of Harvard University, 1869–1909*. 2 vols. Cambridge, MA: Houghton Mifflin, 1930.

Kerr, Clark. *The Uses of the University*. 4th ed. Cambridge, MA: Harvard University Press, 1995.

Kett, Joseph. *The Pursuit of Knowledge Under Difficulties: From Self-Improvement to Adult Education in America, 1750–1990*. Stanford: Stanford University Press, 1994.

Kronman, Anthony. *Education's End: Why Our Colleges and Universities Have Given Up on the Meaning of Life*. New Haven, CT: Yale University Press, 2007.

Lewis, Harry. *Excellence Without a Soul: Does Liberal Education Have a Future?* New York: PublicAffairs, 2007.

Litfin, Duane. *Conceiving the Christian College*. Grand Rapids: Eerdmans, 2004.

MacIntyre, Alasdair. *After Virtue*. 3rd ed. Notre Dame: University of Notre Dame Press, 2007.

———. *God, Philosophy, and Universities: A Selective History of the Catholic Philosophical Tradition*. Lanham, MD: Rowman & Littlefield, 2009.

Marsden, George. *The Outrageous Idea of Christian Scholarship*. New York: Oxford University Press, 1996.

————. *The Soul of the American University: From Protestant Establishment to Established Nonbelief*. New York: Oxford University Press, 1994.

Meilaender, Gilbert. "Who Needs a Liberal Education?" *The New Atlantis* 41 (Winter 2014). www.thenewatlantis.com/publications/who-needs-a-liberal-education.

Morison, Samuel Eliot. *Three Centuries of Harvard, 1636–1936*. Cambridge, MA: Belknap Press of Harvard University Press, 1986.

Newman, John Henry. *The Idea of a University*. Notre Dame: University of Notre Dame Press, 1960.

Noll, Mark. *Princeton and the Republic, 1768–1822*. Princeton, NJ: Princeton University Press, 1989.

————. *The Scandal of the Evangelical Mind*. Grand Rapids: Eerdmans, 1987.

Palmer, Parker, and Arthur Zajonc. *The Heart of Higher Education: A Call to Renewal*. With Megan Scribner. San Francisco: Jossey-Bass, 2010.

Pelikan, Jaroslav. *The Idea of the University: A Reexamination*. New Haven, CT: Yale University Press, 1992.

Peterson, Christopher, and Martin Seligman. *Character Strengths and Virtues: A Handbook and Classification*. New York: Oxford University Press, 2004.

Rentz, Audrey L., ed. *Student Affairs: A Heritage's Profession*. Lanham, MD: University Press of America, 1994.

Reuben, Julie. *The Making of the Modern University: Intellectual Transformation and the Marginalization of Morality*. Chicago: University of Chicago Press, 1996.

Revsine, Dave. *The Opening Kickoff: The Tumultuous Birth of a Football Nation*. Guilford, CT: Lyons Press, 2014.

Ridder-Symoens, Hilde de, ed. *Universities in Early Modern Europe (1500–1800)*. Vol. 2 of *A History of the University in Europe*, edited by Walter Rüegg. Cambridge: Cambridge University Press, 1996.

————. *Universities in the Middle Ages*. Vol. 1 of *A History of the University in Europe*, edited by Walter Rüegg. Cambridge: Cambridge University Press, 1992.

Ringenberg, William C. *The Christian College: A History of Protestant Higher Education in America*. 2nd ed. Grand Rapids: Baker Academic, 2006.

Roth, Michael. *Beyond the University: Why Liberal Education Matters*. New Haven, CT: Yale University Press, 2014.

Rüegg, Walter, ed. *Universities in the Nineteenth and Early Twentieth Centuries (1800–1945)*. Vol. 3 of *A History of the University in Europe*, edited by Walter Rüegg. Cambridge: Cambridge University Press, 1996.

Skalnik, James Veazie. *Ramus and Reform: University and Church at the End of the Renaissance*. Kirksville, MO: Truman State University Press, 2002.

Sloan, Douglas. "The Teaching of Ethics in the American Undergraduate Curriculum, 1876–1976." In *Ethics Teaching in Higher Education*, edited by Daniel Callahan and Sissela Bok, 1-57. New York: Plenum, 1980.

Smith, Christian. *What Is a Person? Rethinking Humanity, Social Life, and the Moral Good from the Ground Up*. Chicago: University of Chicago Press, 2010.

Smith, James K. A. *Desiring the Kingdom*. Grand Rapids: Baker Academic, 2009.

Smith, Ronald A. *Play-by-Play: Radio, Television, and Big-Time College Sports*. Baltimore, MD: Johns Hopkins University Press, 2001.

Snyder, Thomas D. *120 Years of American Education: A Statistical Report*. National Center for Educational Statistics. Washington, DC: National Center for Education Statistics, GPO, 1993.

Sommerville, C. John. *The Decline of the Secular University*. New York: Oxford University Press, 2006.

Sprunger, Keith L. *The Learned Doctor William Ames: Dutch Backgrounds of English and American Puritanism*. Urbana: University of Illinois Press, 1972.

"The Student Personnel Point of View." *American Council on Education Studies*, first series, 1, no. 3 (1937).

Taylor, Charles. *A Secular Age*. Cambridge, MA: Belknap Press of Harvard University Press, 2007.

Taylor, Mark C. *Crisis on Campus: A Bold Plan for Reforming Our Colleges and Universities*. New York: Knopf, 2010.

Thelin, John R. *The History of Higher Education in America*. 2nd ed. Baltimore, MD: Johns Hopkins University Press, 2013.

Williamson, E. G., chair. *The Student Personnel Point of View*. Washington, DC: American Council on Education, 1949.

Witherspoon, John. *The Selected Writings of John Witherspoon*. Edited by Thomas Miller. Carbondale: Southern Illinois University Press, 1990.

INDEX

OTHER BOOKS
ON CHRISTIAN HIGHER EDUCATION
BY PERRY L. GLANZER AND TODD C. REAM

Perry L. Glanzer and Todd C. Ream:

The Idea of a Christian College: A Reexamination for Today's University

Christianity and Moral Identity in Higher Education: Becoming Fully Human

Christian Faith and Scholarship: An Exploration of Contemporary Debates

Perry L. Glanzer:

Christian Higher Education: A Global Reconnaissance (coedited with Joel Carpenter and Nick Lantinga)

Todd C. Ream:

A Parent's Guide to the Christian College: Supporting Your Child's Heart, Soul, and Mind During the College Years (with Timothy W. Herrmann and C. Skip Trudeau)

Finding the Textbook You Need

The IVP Academic Textbook Selector
is an online tool for instantly finding the IVP books
suitable for over 250 courses across 24 disciplines.

ivpacademic.com